STRUCTURED FAMILY FACILITATION PROGRAMS

Enrichment, Education, and Treatment

Margaret H. Hoopes
Brigham Young University

Barbara L. Fisher
Colorado State University

Sally H. Barlow
Brigham Young University

AN ASPEN PUBLICATION ®
Aspen Systems Corporation
Rockville, Maryland
Royal Tunbridge Wells
1984

Library of Congress Cataloging in Publication Data

Hoopes, Margaret H.
Structured family facilitation programs.

An Aspen publication.
Includes bibliographies and index.
1. Family life education—United States—Addresses,
essays, lectures. 2. Family social work—United States—
Addresses, essays, lectures. 3. Family psychotherapy—
United States—Addresses, essays, lectures. I. Fisher,
Barbara (Barbara L.) II. Barlow, Sally H. III. Title.
HQ10.H634   1984   362.8'2   83-22372
ISBN: 0-89443-579-5

Publisher: John Marozsan
Editorial Director: Margaret M. Quinlin
Executive Managing Editor: Margot Raphael
Editorial Services: Scott Ballotin
Printing and Manufacturing: Debbie Collins

Library of Congress Catalog Card Number: 83-22372
ISBN: 0-89443-579-5

Printed in the United States of America

2   3   4   5

To our parents, James and Joyce Howard,
Kenneth and Leone Fisher, and
Wallace and Marjorie Hess

Table of Contents

Foreword

In recent years, right- and left-brain information processing has received a great deal of attention. I originally decided to write a foreword for *Structured Family Facilitation Programs: Enrichment, Education, and Treatment* that would appeal primarily to the right brain. Many of the activities in the structured group treatments are right-brain activities, and, in my associations with Drs. Margaret Hoopes, Barbara Fisher, and Sally Barlow, I have been exposed to strategies for changing human behavior that utilize space and sensory information in very creative right-brain ways. I became convinced, however, that this book had much to offer left-brain thinkers as well. If I had simply created a metaphorical story about the creation of the text, I feared that those left-brain people would be put off by its presentation as a fairy-tale. The result, as you can see, is a combination of both right- and left-brain modalities.

Structured Family Facilitation Programs introduces a unique contribution to those who work with families. It illustrates the differences between enrichment, education, and treatment. More importantly, in its discussion of structured family facilitation programs the book offers a relatively new aproach for individuals, couples, and families. The time-limited concept is cost-effective and allows professional facilitators to focus on specific behavior, feelings, and thoughts. This provides a refreshing contrast to open-ended group therapy.

The programs in this book are replicable. Professionals can use them as is or modify them to fit special circumstances. Most of the programs have been empirically tested and have demonstrated successful outcomes. I hope that others will be encouraged to create their own structured experiences. For those who wish to do so, this book, with its procedures for designing programs, a variety of sample programs, and references for additional study, provides adequate tutelage.

I have watched the evolution of these ideas and the group that wrote this book. A left-brain   description of their efforts loses many of the more subtle characteristics of their working relationships, and the dream that kept them going. For this reason, I would like to dedicate the following metaphor to them.

Once upon a time in a distant woods, three wizards gathered around a fire for a friendly chat. As is the temptation of all wizards, on this particular night our three wizards conspired to create stories of mystical happenings.

In her boastings, one wizard claimed she had discovered the secret of making sunshine and could bring light to the woods that were so often dark even during the day. The other wizards did not at first believe her claim, insisting that even the best of wizardry would surely be destroyed by sunshine itself. But still, with reflections of night-fire dancing in their eyes, the two wizards listened and dreamed of spells so powerful.

"Could it really be done?" queried the one.

To this, the dreamer whispered, "It can be done, but it happens only within particular times, certain places, and in peculiar ways."

"Delight fills my mind at the thought of such daring," replied the third.

"Delightful and daring perhaps, but our wizardry will certainly be defiled if we fail to consider the structure in which it can happen," cautioned the first wizard.

The three, hoping and dreaming, watched that next morning as the sun showed itself through leaves in the roof of the woods. During the night, they had conspired to create peculiar ways, as well as times and places, in which the elusive sunshine would appear.

The wizardous trio called a meeting of forest people—fairies, elves, gnomes, and the like—and told them of the plan. Many of these friends of the woods wanted to help because their lives had been so limited by the shadows of the forest. Now, they might bring sunshine even to their own homes. Each described special ways—those of the elf, of the fairy, and of the gnome—that added a piece to the puzzle of how to structure sunshine.

After much struggle, the wizards finally announced the time and carefully planned a place for the event. All three waited anxiously. With a slow warmth, sunshine did appear. All were at peace for they had given structure and their wizardry was affirmed.

And so this book was born.

James Harper, Ph.D.

Preface

The family is not an endangered species as some purport. It is an institution that will thrive long beyond the lifetimes of future generations. The importance of the family—past, present, and future—cannot be disputed. The family plays a vital role in the development of individuals. It can be a source of nurture, support, safety, and socialization. The family can be a respite; and it can provide the means for fulfilling needs, such as validation and intimacy. Perhaps an entire text could be written on the value and responsibilities of the family. The point here is that it serves a vital and necessary role for society and its members.

However, despite general acknowledgment of the importance of the family, there is a widespread myth that healthy family relationships develop easily and naturally. People tenaciously hold on to this myth in spite of overwhelming evidence to the contrary. In fact, members of families need training and skill to create and maintain healthy family dynamics. To become a competent engineer, chemist, administrator, secretary, clerk, or teacher requires training and practice. This is also true of family members.

For those professionals who share these premises with us we have developed this book. It is designed for professionals and developing professionals who want to enhance their repertoire of skills and approaches that facilitate growth in individuals, couples, and families. The work has a dual purpose: (1) to provide professionals with the information and skills to help them plan, develop, deliver, and assess a structured family facilitation program; and (2) to provide a variety of programs that may be utilized, as they are written or modified, to meet the needs of a specific population.

We have selected three structured family facilitation approaches as our focus. However, in no way are we trying to make a statement about the relative efficacy of these approaches compared to others. Instead, we have narrowed our field of study to ensure manageability of content. We believe that the resulting structured family facilitation programs can be utilized to augment a professional's current skills.

The volume is divided into six parts. Part I is designed as an introduction to structured family facilitation approaches. Its chapters describe and compare our three approaches and provide relevant background information about families, groups, and structures for those desiring to develop or deliver a family facilitation program. Part II is concerned with "how to." Its chapters explain step by step the decisions and procedures required for planning, developing, delivering, and evaluating family facilitation programs. The ten chapters in Parts I and II are by the book's coauthors. The remaining chapters, in Parts III through VI, were provided by the contributors.

Part III presents the rationale and theoretical premises on which a family facilitation program is based and shows the process and procedures utilized in a specific program design. Although the design is not complete, it provides considerable information on preplanning. It includes data on the needs of the target population, directions for selecting and organizing a family facilitation group, a description of the control factors in the program, and the basis for treatment. All of the program's sessions are complete and ready for application.

In Parts IV through VI, 15 programs, illustrating the elements discussed in Parts I and II, and exemplified in Part III, are presented. These programs may be applied as written, or they may be modified for specific audiences. Some (Chapters 12, 13, 15, 16, 17, 18, 22, and 25) have all the sessions and aids necessary to deliver the program. The remainder (Chapters 14, 19, 20, 21, 23, 24, and 26) have two or three complete sessions with the remaining sessions in outline form. In these cases, the programs could also be applied immediately if the users wish to develop the outlined sessions. To acquire the complete programs in these cases, the reader should write or call Margaret Hoopes at the Comprehensive Clinic, Brigham Young University, Provo, Utah, 84602, (801) 378-6510.

Supplementing the above material, Appendix A presents several theoretical frameworks for family facilitation programs. Appendix B describes assessment tools that are often used in evaluating the effectiveness of programs. Appendix C contains an annotated bibliography for the first ten chapters with suggestions for further study.

A final note: One of our goals in writing this book was to synthesize, under one cover, as much information as possible on structured family facilitation programs. This goal emerged from our frustration in trying to "pull together" adequate sources and resources for teaching professionals about family facilitation. In this endeavor, we hope we have succeeded.

Acknowledgments

To my parents, my brother and sisters, and my extended family who have not only loved and supported me, but have taught me to love people, to value and serve the family, and to seek spiritual strength as a source to guide me in my life.

To my two friends and mentors, Clyde Parker and Alan Anderson, who encouraged me to write my first structured treatments for my dissertation at the University of Minnesota.

To my many friends and colleagues who befriend, challenge, and encourage me to create, apply, and share.

To my students, who allow me to participate in their education and in so doing teach me; without them this book would not be.

Margaret H. Hoopes

To my family, especially my parents, who have supported and encouraged me through all pursuits. They have provided a safe and stable environment that has promoted my intrapsychic and interpersonal growth.

To my friends, Terri Dail and Reba Keele, who share the laughter and tears of my professional and personal development and who make me want to be a better human being.

To Lynn Scoresby and Meg Hoopes, who planted the first seeds that led me into developing my first family enrichment programs. Those experiences kindled a desire to contribute to the field of enrichment.

To my students, who developed and researched programs for their dissertations, and to other students who have earnestly studied enrichment under my direction. To them I extend much appreciation. In directing and facilitating their education, I have learned and learned and learned.

To all those who have written in the field of enrichment, especially to those dedicated pioneers with whom I served on a two-day panel at the

1978 Annual Groves Conference: David and Vera Mace, Sherod Miller, Luciano L'Abate, Ed Bader, and Margaret Sawin. I value my all-too-brief interaction with each of them.

Barbara L. Fisher

To my family who taught me that, although life may not often be fair, it can always be rich. Especially to Jackson, whose constant curiosity and three-year-old tenderness have taught me what it really means to be responsible in my love.

To my friends, whom I am lucky enough to have also as colleagues—Tammie Quick, Bill Hansen, and Maren Mouritsen—their support came in all shapes, from good ideas when I ran dry to gentle proddings when I procrastinated.

To my teachers—Addie Fuhriman, Bob Finley, and Ted Packard—who taught me not which technique to use when, but how to be me, always.

To my students, whose interest in helping takes many forms, from the unorthodox and creative to the organized and carefully planned.

Sally H. Barlow

To our competent, hard-working secretaries who "typed their fingers to the bone," and also managed the giant jigsaw puzzle of a multiauthored manuscript: Donna McKernan, Natalie Hawkes, Laurie Leishman, Lisa Lagerstedt, Mary Ann Peel, Janine Gadd, and Kelly Anderson.

To our colleagues, Barbara J. Vance and James M. Harper, who read our manuscript and gave us helpful suggestions.

To Melissa Peterson, who manages the word-processing center and makes manuscripts happen.

To Laurie Wood, who edited our manuscript.

To Suzanne Dastrup, who edited parts of the book, wrote Appendix A and B, and did anything we asked her to do.

To Suzie Hess Slingerland, who also edited parts of the book.

To Kimberly Ford, for her fine graphics.

To students, former students, and colleagues who believe in family facilitation programs and shared their ideas, questions, enthusiasm, support, and, most of all, their programs for this book.

Margaret H. Hoopes
Barbara L. Fisher
Sally H. Barlow

CONTRIBUTORS

Lane B. Andelin, M.Ed.,
Psychomotrist and Corporate
   Materials Manager,
Houston, Texas

Dorothy S. Becvar, Ph.D.,
Adjunct Professor,
St. Louis University,
Instructor and Director of the St.
   Louis Family Institute,
Private practice,
St. Louis, Missouri

Dana N. Christensen, Ph.D.,
Assistant Professor in
   Department of Expressive
   Therapy,
The University of Louisville,
Private practice in marriage and
   family therapy,
Louisville, Kentucky

Suzanne L. Dastrup, M.S.,
Doctoral student in Marriage and
   Family Therapy and therapist/
   researcher,
The Gathering Place,
Provo, Utah

Camille C. Delong, M.S.,
Private practice in Marriage and
   Family Therapy,
Part-time instructor,
Brigham Young University,
Provo, Utah

Thomas J. Delong, Ph.D.,
Organizational Behavior
   Consultant,
Assistant Professor of Education,
Brigham Young University,
Provo, Utah

Leslie L. Feinauer, Ph.D.,
Private practice in Marriage and
   Family Therapy,
Associate Professor of Nursing,
University of Utah,
Salt Lake City, Utah

David J. Gardner, M.Ed.,
Doctoral student in Marriage and
   Family Therapy,
Brigham Young University,
Private practice,
Provo, Utah

James M. Harper, Ph.D.,
Private practice in Marriage and
   Family Therapy,
Assistant Professor of Marriage
   and Family Therapy,
Department of Family
   Sciences,
Brigham Young University,
Provo, Utah

Laura Huelsing, M.S.,
Private practice in Marriage and
   Family Therapy,
Counselor at Care and
   Counseling,
St. Louis, Missouri

CONTRIBUTORS continued

Reba L. Keele, Ph.D.,
Associate Professor of
  Organizational Behavior,
Brigham Young University,
Provo, Utah

Philip S. Klees, Ph.D.,
Executive Director of Family
  Networks,
A day treatment center for
  emotionally disturbed
  adolescents and their families,
Minneapolis, Minnesota

Kayleen Mitchell, Ph.D.,
Private practice in Marriage and
  Family Therapy,
Vienna, Virginia

Charles Ronig, Ph.D.,
Catholic Social Services,
Champaign, Illinois

William R. Steele, M.S.,
Doctoral student in Marriage and
  Family Therapy,
Brigham Young University,
Director of the Community Crisis
  Center,
Salt Lake City, Utah

Marcia R. Stroup, Ph.D.,
Director of Mount Olympus
  Christian Counseling Center,
Salt Lake City, Utah

Part I

Foundations for Family
Facilitation

Chapter 1

Family Facilitation Approaches: An Introduction

The family plays a critical role in the development of individuals. Steinmetz (1977) states that the family is the primary socialization agent and has responsibility for developing appropriate attitudes and behavior in each child. She cites several researchers to indicate the "voluminous research correlating inadequate socialization (frequently defined in terms of family structure and supportiveness) with a wide variety of criminal behavior" (p. 29).

Strengthening the family is a high priority in the minds of both mental health professionals and government policy makers. For example, in 1976 Jimmy Carter, then president of the United States, said that there can be no more urgent priority than to see that government decisions honor, support, and strengthen the American family. This priority is founded in concern about the health of the American family, which is experiencing increasing stress due to rapid social changes that adversely affect family life.

In the field of psychotherapy, the trend in the past 20 years has been toward working with the entire family. This trend began with the realization that problematic families produce problem individuals, and that individuals are products of their family life. Today, family facilitation as a profession has earned both respectability and credibility.

DEFINITIONS

Family facilitation is an approach to mental health that is designed to strengthen individuals and families by utilizing the family context. Family facilitation covers a broad range of activities—from high-school family life classes to family therapy that customizes treatment for pathological families. Since no single text could adequately discuss all of the various forms

3

of family facilitation, we have focused on one manageable and relevant area of study: structured family facilitation programs. *Structure* refers to predetermined parameters that define the nature of a program; a *program* is a formal plan with specific objectives designed to meet the needs of specific populations; *family facilitation* is the process designed to enhance a family's ability to reach desired goals. Therefore, a structured family facilitation program may be defined as a formal plan with predetermined parameters that is designed to facilitate a family's achievement of goals. Structured family facilitation programs involve a group format, including several family units with one or more facilitators.

Several other terms need to be defined at this point. The word *family*, as used in this text, includes many family forms. It includes the nuclear family (husband, wife, and children), the extended family (husband, wife, children, and other relatives), and alternate families (single parent, childless couples, unmarried homosexual adults, stepfamilies, communes, and so on). For our purposes, the term refers to the social unit with which one is most intimately involved. The entire family or any part of it—couples, individuals, parent-child dyads, and so on—may be the target population for family facilitation.

Plan or *design* refers to all the planning decisions, negotiations, and writing necessary to develop, deliver, and evaluate a program. The design is a map that can be followed from the first stages of conceptualizing to the final stages of evaluating. A *program* is what is actually delivered to participants.

Facilitators are the individuals who are responsible for delivering the program. They are called teachers, leaders, therapists, and so forth, in various programs; however, facilitator will be used throughout the book to eliminate confusion.

THE THREE APPROACHES: ASSUMPTIONS AND ROLES

There are three basic approaches that facilitate family change and growth: family life education, family enrichment, and family treatment. Structured family life education programs as discussed in this book do not include high school or college classes in marriage and family living. They do include programs that are primarily instructional in focus, with the intent of imparting information and skills to family members outside of an educational setting (for example, in community based parent education classes). Structured family enrichment programs are designed to enhance skills and healthy family interactions through instructional and experiential activities. Structured family treatment is designed to resolve problems encountered or developed by a family.

Figure 1-1 demonstrates the interrelationships of family life education, family enrichment, and family treatment programs. The three approaches may share some commonalities, as represented by the criss-crossed area. In addition, a program using one approach may share some features with programs that use one, but not both, of the other approaches as shown by the striped areas. Yet, each approach has its distinct and independent characteristics that set it apart from the others. The similarities and differences are elaborated in Chapter 2.

Structured family facilitation is a professional area that requires facilitators who have knowledge, skills, and expertise. There are several different roles that must be assumed for successful family facilitation. These include, but are not limited to, program facilitator, program developer, program modifier, program planner, needs assessor, marketing engineer, and researcher. Each role requires its own competence. A professional who is undertaking several or all of these roles has a big job! The present work is designed for the professional who desires expertise in any or all of these roles.

The first step in role competence is to gain a solid grounding in the underlying assumptions of family facilitation. Family facilitation programs

Figure 1-1 Interrelationships of Family Enrichment, Family Life Education, and Family Therapy

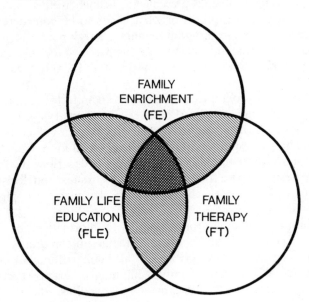

share some common assumptions that provide a theoretical framework. The assumptions, which are articulated in Chapter 2, and the resulting framework guide the practice of structured family facilitation.

Next, expertise in designing and leading structured family facilitation involves knowledge in several areas that could be considered background or related fields. Specifically, this expertise can best be developed by integrating a working knowledge of family dynamics and development; group dynamics and development; concepts related to structure, research and assessment; theories of instruction and learning; theories of change; and the content of other related fields (for example, health, finances, recreation, and so on). Information about families, groups, and structure is provided in separate chapters. Due to space constraints, information concerning the remaining areas is woven into discussions throughout the text, but is not dealt with in a specific chapter.

FOUNDATION ELEMENTS

Beyond these underlying assumptions and background knowledge in specific fields, skills in program planning, development, delivery, and assessment are crucial. Figure 1-2 shows a pyramid that demonstrates the levels of elements in the foundation of family facilitation designs. The first three levels are discussed in Parts I and II. An overview of relevant assumptions and information is presented and complemented with resources for further study. Descriptions of what needs to be considered and the skills to be developed in program planning, development, delivery, and assessment are presented in Part II. In this part, we focus on procedures to plan, develop, deliver, and assess a structured family facilitation program.

In writing about programs, professionals seem to focus on objectives, content, settings, and process (Porter & Chatelain, 1981), but rarely on the guidelines for issues, decisions, and processes involved in designing programs. The assumption seems to be that we all know how to do this. With this incorrect assumption in mind, Part II describes the four stages of program design, with a focus on procedures, issues, and decisions. This information will help prospective program designers to complete each stage of the design successfully.

In addition to providing professionals with information about the relationships, purpose, and content of family facilitation programs (Part I) and about how to design programs (Part II), this book has another major goal: to provide actual structured family facilitation programs (Parts III–VI). Often family facilitators find it expedient, as well as relevant, to use an

Figure 1-2 Foundations of Family Facilitation

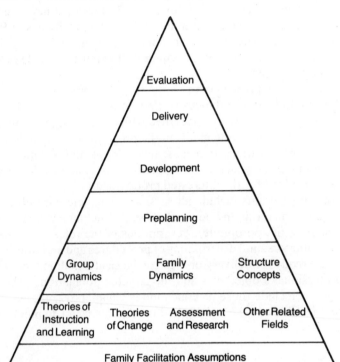

existing program to meet the needs of an identified population. Appropriate family facilitation programs are not easily found, however, because the professional literature scatters specific programs under headings of family life education, therapy, sex education, enrichment, skill development, and communication. In addition, many programs are developed and conducted privately and have positive outcomes but are not made available to other professionals. Some of these are administered as parts of graduate study and are never refined and continued in application. Professionals working with families are thus often forced to "reinvent the wheel" because there is little opportunity to compare or utilize previously developed programs.

The present work is designed to provide an opportunity for professionals to compare programs. Sixteen family facilitation programs have been assembled with instructions for their use. To supplement these programs, we have provided references to many other relevant programs in the literature. Thus, a professional with this book in hand may (1) adopt one of the 16 programs, (2) adapt one of them, or (3) develop a new one.

Part III presents a single program that follows the guidelines in Part II from start to finish. The discussion points out many of the decisions (involving the issues described in Chapter 7) that must be made before a program can be written.

The 15 programs presented in Parts IV–VI represent a variety of approaches, participants, and focuses. Four of the chapters (12–15) focus on education, three (16–18) are concerned with enrichment, and eight (19–26) deal with treatment. Participants in the programs include individuals, premarital couples, marital couples, families, stepfamilies, and religious communities. Program goals, content, methodology, and evaluation procedures are provided for the interested professional.

Some of the programs include all sessions, complete with objectives, lists of required material and equipment, supplementary visual aids and didactic material (if appropriate), descriptions of the roles of the participants and facilitators, and descriptions of procedures and activities. These programs are ready for delivery or they can be easily modified, depending on the professional's objectives and the targeted populations. The complete programs include those on education in Chapters 12, 13, and 15; on enrichment in Chapters 17 and 18; and on treatment in Chapters 11, 22, and 26.

Chapter 2

Family Facilitation Comparisons

Structured family facilitation programs are designed to capitalize on and enhance existing family strengths. These programs can also serve as adjuncts to other forms of facilitation, for example, therapy for a family, couple, or individual. They are not intended to supersede other vital forms of enhancing individual and family growth; rather, they are intended to complement them. Structured family facilitation programs may also be offered to families who may not ordinarily pursue therapy. Thus, structured programs may be used in conjunction with another facilitation form or they may be offered independently.

BASIC ASSUMPTIONS

Basic to planning, developing, delivering, and assessing structured family facilitation programs is an understanding of the assumptions from which such programs are generated. Assumptions are the implicit or explicit suppositions—many of which are taken for granted—upon which structured family facilitation programs are built (Fisher, 1982). Several assumptions underlie the three approaches in the present work. Many of these assumptions apply to other forms of facilitation as well as to structured family programs. The assumptions underlying our approaches were inductively formulated after writing programs, supervising students in writing programs, and examining many different programs. Each of the following assumptions identifies a framework or road map to guide a phase or several phases of the process of program design:

- *Assumption 1: Families proceed through developmental stages.* A family goes through a life cycle just as individuals proceed through developmental stages. The stages of the family life cycle are briefly

9

described in Chapter 3. In terms of family facilitation, this assumption is related to the assessment of the needs of the target population. That is, families at the same stage in the life cycle have common needs that are different from those of families at another stage. For example, parents in families in the "young children" stage of development need to adjust to a lack of privacy and energy depletion caused by young children, while parents in families in the "launching" stage require a rebuilding of the marital dyad and aid in the transition to postparental pursuits. Thus, programs for various families will be quite different, depending on the needs and tasks of each family's developmental stage.

- *Assumption 2: Families have internal strengths and resources.* All family facilitation programs build to some extent on the family's resources. Identifying strengths and resources is an aspect of the programs' needs assessments. In addition, the content and activities of the programs should be geared to utilize and add to the strengths and resources of the families within the targeted population.

- *Assumption 3: Families are the primary socializing agents for individuals and, therefore, play an important developmental role for all family members.* An unhealthy family usually produces dysfunctional individuals. Families range from healthy to severely pathological. Theorists, researchers, and practitioners are beginning to unravel and discriminate the differences between families with different levels of health and pathology. An understanding of healthy family dynamics forms the foundation for establishing the goals of structured family facilitation programs. A common goal of all such programs is to produce healthier, better functioning, and more productive families.

- *Assumption 4: Family facilitation is interdisciplinary.* Professionals in the family facilitation area come from various fields of study, including theology, psychology, psychiatry, home economics, education, social work, sociology, anthropology, health care, family therapy, and family studies. Family facilitation is thus something of a melting pot for professionals. This results in a field that, hopefully, derives benefit from the strengths of its contributing fields. There are, however, certain areas of study in which competence may be considered to be a prerequisite for work in family facilitation. These areas include family dynamics, group dynamics and development, research and assessment, social skills and human relations training, health, education, and instructional development. When they are integrated appropriately, knowledge and skills from a variety of such areas will strengthen family facilitation programs.

- *Assumption 5: Family facilitation fills a void in the interface between family and society.* Family life is not only complex and difficult, it is also the most critical area of human relations. However, normally no formal training is offered to family members to assist in the demanding processes of being a family. Parenting, for instance, often reflects what was learned in husbands' and wives' families of origin. Family facilitation programs offer training, skills, and resources to assist family members in making productive contributions to society. This assumption is related to one's concept of the role of family facilitation, which, in turn, helps to establish the goals of the program.

- *Assumption 6: Marriage and family systems are changeable.* Functional families progress through developmental stages and change in response to the needs of the individuals involved. Structured family facilitation programs are designed to assist in the changes through the developmental stages and to help prevent or remove barriers to normal development.

- *Assumption 7: Family facilitation programs facilitate change.* Such programs assist in changing family systems by providing new information and new behavior, either from external sources (facilitators, other group members) or internal sources (family members). Assumptions 6 and 7 both underscore beliefs that the family can change through the procedures utilized in family facilitation programs. These beliefs about change affect the choice of an approach and the process, method, format, and timing of a program.

- *Assumption 8: Family facilitation generalizes to other settings.* Information gained at a family facilitation program generalizes to other settings, specifically the home. Participants are able to take attitudes and skills home to enhance family life presently and in the future.

- *Assumption 9: There are many short-term as well as long-term advantages to family facilitation approaches.* Short-term advantages are realized when specific needs of the family are addressed and met in a given program. In a parent education course, for example, parents may learn what to expect of their toddlers. In an enrichment program, parents and children may learn to express feelings and communicate more effectively. In a treatment program, a family may learn to cope with the declining health of an aging family member.

  Positive attitudes, developed through a facilitation program, can help families seek outside resources and continue the enhancement of the family. The long-term advantage, then, is that such programs may help families to continue actively working on family-related issues.

- *Assumption 10: Family facilitation programs are successful in groups of families.* Family therapy usually involves one facilitator (therapist) per family. For some families, this is what is necessary for change. However, facilitation programs assume that several families can simultaneously benefit from the same approach and the same facilitator(s). Actually, the group members and families in the program contribute to the growth of other participants by adding more information and experience.
- *Assumption 11: Structured family facilitation is effective in enhancing family life.* This assumption is an impetus for answering research and evaluation questions, such as: What are structured family facilitation programs effective at doing? What variables may be changed with what type of program? What is not affected by structured programs? How may the variables be measured?
- *Assumption 12: There are optimal conditions for structured family facilitation programs.* This assumption addresses the relation of all of the elements of a structured program. It states that certain program elements are most effective for certain participants in specific settings. Basically, this requires that family facilitation discover the blend of elements that make a program most effective.

These assumptions are the foundation of family facilitation programs. They guide one's choices in selecting methodologies, in assessing needs, and in preplanning, development, delivery, and evaluation. They are global, but each professional will operationalize them somewhat differently, thus leading to program variability. Also, individual professionals will have their own idiosyncratic assumptions that will generate program differences.

SPECIFIC ELEMENTS

In addition to shared assumptions, each approach has its own assumptions or assumptions that may be shared with only one other approach. These assumptions relate to the program's function, its goals and objectives, the process of change, the participants, the role of the leader, the direction of information, the generation of energy, the program's format, and the program's cost. Table 2-1 shows some of the relevant comparisons.

Function

Each approach serves a relatively different function for families who seek facilitation. Family life education is the oldest and most widespread

Table 2-1 Comparison of Elements of Family Life Education, Family Enrichment and Family Treatment Approaches

	Family Life Education	Family Enrichment	Family Treatment
Function	Education/Prevention	Prevention/Enhancement	Remediation/Education/Enrichment
Goal	To provide information about a relevant content area	To prevent dysfunction and increase relationship skill and satisfaction	To correct dysfunction or assist in coping with a stressful situation
Change process	Occurs through assimilation of information/knowledge; primarily a cognitive process	Occurs through exercises, activities, and practice of skill; primarily an experiential process	Occurs through discussion of issues; primary focus is on resolution of an area
Information flow and generation of energy	Moves from leader to participants	Moves within family, between families, leader to participant, participant to leader	Moves within family, between families, leader to participant, participant to leader
Participants	Usually includes individual members of a family wanting information	Usually includes whole families or couples wanting to enhance their relationships	Usually includes whole families or family subsystems experiencing specific problems
Facilitator role	To impart information and teach	To direct activities and discussions	To facilitate learning activities and discussions
Process	Uses lecture, discussion, question-answer activities	Uses family activities, discussion, homework assignments	Uses group and family activities and discussion

of the family facilitation approaches (Wright & L'Abate, 1977). It is primarily an educational process, with a close secondary emphasis on prevention. Parent education courses are common examples of family life education programs as defined in this book.

Family enrichment programs attempt primarily to prevent family disorganization. "It is assumed they decrease the frequency, intensity and duration of crises and increase the likelihood that the family will better manage crises and transitions in family life" (Fisher, Sprenkle, & Sheehy, 1980, p. 7). Marital enrichment is one type of family enrichment program.

Family treatment is somewhat of a hybrid of enrichment, education, and treatment. It is remedial in that it is used only after something has "gone wrong." Though its objective is different, it is similar to enrichment and education in that it provides a structured format and group setting for facilitators and participants. The primary objective of family treatment is the resolution or reduction of a problem area. An example of family treatment is a couples' group focused on intimacy problems caused by a lingering illness of one of the partners (see Christensen's program in Chapter 22).

Goals

Goals and specific objectives are closely related to the function of the program. The goal of family life education is to provide useful information to participants about relevant content and skill areas. Courses in an educational setting on child development or parenting are designed to increase the participant's knowledge. Programs that include families or parts of families in a less formal setting tend to integrate enrichment goals with education goals.

The goals of family enrichment are to prevent dysfunction and to increase skills in coping with stress-producing situations. In addition, family enrichment facilitators hope to enhance the quality and intimacy of family life.

Family treatment programs are designed to correct dysfunctional behavior or to assist in coping with or resolving stressful situations. For example, for a family in which one member had been raped, a family treatment program was designed to help each member understand the victim's experience and then acknowledge, express, and resolve that person's feelings about the experience (see Feinauer's program in Chapter 11).

The Process of Change

It is difficult to articulate a single theory to explain the process of change in families. However, a theory of change for a particular program should, at least, include a discussion of who is included in the change process and what techniques facilitate change. Although approaches to family facilitation may have many similarities, each approach operationalizes assumptions about change in slightly different ways.

A family life education program is primarily a cognitive process. However, family life educators currently are stressing the importance of utilizing integrated and participative learning. Typically, change is considered as an assimilation of information, knowledge, and practice in doing things, for example, in using communication skills. Family life education programs may be designed for whole families, for subsystems of families, or for individuals in a family.

Enrichment is primarily an experiential process. That is, family members participate in experiences and activities that are designed to enhance family life. Family enrichment programs attempt to include all members of a system. Thus, if the program's goal is to enhance couple communication, both spouses are expected to attend. If the program is designed to increase family cohesion, all members of the family are expected to attend. The assumption of enrichment is that the most efficient means of changing a system is to work with all parts of that system conjointly.

Family treatment programs may involve individuals, family subsystems, or whole families. The assumption here is that the most efficient method of change is to address directly the unit needing facilitation. Change occurs through such activities as directed discussion. Resolution of specific issues is accomplished through experiential practice of some skill.

All three approaches share common techniques of change: exercises, activities, discussion, and other teaching stategies. However, the emphasis on the technique varies. For example, family life education emphasizes teaching and other cognitive activities and some role rehearsal or practice. Family enrichment emphasizes experiential activities and exercises to develop skill. Family treatment emphasizes discussion and experiential exercises.

Information Flow and Generation of Energy

The movement of information and energy is another source of comparison. Who provides information for whom and who invests the most energy? Family life education is characterized by information and energy moving from the leader to the participants. In contrast, family enrichment participants provide the most energy for the program, though some information and energy are provided, initially and intermittently, by the facilitator. In completing exercises and assignments, the participants generate energy and provide information to themselves about the inner workings of their unique family. Family treatment is quite similar to family enrichment in that both leaders and participants provide information and generate energy.

Participants

All three approaches can be developed and delivered to families of any socioeconomic status, ethnic group, religion, age, and developmental stage. Each approach assumes that the use of a group format is effective. That is, individuals, families, or family subsystems that are selected by carefully chosen criteria meet together with others who share similar concerns.

Family life education is open to all interested participants. However, it is commonly believed (but not empirically documented) that well-functioning family members seem to benefit most from this type of approach. There is rarely any screening of participants. Rather, a family life education program is advertised, and participation is determined by a self-selection process. In addition, family life education is usually voluntary, although, at times, schools or churches may require it.

Family enrichment is always voluntary and usually self-selective. Occasionally, a screening procedure is used by a group facilitator to determine whether an individual or family should be involved. However, most enrichment programs are offered to the public in general. Almost as a contradiction to this practice, most family enrichment leaders assume that enrichment is appropriate only for well-functioning or minimally dysfunctional families. However, without screening procedures and tools, it is difficult to determine whether this is the population that is reached. Enrichment is usually offered for the entire family system or couple. However, enrichment may also be directed at family subunits (parents, siblings, mother-child, father-child, and so on).

Family treatment is offered to families or family subsystems that are experiencing problems ranging from the specific and isolated (for example, an unexpected death) to the pervasive (for example, a generally dysfunctional family system). Thus, families in which one member is chronically ill or families going through divorce could be the target population for a family treatment program. Typically, family treatment is voluntary, although some family members may be required to attend by a higher authority (parents, courts, schools, and so forth).

Role of the Facilitators

Each approach assumes that facilitators are effective if they can perform certain tasks specific to the program's objectives. In all three approaches, the tasks of facilitators are quite similar; the differences are a matter of emphasis. The tasks of facilitators of a family life education program generally include actively teaching and providing information to the participants, with some emphasis on leading discussions and encouraging rehearsals or practices. The tasks of family enrichment facilitators are somewhat less active. These facilitators provide some didactic material, but primarily they direct the process of the program, by leading discussions, explaining exercises and activities, and so on. Family treatment facilitators do little teaching. They facilitate the resolution of issues by structuring exercises and directing key questions for discussion. Facilitators of family treatment may be less directive than leaders of family life education and family enrichment, in that they allow their participants to take more responsibility to meet their idiosyncratic needs.

Process and Format

Two concepts similar to information flow and generation of energy are process and format. *Process* refers to the instructional and activity strategies, facilitator and participant roles, and the procedures for conducting the session. *Format* refers to the frequency and number of sessions, the length of each session, and the sequencing of sessions. Each program has a predetermined format regarding the number, frequency, and length of sessions, based on the objectives of the program. The process and format of a program should be designed to fit the needs of the participants and the goals of the program.

The educational process of family life education is characterized by a lecture or provision of information through other means, for example through movies or readings. Discussions, questions and answers, and other learning activities may be part of the family life education process.

Enrichment is characterized by a brief facilitator presentation and by family exercises and activities, discussions, and homework assignments. Family treatment is similar to enrichment in the performance of activities and group discussions. However, more emphasis is placed on discussion of issues.

ADVANTAGES OF FAMILY FACILITATION

Family facilitation offers many advantages. From an economical standpoint, family facilitation in groups is much less expensive than traditional treatment approaches, such as therapy. Therefore, more people are able to participate at a lower cost; and, because several families are offered service together, a professional's time is used more efficiently.

Another advantage is that, when professionals attempt to teach, treat, or enrich the family in its own context, they solve a number of problems overlooked by delivery systems that focus only on the individual. First, because all members participate in the same program, each individual member has the same opportunity to see and hear what is actually occurring. Interaction does not run the risk of second-hand translation. Members may distort the information that is currently available to everyone else; but, because there are others there who are privy to the same data, the distorting member has a reality check readily available. Second, teaching, treating, or enriching the family as a group defocuses attention on the "problem member" or "symptom bearer." When families stay in the program long enough, each member discovers that responsibility for effective functioning must be shared equally.

When several families are joined together, each family has the opportunity to observe how other families function at different stages. The group can provide a family with a new support network of others who share similar interests, concerns, and problems. Through these contacts, by focusing on family strengths, the stigmas surrounding the use of professional help for family-related issues diminish.

Chapter 3

Family Functioning

Earlier, we noted that the integration of various fields is a necessary building block in the development of effectively structured family facilitation programs. In working with families, the field that provides information about the family is one of the most important. Relevant information about the family may be categorized in terms of the family as a system, family development, and functional or dysfunctional family behavior.

The rationale for including such information should be obvious: all three of the facilitation approaches focus on families. However, there are less obvious reasons. Most programs reflect the values, philosophies, biases, and suppositions of the program developer. While respect and credibility must be given to the experience and expertise of a professional working with families, programs should be founded in theory and research in order to enhance the results. Program creators should rely less on subjective biases and should avoid imposing their own values. They will then be better able to develop empirically and theoretically grounded programs designed to address the assessed needs of a specific population.

THE FAMILY AS A SYSTEM

For at least the past two decades, family professionals have been advocating a new theoretical approach to the understanding of human behavior. This new approach is based on General Systems Theory, first proposed by Ludwig von Bertalanffy, a biologist, in the 1940s.

Systems theory has been applied to families by many theorists and practitioners. While there are significant differences in the theoretical assumptions of different professionals, several basic concepts of systems theory can be delineated to help designers of family facilitation programs.

First, a system consists of interacting parts. In order to understand the operation of the whole system, one must study the parts, the transactions between the parts, and the relationships between the parts and the environment. "A system is characterized by wholeness or unity and must take into account the ongoing interaction between the parts" (Goldenberg & Goldenberg, 1980, p. 29). To understand a system as complex as a family, one must examine the individual family members, their interactions with one another, and their interactions with others outside the family—not an easy task! The fact is, however, that the family cannot be defined by merely observing one member. For example, school teachers often report being surprised when they meet the parents of some of their pupils for the first time. The opinions they have formulated about the child's parents and family based on the child's behavior are often drastically altered when the parents are introduced.

Systems are rule-governed. That is, they have organized repetitive patterns that are initiated, modified, and maintained by the members of the system. All families follow rules that direct members to act in predictable ways. These rules govern the roles, division of labor, power, and patterns of interaction in a family. They keep the system operating smoothly. Some family rules are overtly stated. Overt rules are talked about and often agreed upon, for example, "Jimmy does the dishes," and "Scott takes out the trash." Some family rules are covert; they are not talked about, but they are still followed and understood by everyone. For example, a covert rule may be, "It is easier to borrow money from Dad than Mom" or, "It is acceptable to sass Mom until Dad gets angry." Rules, then, are the governing mechanisms that overlay family roles, interaction patterns, and relationship boundaries.

Roles are the expected behaviors of family members; for example, Mom is the caretaker, Dad is the breadwinner, Cindy is the clown, Julie is the peacemaker. *Patterns of interaction* are redundant sequences of behavior. Every family has countless interaction patterns that define who talks to whom, when, about what, and in what manner. For example, imagine you are sitting around a dinner table with the Jones family. The oldest child, Rob, begins to talk about an experience he had at school. Mom listens attentively while Dad continues eating and Rob's two sisters begin to whisper about a boy they like. Rob gets upset and complains that Dad and his sisters are not paying attention. Mom fusses at the girls and gives Dad a warning glance. Everyone then listens more carefully to Rob's story. This is a fairly simple interaction pattern that will be repeated over and over in the family.

Let's look at another pattern of interaction by a newly married couple. Jan and Ron have been married six months. Ron comes home from work tired and frustrated. Jan wants conversation and affection from him. When he comes in, he sits down on a chair and starts reading a newspaper. Jan sits on the edge of the chair, rubs his shoulders, and kisses him. He ignores her. She gets hurt, goes to their bedroom, and slams the door. Ron calls to her but she doesn't answer. He goes to the bedroom and demands, "What is the matter with you? Aren't we going to have dinner?" She replies, "All you care about is yourself. You don't really care about me. Get your own dinner!" Ron mutters a few words and goes to McDonald's for a hamburger. Jan cries. When he returns home, they go through a cold war and don't speak to one another until bedtime, when they both apologize and. . . . Well, the pattern ends happily, but Jan and Ron have established an interaction that will be repeated in a similar form whenever he is tired and frustrated and she needs attention. Patterns of interaction are powerful; each person behaves in a predictable way as if reading a script.

Boundaries define who and what ideas and things are included in a family, and at what level of intimacy. For example, in a healthy family, Mom and Dad have the highest level of intimacy. The children form a subgroup that interacts with the parents both as individuals and as a parental subgroup. Relatives and friends are included but at a less intimate level. The permeability of a boundary refers to the ease or difficulty of exchanging information across that boundary. If the parents, for example, have a relatively permeable boundary, they will hear more information from their children than will parents with impermeable boundaries. If the whole family has an open boundary to the outside, much new information will enter the family system.

The rules of the system maintain a dynamic equilibrium or steady state. This steady state or *homeostasis* makes the system predictable and comfortable and requires less energy than change requires. If the equilibrium is threatened, the system's rules operate to restore that equilibrium. For example, let's say a family has a rule that says, "Mom doesn't work outside of the home," and Mom decides she wants to get a job. The system either has to change the rule and allow Mom to work, or operate so that Mom conforms to the rule. The rule may be upheld if, for example, Mom discovers she is pregnant and decides to stay home with the newborn, or if a child becomes ill and requires special attention that diverts Mom's interest in working.

In order for a system to change, the rules must be modified. Outdated rules must be updated to allow the system to meet the needs of the individuals involved.

Another property of a family system is *openness*. As stated above, openness is related to the permeability of the boundaries. An open system exchanges information with others outside the system and between members within the system. All living systems are open, but there are degrees of openness depending on the amount of information the system assimilates. The information that enters the family becomes part of two continuous and simultaneous types of feedback mechanisms that form a loop. *Positive feedback* amplifies deviation from the steady state. *Negative feedback* corrects deviation and returns the environment to its steady state. For example, the Jones family car breaks down and requires $1,200 in labor and repair. The family decides to purchase a new auto. They go shopping and find out that a new car is beyond their current budget. They then call the repair shop to find out how soon they can have their car back. The information about the car repair cost initiated positive feedback and caused a change in family behavior (shopping for a car). However, the information about the cost of a new car compared to the family budget initiated negative feedback and caused the family to return to their home without a new car (stop shopping for a car).

Through the feedback mechanisms, information about the system's functioning is reintroduced to the system as feedback (output returns as input to the system) and generates change, if necessary, to keep the system operating in a steady state. The system is constantly changing in response to information entering the system. The degree of change in the system is a function of the amount and type of information that is integrated via the feedback mechanisms.

Systems theory rejects the cause-effect or linear model of causality. Instead, a circular model of causality is adopted in which a person's behavior is a function of, and serves as a function for, that person's system. In order to understand an individual's behavior, the function of that individual's behavior for the system and the system's rules, roles, patterns of interaction, and boundaries must be examined. For example, instead of attempting to determine what caused Billy to misbehave (for example, poor and inconsistent parenting), the function of Billy's behavior for the system is hypothesized and acted upon (Billy is misbehaving in order to strengthen the marital relationship).

The systems approach to family facilitation has spread rapidly. It enables professionals to intervene effectively and efficiently because it defocuses blame and utilizes the whole system in change. Though only a brief introduction to systems theory has been provided here, we would recommend in-depth study of the family as a system. For that purpose, a list of additional readings is provided in Appendix C.

THE FAMILY LIFE CYCLE

The family develops through predictable stages.* Each stage is accompanied by developmental tasks that should be mastered to ensure successful passage into the next stage. For example, a newly married couple's task is to develop a satisfactory relationship before successfully assuming the responsibility of the needs of a child. Unsuccessful mastery of the tasks of one stage creates difficulty in a later stage.

Families in each stage have needs that are idiosyncratic to that stage. Therefore, a professional working with a family in a particular stage should be aware of the family's needs and developmental tasks. Carter and McGoldrick (1980) offer the most current explanation of these stages and tasks. They delineate six stages, beginning with the "unattached young adult." People in this stage need to differentiate themselves from their families of origin, develop intimate relationships with peers, and establish themselves in the world of work.

The next stage is "the newly married couple." Couples in this stage make mutual adjustments and realign friendships and family relationships to include their spouse. The third stage, "young children," is characterized by the assumption of parental roles, adjustments to children, and, again, realignment of friend and family relationships to include children. The fourth stage includes "families with adolescents." These families attempt to balance family life with the adolescents who are striving for autonomy. In addition, midlife crises and career issues are faced during this stage.

The fifth stage is "Launching." This stage is characterized by a rebuilding of the marital dyad, establishment of adult relationships with offspring, realignment of relationships to include inlaws and grandchildren, and a coping with disability and death of parents and grandparents. The final stage is the "family in later life." Here, the developmental tasks include coping with declining health and physiological abilities, supporting the older generation, and dealing with death.

Healthy family systems proceed relatively smoothly through these stages, completing appropriate developmental tasks and modifying rules, roles, and patterns of interaction to adjust to the demands of the next stage. These changes occur as the family assimilates new information via the

---

*Several authors (Carter & McGoldrick, 1980; Duvall, 1977; Haley, 1973) have not only identified family development stages but have also provided excellent treatises on the subject. Since we do not wish to compete with this extensive literature, a detailed explanation of these stages is not provided here. The reader is referred to the references for further information.

feedback mechanisms. An unhealthy family is unable either to change its homeostatic balance to allow progression to the next stage or to achieve the developmental tasks of the present stage. It is "stuck" in a stage, with rules, roles, and patterns appropriate only to that stage.

While family facilitation focuses more broadly, not just on family development, its approaches may utilize information about the family life cycle in various ways. For example, one purpose of family life education programs could be to provide information about the expectations and needs of each stage. Family enrichment programs may be designed to assist in the development of skills to cope with the needs and developmental tasks of each stage. Couples preparing for marriage represent a population in transition. A few of these couples may need therapy, but most of them could benefit from enrichment or education. The education program for premarital couples in Chapter 15 is an example of a program to help couples in one stage move to the next stage.

Often families are faced with an intrastage crisis. This means some event has occurred that disorganizes the family homeostasis. For example, death or illness of a family member would create an intrastage crisis.

Interstage difficulties refer to a family's inability to progress from one stage to another. For example, the family with adolescents may still adhere to rules for young children (for example, bedtime at 8:30 P.M.), thus creating an interstage crisis. A program with a focus on family rules and life cycle issues would help a family move on from this kind of impasse. The divorce adjustment program in Chapter 19 and the drug program for teenagers and their families in Chapter 25 are examples of programs designed to help families with specific developmental problems.

Understanding the life cycle of the family allows family facilitators to zero in on the most relevant and vital issues for the family. For example, in planning a program for families with adolescents, a facilitator can quickly become aware of universal issues facing such families and, with this understanding, proceed to establish a foundation for effective intervention (see Mitchell's program in Chapter 21).

HEALTHY FAMILY FUNCTIONING

While much has been written about dysfunctional families, only recently has the emphasis shifted to explore the healthy family. Previously, it was assumed that the healthy family was one with an absence of pathology. But, since family life education, family enrichment, and family treatment focus on promoting or restoring family health, a focus only on the absence of pathology did not provide an adequate explanation of healthy family functioning. Thus, the shift to the study of family health was important to family facilitation. Empirical studies designed to describe and differentiate healthy families provide goals for family facilitation that are more objective than goals tied to the value system and biases of the facilitator. However, as Gantman (1980) has indicated, "there is paucity of theoretical and empirical information about normal families" (p. 106).

Unfortunately, efforts to describe the healthy family are nascent. Numerous models of both healthy and dysfunctional family behavior are being studied. In this section, we examine three empirical studies that have tested some of these models.

Perhaps the most extensive study of healthy families was that undertaken by Lewis, Beavers, Gossett, and Phillips (1976). Integrating their work with that of Mishler and Waxler (1968) and Westley and Epstein (1969), this group identified five major dimensions of family behavior. They then developed a rating scale to distinguish healthy from disturbed families. Based on the results of rated videotaped interactions and structured interviews with 33 healthy families, the group concluded that no single quality identified the healthy family. The findings did indicate that healthy families have the following qualities:

- strong parental coalition
- an affiliative attitude toward encounters
- respect for the subjectivity of others
- open and direct communication
- an understanding of varied and complex human needs and motivations
- spontaneity
- high levels of initiative
- enjoyment of the unique characteristics of each individual

Stinnett (1979) studied the relationship patterns among families designated as strong. A total of 157 subjects and 99 families identified as strong families responded to a questionnaire with 15 open-ended questions. The families indicated that the following are qualities of a strong family:

- appreciation for one another
- time together that is genuinely enjoyed
- good communication patterns
- commitment to promoting the happiness and welfare of others in the family group
- high degree of religious orientation
- ability to deal with crises in a positive manner

Fisher, Giblin, and Hoopes (1982) asked 208 mothers, fathers, and teenagers to respond to a questionnaire that requested a ranking and rating of 34 aspects of healthy family functioning. The 34 aspects were identified and defined after a lengthy review of the literature on family health and dysfunction. The family members identified the following aspects as most important to healthy family functioning:

- a sense of belonging to the family
- good communication that includes attending to affect and content of a message, listening attentively, and expressing feelings and thoughts openly
- enjoyment of one another, feeling good about each other
- acceptance of and support for each other's emotional needs
- a feeling of security, safety, and trust with one another
- ability to depend on one another to honor agreements and commitments
- protection of individual members against outside threats
- doing things together that are rewarding, fun, and enjoyable

The three studies identify very similar aspects of the healthy family. The implications for family facilitation are numerous. First, the identified aspects of health may be integrated into a program as goals. The objective of the program then is to provide knowledge or skills that facilitate the building of healthier family systems. Second, a family facilitation program may use these aspects as outcome criteria in measuring the effectiveness of the program. The families' development of these aspects could then be utilized in an assessment of the effectiveness of the program. For example, a program's effectiveness could be measured by the cohesion developed by the families as a result of attending the program. Third, family facilitation program facilitators are in an excellent position to add to existing knowledge about family health. Working with many families, facilitators observe the dynamics of various systems. This information is valuable in building and testing models of family health.

In addition, the identified aspects of family health may be used as screening devices for programs. For example, a facilitator may want to deliver a program to mildly dysfunctional families. The aspects of family health could serve to discriminate families in this category.

A focus on family health, family development, and the family as a system is critical in developing family facilitation programs. Each of these areas adds insight and understanding to the complexity of family life and helps unravel the needs of families that can be addressed by a family facilitator.

Chapter 4

Small Group Dynamics

BACKGROUND

Underlying our theoretical focus on families is an assumption of small group dynamics. Because programs for all three approaches of family facilitation—enrichment, treatment, and education—are delivered in groups, the professional needs to know something about group dynamics. A family is a small group of related individuals who possess a history. Small group dynamics, as well as history, influence roles, conflict, and expectations.

However, *family* and *small group* are not necessarily synonymous terms. Thus, professionals should have information not only about the family but also about small group dynamics. For example, why are small groups valuable as vehicles for teaching, enriching, and treating the family? What change factors occur in groups? How do developmental stages progress in groups? What facilitator skills are necessary to lead small groups? What misconceptions are promoted about small groups (misconceptions held by both the professional community and the lay public)? Finally, which properties and processes of the family are similar to the small group and which are not?

There is a paucity of research comparing and contrasting the two types of groups—the family and the ahistorical small group. One of the reasons for the lack of data centers on the circumstance of the family; that is, once families reach professional attention (within any of the areas of education, enrichment, or treatment), their formative processes have long been completed. They have the added dimension of long-term histories as small groups. They have a complex set of implicit and explicit rules, inside jokes, deep secrets, and years of joys and sorrows.

Research has accumulated on both the historical family and the ahistorical small group, though it is the exception rather than the rule when the two areas of research combine data. Both areas are compatible, complementary, and most likely synergistic. This means that the appropriate combination of research on small group and family dynamics may produce a powerful knowledge base from which professionals in the area of family facilitation can more effectively aid the family unit.

One of the original inhibitions to combining the two areas of knowledge has to do with the complexity of the variables. Not only do facilitators need to attend to the present-tense variables of family structure, they must also catch up on all the pertinent past-tense variables. For example, when meeting a family for the first time, an outsider to the family (a workshop facilitator, a therapist, a clergyman) may have the feeling of walking into the middle of a movie with a complex plot. Thus, facilitators who start groups of several families need to be aware of both family dynamics and ahistorical small group dynamics. This is a complex task to say the least.

LITERATURE REVIEW

Small groups have been studied extensively in the last 40 years, particularly during the height of the group movement from approximately 1945 to 1965. Most professionals are familiar with the names Bethel, Big Sur, and the Esalen Institute. These are just some of the places interested in providing a "group experience" for interested participants. These past 40 years were a time of tremendous growth and proliferation of knowledge, involving a number of disciplines. The social sciences, psychology, psychiatry, communication, and business continue to be the main areas in which various facets of the group are studied.

Groups vary in terms of their purpose, size, format, and focus. Recognition of the importance of the group process grew out of Lewin's World War II conclusions that "certain methods of group discussion and decision making were far superior to lecturing and individual instruction for changing ideas and social conduct" (Luft, 1963, p. 2).

Groups are valuable media of communication. From the moment we are born, we spend our lives moving in and out of groups. A lifetime of group memberships covers a broad spectrum of forms, ranging from vast ideological networks that span decades and continents (such as political affiliations or racial ties) to the small and intimate circles of families and friends where our innermost secrets, successes, and failures are known.

Apart from the findings of researchers, it is a common belief that individuals reach their highest potential as members of groups or teams. The accounts of the value of small group affiliation—from John Donne's *No Man Is an Island* to sophisticated experimental designs—suggest that, at an optimal level of group size, people perform their best when not isolated from one another. Humans learn from one another.

A number of learning tools are used in groups. Feedback is used by members to give information to each other about how they see or experience one another. Also, if individuals feel too threatened to venture out on their own, they can watch for a time while others try new ways of feeling, thinking, and behaving. In other words, we change in groups.

Change is a multidimensional construct. It has been defined as a transformation or difference and also as removing or replacing. Changes occur in attitudes, beliefs, values, and behaviors. These changes occur in different ways as a result of education, enrichment, or treatment. The assessment of change also takes various forms in the research literature (see Chapter 10).

Yalom (1970), referring to ahistorical small groups, particularly in the area of treatment, has cited several change or "curative" factors that apply in differing degrees to education, enrichment, and treatment groups: imparting information, instillation of hope, universality, and recapitulation of primary family processes. Thus, individuals who are originally strangers learn to trust one another and allow each other to redo the behaviors that are used in the family. The revised behaviors are often the reason a person seeks education, enrichment, or treatment, since many of the habitual behavior patterns that are reinforced in the family are not appropriate in society's other groups.

Yalom's change or curative factors can be viewed in relationship to ahistorical groups. It may be possible to expand Yalom's list to include historical groups as well. There are obvious similarities between the two types of groups. Whether strangers or siblings, we all need to feel helpful, to feel hope, and to experience emotional catharsis. (In Chapter 19, on divorce adjustment, group members are encouraged in a strength-bombardment exercise to extend positive reinforcement (or in other words, hope). In Chapters 13 and 24, there are several exercises designed to give group members a sense of universality or, "I'm not alone."

The small group literature points up several advantages of group intervention over individual intervention. Group members do not necessarily need to "describe" their problems or issues, since those problems and issues may arise within the microcosm of the group. Individuals cannot remain insulated from reality. Sooner or later, group members will give an individual feedback about reality. In the "critical incidence" research of Leiberman, Yalom, and Miles (1973), individual members in small groups reported that feedback from their group peers had much more impact on them than feedback from their group facilitator. In a one-on-

one encounter, the individual has only one "wall" on which to bounce off ideas, whereas in a group encounter there are many walls. For example, in the program for professional couples in Chapter 14, the exercises are designed to introduce a heterogeneity of ideas or problem-solving techniques that differ from couple to couple, thus allowing individuals a wide variety of models and behavioral alternatives to add to their repertoire of coping skills.

PROPERTIES OF SMALL GROUPS

All groups—from Eaters Anonymous and Marriage Encounter to neighborhood PTA meetings and sewing circles—share common properties. These properties are purpose, membership, developmental stages, and leadership.

Group Purpose

The purpose of a group often determines what the group is called, for example, Alcoholics Anonymous and the Save-the-Whales Foundation. However, there are a number of other ways a group can be categorized. Since here we are most interested in small groups—that is, groups that have face-to-face interaction—Tuckman (1965) provides a useful model as a basis for classification. He classified small groups into (1) therapy groups, in which the task is to help individuals with already existing problems they would like to solve and in which, therefore, the treatment is remedial rather than preventive; (2) training groups (also known as T-groups or sensitivity groups), in which the task is one of enhancing interpersonal sensitivity; and (3) natural groups, which exist as a social function in which members participate to accomplish an assigned task. What distinguishes this last type of group from the others is that, since it already exists, the researcher has no experimental control over it, as, for example, in a governor's task force on the status of minorities.

In addition to Tuckman's model of classification, two other hybrid models deserve mention as relatively new and powerful forms representing the group process. The first is the enrichment group model. While an enrichment group may be made up of parts of other groups, it has a separate identity in that it incorporates experiential exercises or "hands on" experiences. It is usually designed for normally functioning people who desire enrichment in a certain area. The second hybrid model is that of the educational group. The main purpose or task of this group is to impart cognitive material rather than affective or experiential exercises, though there is a recent trend to include more experiential information.

The five group models we have described share an important variable that helps to determine part of their purpose. This variable is structure. Small groups may range from the highly structured to the highly unstructured. Structured groups achieve their purposes through planned or structured exercises. In unstructured groups, few if any specific experiences are planned ahead of time. (Chapter 5 provides further information on the issue of structure.)

Group Membership

In examining the group process, the question of who attends the group and why they do so is important. The groups we have described are all small groups whose membership ranges from 2 to 20. For example, therapy groups may have from 4 to 10 members; an optimal number, according to Yalom (1970), is 7 or 8. However, treatment groups of multiple families may have a much larger number; five families of 6 members each would total 30 members.

Using Tuckman's classification scheme, members of therapy groups are usually referred by professionals, clergy, or friends for remedial help and usually volunteer to attend. That is, unless referred by the courts, group therapy members come of their own accord. Tuckman's training group or T-group may comprise a somewhat larger number of members, perhaps 8 to 15. Once again, if multiple family groups are involved, the membership may be much higher. Membership in such a group is voluntary, and those attending are generally curious about themselves and their interpersonal relationships. Membership in natural groups may be assigned, and it is ended once the group task has been accomplished. Membership in such groups ranges from 5 to 15, and how long the members meet is determined by the complexity of their task.

Enrichment and educational groups usually solicit members from those areas of society that are interested in enhancing their lives with additional affective or cognitive information. Their membership may vary from 5 to 50, or even more if multiple family groups are involved. For example, seven or eight families participating in an educational group with 4 to 5 members each may total 40 or more members. Enrichment and educational groups can deal with larger memberships, sometimes with as many as 100 members, when they are in the form of classes in which general instruction is given. Membership in both types of groups is voluntary.

Group Stages

The stages of development of groups have an interesting similarity of progression, regardless of the group format. In Tuckman's study (1965), many different kinds of small groups appeared to follow the same general pattern of development, whether they were in the form of one 10-hour session or several sessions totalling 50 hours. In Tuckman's now famous nomenclature, the four stages of development are forming, storming, norming, and performing. Each stage accomplishes certain tasks, regardless of the type of group:

1. *Forming,* the first stage, is characterized by group members testing out certain expectations and acceptable behaviors and looking to the facilitator for guidance.
2. *Storming,* the second stage, occurs after members have tested the boundaries and have begun to risk more. They begin to realize that their individual needs may conflict with each other, the facilitator, or the overall group goal.
3. *Norming,* the third stage, is the stage in which group members become more willing to accept each others' idiosyncrasies and begin to define expectations or rules that they agree upon.
4. *Performing,* the final stage, occurs after the initial chit-chat, after the conflict of individual personalities, and after the definition of group goals. The group members finally "get down to business." They begin to work on the group task.

In other group developmental research it has been determined that even those groups that deliberately attempt to avoid the initial stage of forming or conversational chit-chat eventually go through all four stages, though not sequentially. Hill's (1971) hypothesis was that educated "group-wise" psychologists would skip over the first few stages and begin to work right away. She found, however, that, although they started out working (performing) diligently, they eventually went back through all three of the previously missed earlier stages. Thus, group "life" appears to go through predictable stages of development, though the progression may not always follow the same sequence.

Group Leadership

One of the more obvious differences between individual and group settings is leadership or facilitator behavior. In individual settings, the facilitator (the therapist, counselor, leader, tutor, teacher) is dealing with a one-on-one experience. While we are highly complex human beings, it is still less complicated to deal with one person than with many.

Variations in leadership style among different kinds of small groups include differences in training, in professional background, activity level, and responsibility, and in the facilitator's overall intent or purpose. Research indicates that facilitators in therapy and T-groups are less directive, spend less time talking, and depend more on peer-to-peer interaction of group members. Leader directiveness, activity level, and responsibility depend on the particular leader's theoretical orientation. For example, a Rogerian would be far less directive than a behaviorist or a gestaltist. Nonetheless, in comparison to other forms of small groups, therapy and T-group leaders are still considered generally less directive (Leiberman et al., 1973). However, this does not necessarily diminish the facilitator role in such groups. Although the change factors of small groups appear to be mediated through the group members, the facilitator must know how to facilitate what has been called second-order change or subtle social engineering in order for the group to experience the power of small group interaction (Yalom, 1970). Hoffman (1981) defines a first-order change as a connective response that causes minor fluctuations, while a second-order change creates more drastic differences that impact the whole system.

An inaccurate interpretation of the critical incidence research cited earlier might suggest that the facilitator is unnecessary. Indeed, group clinicians have long since given up the Ptolemaic idea of group leadership—that all interaction revolves around the power of the facilitator. However, the opposite view is equally inaccurate—that facilitators generally are not essential to the group process. An appropriate analogy might be the image of an electrician who quietly connects the circuits so that interactions can be completed rather than left dangling.

Members in training and educational groups place more responsibility on the facilitator; they expect an increase of directiveness and activity, particularly in accomplishing the common task at hand. The facilitator or teacher in an educational group is generally responsible for most of the information flow.

There is, however, an array of general facilitator skills that enhance all groups toward   the establishment of goals and the development of change and curative factors. Some of these skills are more aptly developed in a therapy group, others in an educational group, still others in enrichment groups. Their appropriateness depends upon the particular emphasis on task or maintenance.

The basic differences in facilitator style among different kinds of groups depend on the group purpose. In all groups, two variables exist: content or what occurs, and process or how it occurs. These two variables relate, respectively, to task and maintenance skills. Task refers to the accomplishment of the purpose for which the group is assembled; maintenance refers to keeping the group climate or atmosphere conducive to eventual accomplishment of the task. In Exhibit 4-1 is a list of facilitator behaviors that

Exhibit 4-1 Group Facilitator Skills

Task Skills (Accomplishing Goals)

1. Help set goals
2. Keep self working on goals
3. Keep group member working on goals
4. Define group task/tasks
5. Discuss, decide group procedures
6. Operationally define material
7. Place responsibility on members
8. Set action programs
9. Initiate
10. Give information

11. Ask for information
12. Give positive reactions or opinions
13. Give negative reactions or opinions
14. Ask for restatement
15. Restate others' contributions
16. Ask for examples
17. Give examples
18. Give clarification, synthesis, or summary
19. Ask for clarification, synthesis, or summary
20. Assess accomplishment of goals/tasks

Maintenance Skills (Influencing Atmosphere)

21. Acknowledge member's behavior
22. Focus on behaviors member wants to change
23. Reinforce nonpositively:
    - physically (tap)
    - nonverbally (ignore)
    - verbally ("That wasn't useful.")
24. Reinforce positively:
    - physically (hug, pat)
    - nonverbally (head-nod)
    - verbally ("That was good.")
25. Actively confront or reality-test
26. Sponsor, encourage, help, or reward
27. Physically move (so as to enhance atmosphere, e.g., move a chair, move next to someone)
28. Ask for comment on group's movement, progress, or lack of it
29. Give comment on group's movement, progress, or lack of it
30. Test for concerns
31. Express group feeling
32. Establish group rules (norms)
33. Acknowledge group rules (norms)
34. Change group rules (norms)
35. Relieve group tension

36. Express negative feeling
37. Express positive feeling
38. Accept/acknowledge negative feeling
39. Accept/acknowledge positive feeling
40. Actively reinforce new behavior
41. Actively discourage old behavior
42. Create anxiety/cathartic situation
43. Experiment with own behavior
44. Move in a variety of roles
45. Diagnose group processes
46. Identify/understand anxieties and pressures of groups
47. Inform as to what is going on
48. Establish ties between members (e.g., "Tom, can you check that out with Fred?")
49. Interrogate, probe
50. Show support, reassurance
51. Interpret
52. Crystallize (conceptually make more clear, concise)
53. Join members' resistance
54. Elicit "beneficial uncertainty" (ambiguity)
55. Make issues more concrete
56. Debrief-process termination of group activity

Source: Reprinted from A. Fuhriman, *A Compilation of Task and Maintenance Skills for Group Leaders,* Unpublished paper, 1975, with permission of the author.

relate to maintenance and task. These behaviors can be used in differing degrees within structured, unstructured, education, enrichment, or treatment groups.

THE FAMILY AS A SMALL GROUP

Early workers in family therapy, particularly those whose backgrounds were in small group dynamics, stressed the similarities rather than the differences between the family and the small group (Bell, 1976). Many assumed that skills in one area were readily transferable to the other (Kaplan & Sadock, 1971). Studies by Nye and Berardo (1966), Bales and Slater (1955), and others used family and small group as synonymous terms.

One of the obvious factors that produces differences between the family and the small group, a factor that was overlooked by early researchers and clinicians, is history. Families clearly have histories. Looking back, it is surprising that such an important difference was relegated to an obscure research corner. However, the historical dimension was eventually taken into account by, among others, Kaplan and Sadock (1971) who asserted that small groups that are not families "have no childhood, no expectations based on experience that their needs would be gratified, their thoughts and feelings understood" (p. 370).

In fact, history is perhaps the most powerful variable governing the differences between families and small groups. All family variables can be subsumed under history. Exhibit 4-2 presents a summary of variables—such as group norms, roles, conflicts, and cohesion—that are pertinent to understanding the impact that groups have on individuals, families, and parts of families. The summary list is divided into quadrants of potential pros and cons for historical and ahistorical groups, permitting easy comparison across variables.

The following sections examine four areas that are important in the functioning of the family as a small group: roles, norms, cohesion, and conflict. The process of taking on certain roles in a family is an essential element in family interaction. The norms family members develop as a group help determine how the family operates. Small groups experience both conflict and cohesiveness. An understanding of the differences between the development of these two variables in the family is important in implementing family facilitation programs. Conflict cannot be ignored until the group ends; families do not end. T-groups may be able to endure unresolved conflict for ten hours or so; families generally cannot. Finally, cohesion develops differently and with different consequences in small

Exhibit 4-2 Comparison and Contrast of Historical vs. Ahistorical Group Variables

	Historical	*Ahistorical*
Pros	• known or "at home" • previously established ties • predictable roles, expected reciprocity, and complementarity • indirect asking of needs • predictable group rules prescribing most member behavior • family continues even though treatment ends	• members' wants expressed directly in order to be met • less investment in rules; may examine and change more freely • less need to protect homeostasis since group will end • disclosures more likely since there are no "group secrets" • authority struggle with facilitator or powerful members • emphasis on achieved roles; free to try out new roles
Cons	• members less direct • resist examination of implicit rules • protect family homeostasis at cost of individual needs • fear family will break if secrets are known • authority struggle between historical leader and group leader • emphasis on ascribed roles in which member may feel trapped	• members feel as if they are strangers • no previous ties established • roles yet to be established • members ask directly for needs to be met • struggle to establish rules or norms out of nothing • group ends when treatment ends

groups and families. As Haley (1976) has pointed out, families enter the arena with a hierarchy, an already-formed cohesive unit of predetermined statuses and loyalties.

Roles

Family interactions can be explained to some extent by role theory. When interaction is frequent or when the situational context is such that it is highly important for each party to behave in a predictable and inter-dependent way, well-established expectations arise that have an obligatory or normative quality (Johnson, 1970).

Both in and outside the family, people have many kinds of selves or roles. Sociologists have divided roles or positions into two basic types: achieved and ascribed. Ascribed positions are assigned on the basis of factors over which the individual has no control, for example, sex and race. Achieved positions are earned on the basis of individual achieve-ment, for example, becoming boss, peacemaker, breadwinner, or scape-goat. The two kinds of roles overlap and are present in both families and small groups. However, family role structure is often so obscured in its early development that family members may not know the origins of their role as the family peacemaker, for example, and they may feel trapped in it.

In addition to these basic divisions of role, family theorists have devel-oped other categories to explain family roles. Ackerman (as quoted in Foley, 1974) writes about a social role, defining it as "the adaptational unit of personality in action," and regards it as synonymous with the concept of social self (p. 58). The social role is "a permeable membrane that permits a limited penetration in both directions, between environment and self" (p. 58). Further, social roles can be either complementary or reciprocal.

Role differentiation is an important concept in both families and small groups. Differentiation is viewed as a defensive effort to restore a sense of self. The cost of such differentiation, to the individual and to the group, is that, in order to remain a part of the group yet still have individually unique qualities, the individual may distort or simplify personal emotions (Gibbard, Hartman, & Mann, 1974). Each person experiences pressure to be both a unique individual and a valued member of the group. Gibbard argues that individuals in groups wish that they could be distinctive, with their idiosyncratic needs acknowledged, and at the same time maintain a sense of unity and sameness with other group members (Gibbard et al., 1974).

Role differentiation may cause distance, a sense of "I can't be me in this group." On the other hand, role differentiation may serve adaptive functions: a division of labor, an ability to compromise, an increased skill in dealing with conflict, and an appreciation of differences.

Norms

Norms develop when controls are needed to enforce certain attitudes and behaviors that would not normally exist. Normative structures require (1) an initial definition of the attitudes and behaviors in question (for example, dinner is at 6 P.M.), (2) some way of monitoring those members who conform and those who do not (Dad sees who is 15 minutes late), and (3) rewards or punishments for conformity or nonconformity (those who are late go without dinner) (Thibaut & Kelley, 1959).

Normative controls exist in groups whose members have come to depend on the group for need satisfaction. Group members abide by the normative structure because of the mutually satisfying contract, and they disapprove of interference with satisfaction. As we have seen, family researchers refer to this phenomenon as homeostasis. When the cost-benefit ratio of certain norms becomes too high, the member can either leave the group (this is difficult to do if in a family) or encourage the group to change the norm.

Because norms develop more rapidly in highly cohesive groups, the family is likely to have an initially firm or cohesive normative structure. Ahistorical small groups may imitate that style of cohesion but lack some of the more powerful presuppositions for cohesion.

Cohesion

Cohesion refers to the complicated ties that indicate the strength of interrelationships among group members. Authority and power struggles, rejection and isolation, subordination, superordination, and equality are all processes that affect cohesiveness in a group.

Ahistorical small group members differ from members of families in a number of ways. Most small groups generally begin with equal power among the members, although the emergence of experts or leaders may alter that. On the other hand, families or historical groups have well-established positions of power. Mills (1953) and Stredback (1969) studied power alliance inside and outside the family. Their consistent finding was that individuals in groups or families form a variety of alliances that determine decision making as well as power bases. Mills and Stredback differ as to how individuals form alliances. Nevertheless, they agree that alliances are integral to family dynamics. The multiple family group may develop multiple power bases, as the ascribed head of each household vies with four or five leaders from other families for positions of power.

Previous history may or may not prove helpful in developing family cohesiveness. The higher the level of member involvement, the more myths and fantasies the group uses to defend itself against reality (Bion, 1961). Thus, cohesion may inhibit individual expression, particularly if it is synonymous with consensus in family groups.

Conflict

Group compatibility is a key variable in building cohesiveness (Yalom, 1970). Especially if compatibility means agreement or consensus, agreement-at-any-cost can be a tempting option. For groups that have survived a variety of disagreements, conflict and compatibility have been resolved. However, for groups that fear group dissolution and may not have practice with successful conflict resolution, conflict phobia may occur. This is particularly true of families. A family may subtly coerce its members into a pseudocohesion for the sake of blood-line loyalties or for fear of the proverbial "family skeleton" or secret. For ahistorical small groups that share an important group identity, such pseudocompatibility may serve as a front. Laing (1969) described this situation somewhat whimsically in the following verse:

> So we are a happy family
>   and we have no secrets from one another.
> If we are unhappy
>   we have to keep it a secret,
> and we are unhappy that we have to keep it a secret
>   and unhappy that we have to keep secret
> the fact
>   that we have to keep it a secret and that we are keeping all that
>   secret.
> But since we are a happy family
>   you can see this difficulty does not arise. (p. 100)

An even more complicated group is one that combines historical members and ahistorical members, as in multiple family groups. While within the family unit, members do indeed know one another, the combination of families whose members are strangers to each other adds the ahistorical dimension.

Authority involves conflict. Most people struggle with authority at one time or another in one of three general ways: (1) they join the "opposition" by becoming authorities themselves; (2) they are seductive or oversolicitous, thereby hoping to close the distance between themselves and the authority; or (3) they resist or rebel against authority figures. All three behaviors occur in both ahistorical small groups and families.

Ahistorical groups whose facilitators present themselves as experts (the therapist, the teacher) are more authority-like than those whose facilitators profess no expertise or those without appointed facilitators. The "expert" facilitators invite conflict simply by virtue of the positions they occupy. In multiple family groups, there are several ascribed authorities (for example, parents) in addition to the group facilitators; thus, the authority struggle takes on an added dimension.

The struggle with authority can be resolved in a healthy, developmental process. Though labeled differently, this process follows the group development stages of forming, storming, norming, and performing. Reid (1965) calls these stages dependence (facilitator is expert, member depends on that expertise), counterdependence (member realizes facilitator may not be all-knowing and resists original dependence), and consensual validation (facilitator and member develop a give-and-take relationship).

Another interesting authority phenomenon that occurs in historical and ahistorical groups is that of transference. A great deal of speculation as well as documented research has centered on transference. Group members "transfer" onto the group facilitator feelings that originate in the family. This powerful projection of feelings may be the result of many factors: unfulfilled longing for a perfect father, anger at an imperfect parent, and so on. Another factor may be society's expectations about parenting. On the one hand, we expect parents to be good parents, yet, on the other hand, we rarely teach people to be good family leaders. Thus, when a member transfers needs onto the "father figure" of the group facilitator, many variables are at play. The multiple family group has a number of such transferences going on at one time. For example, a son of one family may have problems with his father and transfer these negative feelings to a leader in one of the other families, or may transfer those feelings onto the group facilitator.

If, according to Yalom (1970), the best facilitators are spontaneous, open, active, and risking, we may be putting the ahistorical facilitator and the historical family leader in a compromising position. The ahistorical facilitator may feel free enough to be spontaneous and open, especially if the group is not going to last long. The historical leader, who remains invested in the family, may confuse authoritarian with authoritative and lose openness and risk-taking behaviors in an attempt to be "in control" of the family. Authoritative refers to a leadership style that encourages freedom within reasonable limits. Authoritarian, however, is a leadership style that is highly restrictive.

As group members experience authority struggles and individual differences, conflicts may emerge either in identifiable ways (anger, blaming) or in less identifiable ways (silence, nervous laughter, avoidance). Conflict can undermine a group if it remains beneath the awareness of group members. Such conflict may result in dangerous indifference ("Well, who cares about this group anyway. I guess I'll leave") or in an eventual explosion that threatens the group's existence.

Families experience many types of conflict: value conflicts, conflicts between family siblings, conflicts between parent and child. However, conflict is a predictable part of development and can lead eventually to cohesion.

SOME MISCONCEPTIONS ABOUT GROUPS

Misconceptions about the group process may contribute to the resistance of professionals and family members to utilize the group process. Exposure, lack of trust, rejection, and potential harm all may reinforce a person's hesitation to become part of a group. When an individual joins a group as part of a family unit, the same fears may exist. Within the family unit, members may fear rejection or lack of trust, they may feel things are getting worse rather than better, or they may discover that they really are the "oddballs" who have values that are different from those of the other family members. Some may have heard horror stories about people becoming worse after they joined a group. They may fear losing their identity, being expected to "tell all," or actually telling all and being rejected for it. These fears, some real and some not, are part of the group mythology. To pretend they do not exist is akin to pretending that conflict does not exist. Nevertheless, all these misconceptions can be dispelled by appropriate education and positive experience.

Why should we treat, teach, or enrich the family in a group context, given all these limitations, complexities, and potential misconceptions? Leiberman (1975) suggests five reasons for using groups that may be applied to families.

1. The group process allows for the development of cohesiveness or a sense of belonging. Some family members may feel like outsiders regardless of the external label of "the family."
2. Groups have the capacity to control (reward and punish) behavior. Often, families seek help because they experience a lack of control regarding reward and punishments.

3. The group has the capacity to define reality for the individual. This is particularly important for enmeshed families who concoct their own reality and impose it on all members.
4. The group has the capacity to induce and release intense emotions. Many families have implicit rules that constantly smother powerful feelings for fear their release will shatter the family.
5. The group's capacity to provide a contrast for social comparison and feedback is readily available. Families can actually see how they compare with other families and determine if some of their behavior is dysfunctional.

These are just some of the reasons why working with the family in a group or in multiple groups is a powerful tool with great potential.

Chapter 5

Structure in Family Facilitation

Structure places parameters around a program. Structure is a multi-dimensional concept that is generally concerned with influencing the group process by focusing and controlling group attention and behavior (Bednar & Battersby, 1976). Melnick and Woods (1978) define structure as the context within which the group process unfolds. As used in this book, the structure of a program defines the roles of the facilitator and participants, the methods, and the time sequencing of activities.

Family facilitation programs can vary in degree of structure from those with little structure to those that are semistructured or highly structured, from those with only a few preplanning variables to those with many such variables. Family life education, family enrichment and family treatment overlap, not only in terms of content, but also in terms of the degree of structure involved. Figure 5-1 illustrates the overlap of the three facilitation approaches with regard to structure.

ADVANTAGES IN THE USE OF STRUCTURE

There are a number of advantages in the use of structure in programs. Drum and Knott (1977) list the following:

- Individual goal attainment can be structured in such a way that self-discovery and self-enhancement are not mystical.
- The learning process becomes less threatening.
- Peer and professional feedback relating to specific interpersonal skills and life issues is provided.
- The use of structured treatment is economical.
- Change and growth are encouraged by providing a mechanism for active problem solving.

Figure 5-1 Overlap among Structured and Unstructured Family
Enrichment, Family Life Education, and Family Therapy

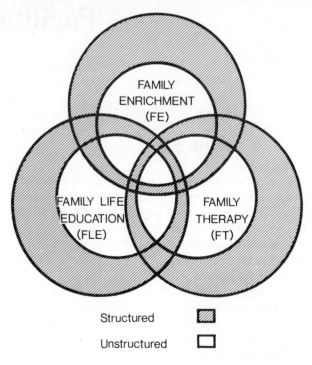

Structured   ▨

Unstructured   ☐

- Participants become more aware of the frequent occurrence of the type of problem situations they are solving.
- The stigma associated with seeking help is reduced by focusing on common developmental needs.
- The facilitator is usually responsible for helping the participants set boundaries and limitations, thus providing a sense of psychological security.

A review of the literature suggests that structured groups are effective in helping people change. Bednar and Weinberg (1969) found that structured counseling programs for underachievers in school were far more effective than unstructured programs. Increased self-disclosure and openness occurred more in structured than in unstructured treatments aimed at increasing self-concept (Ware & Barr, 1977). Bednar (1978) agrees that structure increases the likelihood of risk-taking by group members. Bednar, Melnick and Kaul (1974) conducted an empirical study to test this hypothesis, and concluded that risk-taking behavior was a critical component in change and that risk taking was facilitated by structure. DeJulio, Bentley, and Cockayne (1976) found that early structure in a group helped member participation and performance.

Structure may be most important at the beginning of a group (DeJulio et al., 1976). Later, anxiety may be high as members realize that they may have to make personal changes. Activities that encourage change may be more successful if structured initially. Persons tend to change if they see others changing, particularly when the direction of change is valued by other group members. That may explain why group members who are resistant at first begin to change later.

Structured format has advantages in some aspects of program delivery. For example, some structured programs with specified approaches allow preprofessionals in training to administer groups. Facilitator manuals help preprofessionals run some groups without special training.

Another advantage involves research. When groups are structured, the comparison of variables in enrichment, education, or treatment programs is a much more definable process. By holding certain variables constant (amount of time, number of sessions, kinds of group exercises), researchers can more readily study outcome and process variables among, as well as between, groups. Feedback provided by researchers may then encourage group facilitators to refine their group structures in a more systematic manner.

THE STRUCTURE CONTINUUM

Structure and ambiguity are often viewed as opposite ends of a continuum. Some theories of change emphasize ambiguity as an essential part of the change process, particularly because it increases anxiety and may bring into focus the behaviors an individual would like to change. These theories, in which change emerges from ambiguous situations, do have merit. Indeed, many professionals have wondered what advantage there is in reducing ambiguity, hence in reducing anxiety, by introducing structure. This issue is resolved if one views structure *along* a continuum, from low structure to high structure, rather than as a discrete end of the continuum.

A number of studies have indicated how and when more structure might be useful. Lee and Bednar (1976), in studying the effects of clarity and structure on member performance, found that ambiguity tends to be associated with increased anxiety and decreased learning. Barlow, Hansen,

Finley, and Fuhriman (1982) noted the tendency of groups (highly unstructured situations) to stay within the "safer" communication styles, as measured by the Hill Interaction Matrix (Hill, 1965), when they were experiencing too much anxiety and had no immediate support from the group facilitator to venture into a more therapeutic (change-oriented) style. Bentley (1974) found that, although persons tended to resist change to the degree that they felt it had been imposed upon them, they were more apt to support the group goals if they had more control in manning them (as in Tuckman's "norming" phase). Other findings (Bednar, 1978) in a variety of group settings indicated that high anxiety and low risk-taking were correlated with fewer member gains, which might suggest that a certain amount of structure is needed in order to lower anxiety and that increased risk-taking might increase member gains.

Some researchers and clinicians question the value of "imposed" structure as a means of facilitating the group process. Ambiguity (which could be defined as the lack of planned structure or the absence of explicit expectation) may, in fact, encourage people to encounter and resolve individual issues as they develop (Bednar & Battersby, 1976; Corey & Corey, 1977; Yalom, 1970). Perry (1970) suggests that ambiguity is one of the stages in a necessary progression of development from adolescence into adulthood. That is, as life becomes more complex, we cannot simply choose options that are black or white. Rather, ambiguity plays a major role in our development of abstract thought and complex commitments. Wright and L'Abate (1977) found that, although there were some gains between marital couples in structured as opposed to unstructured groups, there were more gains in a third group, focused on clinical treatment, whose members were given unstructured therapy.

Rogers (1961) asserted that anxiety is the client's friend. Though he was speaking in particular about therapy, he believed that anxiety, the fear of the unknown, occurs when the individual is standing on the very edge of uncertainty, a cliff that represents a leap into discovery. The individual has the choice between the known and the unknown and may accept, in the words of Hamlet, "the ills we have rather than fly to those we know not of." Researchers and writers alike view the unknown or anxiety as an invitation into what may be a new and more helpful way of being.

Anxiety is not a byproduct of ambiguity or low structure. Other variables create anxiety: the element of risk, the newness of an experience, performance in front of others, a sense of loss of control (someone else is in charge), and so on. Thus, even highly structured programs have elements of anxiety. However, a highly structured program reduces irrelevant anxiety or ambiguity by placing parameters around the program. For example, a group member may not be anxious about when a group will end, but may be anxious about how to perform an exercise in front of others. Thus, anxiety and structure both move along a continuum.

The move toward more structure as a treatment of choice may have been the result of several events during the height of the group movement. For example, during the 1960s, when ambiguity was associated with "letting it all hang out" in sensitivity groups, the term was cast in an unfavorable light. However, the renewed effort to study the impact of small groups on individuals has shed more light on group process and outcome variables to increase our knowledge about when to use ambiguity therapeutically in both structured or unstructured groups (Leiberman et al., 1973).

The impact that structure has on facilitators is also important. The facilitator's personality should not be restricted by structure. Facilitators should choose the level of structure that optimizes their skill level. This can be done by experimenting with different levels of structure in groups. In this way, facilitators will be able to identify the kinds of structured exercises that enhance or reduce their skill level.

Facilitators' beliefs about how people learn and change have a great deal of influence on how they work within a range of structures in education, enrichment or treatment groups. For example, if a facilitator believes that people learn only if they can consciously understand and that anxiety in any degree is harmful, the group members will be "protected" by the facilitator from cognitive confusion or emotional stress. This protection may come in the form of one highly structured exercise after another. If, however, the facilitator believes learning can occur even in the midst of confusion and that a certain amount of anxiety helps the group members repattern old ways of behaving, the facilitator would be more likely to wait for members to arrive at the insight on their own through the use of less structure.

As stated earlier, the range of structure is optional. If structured programs are so tightly designed that there is no room for ambiguity and subsequent anxiety (in moderate doses), they may lose one of their more powerful tools for change. A program that has enough structure to hold up the roof, but leaves enough room to move underneath the roof, will be able to allow for individual, couple, and family growth and for facilitator variation.

WHY USE STRUCTURE WITH FAMILIES?

Structured approaches tend to encourage professionals to relate theory, assessment, technique, and evaluation in a much more organized manner. The rationale for time-limited and content-structured groups is multifaceted. First, structured programs are cost- as well as time-efficient. The use of preprofessionals for some programs (graduate students, paraprofessionals) reduces the expense for the client and is more cost-efficient. A structured program that is initially written, using a small portion of a professional's time, and then packaged for later multiple use is particularly efficient. For example, the popular Couples Communication Program (CCP) was originally written by several professionals who then packaged it in a very usable facilitator's manual that has been used with thousands of people.

Second, structured programs can use action-oriented approaches or interventions. The target groups (single parents, overweight people, families in crisis), feel immediately involved. The deliberate intervention attempts to alter the ongoing system of the family as soon as possible. Patterns the family members may have been immersed in for years are brought to light and repatterned almost immediately.

Third, structured programs focus on observable behavior, on interactions in the present. "Minor changes in overt behavior or its verbal labelling often are sufficient to initiate progressive developments" (Weakland, Fisch, Watzlawick, & Bodin, 1974, p. 145). The primary task in treatment programs is to alter patterns in the family that have not worked before, yet have been maintained due to lack of alternatives or fear of change, and to intervene as quickly and pragmatically as possible.

Fourth, a professional's theoretical orientation need not be changed. Generally, structured exercises or interventions can be superimposed on the facilitator's style and theoretical orientation.

Structured programs attempt to take what might appear to be a body of nebulous life skills and turn them into concretely described techniques. Structured programs have been regarded by some as "nondynamic," simple-minded interventions for a complicated phenomenon. But research suggests that many such "simple" interventions have been successful in producing change, for example, Assertive Training and Marriage Encounter.

Structured programs combine many of the advantages of treatment, education, and enrichment. They can be used in conjunction with other kinds of intervention, or as the sole intervention mode. They can be used with a variety of populations and in a number of settings. Finally, they can better utilize professionals' time and talents by structuring for them those elements that help the most in operationally definable ways. Those elements can then be replicated by other professionals or preprofessionals in research or service.

Part II

How To Design Structured Family Facilitation Programs

Chapter 6

Introduction to Program Design

The variety and availability of structured family facilitation programs have increased greatly in the past decade. However, this proliferation does not guarantee a magic fit between what is available and what is needed for a particular group of people in a specific context. Consequently, the ability to modify a program or to create a new one becomes a valuable asset for professionals. Thoughtful consideration of the numerous possibilities for programs and acquisition of skills in designing family facilitation programs becomes the cornerstone for successful experiences for all concerned—designers, deliverers, and recipients. In this context, the following four chapters show professionals how to design and modify their own programs.

The recognition of a need for a family facilitation program may come from a variety of sources: public agencies, educational or religious institutions, government policy makers, professionals working with a specific population, researchers, or a group of families with similar needs that request help. Regardless of its origin, however, many questions surface quickly and need immediate attention in order to design an effective program. For whom is the program planned? What approach should be used? Who should design and deliver the program? What are the goals of the program? What should the program include? Do these goals meet the needs of the targeted people? These are but a few of the questions answered in Chapters 7 and 8.

A design is a map that can be followed from the first conceptual stages to the last evaluation stages of the program. The program is what is delivered to the targeted group. All of the elements of the design should be written clearly and simply, with enough detail that the entire procedure can be followed easily and replicated if appropriate.

The design has four stages: (1) preplanning (Chapter 7), (2) development of the program (Chapter 8), (3) delivery of the program (Chapter 9), and (4) evaluation of the program (Chapter 10). Figure 6-1 illustrates the progression of these four stages. Each stage has a number of important interrelated variables. Each stage is described in the appropriate chapter by examining the issues and explaining the decisions that are needed to complete the design.

Because of the unique features of each program, the order in which decisions are made for the various parts is not always the same. For example, the point at which decisions are made about who will design the program and what personnel configuration to use varies for each program. However, the guidelines presented in each chapter will facilitate decision making with regard to program design. To this end, the examples that are used illustrate a point rather than set a prescribed sequential model.

Figure 6-1 The Four Stages of Program Design

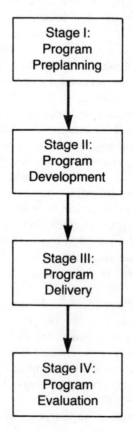

Chapter 7

Stage I:
Program Preplanning

The quality and timing of preplanning of the program often determine its effectiveness (Drum & Knott, 1977). Lippett and Schindler-Rainman (1975) clearly identify the task for designers: "Planning for the mobilization and use of all the resources which will facilitate learning and problem solving is the focus of the design task" (p. 189).

Preplanning strategies focus on design decisions that help develop, deliver, and evaluate a program's effectiveness. However, as we have noted, decisions do not always follow the same order; the order can vary from design to design. Planning is facilitated by knowing how to make decisions about the following:

- identifying the target population
- assessing the needs of the target group
- establishing goals for the program
- selecting an appropriate approach
- selecting a designer
- developing a timetable
- making decisions about design variables
- choosing a delivery base

Although the other stages—development, delivery, and evaluation—of the program also require preplanning, the preplanning stage, with all of the variables mentioned above, is basic in preparing for the later stages. Figure 7-1 illustrates the various components of preplanning and its relationship to the other three stages of design.

Figure 7-1 Components of Program Preplanning

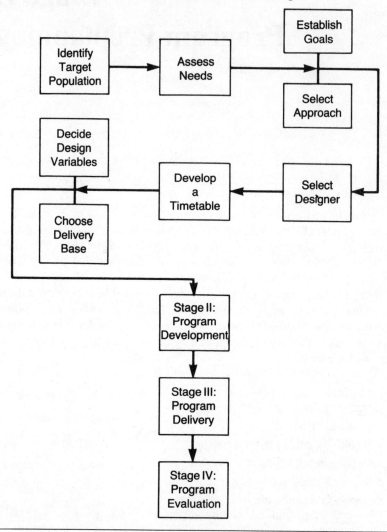

IDENTIFYING THE TARGET POPULATION

To target a population means to select a group of individuals, couples, families, or parts of a family that would, because of common characteristics, benefit from a family facilitation program. Common characteristics give definition to the group and are endless in nature. Some examples are issues (surviving on limited or reduced income), problems (preadolescent children having difficulty adjusting to the death of a parent), life style (single-parent families), and developmental experiences (families with the first adolescent).

Groups, given their common characteristics, arise in a number of settings: church (for example, premarital couples who want education correlated with religious values), community (families with adolescents who commit vandalism or housebreaking), schools (children identified as gifted or as having social problems), work (executive families with a parent who is in and out of the family), agencies (parents who are experiencing stress), medical services (women with mastectomies), mental health services (anorexic young women), and prisons (inmates who are reentering their families). These are but a few of the many types of target populations.

Who targets the population for a program? A few groups target themselves, by identifying needed programs and actively seeking someone to design a program. Other groups are identified and selected by educators, family facilitators, nurses, doctors, psychologists, social workers, administrators, politicians, or other professionals.

Because of the glaring needs of some populations, the selection of a target group may be obvious or may be mandated by policy or administration. For instance, an agency serving handicapped children may recognize that parents need help in coping with their children's handicaps and the effect on them and the family. Or the policy of the agency may be to provide supportive help to parents. If either or both of these situations exist, an assessment of parental and family needs could then be conducted by surveying the parents and staff involved. This assessment could then be used to develop an appropriate program.

Targeting a group is related to decisions about which approach to use. For example, a current national problem arises from the large number of divorces each year and their effect on both family members and society as a whole. Which approach should be used with which population to help resolve this problem? Programs of enrichment and family life education have in fact been developed and delivered to improve existing marriages and reduce the number of divorces (Bosco, 1976; Campbell, 1980; Mace & Mace, 1976; Ridley, Avery, Harrell, Leslie, & Dent, 1981; Witkin & Rose, 1978). Premarital classes for engaged couples and preparation-for-marriage classes are a part of this trend (Bader, Microys, Sinclair, Willett, & Conway, 1980; Guerney & Guerney, 1981; Stahmann & Hiebert, 1980). Finally, individual, family, and group therapy is available in agencies and the private sector in an attempt to meet the needs of those suffering from the trauma of divorce (Hozman & Froiland, 1976; Vogel-Moline, 1979).

The program in Chapter 19 is an example of a professional responding to the needs of a divorced population in the community and thus pinpointing the group to be served. The targeted group is described as divorced individuals having psychological and/or social adjustment problems manifested in some or all of the following symptoms: depression, anxiety, withdrawal from social situations, and an expressed lack of confidence and ability in handling family problems. The purpose of the program was to help divorced people (the targeted population) gain relief from these symptoms.

ASSESSING THE NEEDS OF THE TARGET GROUP

Specific information about the needs of a group is essential in choosing an approach and developing the goals for a program. The process of collecting, analyzing, and categorizing this information is described as assessing the needs of the group. In determining how to do this, the sources of the information must be considered. The group itself obviously knows something about its needs. Group interviews, questionnaires, surveys, and formal assessment instruments can provide a great deal of information about the needs of the group.

People who are not part of the group or an outside agency can also provide valuable information. Professionals and journalists often review studies, articles, and reports and summarize their findings. Some research projects are aimed at learning about specific groups. Also, government and private agencies collect information about those they serve. These sources and others can provide a body of knowledge that can help to pinpoint needs.

Sometimes the assessment is made easier because increasing numbers of the target population appear in agencies, schools, or other institutional settings or make their needs known in other ways. Newspapers, popular magazines, TV, radio, professionals in mental health, and other researchers may begin to focus on the population, thus creating a pool of knowledge from which to draw.

Whatever the method or combination of methods used to assess the needs of a population, the analysis of the collected data should clearly identify the needs. For example, in the Chapter 11 program, Feinauer found, through a review of the literature, that rape victims need to work through internalized guilt, shame, and vulnerability that immobilize their growth. Their parents need help in working through their feelings and in learning how to support their daughters. Thus, the needs of any given group—however numerous, complex, and demanding—guide the selection of goals and approach for a program.

DETERMINING GOALS

No matter what the approach, all program designs call for changing something within individuals and/or families—whether it is behavior, attitudes, affect, or interactional patterns. In order to do this, the design must take into account the needs of prospective participants and the program must be planned accordingly. There must be a clear connection between the needs of the participants and the nature of the program. This connection will be clear only if the goals for the program guide the total design of the program (Bagarozzi & Rauen, 1981; Mager, 1972).

Three kinds of goals—overall, intermediate, and specific—guide the design of the program. Each kind of goal has its unique functions. The overall goal is very general in nature, but it helps designers focus on a selected population and on what they want to do for that population. For instance, in selecting an overall goal for a program to help divorced people, Hoopes (Chapter 19) chose to focus on reducing psychological and social adjustment problems for individuals experiencing divorce. Because this goal is so general, the approach—education, enrichment, or treatment—is difficult to select unless chosen arbitrarily. Nevertheless, in order to ascertain the structure, content, and process of the program, intermediate goals must be determined.

Intermediate goals are formulated from the identified needs of the selected group, thus narrowing the range and focusing on particular group needs. Because all needs cannot be addressed, intermediate goals help select those that will receive attention. The intermediate goals will also specify the group to receive the program, select the appropriate approach, structure the program, and select outcome evaluation objectives. These decisions interrelate, often making it difficult to determine what should be done first. In the example of the divorce adjustment program, the following four intermediate goals might be formulated:

1. to increase understanding about the psychological and social impact of divorce on families
2. to reduce depression of divorced spouses
3. to increase social interaction and reduce social withdrawal of children of divorced parents
4. to train divorced parents and current spouses how to communicate with children during visitations

An examination of each goal can lead to the selection of a particular group that could benefit from the program. This kind of decision can be made arbitrarily by the designer, or more specific goals can be formulated that clearly stipulate the approach to be used. Each of the intermediate goals listed above identifies a group that could use a family facilitation program. The first goal would be appropriate for all families; the second, for divorced spouses; the third, for children of divorced parents; and the fourth, for divorced parents, their current spouses, and the children of the former marriage who move in and out of the home.

The specific group for the first goal is still vague, since the term *families* does not narrow the focus enough; whereas the other three goals are much more specific. Thus, the selection of an approach may still be uncertain for the first goal, while the designers decide on treatment for the second, education for the third, and enrichment for the fourth. The choice of the approach could then guide in the selection of more intermediate and specific goals. Conversely, the selection of additional goals might determine the selection of the approach. In any event, once the approach and the set of intermediate goals are selected, the basic structure of the program—content, process, and format—can be determined. Also, the intermediate goals, or at least some of them, can be refined for outcome evaluation. The intermediate goals thus lead to the development of specific goals or objectives for each program session.

The following goals are taken from Feinauer's program of multiple family therapy for single rape victims and their parents (Chapter 11). They are presented here to show the relationship of overall, intermediate, and specific goals.

- *Overall goal*. The purpose of Feinauer's program is to counteract the rape victim's internalized guilt, shame, and vulnerability that immobilize her growth and to aid her parents as they attempt to resolve their feelings and function as a healthy support system.
- *Intermediate goals*. The following intermediate goals were formulated:
  a. to facilitate an emotional response
  b. to explore misconceptions about rape and the expectations surrounding rape
  c. to explore and resolve the unique problems resulting from rape experiences, with emphasis on developing constructive strategies for dealing with them
  d. to focus on the future with an emphasis on growth
- *Specific goals*. Goals are often written in terms of objectives, especially when they get to the specific stage. Three of Feinauer's ten specific objectives were:
  a. open, direct communication among members of the group as they discuss their shared life crisis

b. ventilation of feelings, including resentment and anger
c. decreased evidence of depressive (helpless, out of control) affect in the family

This chapter shows how to match goals, content, and process in developing a program. Feinauer's program illustrates how sessions are connected to goals through the use of content and process.

Earlier, we emphasized the use of structured programs to aid in evaluating the value of programs to families. The specificity of goals is a basic, necessary part of a structured program. Appropriate assessment measures and procedures correlated with the goals can then be used to evaluate the effectiveness of the program (see Chapter 10).

SELECTING AN APPROACH

As already indicated, the selection of an approach and the determination of goals are so interrelated that it is difficult to determine which comes first. The matching of intermediate goals with the approach determines the appropriateness of the program for the selected group and the program's potential effectiveness. In this section, we describe a process for determining which approach to use for specific groups.

Assume that a needs assessment has divided divorce adjustment problems into three general categories: (1) divorced individuals and their families who seem to be making adequate psychological and social adjustments but who feel isolated and discouraged at times; (2) divorced individuals and their families who seem to be making adequate psychological and social adjustments but flounder in certain areas because they lack skills and information in specific areas (such as getting credit), experience difficulty living on a reduced income, and make poor decisions with only one parent as a resource; and (3) divorced individuals and their families who are having psychological and social adjustment problems manifested in such things as depression, withdrawal, truancy, and fighting within the family.

The first category of problems indicates that the families seem well-adjusted but also feel isolated and discouraged. Here, an enrichment program that focuses on the families' strengths, provides interaction with other families, and gives them information and strategies to keep them active and integrated with other families may be an appropriate choice.

The second category indicates that the families lack information and skill but are well-adjusted. Here, the provision of information and teaching skills seems best suited to an education program that will buoy family and individual confidence and give the family members what they need to adjust to their life situation.

The third category clearly identifies families with psychological and social adjustment problems. Some in this group may respond very well to either enrichment or education programs, but it is more likely such programs will not emphasize the solutions to specific problems nor provide remedial help. In this case, therefore, treatment would be most appropriate.

SELECTING A DESIGNER

When an approach is chosen, based upon the assessment of the needs of a group and the decisions about goals that are clearly tied to those needs, the design of the program can move forward. The next step is selecting a designer. In some situations, a designer may be designated before the target group is identified, before the needs of the group are assessed, before goals are identified, or before an approach is selected. This may be done out of need, by assignment, or because of ignorance of what is needed.

The designer of a program has the responsibility of putting the four stages of design into a map with enough detail to ensure that a program gets written, delivered to an appropriate audience, and evaluated for its effectiveness. This requires wise and timely decisions, collaboration with other people, and management of time and resources.

Assuming that the need for a family facilitation program has been established by an agency, institution, or a professional working with families, a number of questions about the program should be answered before a decision is made as to who will design the program. What personal qualifications are necessary for effective family program design? Is the potential designer qualified to design education, enrichment, or treatment programs? Will the program be designed primarily for service or research? Does the design originate from within the agency or from outside? Which personnel configuration will work best in designing the program?

Sometimes the answers to these questions are readily available, and the decision of who will design the program can be answered quickly. Or it may be that the designer of the program is self-selected or designated because of the person's job description. In some circumstances, because of complex issues, more intensive study and deliberation may be necessary. In this section, we examine the issues posed by each of the above questions.

What Personal Qualifications Are Necessary?

Whether the program is for enrichment, education, or treatment, the qualification of the designers of programs are basically similar, though specific qualifications are necessary for each approach. Appropriate interpersonal skills, experiences, and personal characteristics will increase the likelihood that the designer will enjoy the work and produce an effective and appropriate program. In addition to personal experience, a background or working knowledge in several fields is most helpful in developing programs. Some of the related fields that seem particularly relevant are healthy and dysfunctional family development, group dynamics and development, human relations training, social skills training (assertiveness, value clarification, communication, parent effectiveness, sexuality), and health and recreation. Also knowledge in the following areas will facilitate the development of good programs: organizations (budgets, funding, decision-making policies, hierarchy, power), change (particularly in families), approaches to design, and group dynamics in a structured format. The ability to get along with people, to make decisions and follow through, to speak and write effectively, and to organize time, talent, and resources will enhance use of this knowledge. Designers need not have all this information or possess all the cited skills, but they should be aware of the basics and be able to go after the information and arrange consultations when appropriate.

Experiences and personal characteristics vary a great deal among successful designers. Past experience in designing any kind of a program will prove very helpful. The ability to generalize from past experiences, blended with optimum use of personal strengths, is a powerful combination. Intelligence, creativity, flexibility, and adaptability also seem to be personal characteristics of successful designers.

Qualifications for designing a specific program must be matched with fundamentals about that program. Knowledge about the targeted population, writing ability, and methodological soundness are obvious qualifications (Gurman & Kniskern, 1977; Mace & Mace, 1976; Sporakowski & Staneszewski, 1980; Sullivan, Gryzlo, & Schwartz, 1978).

Do Designer and Approach Match?

The three approaches to family facilitation programs overlap each other, but each serves a unique purpose, depending on the needs of the target population and the goals of the program. Let us assume that the appropriate selection for a given program has been made. The important consideration then becomes one of matching the overall design, session activities and procedures, and delivery with the basic intent of the program, that is, enrichment, education, or treatment.

The person selected to design a program must meet the criteria for writing that particular program. Someone may be an excellent teacher who can develop learning activities effectively for enrichment and family life education but may not know enough about dysfunctional patterns and how to change them for a given population to write an effective treatment program. The reverse of this is a person who understands therapy but does not have adequate experience with enrichment or family life education. Thus, the selection of a designer should be based on the ability to do a particular job.

Service or Research?

When considering group family facilitation programs, professionals in agencies and private settings often respond to the needs of people by designing programs for efficiency of service. Usually their interests focus on serving more of the same population or on serving a new population with surfacing needs, and doing so in more effective ways. Thus, some programs are designed primarily for service. Though assessing the quality of service or doing outcome evaluation may receive attention and be important, it is secondary to meeting the needs of the people. Designers of service-oriented programs do not have to focus on research issues (although they might), and they do not need as many research skills as those who develop programs primarily for research.

On the other hand, researchers who are developing major research projects or graduate students who are looking for theses or dissertation topics—both creating designs to serve families—have specific questions they want answered about the population, about the methodology of service, or about the outcome or effects of a program. Although quality control of service and concern for the needs of the targeted population are evident in the design, the major concern here is research. The designers of these kinds of programs need to be conversant with research design, internal and external validity issues, control factors for program delivery, and assessment instruments and procedures. They also may need consultants to help with the content of their programs.

Thus, in considering who will design a program, the question of research or service, or a combination of the two, is important because of what it implies about the emphasis in design. Prospective designers may not have equal qualifications for designing research and service programs.

From Inside or Outside?

If the design of a program is to originate within the institution or agency, the question of who designs the program can be confined to the staff in the agency. Does anyone have the qualifications to design the program, or do the staff or designated individuals need training? If no staff members are available to design the program, one may be selected from outside the agency. Programs found outside the agency may be used as they are or modified. Existing programs may be selected from a variety of sources. The following list is not exhaustive, but it is exemplary:

- other agencies with the same needs who have developed programs
- review of theses and dissertations, for example, Cauthorn (1976) on teaching leadership skills to fathers, Fisher (1974) on teaching observation skills to couples, and Vogel-Moline (1979) on divorce/separation adjustment
- published programs in books and articles, for example, Avery, Ridley, Leslie, and Handis (1979) on family life education and dating couples, Campbell (1980) on couples groups and weekend workshops, Dinkmeyer and Dinkmeyer (1979) on step-parent education, Hawkins and Killorin (1979) on one-day workshops, Hof and Miller (1981) on marriage enrichment, Ridley et al. (1981) on educational premarital programs, and Robin (1979) on a family program that could be adapted to multiple family therapy
- marketed programs

Contracting with an outside designer to create a program is an alternative for agencies who must, or choose to, look outside their own staff resources. Finding an appropriate outside designer requires a knowledge of what kind of design is wanted and a search for someone with appropriate qualifications. The community grapevine can provide good information about professionals who are designing and delivering programs. Universities and colleges have a wealth of talent among their faculties, staff, and graduate students. Professional consultants also provide this kind of service.

Which Personnel Configuration?

The primary questions here are: how many people will be involved in designing a program and, of those involved, who will work on what stages of the design? To look at the range of possibilities, it is necessary to review the stages of design structure.

The first stage, program preplanning, includes suggestions, limitations, and directions for the other stages. The second stage, program development, entails writing the structure of all activities and procedures, including a training program for those who will facilitate the groups. The third stage, program delivery, is the actual presentation to the people in need, with considerations for further marketing and delivery. The fourth stage, program evaluation, contains issues relevant to the other stages, since evaluation must be preplanned, written into the program, and executed where the program is delivered.

Table 7-1 lists some of the personnel configurations for designing family programs. For ease of explanation, three roles and three people are presented. However, these do not represent all the roles or people needed to complete a design. Nor are all of the variations shown in the table; more people and more roles could be involved, which would make the variations even more numerous. Still, as can be seen, even with three people, a great many variations are possible.

The selection of one person to design the entire program, develop the learning activities and procedures, and deliver and market the program is represented on line 1, with Person A performing all three roles. Line 2 suggests that Person A could not deliver the program; therefore, Person B was designated to do so. The other variations represent total-team (line 5) and partial-team (lines 6–13) approaches.

The possibilities for personnel configurations take on greater complexity if an agency utilizes people from inside and outside the agency, hires

Table 7-1 Sample Personnel Configurations for Designing Family Facilitation Programs

Personnel Configuration	Preplanning	Developing Activities	Delivery of Program
1.	Person A	Person A	Person A
2.	Person A	Person A	Person B
3.	Person A	Person B	Person B
4.	Person A	Person B	Person C
5.	Persons ABC	Persons ABC	Persons ABC
6.	Persons AB	Person A	Person A
7.	Persons AB	Person B	Persons AB
8.	Persons AB	Person B	Person C
9.	Persons AC	Persons AB	Person C
10.	Persons AC	Persons ABC	Persons AC
11.	Persons ABC	Person B	Person C
12.	Persons ABC	Persons ABC	Person A
13.	Persons ABC	Person A	Persons ABC

consultants, and emphasizes research or service. For example, line 11 assumes that Persons A and C from within the agency have prepared the overall design, using a structured program developed by Person B, who is a professional in the community. It assumes that Person B has worked extensively with the population targeted for the program and is therefore qualified to consult with Persons A and C as they design the program. Then Person C delivers the program. If this particular program were designed more for service than for research, there would be less emphasis on research measures.

Thus, the choice of who will design a program is more complex than one would suspect. The personal qualifications of the designers, the variety of personnel configurations, the location of origin of the program (from inside or outside), the type of program desired (enrichment, education, or treatment), and whether research or service is emphasized must all be considered in making the choice.

DEVELOPING THE DESIGN

Timetable

The timing sequence designates the order in which things are done and who will be responsible for each part. Some activities may overlap others. Each design and its timing sequence will be unique and tailored to the needs of a particular program. Exhibit 7-1 illustrates an initial timing sequence for a program. As more details are planned, the timing sequence for the program can be elaborated.

Design Variables

Selecting an appropriate design for a program challenges the designer because of the myriad of alternatives (Lippett & Schindler-Rainman, 1975). Variations in types of participant relationships, procedures for placing participants in groups, size of the groups, types of interactions desired, formats, settings, and cost and facilitator variables all provide rich choices for design alternatives. The following examination of the variations in each of these areas will guide designers in making appropriate choices.

Participant Relationships

For family facilitation programs, the issue of the relationship of the participants must be considered carefully. Whether strangers, casual acquaintances rarely encountered, acquaintances encountered in a routine

Exhibit 7-1 Illustrative Timing Sequence for Program Design

Designers: S. Akers and J. Lambert
Program Title: A Structured Group Treatment for Divorced Individuals.
Purpose: To reduce psychological and social adjustment problems.
Projected completion time: September–August

	September	October	November	December	January	February	March	→	September
Design Stage	Preplanning	Development of the program, pretesting, revision, packaging and marketing —Advertising 　—Orientation 　—Preassessment 　—Selection of participants 　—Training of facilitators			Delivery of the program		Post assessment	(Revision?)	Follow-up
Who is Responsible	(Akers/ Lambert)	(Lambert)	(Akers)	(Akers)	(Akers/Lambert)		(Akers/ Lambert)	(Lambert)	(Akers)

pattern (for example, through work, educational class, neighborhood, religious or professional affiliation), friends, or family members, they may affect the content and structure of the program.

Many groups will have some combination of such relationships. For example, a divorce adjustment group might have five people who are strangers, two friends who jointly decided to attend the group, and one person who works with one of the two friends. In a group for multiple families, none of the families may know each other; but the possibility of school, work, or neighborhood affiliation always exists. Thus, the combinations are infinite and unique to each program, and it is important to consider these relationships when designing a program.

Procedures for Forming Groups

Often, the first step toward placing participants in groups is to advertise the program through radio, TV, bulletin boards, mailing lists, newspapers, or professional groups and thus get information to the targeted population. Decisions about the number to be enrolled, the place, time, date, how to obtain additional information, and how to enroll in the program must be made before advertising the program so that such information can be included in the advertisement. The designer of the program is responsible for securing this information and making it available for dissemination. These decisions should be in harmony with the approach, the criteria for participant selection, the goals of the program, and the learning environment designed to fit the structure of the program.

Orientation meetings are helpful. In such meetings, prospective participants can get more information about the program and make decisions about participating in it. Orientation also serves as a method of advertising, because participants are likely to share the information with acquaintances.

Selection criteria and a process for preparing participants for each program help determine who will be in the group and if they are suited for the program. For example, interviews or preassessment instruments are needed for screening divorced individuals to determine if they have psychological and social adjustment problems. In this case, such screening would help eliminate people without problems and those with extreme pathology, since neither group would benefit from the treatment program.

Although selection criteria may not be as important for enrichment and education programs as for treatment programs, they should still be very specific in the design. (Parts IV–VI describe the criteria used to select participants for specific programs.)

Size of Groups and Types of Interaction Desired

Sometimes the size of the group may be predetermined by circumstances. For example, a program for marital enrichment in a church setting may be controlled by the number of people the scheduled room can accommodate and/or by the enrollment for the program. The structure of the activities and the objectives may not have to be modified based on space, but these factors should be considered.

The size of the group is also important in designing the optimal program, on the assumption that the size of the group can be controlled. In this case, the designer plans the size of the group as one way of meeting program objectives. For instance, if a program is designed as a structured multiple family therapy program to serve single parent families and their adolescent children who have been identified as truant and failing in school, the size of the group must be considered. Too many families and too many individuals in the same time frame, given the available accommodations, may inhibit the kind of interaction desired in the program. On the other hand, too few members may not provide the variety of experience or the beneficial effects of being in a group.

Thus, the size of the group has an effect on what can be accomplished. The types of interaction desired affect grouping variations within the group and must be planned for when designing the program. A program may call for small group activities, for example, two people (husband and wife, parent and child, adult to adult, child to child), or three people (parents and child, couple plus an observer). In other groups, interaction may occur in many ways. In small groups, individuals can learn interpersonal skills. In larger groups, fishbowl discussions may involve a group with 10 to 15 members being observed by a group with 15 to 30 members. In other groups, didactic information may be given by a facilitator to a group of 50 people, with time for appropriate discussion. Thus, all kinds of combinations and different sizes of groups are possible. Groups for some education or enrichment programs might have as many as 100 members, with accompanying small group activities with participants varying from 2 people, to four couples, to 30 people.

Format

The format of a program is concerned with the total time needed to deliver the program, the number and length of the sessions, and how the sessions are sequenced over time. This combination of factors can provide a great variety of formats. Given this variety, designers must be guided in their choice of format by the goals of a program and the development of session content and procedures. Sometimes, however, factors outside the control of the designers may dictate the format or part of it, for example, the amount of time available, the type of facilities, and when participants can attend.

The length of programs can vary a great deal in total hours of delivery time, in the number of weeks and/or weekends needed to complete the program, and in the sequencing of the sessions. The amount of time given for each session may also vary, for example, 30 minutes, two hours, or eight hours. Because of the nature of structured experiences, family facilitation programs are usually limited by the number of sessions and the amount of time available for each session.

The hours for a program can be sequenced in a number of ways. To illustrate, let us examine two programs, A and B. Each had a total of 16 hours to deliver the program. These hours do not include orientation or the collection of assessment information. Participants in Program A meet two hours weekly for eight weeks. Participants in Program B meet for six hours, on Saturday from 4:00 to 10:00 P.M., for the first meeting. Then they meet for three weekly sessions of two hours each on successive Wednesdays. The final session is held again for four hours on a Saturday.

In another example, a structured program designed to enrich marriage, Travis and Travis (1975) designed two formats: (1) a weekend format with five three-hour sessions and (2) a three-week format with six three-hour sessions. The content and process of the sessions remained the same, but couple contact and intensity of interaction between the two were different.

Settings

A setting is the space or spaces with attending characteristics in which the targeted group meets to participate in scheduled activities. The important issue in design creation is what setting will best facilitate a program. For one thing, the setting should be pleasant and be able to accommodate the size of group expected and the types of interaction planned. If the plans for a program call for the group to meet for two hours weekly and the group will be six single-parent families with parents, one or two adolescents, and two facilitators, the setting must accommodate 14 to 20 people. The furnishings and location should be accessible and comfortable for the people being served, while at the same time usable for the activities structured in the program. Appropriate lighting, seating, restrooms, and ventilation will help participants to be comfortable and take part in the activities. Facilities for food preparation and recreation may also be important.

Some programs may be designed for a retreat situation, that is, to move the population away from its usual setting to a place where telephones, routines, and other people cannot interfere with the objectives of the program. Hotels, resorts, and designated retreat centers are often used for this purpose. Again, the facilities should be appropriate for the inter-actions desired and the comfort of the participants.

Settings may differ depending on which of the three approaches to family facilitation programs is being followed. In enrichment programs, the set-tings are generally informal and semi-structured. Some are planned for weekend retreats. Education programs usually have a classroom setting. If they are conducted in less formal settings, many of the characteristics of a classroom may be simulated. That is, a chalkboard or an easel for writing may be brought in, and the audience may be seated facing the facilitator in the front of the room. In treatment programs, the setting may be formal or informal, but the room should be chosen with regard to the size of the group and the activities planned.

Costs

The costs of a program will affect the design. The setting has a cost factor, whether or not it is a part of the agency. The space, lighting, heating or cooling, restrooms and kitchen facilities, and janitorial services all contribute to cost. Advertisements, salaries of the designer, facilitators, and secretarial staff, and any equipment or materials needed for delivery of the program must also be considered when determining the budget.

The cost of supportive resources may be overlooked or may be more difficult to isolate and identify in specific dollar amounts. Supportive resources may include staff members of the sponsoring agency who answer the phone, order supplies, arrange for the setting, do janitorial tasks, conduct orientation and assessment sessions, or handle the advertisements and public relations aspects. Other supportive resource costs may involve equipment, films, visual aids, paper for advertising, assessment tools, and specific materials or objects required for learning activities.

Funding for programs may be provided by a variety of sources. A fee may be charged to the participants for the program. Agencies often have funds set aside for program development (Hawkins & Killorin, 1979). Though programs may or may not be based on written proposals, formal written proposals are usually required to obtain support money from uni-versities, nonprofit organizations, and government agencies. These sources also usually have requirements for research controls (Robin, 1979). Some-times, community funding is not only possible but very appropriate, depending on the purpose of the program (Hynson, 1979). (See Chapter 15.)

Facilitator Variables

In selecting a basic design for a program, there are a number of facilitator variables to consider. The facilitator's sex, age, race, experiences, and qualifications and the number of people to be served must be considered in relationship to the approach, the characteristics of the group, and the program goals. Does the program need both male and female facilitators? How many facilitators are necessary? Are the age and race of the facilitators important in any way to the goals and success of the program? What experiences do the facilitators have that will give credibility to their leadership? For example, if a program uses all-male, white facilitators for marriage enrichment seminars, will some women or nonwhites question the selection?

The range of training is also an issue in the facilitation of programs. The type of facilitator may range from self-help books and tapes used without facilitators, to community volunteers and paraprofessionals, to highly trained professionals. Any of these alone or in combination may be appropriate for a given program. In any case, facilitator variables must be carefully considered in selecting a program design. Indeed, the decisions about the qualifications of the facilitators should be written into the design.

DETERMINING THE DELIVERY BASE

The determination of the delivery base involves (1) designation of a sponsor for the program, (2) selection of the setting for the delivery of the program, and (3) cost factors, including staffing.

The sponsor of the program works closely with the designer. The main function of the sponsor is to provide a base for planning and expediting the components of the design. The provision of a mailing address, telephone number, and common meeting place will facilitate the development of the design. Sometimes, the sponsor meets all the costs of a program not covered by fees collected from participants.

A program may be sponsored privately or by a community, institution, or agency. Those who develop programs with a research emphasis or those with programs in the private sector often seek sponsors for their programs.

In determining a delivery base, the setting should be carefully considered, since the sponsor may or may not be willing to provide it. Sometimes, programs are developed with a particular sponsor or available space in mind. For example, an agency may have a room that is particularly appropriate for a specific program. Thus, a program may describe the setting needed and then contract for that setting or expect the sponsor to procure it.

Cost becomes a priority issue when the sponsor does not provide financial support. In such cases, of course, other financial backing for the program must be obtained.

Chapter 8

Stage II:
Program Development

The product produced by program development in Stage II is a written document that can be followed by facilitators in delivering the program to the intended participants. Sometimes a program that is already developed may be selected. Here, however, we are concerned with helping professionals write their own programs. To this end, the following sections provide guidance in three areas: (1) expanding preplanning decisions, (2) writing the programs, and (3) pretesting and revision. Figure 8-1 illustrates the relationship of these key components of program development to the other stages of program design.

EXPANDING PREPLANNING DECISIONS

In Stage I, program preplanning, a number of decisions are made that affect program development. These decisions must now be re-examined and amplified to guide development of the program. They involve the following components: the program's specific objectives, choice of a theoretical change model, selection of the appropriate content and process for each session, establishment of facilitator qualifications and roles, and selection of outcome evaluation measures.

Specific Objectives

The development of a program—session by session, activity by activity—has to be guided by the specific objectives derived from the overall and intermediate goals (see Chapter 7). Some of these objectives are specific to the changes desired, others relate to process, and still others relate to evaluation of outcome. The selection of content and process depends on the specific objectives. (See the objectives, activities, and procedures for specific program sessions in Parts III–VI.)

Figure 8-1 Components of Program Development

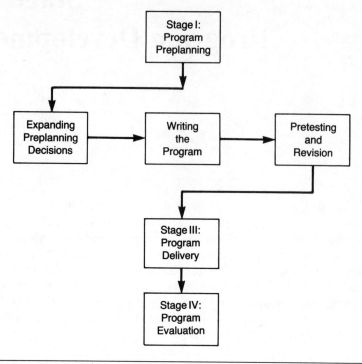

Theoretical Models of Change

Family facilitation programs delivered in a structured group format are grounded in theories about change that can be grouped in three categories: (1) systems theory as it applies to healthy and dysfunctional families, (2) theories about group dynamics, and (3) other theories, like gestalt, theme-centered, educational, and growth, that guide the program developer in choosing activities and procedures to reach specific goals.

Although they share some common theoretical bases, our three approaches to family facilitation programs imply different theoretical models. Which theories best lend themselves to an enrichment program? Which ones to education and treatment programs? These questions confront each program developer. However, they can be only partially answered, in that all three programs share elements of systems and group dynamics theories. Consequently, each program developer must be careful to choose a theoretical model that will reach specific program objectives to foster change in the participants (Guerney & Guerney, 1981; Hof & Miller, 1981; Mace, 1981).

Although all professionals operate on the basis of theoretical models of change, the task in developing a program requires that such models be used specifically to guide the developer in matching theory, objectives, and activities, and that they complement systems and group dynamics theories. For instance, if the objective is to develop greater intimacy in mother-daughter dyads, what theoretical model will help to do that? Gestalt—by creating intimacy in the here and now? Behavioral—by teaching skills that facilitate intimacy? The choices are numerous.

Appendix A describes briefly the theories used in the development of programs in Parts III–VI. The factors believed to create change are noted and references for each theory are listed. In Chapter 11, Feinauer shows how a theory lends itself to the development of a program. Although her program is based primarily on theme-centered interaction, Feinauer also utilizes concepts and techniques from social learning, gestalt, and encounter group theories. For example, Outcome Objective 7 in that program is directly tied to theme-centered interaction theory. Some of the program's ground rules for group interaction are also tied into that theory.

Content and Process

The three approaches to family facilitation all have content and process as parts of their programs. Content is usually thought of as information that helps participants reach their goals and achieve the objectives of the program. Process refers to the methods used to achieve those goals, for example, listening to minilectures, participating in exercises, watching a film, reading printed material, receiving feedback, filling out questionnaires, or making family maps. The major focus with regard to content has been on textbook or written information that can be incorporated in reading assignments, lecture, and discussion-type activities. Family life education programs require less content than family life education courses, but somewhat more than enrichment programs and considerably more than treatment programs.

If we include in our sources of content the instructions and procedures for educational games, exercises, and activities, program content takes on even greater significance. In this broader context, content can be drawn from textbooks, workbooks, manuals, films, filmstrips, slides, audio and video cassettes, pamphlets, stories, posters, transparencies, pictures, journal articles, educational games, exercises, and prepared programs. Whether or not the content from these sources enhances learning and helps meet specific objectives for the program depends of course on the quality of the information and whether it matches the stated objectives of the program.

In addition to the common sense and expertise of the designers, guidelines are available to help determine the quality of information in programs. Ridenour (1979) used the categories of substance, validity, balance, authority, and integrity with appropriate questions to evaluate materials for family life education. The following questions and categories are equally applicable for enrichment and treatment:

- *Substance*. Is the information of professional quality? Is it significant? Does it have depth?
- *Validity*. Have the concepts or activities been tested and supported by research? Are the concepts developed with sufficient evidence? Do the concepts and/or activities seem to produce what is needed?
- *Balance*. Are the generalizations too broad? Are there significant omissions or half truths?
- *Authority*. Who is the author, and what credentials, training, or specializations give authority to the materials presented? What other evidence of authority is present?
- *Integrity*. Does the information reflect honesty, accuracy, and soundness?

In selecting content to meet the needs of a targeted population, biases in educational materials, games, and activities must be eradicated as much as possible (Griggs, 1981). Information about life styles, sex roles, socioeconomic class, age, race, culture, spiritual values, and so on may contain biases that may be offensive to participants and/or inappropriate for the program. The biases may interfere with intended learning and planned change. Games and activities with content, instructions, and procedures may also contain biases. A careful screening for biases in available or original content will facilitate appropriate selections.

Criteria have been compiled for evaluating family life education materials (Griggs, 1981), human relations material (Rinne, 1974), and educational games (Spitze, 1979). These can be applied, when appropriate, in selecting criteria for the three approaches to family facilitation programs. They apply equally well to the content and activities developed by designers of programs. Designer creativity is valuable, but designers also have biases and consequently may neglect to use such criteria in evaluating their creations.

Decisions about the specific content of a program can be difficult. The decisions must be made not only about what is to be taught but also about the order of teaching. For example, if skills are to be taught, the level of difficulty of each skill must be ascertained. There is often a hierarchy of skills, in that one skill must be mastered before another may be learned. The age of the participants and their ability to learn content must also be considered.

In Chapter 17, Fisher and Romig describe an enrichment program for families with children six years of age and older. For the program, they carefully selected content, appropriate for the age groups, that would help teach basic rules of communication (see the minilecture in Session 1). The poem, "Six Men of Indostan," provided relevant content and humor. By using transparencies of pictures, family members of various ages could understand the basic points presented in the lecture.

Some material and skills can be addressed directly, while others are more appropriately addressed implicitly. For example, family enrichment leaders may want their program to increase family closeness. However, a direct approach may arouse defensiveness (particularly in a teenager attempting to differentiate from the family) and therefore be unsuccessful. Instead, the facilitator might introduce an exercise in building self-esteem and request family members to write down one thing they like about each other (content) and then share what they have written with the family group (content and process). This exercise focuses explicitly on self-esteem through strength bombardment and implicitly builds family closeness.

Content and process are determined in terms of the following questions: What specific needs of the target population will be addressed as goals of the program? (Rarely can all be addressed, so choices must be made about the most relevant.) In what order will the content be delivered? Which goals will be addressed explicitly? What methodology will be used to impart the content? A lecture, discussion, reading, experiential experience?

The following questions about structure are also involved in decisions about content and process: How long will the program last? How many sessions will be included? How long will each session last? How often will the participants meet? These questions relate to how much information can be exchanged using what methodology, or how many experiences with a concomitant process can be completed in a given amount of time. The difficulty of what is to be attempted and the readiness of the participants also influence the amount of content and time in learning the content or skill.

The professional's opinion of the optimal time required to achieve the goals of the program guides the development of the content of the program. A session of 30 minutes would not be appropriate for families learning a new and difficult skill. By the same token, a session of several hours in length would not be appropriate for families with small children.

Facilitator Qualifications and Roles

In Stage I, preplanning the program, we examined facilitator variables that help a designer make decisions about how many facilitators are needed and what combination of sex, age, race, experience, and other qualifications would enhance the program. Once those decisions are made, the writer of the program now must consider carefully how the designated combination of facilitator qualities will work in each session. Questions about facilitators in relationship to a given program take on new meaning when procedures and activities for each session are documented. The writer of the program activities and procedures must plan carefully to ensure a fit between content, procedures, and facilitator abilities.

The designer configuration selected in the preplanning stage will indicate whether part of the designer team will deliver the program or if the facilitators are to be selected and trained when the program is ready. Regardless of the procedure to be followed, the selection and training of facilitators are key links in a successful program.

The quality of leadership is important for participants as well as for developers of programs. The developer must plan for facilitators who can do what the program requires them to do. Some facilitators find it difficult to follow a structured program. Therefore, the choice of facilitators who can abide the structure and still apply their unique personality and strengths in delivering the program will be crucial in producing satisfied participants. Participants want facilitators who are both personable and obviously capable. These qualities often determine how involved the participants are and how much they benefit from a program.

Professionals in the three areas of family facilitation—education, enrichment, and treatment—continue to raise questions about the selection of trainees, the kind and quality of training, and licensure or certification requirements. Because many facilitators are drawn from the three areas, program writers need to be aware of the quality and breadth of training being received and whether the people trained in a given area can do what the program requires (Bowman, 1981; Mace & Mace, 1976; Sullivan et al., 1978).

Selection of Outcome Measures

The selection of outcome measures in the preplanning stage helps designers to determine adequate procedures and valid evaluative techniques to determine the effectiveness of programs. Chapter 10 describes the relationship of the four design stages to evaluation and quality control. Refer to that chapter for an understanding of preplanning decisions essential to wise choices of outcome measures.

WRITING THE PROGRAM

Writing the program refers to the writing of a format for each session that the participants and facilitators are to follow. The format includes an outline that describes the program briefly and generally, lists the objectives and appropriate outcome measures, provides detailed session-by-session descriptions of the program, and sets forth guidelines for training the facilitators.

Description of the Program

The brief description of the program introduces the reader to what will follow. The following is an example from Mitchell's program in Chapter 21:

> This treatment covers a period of ten weeks, with the first session on orientation and preassessment, eight sessions of structured treatment, and one session on postassessment data collection. Each session lasts one hour and forty minutes. Recommended group size is six to eight persons (three or four sibling dyads). The treatment can be conducted by one therapist, male or female, or it can be adapted for therapy with two therapists. Although written for adolescent sibling dyads in a public school setting, it is applicable in public or private settings and in government or private mental health agencies.

This kind of description appears at the beginning of a program to briefly introduce the program and highlight its intention and structure. Often a clear description cannot be written until the overall design decisions are made, sometimes not until most of the program is written. In any case, at least the preliminary planning must be completed before the program can be described as shown above.

Objectives and Outcome Measures

Objectives for evaluation of the program are derived from the specific objectives developed from the overall and intermediate goals. For example, if the overall goal of a parent effectiveness program is to promote more effective interaction between parents and children, an intermediate goal might be to increase the quality of parent-child interaction. Specific objectives might be to improve interaction in four areas: (1) listening skills,

(2) sharing personal experiences, (3) admitting mistakes, and (4) negotiating privileges. Measurement instruments—paper and pencil questionnaires or behaviorally rated interactional tasks—must then be found or devised to measure predicted changes in each of the four areas. Once that is accomplished, outcome objectives can be put in the language of the measurement used. For example, sessions may be taped and later coded for specific behaviors that fit in one or all of the four areas. By establishing a baseline for behaviors in early sessions and comparing behaviors in later sessions, change in these areas can be measured as outcome resulting from the program. It is important to remember that in writing a program, measurement instruments and methods must be included.

Session-by-Session Descriptions

In writing the program, an outline that is used consistently through each session or phase will help the writer. The order may vary and parts may be combined, but the following parts should be included in the outline: number and title of each session or phase, objectives, roles of the participants and facilitators, a list of materials and equipment needed, activities and procedures, homework assignments, and, if appropriate, data collection.

A program may be divided into sessions, each with specific objectives, or it may be divided into phases, each with a set of objectives for two or more sessions to accomplish the objectives. Hoopes' program for divorced individuals in Chapter 19 has three phases. Phase 1 has one session, Phase 2 has four sessions, and Phase 3 has three sessions. The three phases each have specific objectives and are designed to be additive in nature. For example, learning how to be supportive, an objective in Phase 1, is practiced in Phases 2 and 3.

The objectives for each phase or session guide the selection of activities. The activities may be original with the writers, or they may be drawn from other sources and either used as described by that source or modified for purposes of the program.

Similarly, program developers can either create their own exercises or modify those created by others. To create an exercise, information is needed on the approach (enrichment, education, or treatment), the setting, the participants, the needs assessment of the participants, the general objective, and the specific session objectives. Materials and equipment are determined by the nature of the exercise. The following demonstrates how exercises can be created. We have used this exercise repeatedly with students learning to write programs:

Approach: Multiple Couple Therapy
Setting: Small group room with space to move around
Participants: 5 couples, 2 therapists
Source of information about the participants (preassessment):
   (1) paper and pencil questionnaire. (2) video-taped couple interaction—coded for affect, risk, and amount and quality of
   exchange
Findings: All couples are low risk, have a blaming style in communication, and rarely confront or share affect
General objective: To achieve higher quality interaction and more
   information exchange between husband and wife
Specific objective: To share high-risk information with appropriate affect and facts

With this type of format, we have found that students in training can generate several original activities in a ten-minute period.

Answers to the following questions—and to many others that can be generated depending on the situation—will affect the type of activities developed to fit specific objectives: Shall the participants be asked to share high-risk information with their spouses or in the big group? Should the sharing be verbal or nonverbal? Would a metaphorical story help some individuals? How can the couples generate high-risk information? How can they generate high-risk behavior? Do they generate their own definition of risk, or should we, the therapists, define it? Have we done any activity similar to what we are considering? How will the activity fit in with the rest of the program? (For examples of multiple activities for objectives, see Klemer and Smith (1975) on teaching family relationships.)

Time to process an exercise should be included as part of structured activity. Often novice program writers write too many activities for a time slot. Also, the time needed for talking about activities and learning from the process is often underestimated. Process time is as important as the activity itself. To do an activity and not process it is like cooking a steak and not eating it. The value of pretesting session activities and the program as a whole to determine the time requirements cannot be overemphasized.

Session-by-session procedural statements help greatly in writing the program. Procedural statements may be directions that tell the order in which things are done, suggestions as to how to arrange chairs or how much space is needed for a given activity, or instructions for collecting data. Take-home assignments, forms to be filled out in a session, such as brief content quizzes, and weekly assessment instruments are examples of data-collecting activities. Decisions about when to do something and who should do it should also be included in the procedural statements.

Ways of writing a program are as numerous as writers. No matter what form the program takes, the test for clarity and completeness is whether someone can facilitate the program without the writer being there to interpret. A variety of formats and style in the presentation of programs is presented in Parts III–VI. For example, Feinauer, in Chapter 23, lists procedures for an entire session before describing the first activity in detail. On the other hand, Andelin and Dastrup, in Chapter 12, embed procedures in the description of each activity as it occurs.

Clear directions about the roles of the facilitators and participants must also be included in the written program. Equipment, materials, and special directions—such as the arrangement of the room or required space—must also be described for each session. This will help the facilitators to prepare adequately for each session. Reading references to help facilitators understand and deliver the program should also be included.

Thus, each session develops from the overall goal, the intermediate goals, and the objectives of each session or phase. These goals and objectives guide the selection of activities for each session. Procedural information describes the order of events, that is, who will do what and when, with time guidelines provided to facilitate the accomplishment of the objectives.

The decisions about the facilitators' qualifications, age, and sex and the number of facilitators needed for the program are made during the preplanning stage. A particular task for the writer of the program is to prepare guidelines that will be helpful in the training of the facilitators. This training usually requires that the facilitators read the program, discuss and practice their own roles and also sometimes those of the participants, and read background information to establish appropriate content knowledge. These activities should take place before delivering the program.

If the writer of the program thinks supervision of the sessions is appropriate and necessary, this suggestion can be written into the guidelines. Specific instructions might also be included regarding the qualifications of the supervisor, how often the supervision should occur, and the type of supervision. Further details on the training of facilitators are provided in Chapter 9.

The guidelines for training facilitators may vary in length, depending upon the program. However, the procedures for such training should be written clearly and followed carefully to ensure the integrity of the program.

PRETESTING AND REVISION

Before a program is ready for marketing, delivery, and/or research, it should be tested and revised, sometimes several times. A group that is representative of the targeted population can serve as a recipient of a trial presentation. The following are some of the aspects of a program that need to be checked during the testing-revision process:

- clarity of instructions for participants and facilitators
- the training program for the facilitators
- the orientation and commitment of the participants and the assessment procedures
- appropriateness of goals for the participants
- effectiveness and appropriateness of specific content and activities
- how the total program is accommodated in the space and time allotted

In planning a timetable for the total design, the designers should allow for delivery on a trial basis so that adequate revisions can be made. Hastily developed and delivered programs may be ineffective and, in some cases, even harmful to the participants.

Chapter 9

Stage III: Program Delivery

After much effort, planning, writing, testing, and rewriting, a program is finally ready for delivery. All of the decisions, the preparations, and the writing of the program have led to this stage. The program is now ready to be marketed. Facilitators must be trained, envisioned participants will become real, and activities and procedures will assume form and movement as the program is delivered.

Marketing a program involves strategies for selling the program and packaging it so that it can be delivered to its intended audience. It does not necessarily mean a huge selling and advertising program in a business sense. The interrelated marketing activities may be simple or complex, demanding much or only a little time, depending on how often the program is delivered, and whether the audience is local, national, or international. Figure 9-1 illustrates the components of Stage III and their relationship to the other stages.

SELLING THE PROGRAM

In the timing sequence of designing a program, two key times for selling the program are evident, and a third one may also be present. Table 9-1 shows these three points in time for selling the program, to whom the selling is directed, the stage of program development at the time, and related money concerns. The first selling point is during the phase of examining the needs of a given population. Someone has to be convinced of the need for a given program in order for the design to begin. For example, those interested in designing the program may have to sell administrators on it in order to get funds and/or time to work on the design. Or people in the targeted population may have to sell a professional on the need for a particular program.

Figure 9-1 Stage III: Components of Program Delivery

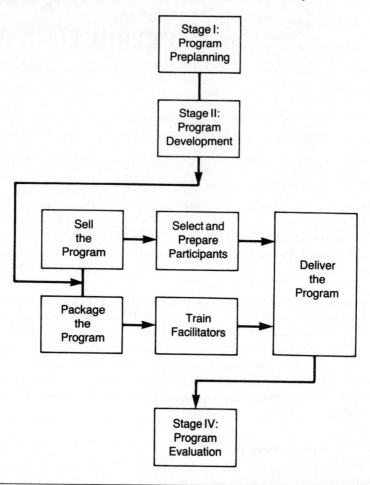

The second time for selling the program is at the point when participants are attracted to it. At this point, issues about who will participate, how to identify and process them into the group, and where the program will be delivered are of paramount concern. These issues involve getting the information to the targeted population in such a way that its members will choose to participate in the program. People may need what the program offers, but if it is not presented appropriately, they may not buy it. At this stage of selling, the program must be fully developed and written so that it can be fully described to prospective participants.

Table 9-1 Steps in Selling the Program

Steps	To Whom	Stage of Development	Money Concerns
1.	To sponsor and professionals who can design a program	Identified target group Selected approach	How much money is required to develop the program?
2.	To participants	Program developed and packaged for delivery	Cost of delivery of program may be absorbed by participants and/or sponsoring agent; may or may not be profit based.
3.	To a wider audience of professionals and participants	Program judged effective Packaging may be more elaborate	Strategies for selling are based on a profit plan.

Family enrichment, family life education, and family treatment programs sometimes challenge popular attitudes that deter people from seeking resources outside the family. Culturally held attitudes of family sanctity and self-sufficiency do not encourage people to attend family facilitation programs. Some people feel as if it is an admission of failure to seek help outside the family, even if the help is not clinical. A marketing strategy must be designed that not only supplies information about the program but encourages active participation for reasons that will appeal to the target population. It is not enough just to get the participants there; a quality program must also help to dispel negative attitudes. Consequently, the program must do what it claims to do. The satisfied consumers then become sellers of the program.

After selling the program twice—the first time to get it sponsored and written, and the second to get it advertised and delivered to participants— a third time for selling the program may be appropriate. If the program has been judged effective, fellow professionals and a larger audience may become the target for a sales promotion. This type of marketing requires different advertising strategies, ones that reach a larger population and have greater visual appeal. Whatever the strategy, however, the packaging must be efficient and attractive.

PACKAGING THE PROGRAM

Packaging occurs in the second and third steps of selling a program. Packaging refers to how the program is written and presented for facilitators to deliver. It may be simple or elaborate, depending on how it is to be used and for what type of audience. Packaging can vary from a few written pages to a formal format. The latter may include a training manual for facilitators and a manual for the program with appropriate supplementary materials, for example, books, filmstrips, transparencies, or games. The minimum requirement for packaging is to provide a written description of the program with enough content and procedural information that facilitators can deliver the program. Unless this simple package is provided, the program should not be sold to participants.

The packaging of a program is an essential part of the marketing strategy and the training of the facilitators. Structured programs that are written clearly, concisely, and completely in an easily followed format facilitate delivery. The essentials in selling the program to facilitators and sponsors are the appearance and quality of the written program, the availability of the equipment and materials needed to deliver the program, and the qualifications of and training instructions for the facilitators.

Ideally, the package should include procedures for (1) the sale of the program to the targeted population, (2) the selection of participants and their orientation to the program, (3) activities and procedures to be followed, and (4) data collection for evaluation. The major part of the package should be a detailed description of the program and the training information for facilitators.

TRAINING FACILITATORS

The packaging of a program results in a complete, written description of the program as it is to be delivered. This description should be provided to each facilitator. In addition to "session information," it should include information about the targeted population, the theoretical model, ways to get participants into the program, the structure for orientation, preassessment and postassessment, content and learning activities, and procedures for delivering the program. Again, programs will vary greatly with regard to the specifics of what is included.

In the preplanning stage, the designer of the program established guidelines as to what kind of facilitators could successfully deliver the program. Now those guidelines are to be used in selecting appropriate facilitators. The facilitator's age, sex, ethnic considerations, preparation, availability, desire to be involved, and match of schedules are but a few of the factors to be considered. Once the facilitators are selected, the training for a particular program can commence.

The core of facilitator training is in reading, studying, and rehearsing the program. Audiorecording or videorecording of the sessions and then reviewing the tapes as part of the training program will help guarantee that the program gets delivered as written. These tapes can also be used for future training.

The training program helps to control the quality of leadership by guiding the facilitators through the sessions through supervision, team planning, and rehearsals. Selection criteria for the screening of applicants and commitment procedures in the program can also help to control the quality of the program.

Circumstances sometimes cause variations in procedures. For instance, a group may go over its allotted time for a session. All such variations should be recorded for purposes of revision and research. An awareness of possible variations in procedures is also a part of training.

Checklists are invaluable, both in helping facilitators follow the structured program and in providing supervisors and/or researchers information about what was done. Exhibit 9-1 is an example of a checklist that was

---

Exhibit 9-1 Screening Interviewer Checklist for a Stepfamily Program

---

Check when complete
_____ 1. Introduction to Research Project given.
_____ 2. Ground Rules discussed.
_____ 3. Family Goals discussed.
_____ 4. Release Form signed.
       5. Assessment Instruments completed.
_____   a. Demographic Information Sheet for both husband and wife.
_____   b. MAT for husband and wife.
_____   c. MAT Child's Form (Child's perception of marriage).
_____   d. SCL-90 for all those 12 and over—fill in the time space—7 days!
_____   e. Moos Family Environment Scale for all family members 6 and over. Remember, don't write in the booklet—use separate answer sheets. Therapist may have to read questions to younger children. Parents should not read these questions to their children.
_____   f. Relationship Intimacy Barometer (RIB) for husband and wife.
_____   g. Kvebaek Family Sculpture test.
          i. Individuals—everyone over 6.
          ii. *Video Tape* Family Conjoint task.
_____   h. Make sure all materials are filled out completely.

Note: See Appendix B for descriptions of instruments used in this checklist.

used to conduct orientation interviews and to preassess a program for stepfamilies.

Decisions need to be made about who will do the training, how many sessions there should be, and the timing and content of the training sessions. Sometimes, facilitators develop their own training programs with no supervisors involved. They read the program, negotiate their roles, read additional content if appropriate, and rehearse activities as necessary. In addition to managing the content of the sessions, facilitators should assume supportive responsibilities that are necessary for a successful program, for example, audiotaping, videotaping, preparing or checking assignments, making announcements, contacting absent members, and arranging for equipment and supplies.

Questions as to who is to do the orientation and administer the preassessments and postassessments may have to be resolved. The designer needs to consider whether or not having the facilitators do the orientation and assessment is beneficial for the facilitators and the participants. It could help both know each other more quickly and thereby gain time in establishing trust and cohesion. However, if research hypotheses are an important part of the design, the facilitators normally should not be made aware of the hypotheses, the results of assessment, or the selection criteria for participants. Such awareness may preclude use of the facilitators as administrators of the assessment measures.

DELIVERING THE PROGRAM

Delivery requires presentation of the program to an appropriate audience by qualified facilitators in the setting for which it was designed. All of the preplanning leads to this reality test. The targeted population becomes a group of real people with personalities, needs, and responses. The content, and whether the planned activity will get the anticipated participation and reaction, are no longer matters for speculation. The facilitators have been chosen. The focus now is on what the facilitators and participants are doing. The program is happening. The quality of the preplanning and the written program and the ability of the facilitators can now be examined for effectiveness. This involves the evaluation procedures and controls that are applied to guarantee a quality program.

Chapter 10

Stage IV:
Program Evaluation

The development of procedures for evaluation and the application of appropriate controls to ensure quality are important elements in the design of a program. Only through such procedures and controls can the validity and effectiveness of a program be ascertained. The main objective of evaluation is to determine if a program has done what it claimed to do. The effectiveness of a program can be determined only after it is delivered.

EVALUATION AND CONTROL FACTORS

Although we have designated evaluation and quality control as a fourth stage in program design, evaluation issues and procedures in fact manifest themselves in all three of the earlier stages. The evaluation issues involve determining what is to be measured, when, and how; planning procedures that will guarantee the data will be collected; and establishing controls to ensure quality of products in all stages of the design. Figure 10-1 illustrates the interrelationship of evaluation components and the other stages of design.

What is to be evaluated in testing the effectiveness of a program can be categorized by (1) content and procedures of the program, (2) participant responses to planned change, and (3) performance of the facilitators. By identifying when and how evaluation is to proceed, the purposes of the evaluation, and what controls can be built into the design, the complexity of program evaluation can be portrayed. Table 10-1 presents this complex picture in abbreviated form.

A major evaluation concern before delivery is to develop the program to meet the needs of the targeted population. To do that, the content, activities, and procedures of the program need to be grounded in research and theory that have, at least in part, been applied previously in some

Figure 10-1 Stage IV: Components of Program Evaluation

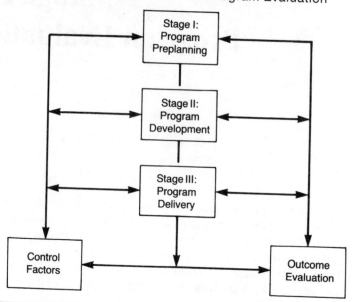

manner. The ability of the developer of the program to blend personal experience, professional speculation, and tested theory into a creative program will determine the quality of the product. The writing, pretesting, revising, and then packaging for delivery to the targeted population constitute the first phase of evaluation. This sequencing of the evaluation process in program development is very important.

The use of selection criteria for placing participants in the program and procurement of commitments to the program from participants and facilitators reduce dropouts and guarantee that the appropriate audience receives the program. How to screen applicants using selection criteria and how to get applicants committed to a program is described in Gardner's program for conflicted couples in Chapter 20. See particularly Session 1 of that program concerning screening and preassessment.

To determine if a program was delivered as designed, any of the following techniques can be used: (1) analysis of audiotapes or videotapes of the sessions, (2) analysis of systematic, formal or informal feedback from participants and facilitators, and (3) the use of a qualified supervisor who can view the process of delivering the program from an outsider's perspective.

Preassessments, postassessments, and follow-up assessments on outcome measures for the participants will give information as to whether the

Table 10-1 Evaluation and Control Factors in Program Design

What to Evaluate	When to Evaluate	Procedures	Purpose of Evaluation	Quality & Evaluation Control Factors
Content and Procedures of the Program	Pre-delivery (A)	Write—test—revise package (B)	To determine if the needs of the population are met (C)	—Research —Experience —Qualification of designer —Consultation (D)
	Delivery of program (E)	Participants and facilitators follow the program and provide feedback (F)	To assess relevance, effectiveness of content, and process	—Selection criteria for participants —Commitment of participants —Audio/video tapes —Feedback of participants and facilitators —Supervision feedback (H)
			To determine if the program was delivered as written (G)	
	Post-delivery of program (I)	Utilize assessment instruments and procedures (K)	To evaluate outcome objectives and to determine if program was effective (L)	—Selection of assessment instruments (valid and reliable) —Procedures for data collection (M)
Participants' Responses	Pre-program, post-program and follow up (J)			
Facilitators' Responses	Pre-delivery of program (N)	Choose based on qualifications (O)	To have facilitators who can deliver the program as planned (S)	—References about performance (P)
	Delivery of the program (Q)	Examine results of outcome evaluation (R)		—Quality of the packaged program —Check off lists —Same as H above (T)

Note: Letters following each factor are for ease of reference rather than to indicate a sequential order.

content, learning activities, and procedures of the program did indeed create the changes planned in the design. The assessments will determine if the needs of the participants were actually met. The validity and reliability of the instruments, the procedures used to collect the data, and the ability of the facilitators to deliver the program as planned are interactive factors in the evaluation process. All evaluations of effectiveness should take these interactive factors into account. Through such factors, the choice of facilitators, the quality of the packaged program, the quality of the training program, and the choice of assessment instruments will all affect outcome evaluation.

As noted earlier, not all the programs in Parts III–VI have been completely evaluated. However, all have identified evaluation procedures and assessment instruments. An examination of the relevant descriptions will provide adequate guidance.

The practicality of program evaluation is particularly well-demonstrated in Hoopes' program in Chapter 19 for individuals who are trying to adjust to separation or divorce. This program was written, tested, and rewritten in 1974. It was developed to meet the needs of participants and to train group facilitators. Over time, its activities and procedures were refined, but evaluation was sporadic, with a variety of interests reflected in the choice of assessment instruments. Consequently, although the program was viewed as effective by participants, facilitators, and supervisors, no systematic evaluation of it was attempted.

However, in 1978 a research project was developed to test the value of the Hoopes program. An experimental group (seven groups, 49 members in all) received the program; a control-wait group (28 members) received the program ten weeks later. Assessment instruments were selected, and seven pairs of male-female facilitators were trained. Analysis of the findings indicated that the treatment was effective. Some of the results were reduced depression ($P > .01$), increased levels of self-esteem ($P > .05$), decreased nervousness ($P > .01$), and decreased hostility ($P > .05$). The program is currently being used in a number of settings. See Chapter 19 for specific research reports in theses and dissertations that have emanated from this project.

ASSESSMENT

In the past, for a number of reasons, many programs did not include adequate assessment procedures. Often the developers of the programs focused on the immediacy of serving a given population. If the population responded in a positive way, there seemingly was not a pressing need for formal evaluation. Also, many times the developers of the programs were not trained to evaluate; they either did not think about evaluation or did not know how.

Often, assessment procedures in family facilitation are not used because it is difficult to find instruments that are appropriate for family facilitation approaches. Difficulties in pinpointing salient change-inducing components, specific manifestations of goal attainment, and appropriate measures to produce effective research results continue to constitute a weakness of family facilitation programs (Clinebell, 1975; Gurman & Kniskern, 1977 & 1981; Schumm & Denton, 1979).

What to measure, and how to measure it, continue to be difficult questions for program designers. Program criteria for outcome evaluation have ranged from self-esteem to knowledge attainment. Other outcome criteria are marital satisfaction, cohesion, adaptability, intimacy, removal of problematic behavior, and development of communication skills. Though group outcome research also has its critics (Bednar & Kaul, 1978), the appropriate criteria and adequate measurement and procedures for data collection are obviously important in determining the effectiveness of a program.

In selecting instruments or procedures to assess interaction, many issues must be examined. The instruments should measure behaviors, thoughts, attitudes, and interaction patterns that are expressions of the outcome objectives. Designers must evaluate couple and family interaction as well as individuals and groups. A variety of measures—subjective and objective, individual and interactive—that is focused either directly on the person, relationship, or family or indirectly via someone outside the person, relationship, or family will ensure an accurate assessment of the effects of the program (Olson, 1977).

The means of evaluating the program should include measures that assess the effectiveness of activities designed to meet program objectives that meet the needs of the target population. Thus, assessment helps determine the overall effectiveness of the program, as well as its specific content and process.

Structured programs lend themselves more easily to evaluation than do open-ended programs or less structured programs. All of the programs in Parts III–VI have assessment procedures and instruments that measure outcome objectives. Appendix B lists additional assessment instruments and their sources. The list is not exhaustive, but it does provide alternatives for various programs.

Part III

An Example of a Structured Family Facilitation Program Design

Chapter 11

Multiple Family Therapy for Single Rape Victims and Their Parents

Leslie L. Feinauer

The treatment for single rape victims and their parents requires ten weeks' total time. This covers an initial assessment and orientation meeting followed by nine weeks of treatment, with the last session including postassessment and evaluation. A pair of male-female cotherapist (preferred) facilitators conducts weekly two-hour sessions with a group membership of 10 to 14. This program is applicable to both private and public agency practice.

The group treatment presented here requires few resources beyond qualified group leaders. Needed materials include large sheets of paper, posterboard, marking pens, and assorted magazines. A video-taped review of the sessions would be helpful but is not essential.

The purpose of the program is to counteract the rape victim's internalized guilt, shame, and vulnerability that immobilize her growth and to aid her parents as they attempt to resolve their feelings and function as a healthy support system.

Rape of young women is the most common violent crime in America. The victims are of all ages, but the majority is 17 to 24 years of age. Silverman's (1978) clinical evidence indicates that the young woman's significant support system must be involved in therapy if it is to be successful. If the parents are involved and the family's resources are mobilized, the young rape victim has more adequate coping mechanisms available. If the family is not included, there is an increased chance that she will become increasingly burdened and revictimized by her family as they attempt to deal with their own struggles over the experience.

THE NEED FOR FAMILY THERAPY

The consequences of a rape experience may be apparent or hidden, temporary or enduring, depending upon the nature of the victim's experience and the life situation to which she must return. Generally she will blame herself and find herself somehow responsible. The feelings of shame she has, though usually irrelevant and unfounded, may prevent her from sharing with her family her feelings and problems related to her experience. She may think she must protect them from the experience she finds so terrifying, as well as protect herself from their possible rejection and withdrawal. If these feelings persist, she will be alone to face an overwhelming situation.

Rape victims and their families have a sense of isolation and estrangement from others. They may feel violated and different. They may lose their sense of community and belonging. Meeting in small groups of families that have had similar feelings, fears, and experiences provides a sense of support and shared experience. This may lessen some of the burden of facing the crisis alone, and enable the families to explore coping alternatives previously unknown to them.

Holmstrom and Burgess (1977) indicate that, to be viewed as a "genuine" victim in our society, other people must be available who can accept and acknowledge that something terribly disruptive has occurred in the victim's life. To prevent a debilitating denial of the occurrence, there needs to be confirmation by others. This may be provided with appropriate support in a group setting.

General Treatment Objectives

There are four major goals in this program:

1. to facilitate an emotional response among the participants
2. to explore the misconceptions about, the attitudes toward, and the expectations surrounding rape
3. to explore and resolve the unique problems resulting from the rape experience with emphasis on developing constructive strategies to deal with them
4. to focus on the future with direction toward growth

Theoretical Basis for Treatment

This program is based primarily on a theme-centered interaction method with elements of gestalt and social learning theory and encounter group techniques adapted to facilitate multiple family interaction. The core philosophical concepts in the theme-centered interaction model include autonomy and interdependence (Shaffer & Galinsky, 1974).

In multiple family therapy, the therapists are generally active and more directive than in peer group therapy (Benningfield, 1978; Laqueur, 1972). Their primary responsibility is to encourage the members to be responsible for themselves and for their own growth. The therapists enforce the ground rules; help the members be direct in their statements about ideas and feelings; maintain a relative balance in the "I-We-It" triangle and in content-process, cognition-affect, and the here-and-now versus the there-and-then; and keep an equal focus on intrapsychic and interpersonal aspects.

The therapists use a variety of techniques based on appropriateness. They keep the group from avoiding issues and feelings through intellectualization and, at the same time, protect the members from excessive probing that may be uncomfortable for members who are not yet ready to make such disclosures (Benningfield, 1978). In this way, the therapists guide the families to deal with issues related to the crisis of rape and the subsequent problems rather than deal with clearly unrelated personal agendas that distract from the therapeutic goals. It is also important for the therapists to allow the theme to recede from focus occasionally to avoid fatigue and distress. They do this by encouraging expression of the members' immediate experiences and awarenesses. As much as possible, the therapists support the group in controlling itself, but they subtly or obviously return the group to the theme if the group members do not spontaneously do so within a certain time. It is appropriate for the therapists to disclose their own experiences in the group, especially as models or working examples, to increase the growth of the members.

The cotherapy team should be composed of a male and a female therapist whenever possible. Although male therapists may work well with the families, some young rape victims are not able or willing to relate to men in an intense, intimate way. However, some victims are relieved and reassured to see a man respond in a sensitive, accepting manner, and they respond easily to male therapists. Also, fathers may find the male therapist an effective model and experiment more willingly with new behaviors.

It should be noted that the dynamics of rape are similar to those of family sexual abuse, where multiple family therapy has been effective. However, the program presented here has also been conducted successfully with individuals in single family therapy.

ORGANIZATION OF THE GROUP

Selection and Screening of Group Participants

Rape crisis centers, district court rape victim programs, area physicians, emergency treatment centers, religious organizations, college health centers, school counselors, crisis telephone lines, and individual contacts all can be instrumental in advertising the availability of the program for potential participants, including the rape victim's family. Although the rape victim is usually identified as the most sensitive member of the family group, it is essential that the family or parents who express interest in the program be interviewed as well as the rape victim.

Before determining that multiple family therapy is more appropriate than individual family therapy, several aspects should be evaluated. These include (1) the family members' willingness to be open about their concerns (keeping secrets from other members of the family will interfere with their effectiveness as participants), (2) their ability to function as a family group in some fashion, and (3) the amount of family dysfunction (chaotic dysfunction in the family may make it difficult to participate in the group). Isolated, rigid families may benefit more from a multiple family approach because of the exposure to a different system (Leichter & Schulman, 1974). In the event that the rape victim has a single parent, a sibling, or a substitute parent, that person should be included as part of her family.

If the rape victim is seeking support from others and is able to acknowledge and discuss her responses, concerns, and fears related to her experience, a group might be helpful. However, if she is attempting to maintain a denial, unwilling to participate in discussion, and fearful of exposure, multiple family therapy is not advisable.

Procedures

Facilities

A large, sound-proofed, well-ventilated room with comfortable, easily movable chairs in a clinic or agency should be used. The room must be large enough to allow movement and activity away from the chairs. A large carpet or floor rug is helpful, and a chalkboard should be available.

Membership

The membership is composed of family groups. Usually this includes the two parents and the rape victim, but it may also include a single parent, a parent and a sibling, or a substitute parent to the rape victim. The group size should be four families or 12 to 14 members, depending on the number in each family. The inclusion of siblings is a sensitive issue and should be handled with appropriate care for each family.

The group should meet for the initial interview and nine regular sessions. The initial interview and last session also serve as testing periods. The sessions should be two-hour weekly meetings conducted by the cotherapy team.

Pregroup Preparation

As indicated earlier, the cotherapy team conducts the selection interview. In addition, this initial session begins the rapport building and helps resolve common misconceptions and unrealistic fears and expectations about the group experience. The ground rules and the roles of the leaders and members should be discussed, and an overview of the program should be provided (see the initial interview section for details).

At the conclusion of the interview, the members are given the Moos Family Environment Scale (FES), the Depression Adjective Checklist (DACL), and the Derogatis Symptom Checklist (SCL-90R) (see Appendix B). These are to be completed prior to leaving the clinic.

THE TREATMENT PROGRAM

Using a structured group treatment model, this ten-week program is designed to help the families of the young single rape victim deal with the terrifying crisis they have experienced. This crisis has threatened the young woman's sense of autonomy and her ability to cope with life. It interferes with her family's normal developmental progression and may result in family dysfunction, which becomes apparent in communication patterns, depression, disengagement, illness, and dependency.

Outcome Objectives

The following objectives define the expected outcomes of the sessions.

1. to establish open and direct communication among members of the group as they discuss their shared life crisis
2. to ventilate feelings that may include resentment and anger
3. to develop an awareness of communication patterns being used in the family
4. to create cognitive understanding of what the experience of rape means to the individuals in the family and especially the victim
5. to establish active problem solving by the family to deal with changes in the family as a result of the crisis
6. to increase the variety of alternatives to current coping skills to help family members support one another
7. to increase the sense of interdependence and autonomy in the family

8. to decrease evidence of depressive (helpless, out of control) affect in the family
9. to increase a sense of satisfaction among family members through their family's support, acceptance, and understanding

Measurement

The outcome objectives are measured by three instruments: the Derogatis Symptom Checklist (SCL-90R), the Moos Family Environment Scale (FES), and the Depression Adjective Checklist (DACL). The SCL-90R is administered during the initial interview and again during the final session. The FES is administered during the initial interview, and again during the post-testing and termination session.

Form A of the DACL is administered at the initial interview. Form B is given to the participants to be completed three days later and returned at the first session. The participants are given consecutive forms at the beginning of each of group sessions until Form G has been completed. Form G is followed by a second completion of Forms A through C. These three forms are used to collect baseline data to compare changes in the families' affective state. The DACL forms are also compared within each family system to detect relationships.

Control Factors

The treatment program is never repeated exactly the same way because of a number of uncontrollable variables, for example, the responses of the participants and the personalities of the group members. However, the following measures can be used to impose control and consistency in the model.

Initial Screening

As indicated previously, family groups are assessed by the cotherapy team to determine if there is pathology or dysfunction in the family that would interfere with the effective functioning of the group or indicate a need for individual family therapy.

Measurement Instruments

The measurement instruments are designed to measure the individual personality and interactional components and the perceived aspects of change in the family system. If it were imperative that the format be adhered to, as in a research project, the sessions could be taped and reviewed or observed and rated according to identified criteria. In the clinical approach, however, reliable therapists who are trained in the use of the structured treatment method and familiar with the measurement instruments should be sufficient.

Training the Therapists

In multiple family therapy, a theme-centered interaction model is not commonly utilized, even though the techniques used in the program are primarily gestalt and encounter group experiential exercises. Thus, to ensure that the leadership roles are carried out effectively, it is important that a training session be held. Prior to this session, the treatment sessions should be written carefully for the therapists to read and study. It is helpful if the group process of the theoretical model can be observed and discussed by a new therapist prior to entering a leadership role. The sessions should be addressed individually and supervised directly, with training in each technique. Tapes of each session could be evaluated to be sure the methods and objectives were adhered to.

The therapists' roles are directive, facilitative, and modeling. They must work well together as a team. Their roles are clearly defined for each session, but their knowledge of, and sense of comfort with, one another can only be developed through working together and processing the group interactions. The therapists can have an important impact upon one another, providing a system of support and understanding that will help them learn more effective ways of communicating and solving problems.

Commitment of Members

In the initial screening session and again in the first session, the group should discuss commitment, attendance, and participation. The member families should be asked to commit themselves verbally to the group. As group cohesion increases, this commitment should also increase.

PROGRAM OUTLINE

The following outline describes the content, procedures, and materials used in each program session.

1. Initial Interview
   - Objectives
     a. To interview each family that indicates its members are interested in the program. The criteria for elimination from multi-

family therapy include a family's or family member's (1) unwillingness to be open about their concerns, (2) obviously disruptive, dysfunctional, or bizarre behavior, (3) unwillingness to commit to the eight-week program, or (4) unwillingness to be involved in the program.

    b. To discuss common misconceptions about procedures, purposes, and functions of the therapy group.

    c. To review ground rules and member and leadership roles.

    d. To provide an overview of the program.

    e. To administer pretreatment evaluation measures.

- Materials
    a. The Moos Family Environment Scale (FES), the Derogatis Symptom Checklist (SCL-90R), the Depression Adjective Checklist (DACL), and the handout on general ground rules (Exhibit 11-1).
- Session Procedural Outline (1½ hours)
    a. Involve both therapists in interviewing the families and discussing their fears and expectations. (20 minutes)
    b. Review and discuss the handout on ground rules (see below) and also a handout on common fears that the therapists should construct from the literature, describing the fears that are common to rape victims. (15 minutes)
    c. Administer the FES and DACL Form A. Read the instructions of the FES and DACL forms to the families or allow them to read them and answer any questions they may have. The two forms are to be filled out independently by each participant without consultation among them. (30–40 minutes)
    d. Direct the family to come to the next week's session. Provide the time and place of the meeting. (5 minutes)
    e. Send DACL Form B home with the family to be filled out in three days and returned to the therapist at the first session. (3–5 minutes)
- Information
    a. Handout on ground rules (see Exhibit 11-1).

2. Session 1: Introductions, Commitments, and Beginnings
- Objectives
    a. To make introductions that will result in the group being able to use first names by the end of the session. This will reduce anxiety and get the group involved in an interesting and enjoyable way.
    b. To review the ground rules established in initial interview.

Exhibit 11-1 Handout on Ground Rules

(1) Be Your Own Chairman. Members are responsible for themselves. They have the freedom to choose what they want to obtain from the group during each session. Participants are reminded throughout the program that they have committed themselves to be actively involved; however, ultimately each member must determine how involved that member should become.
(2) Speak for Yourself. Participants should speak for themselves as clearly and directly as possible. They should avoid making generalizations or speaking for someone else in the group.
(3) State the Concern behind Your Question. Most questions that a person asks of another hide unstated concerns or curiosity.
(4) Disturbances Take Precedence. Participants are encouraged to let the group know when they are distracted or preoccupied with something they are experiencing or something taking place in the group.
(5) Speak One at a Time. To avoid mass confusion, members are expected to listen to the person speaking and to try to understand what is being said. Members may say anything they wish but sometimes may have to "fight" for the floor to express themselves.
(6) The group will always begin at 7:00 P.M. and end at 9:00 P.M.
(7) Members must hold all information revealed in the group in strict confidence.

c. To discuss the expectations and concerns of the group.
d. To explore common misconceptions about rape. This should be kept at a general level in this phase.
e. To establish commitment to the group. Each family should be supported and reinforced as it shows its willingness to participate in the group.
f. To introduce the topic of support as an important aspect of the program (see the handout, Types of Supportive Behavior in Chapter 19).

- Materials
    Multicolored sheets of construction paper, felt tip pen, scissors, pins, chalkboard, chalk and eraser, and list of myths about rape.
- Procedural Outline
    a. Introductions. (40 minutes)
    b. Brainstorming myths and misconceptions about rape. (30 minutes)
    c. Family commitment. (30 minutes)
- Procedures
    a. Introductions, a self-description exercise (40 minutes): Have each person take a sheet of construction paper. The color of the paper the members take should in some way describe what

they are like or relate to their past experiences. The members should then cut something out of the construction paper that reflects what they are like. The shape of an object, the color of the paper used, and the symbol chosen all reflect aspects of the person. The cutouts may be a green bridge, a small blue bird, or a red church. After the project is completed, the members put their first name somewhere on the cutouts and place them so that everyone can see them. Then, in turn, the members should explain in what ways the cutouts reflect aspects of themselves. Other members may respond or ask questions. (This exercise is adapted from Johnson, 1972.)

b. Brainstorming—myths and misconceptions about rape:
(1) Divide the group into two groups of about 6–7 people each to brainstorm myths and misconceptions about rape.
(2) Allow no criticism, negative comments, or evaluation of ideas.
(3) All ideas are acceptable no matter how farfetched, far-out, or untrue.
(4) Keep ideas flowing.
(5) Write everything down that is said.
(6) Encourage building on ideas.
(7) Discuss the ideas presented only after no new ideas can be identified.
(8) Recombine the groups and discuss the myths generated by each group. A list of nine myths about rape is provided below. If brainstorming does not bring out all of the myths, the leaders should use this list to add to the myths generated by the group.
(9) Process the experience of discussing myths. Focus on the affect generated during the brainstorming exercise.

c. Family commitment: Divide the group into family groups. Give them a list of expected behaviors that reflect commitment to the group. The list should include attending all the sessions; supporting one another by listening, being honest, and being responsible; sharing feelings, experiences, and ideas with the group; and asking for the group's attention when feeling uncomfortable or distressed about something. Give the families five minutes to discuss their willingness to do these things as individuals. Have them commit themselves to doing them in their family groups, and then return to the group as a whole. At this point, they should verbally express their commitments as family groups to the rest of the group.

- Information
a. List of myths about rape:
    (1) *All women want to be raped.* This assumes that women wish to be out of control and to be forced into a sexual act against their will. If the rape victim has ever had fantasies of this kind in the past, it is important to remember that, in the fantasy, she was in control over who the other person was (the person's speech, dress or action) and the circumstances.

    (2) *You can't thread a moving needle.* This usually implies that a woman cannot be raped against her will. This does not take into account the fact that male rape takes place in prisons between very strong men. It also does not account for gang rapes or the fact that women are usually taken by surprise and sometimes knocked unconscious, that the rapist is usually larger in size, that women are often attacked while asleep, that a weapon or the threat of a weapon is used, or that women might succumb to verbal threats to their safety if they resist. To suppose that a struggling woman can always avoid being raped is to assume that a struggling man can always avoid being mugged or robbed.

    (3) *She was asking for it.* This shifts the blame onto the victim. It assumes the woman is somehow responsible. But, by the same token, if a man takes a walk at night, is he asking to be mugged or beaten? Studies from the Florida State Prison indicate that rapists are not interested in the woman's appearance; rather thay want to make the act as violent as possible. The rapist inmates all had available sexual relationships and were not looking for sexual satisfaction.

    (4) *Rape only occurs in secluded places; if women stayed at home, they would be safe.* Statistics indicate that one-half of all recorded rapes occur in the rapist's or victim's houses.

    (5) *Women are raped only by people they do not know.* The chances are better than 50 percent that the rapist will be someone the victim knows, someone that is trusted and allowed into the home—a neighbor, relative, a repair/delivery/service person, or a so-called friend.

    (6) *Only bad or easy girls are raped.* This probably originated as a protective statement by parents to reduce their

daughter's fear of being raped: "It can't happen to you." Thus the victims of rape conclude they must be bad. Was it the hour, their dress, the location, or what? They then develop guilt feelings that they may carry around for the rest of their lives.

(7) *After being raped, a woman can never enjoy sexual relationships again.* Memories of the experience can be resolved and do not make it impossible for a young woman to go on living a rich and satisfying life, if she has the opportunity to work through her feelings.

(8) *No man would ever want a raped woman—she is used merchandise.* This response reinforces the victim's feelings of shame, worthlessness, and humiliation. It is putting a "scarlet letter" on her forehead. How does the act of sexual violence become more significant than any other in terms of being "used?"

(9) *Women who have been raped secretly enjoyed the experience.* Again, rape is not primarily a sexual act; it is a violent, terrifying experience of being overpowered by an aggressive man who may kill his victim.

3. Session 2: Secrets and Feelings
   • Objectives
   a. To create an experience that allows everyone to experience a situation in which something "private" becomes known and produces potential vulnerability.
   b. To provide an opportunity for rape victims to become aware that others share their fears of exposure and that they are not alone in their need for control over their environment.
   c. To explore the need for confidentiality and privacy about personal experiences.
   d. To provide an opportunity to explore the responsibilities, binds, and roles that people perceive for themselves because of external forces and expectations.
   e. To increase the participants' awareness (revelation of their own perceptions and meanings observed by themselves) of the way they respond to their environment.
   f. To focus on the added stress on each individual because of the assault on the family.
   g. To provide an experience in which the group is able to experience themselves as supportive, understanding, and empathic with others in the group.

- Procedural Outline
  a. Fill out DACL Form C. (3 minutes)
  b. Discuss last week's experience and any questions and/or concerns brought up by the group. (5 minutes)
  c. Introduce "Secrets" as outlined below. (50 minutes)
  d. Discuss similarities in feeling vulnerability and loss of control because "secrets" are known, and in feeling out of control because of external pressures and demands. (10 minutes)
  e. Sculpting exercise as outlined below. (50 minutes)
  f. Have group members fill out "Self Rating" sheet (see below) for use at a later date. (5 minutes)
- Materials
  a. DACL Form C, paper and pencils, self-rating sheets.
- Procedures
  a. Secrets
    (1) Tell the group that everyone keeps secrets because they imagine that, if they were honest and open, there would be some kind of unpleasant consequence—others would not like them, would take advantage of them, would be disgusted, or would reject them. Explain that the present group experience gives them a chance to become more aware of the fear involved in revealing secrets, without suffering any consequences. Hand out pieces of paper, explaining that you want to collect their secrets anonymously in order for them to see how people in the group respond to their secrets without knowing whose they are. Explain that they should also get some idea of what kinds of things others are keeping secret. Have them close their eyes and think of two or three secrets that they would *least* want the others in the group to know. What information about themselves do they think would be most difficult to reveal or would be most damaging to their relationship with the people there?

    (2) Next, have them write their secrets on the pieces of paper. They should write them clearly and with enough detail that anyone reading them will know exactly what they mean. For instance, they should not just write, "I'm afraid of people," but rather say exactly which people they are afraid of and what they fear from them, such as, "I'm afraid of strong men who might injure me physically." Ask them not to be phony. They should either

write a real secret that is important, or just write that they are unwilling to write down any secrets.

(3)   When they have finished writing their secrets, have them fold the papers twice and place them in a pile in the middle of the floor. As they put the papers on the pile, have them shuffle the pile a little and go back to their place. After everyone has put a piece of paper in the pile, have each person go to the pile and pick up one piece and then sit down again.

(4)   Next, have one person read the secret on the piece of paper they picked up *as if it were that person's own secret*. Have the person begin by saying, "This is my secret: I . . ." The participants should try to imagine that they really become the persons who wrote the secrets and should try to express something more about how they feel *as the person with the secret*. Even if the secret does not seem important to them, it was to someone, so they must respect that. After each person has read a secret, have the others in the group say how they feel toward the person who has just revealed the secret. They should not show anything except a feeling response, such as, "I feel disgusted," "I am surprised," or "I don't care if you do that." If any of the participants feel the same fears, encourage them to share it with the group. After all have given their responses, go on to someone else who, in turn, reads a paper as if the secrets on it were the person's own, while the others give their feeling responses.

(5)   The group should then take ten minutes to discuss anything they want to share about what they experienced or discovered through the experience. How did they feel as someone else read their secrets and as the others responded? How did they feel as they heard others' secrets? (This exercise is adapted from Stevens, 1971.)

b.   Individual sculpting exercise. In doing the sculpting exercise, the cotherapists may find the following guidelines helpful, but they should not be limited by them:

(1)   Choose someone from the group who is likely to respond spontaneously.

(2)   Use your own enthusiasm and conviction as catalysts to overcome the families' initial hesitation.

(3)   Encourage body movement and physical activity during the creation of the sculpture.

(4) Outline the activity, select the sculptor, and encourage the families to move out of their seating positions so that they can begin.

(5) After the rules are set, allow the sculptor to take over. Move into the role of observer, commentator, and interpreter.

(6) Reduce the anxiety of the sculptor by indicating you are aware that the group is being asked to respond to one person's view of the situation and that there are, of course, other views. This allows the sculptor to create something others may not agree with.

(7) As the sculptor proceeds, engage the sculptor in an ongoing dialogue, providing encouragement as the sculptor encounters difficulty, asking if each person is placed as the sculptor intended.

(8) Allow the sculpture to unfold at its own pace.

(9) After the sculptor has indicated completion of the sculpture, have the sculptor find a position in the finished work.

(10) Have the sculptor explain what the positions, gestures, and expressions are meant to represent.

(11) Ask the participants to share some of their feelings about the physical positions they are in. This should be confined to the immediate experience.

(12) Following this processing, encourage the other members to show how they perceive their position in our society.

(13) Process any general comments from the group about the sculpting experience, including any new or different ways they perceive themselves or their experience.

(14) Tell the participants that you want them to try out something a little bit different and that all of them will be involved in some way in the experience. Ask one member to come to the middle to act as the first sculptor. (Others will have an opportunity later to be the sculptor.) The rest of the group stands up and moves into whatever part of the room and to whatever position the sculptor directs. The sculptor shows the group members how they feel as (man and father, woman and mother, young woman and daughter) in our society by putting some or all of them into physical postures that create pictures symbolizing how they see themselves. The participants should do the exercise without talking, unless clarification is needed. When they are finished, the participants should talk about

their experience. Everyone should have an opportunity to demonstrate how they see themselves. (This exercise is adapted from Duhl, Kantor, & Duhl, 1973.)

  c. Self-rating. Hand out the rating scale in Exhibit 11-2 to the members of the group. When they have finished, collect the scales for use in the post-test session.

4. Session 3: Openness, Vulnerability, and Support
    - Objectives
      a. To encourage open expression of affective and cognitive responses to the crisis experience.
      b. To facilitate listening and understanding by parents vis-à-vis their daughters and daughters vis-à-vis their parents as they discuss their unique perspectives on the rape.
      c. To examine the roles assumed by the members of the family in relation to one another.

Exhibit 11-2 Self-Rating Scale

Rate yourself on the scales listed below. Rate yourself as you are now. The ratings should apply only to yourself. Place a check in the appropriate space (:___:) on each continuum.

acceptable	:___:___:___:___:___:___:___:	unacceptable
inaccurate	:___:___:___:___:___:___:___:	accurate
alert	:___:___:___:___:___:___:___:	unaware
tense	:___:___:___:___:___:___:___:	calm
incompetent	:___:___:___:___:___:___:___:	competent
confident	:___:___:___:___:___:___:___:	unsure
inconsiderate	:___:___:___:___:___:___:___:	considerate
kind	:___:___:___:___:___:___:___:	cruel
dependable	:___:___:___:___:___:___:___:	undependable
inefficient	:___:___:___:___:___:___:___:	efficient
friendly	:___:___:___:___:___:___:___:	unfriendly
unhelpful	:___:___:___:___:___:___:___:	helpful
illogical	:___:___:___:___:___:___:___:	logical
merry	:___:___:___:___:___:___:___:	sad
immature	:___:___:___:___:___:___:___:	mature
calm	:___:___:___:___:___:___:___:	nervous
abnormal	:___:___:___:___:___:___:___:	normal
optimistic	:___:___:___:___:___:___:___:	pessimistic
awkward	:___:___:___:___:___:___:___:	poised
reasonable	:___:___:___:___:___:___:___:	unreasonable
unworthy	:___:___:___:___:___:___:___:	worthy
useful	:___:___:___:___:___:___:___:	useless
irresponsible	:___:___:___:___:___:___:___:	responsible

    d. To review the ways the individuals currently communicate in their families.

    e. To explore other persons available and involved in the family support system, to determine how such persons have responded to the disruptive occurrence in the family's life.

- Materials:
  a. DACL Form D, information about the rape experience, large pad of paper, colored felt tip pens.

- Procedural Outline
  a. Fill out DACL Form D. (3 minutes)
  b. Review the previous session. (5 minutes)
  c. Introduce the "fish bowl" technique (see outline below). (30 minutes)
  d. Effect the transition from parent to daughter communication to family communication and support systems. (10 minutes)
  e. Introduce the "Family Circle" (see outline below). (60 minutes)

- Procedures
  a. Fishbowl technique. Split the group into two groups. The young women move into the center of the room in a small circle and talk to one another about their experiences and feelings as rape victims while the parents remain in the outside circle and are asked to listen without talking. After about 10 to 15 minutes, the discussion is halted, and the members of the inner circle are silent while the parents discuss what they have heard and what they now know about their daughters that they did not know before. This requires another 10 to 15 minutes. After the discussion is concluded, bring the entire group back together and discuss the experience for another 10 to 15 minutes. (This exercise is adapted from Egan, 1976, and Goldenberg, Stier, & Preston, 1975.)
  b. The family circle
     (1) Divide the group into families. Give each family a large easel pad, and have each member choose a different colored felt-tipped pen. Draw a large circle in the middle of the paper. Tell the family that everything inside the family circle represents what they feel is part of their family. Persons and institutions felt not to be part of their family are placed in the environment outside their family circle. The family circle and the environment together represent the family life space.

(2)   Ask members of the family, in turn, to place a small circle representing themselves in the family circle. It is recommended that the daughters not be the first to place themselves in the circle in positions relative to the other family members and the environment. Give immediate feedback to the family members as they place themselves, by such remarks as, "You feel you're in the center in your family, very far from your parents."

(3)   After everyone has placed themselves, explore the social network by asking the family questions such as, "Are there any other people who you feel are important to you and should be included in this drawing?" The family members then place important others (that is, absent family members and/or friends, deceased or living) somewhere in or outside the family circle, as they perceive them. There is often considerable disagreement among family members about the placement of absent extended family members. When this happens, note the perceptual differences diagrammatically by asking the dissenting family members to place the disputed person where they feel that person should be in the drawing. Occasionally, a family does not include anyone not present in the session. In these cases, it is useful to probe for information regarding at least siblings and paternal and maternal grandparents. This may elicit information about multigenerational patterns, family secrets, and past traumatic experiences.

(4)   Then ask the family to place significant social institutions (schools, churches, community agencies, work groups, and so on) in the environment. After this has been done, instruct in the following way: "I would like to know how you feel you communicate with the people and institutions in this drawing. By this I mean, how you feel you can talk with another person, and whether or not that person understands you. If you feel that you have good communication with another person, draw a straight line from you to that person, like this (0____0). If you feel you have 'so-so' communication with the other person—sometimes good and sometimes not so good—draw a dotted arrow from you to that person, like this (0<----->0). Finally, if you have poor communication with that person, draw an arrow slashed twice from you to that

person, like this (0<-//->0). Thus, you have three choices: good, 'so-so,' and poor communication."

(5) Now have the participants indicate how they perceive the communication they have with others in the drawing. Again, provide feedback to each person, reflecting the quality of communication the person has noted: "You have good communication with your mother," or, "You feel you have poor communication with your school." The purpose of the comments should be to involve the family in the process of self-observation (Geddes & Medway, 1975).

(6) Process this exercise as a group. How do they like their current style of coping with pressure? What new information do they have about themselves?

- Information
  a. In the above procedures, be alert to the following:
    (1) The rape experience adds stress to the already vulnerable areas of relationships.
    (2) The father may view the rape as a failure to fulfill his responsibilities and may compensate by being overly protective.
    (3) The father may have lost status in his wife's perception because he failed to protect the family.
    (4) To overcome their feelings of inadequacy and powerlessness, the family members may attempt to rally the support of the victim's friends, teachers, coworkers, relatives, church leaders, neighbors, and so on. However, this may seem invasive to the victim. It should therefore be explored and related to the issue of providing confidentiality and privacy and of including only a chosen few.
    (5) The family may decrease their communication in an attempt to deny or avoid communication about the crisis. This should also be explored. Another method of avoidance is to create conflicted communication patterns.

5. Sessions 4 to 7: Problem Solving
  - Objectives
    a. To focus on the unique problems perceived by the individual families.
    b. To begin looking at problems the family encounters in a systematic way that will help them arrive at solutions more quickly and effectively.

    c.   To involve members of the group in supportive, confrontive, empathic, and clarifying roles.

- Materials
  a.   DACL Forms E, F, G, and A.
- Procedural Outline
  a.   Give DACL Forms E, F, G, and A at successive sessions. (5 minutes)
  b.   Identify the problem. (20 minutes)
  c.   Gather information from previous sessions and experiences, including previously tried solutions, that will help solve the problem. (20 minutes)
  d.   Have the family analyze and select from the gathered information things they feel would be helpful to them in solving their problem. (15 minutes)
  e.   Form a tentative solution to the problem. Make it very specific and operational so that the family knows exactly what they are to do differently. (15 minutes)
  f.   Commit the family to try the solution and report the results at the beginning of the next session. (5 minutes) At the beginning of the next session, allow the family members to take the first 10 to 15 minutes to discuss their experience, using the solution they agreed to try. Then move to a new family and repeat the process.
- Procedures
  a.   Discuss the roles of the group members briefly, indicating that the family that is presenting its problem is risking something. Be sure to give supportive and reinforcing comments to the family members.
  b.   Emphasize clearly the need to identify a specific problem. This may require use of multiple therapeutic techniques, including role playing, sculpting, fantasy trips, and role reversal.
  c.   Have the family members describe how they would like their experience to be different.
  d.   Help the family members move through this experience in a way that leads to discovery about themselves—to learning about their interactions and how to use their own resources.
  e.   Guide the group interaction toward solving problems, defining the limitations, unrealistic expectations, or limited resources that might inhibit solutions.
  f.   Provide an accepting, safe environment into which the victim and family can release their thoughts and feelings without fear

of condemnation or critical responses born out of shared help-lessness.

g. With poise and gentle reassurance and avoidance of overdirec-tiveness, model empathy and willingness to address difficult material.

h. Support the solution and get commitments for follow-through by reporting to the group at the next session.

i. Write down on the chalkboard the possible solutions and influ-encing factors as they are identified for each problem so that the group can see what has been accomplished.

j. Repeat this process with a different family and a new problem.

6. Session 8: Focus on the Future
   • Objectives
     a. To focus the group members on their individual growth, uniqueness, and future orientation.
     b. To provide an expressive medium that allows them to generate their feelings, fears, and expectations.
     c. To allow group expression of support to the individuals within the group, much as they have to the family groups in the previous sessions.
     d. To prepare for termination.
   • Materials
     a. A variety of magazines, scissors, variously colored poster-boards, and glue.
   • Procedural Outline
     a. Administer DACL Form B. (5 minutes)
     b. Present the future direction in collage (see below). (90 minutes)
     c. Discuss termination. (10 minutes)
     d. Emphasize the importance of returning for the final session. (5 minutes)
   • Procedures
     a. Roles of the therapists and participants
        (1) Continue enthusiastic support for and confidence in the use of activities as a means of discovery.
        (2) Focus on future direction and growth during the sessions.
        (3) Begin to talk about termination of the group and its mean-ing for both therapists and members.
        (4) Provide the members with a feeling that there are avail-able counseling resources if they think they need further help.

b. Future direction in collage
   (1) Instruct the participants to go to the stack of magazines at the front of the room and select several magazines. Then silently, without any consultation, have them select from the magazines pictures, words, headlines, colors, or shapes that somehow represent where they see themselves in five years. If this is difficult for them to do, they might try glancing through the magazines and cutting out things that they like or are somehow attracted to. After the group members have accumulated as many pictures, symbols, words, and headlines as they want, each member should select a piece of poster paper. The color of the paper should fit their images of themselves in the future. They should then begin to organize their assortments onto the paper in a way that reflects where they will be in five years if they continue in the direction they are going. The activity should take 15 or 20 minutes to complete.
   (2) Then, holding each collage so others can see it, each member should take three or four minutes to describe the project. The description should be in the first person present tense, as if they were describing themselves. They should say, for instance, "I have a lot of red and yellow shapes surrounded by headlines on my right side. On my left side and at the top, I have peaceful blue and green mountain scenes that fill me with pleasant warm feelings." Ask the members to be aware of how they feel and what they notice as they describe themselves.
   (3) After all the participants have described their collages, ask the group to silently reflect on this experience. Ask what they discovered about themselves and others as they expressed themselves through their collages. What similarities and differences did they notice in the collages? Then take another five or ten minutes to share the observations and discuss them.

7. Post-Test Session
   • Objectives
      a. To obtain measurement data.
      b. To finish up the sessions and terminate the group.
      c. To provide individuals with feedback about their individual growth.

- Materials
  a.   Self-Rating Scale, Derogatis Symptom Checklist (SCL-90R), Moos Family Environment   Scale (FES), and DACL Form C.
- Procedural Outline
  a.   Readminister the self-rating scale (Exhibit 11-2) to each participant. (5 minutes)
  b.   Discuss the changes the participants see in themselves and in their families and how they feel about them. (30 minutes)
  c.   Administer DACL Form C. (5 minutes)
  d.   Administer FES. (30 minutes)
  e.   Provide punch and cookies for socializing.
  f.   Terminate the group. Indicate that follow-up counseling is available if desired.

Part IV

Structured Family Facilitation Programs: Education

Chapter 12

The Lonely Marriage: Couples Coping with Prison Separation

Lane B. Andelin and Suzanne L. Dastrup

This is an educational, group-structured program that is designed specifically for a population of couples separated by incarceration of the husband. The total length of the program is eight to ten weeks (dependent upon the number of problematic areas that group members choose to address), with two-hour sessions held once each week. The suggested group structure involves three to five couples (voluntary participation) and male and female coleaders.

BACKGROUND

Group psychotherapy has been utilized in prison rehabilitation since World War II. It was begun to help conserve the time, energy, and number of staff members, but was soon found to be useful also in helping to instill inmates with values conducive to law abiding behavior and to alienate them from peer groups conducive to criminality (Stephenson & Scarpitti, 1974). It was also found to be useful in improving relations between prison staff and inmates by providing new, more rehabilitative roles for staff members, helping prisoners recognize and solve emotional conflicts underlying their criminality, giving inmates a chance for feedback from their peers as to the social aspects of their personality, and in improving the emotional climate of the prison (Fenton, 1961).

As groups have become more accepted and more frequently used in corrective settings, a wide variety of approaches has been incorporated in group psychotherapy: criminals working with noncriminals to help rehabilitate other criminals (Stephenson & Scarpitti, 1974), Alcoholics Anonymous groups, in-service training groups (Fenton, 1959), family night groups, drug rehabilitation groups, sexual offenders groups, sexual inadequacy groups, and many more.

For couples and families with prisoners, various marriage and family counseling groups have been formed: orientation groups to help families be aware of prison facilities, prison life, rehabilitation, and services available; group counseling for parents, wives, and families of prisoners (Fenton, 1959); conjugal visits for purpose of sexual relations (Hopper, 1969); and wives' groups to help wives of prisoners cope with problems of separation (Crostwaite, 1972). These group programs recognize that the attitudes and behaviors of wives (and families) of inmates greatly influence how the inmates behave in prison and the extent to which they utilize a treatment program while there. Their adjustment after release is also facilitated if they have families waiting with an awareness of their welfare and of solutions to problems arising during their sentences (Fenton, 1959).

The present program is designed to intermesh with existing treatments by spanning the gap between marriage and family counseling groups and outside wives' groups. The intent of the program is to help husbands and wives understand and overcome problems caused specifically by the separation of the husband and wife due to the husband's prison sentence. Although many families are also separated by the imprisonment of the wife/mother, a greater number of separated families involve an incarcerated husband/father. Hence, our program addresses the family structure of the imprisoned husband/father and custodial mother. It is not designed to solve normal problems of interaction faced by most couples living together, nor is it designed to change dysfunctional interaction patterns. Although there is some overlap with interaction problems, the sessions specifically address the difficulties of prison separation. Some of the problems inherent in the separation may have been present before, but they could be intensified by the separation and the husband's absence from the home.

The problems of separation are many. Financial trauma is particularly prevalent for the wife or mother at home. Delinquent rent payments and possible threat of eviction, loss of utilities, the need for children's clothing, reliance on and lack of information about social security and welfare—all these are involved in financial trauma. In short, wives of incarcerated husbands may have all the problems of the very poor. Financial problems are often the biggest practical problem and affect both husband and wife.

Other problems that wives face include the emotional problems of loneliness, sexual deprivation and frustration, possible extramarital relationships, feelings of injustice over her husband's imprisonment, and reliance on agencies for subsistence (Crostwaite, 1972). Additional emotional concerns stem from shame, remorse, guilt, hostility in the community, fears of readjustment upon the husband's release, and concern over how the husband is progressing or coping in prison.

Child-rearing also presents a problem, in that the father's imprisonment is often traumatic for the children and discipline problems may occur in his absence. The children also can face degradation and humiliation from their friends. As they grow up, if the husband's sentence is a long one, the wife is faced with trying to maintain the children's loyalty to their father, and yet instilling important values in them. Often loyalty to father is strong, and the children identify with the father by acting out and getting into trouble. With all these problems facing the wife, she sometimes feels that she is the one serving the sentence, not the father. Sometimes, pressure from parents and significant others for the wife to separate from her husband causes additional stress (Crostwaite, 1972). Of course, all of these problems likewise affect the husband and the relationship between the wife and husband. He often feels frustrated in not being able to help his wife solve these problems and is also faced with his own feelings of remorse, guilt, and shame (Fenton, 1959).

GROUP TREATMENT

Theoretical Basis

Theme-centered interaction theory and basic communication theory are the basis for the treatment. See Appendix A for a brief description of these theories.

Role of the Leaders

The role the leaders play is important in fostering those factors that are beneficial to the group. The pair of male and female leaders is responsible for the following:

- modeling good communication skills
- reminding the group of the ground rules as needed
- balancing the focus between the theme, group or interactional process, and intrapsychic process (the "I-We-It" triangle of theme-centered interaction groups)
- preventing acting-out
- providing a positive, nonpunitive atmosphere
- bringing in community resources that are applicable to the theme
- screening the participants and informing them of the nature of the group

Forming the Group

Upon the husband's incarceration, the husband and wife are informed together at a monthly or bimonthly orientation at the prison regarding prison life and the services available through the prison. One of the services mentioned is the theme-centered interaction group. In other words, the couple is able to join the group upon incarceration or at any time during the husband's imprisonment. Participation in a group is strictly voluntary. However, an interview is required of each couple to screen out severe marital interactional problems.

Problems of a minor nature can be handled by the group, although these are not the group's major focus. The group's main concern is with problems related to imprisonment. Specifically, these problems include divorce encouraged by family members and significant others when the wife does not desire a divorce; families who are subjected to criticism and community hostility because of the father's offense; the children's need for male discipline and interaction modeling; the children's maintaining loyalty to the father without adopting his values; financial problems accentuated by lack of unemployment insurance and Social Security benefits; and the loneliness and sexual deprivation of both husband and wife.

The initial interviewer screens out the following: inmates on "death row," prisoners in maximum security, homosexuals, and psychopaths (the MMPI is used to help screen out psychopaths). Though none of these are allowed to be members of the treatment group, referrals to other sources are made whenever possible.

During the initial interview, the leaders seek to establish good rapport with each couple. This is important because rapport with the leaders is often one of the few elements of initial cohesion that the group has. The interview is also used to eliminate misconceptions and fears that the couple might have about the group. For example, the couple might feel that they will be forced to reveal things that they do not want to reveal. The removal of such misconceptions can aid greatly in making each couple comfortable in the group and in facilitating group cohesion.

The expectations for participating couples in the group are specified by the leaders. This enables the group participants to be aware of their responsibilities and commitments in the group. In addition, the MMPI and a questionnaire that assesses the nature of the participants' current support systems are administered.

The Treatment Program

The program consists of four interrelating phases. This format enables the group members to achieve trusting relationships and rapport as a group, to increase their interpersonal communication skills (both with spouses and other group members), to use these skills in addressing specific difficulties associated with prison separation, and to terminate the group process while maintaining the support systems and supportive skills achieved within the group.

Phase I (Session 1) is designed to develop rapport and commitment. Mutual trust among group members precipitates an atmosphere that is conducive to interactional and intrapersonal growth. This trust is achieved through prescribed commitment and rapport-building exercises during the initial session.

Phase II (Sessions 2 and 3) is designed to increase the quality of communication between the husband and wife. An essential ingredient of effective relationship management, and problem solving in particular, is a basic familiarity with communication skills. In our specific population, the skills of explicit communication (to overcome misperceptions), self-disclosure (to enhance relationship cohesion), and intimacy (to maintain mutual support) are critical. Two consecutive sessions are recommended to focus on these skills.

Phase III (Sessions 4 to 8) is designed to help the couples solve their problems. As has been suggested, the number of sessions of the treatment group is somewhat dependent upon the needs of the group. Thus, Phase III requires that group members identify specific problematic areas that are affecting their family life. Topics could include child-rearing in separated families, financial stress, loneliness and sexual needs, family or community nonsupport or hostility, and so on. The group chooses a specific problem or theme focus for each session in this phase.

Phase IV (final session) promotes closure for effective termination. This final session should prepare the group members to create and maintain their own support networks, similar to the one created during the group process. These networks may be informally maintained, either with group members or in other relationships (extended family, neighbors, inmates).

Three assessment procedures are used to determine individual progress and attitudinal change during the four phases. Some measures that could be used for this purpose are the Caring Relationships Inventory (CRI), the Taylor-Johnson Temperament Analysis (T-JTA), group attendance, the Marital Happiness Scale (MHS), and the Marital Adjustment Test (MAT). See Appendix B for descriptions of these instruments.

PROGRAM OUTLINE

The following outline describes the content, procedures, and materials used in each program session.

1. Session 1: Ability To Cope with Prison Separation
   • Objectives
      a. To reduce anxiety.
      b. To get acquainted with group members.
      c. To attain individual commitments to confidentiality, attendance, and responsibility.
      d. To become involved with the general theme of "my personal ability to cope with prison separation."
      e. To establish subthemes for each session.
      f. To introduce ground rules (where appropriate).
      g. To give assignments for next week.
   • Roles
      a. Leaders. The leaders are responsible for outlining the procedures in the session and ensuring that activities are accomplished in the allotted time frames. They must also strive:
         (1) To reduce anxiety and establish rapport.
         (2) To help in the establishment of ground rules for group operation and obtain commitments to them.
         (3) To help members discuss and understand the theme.
         (4) To facilitate the group's decisions about subsequent subthemes.
         (5) To discuss members' opportunities to use the group for support during the week and after termination of the group.
      b. Participants. The participants are told that it is their responsibility to get out of the group what they want and need and also to give what they want to the group. This is the basic ground rule, known as "be your own chairman," that the leaders establish during the commitment phase. In other words, it is up to each member:
         (1) To use the group to help them with their concerns.
         (2) To make sure they understand other members' communications.
         (3) To bring up and deal with those aspects of their own environment that are interfering with the process of the group.
         (4) To be responsible for sharing experiences and resources that will be helpful to the group.
         (5) To participate in decisions that affect group activities.
         (6) To establish the ground rules for the group that they feel are important and commit to them individually.

- Procedures. In the following activities, the leader attempts to reduce anxiety by responding warmly and positively to comments made by members, using empathic and reflective responses. Each person is made to feel welcome and an integral part of the group.
  a. Introduction (40 minutes): Give each participant a pencil and a card and instruct them to draw a picture representing themselves (or write two descriptive adjectives about themselves). Then ask each person, by choice, to take one to two minutes to explain that person's card and answer group members' questions. (3 minutes maximum per person)
  b. Commitment, using silence exercises (40 minutes): Instruct the group members to close their eyes and think silently about the general theme, "my personal ability to cope with prison separation." This theme is established in advance and serves to let potential members know what the group is for and to facilitate interaction focusing upon the common theme and how it relates to them personally (2 minutes). Then have the members (still with eyes closed) think about how they feel regarding their membership in the group, what they expect to do for the group, and what commitments they feel are important. Ask them individually to commit themselves to those rules identified by the group, especially those concerning confidentiality, responsibility, attendance, and honesty. Be sure to discuss the ground rule of "be your own chairman."
  c. Other ground rules may be brought up by the leaders as the need arises. One possibility is the rule to speak one at a time. When several group members speak at once or when there is a whispered conversation, encourage the members to share their whispered conversation with the group. A second, often needed, rule concerns owning statements. Members who, when speaking of their own experiences, tend to generalize to a second-person "you" statement ("You try so hard to please everyone, and where does it get you.") should be asked to rephrase the statements, using "I" instead of "you." Another rule applies to situations in which members are too upset or otherwise distracted by events in their lives or environment to participate effectively. Such members can be encouraged to deal with their feelings by talking about them, by going around the group asking for some feedback, or by using any number of gestalt or encounter techniques deemed appropriate by the therapists. These disturbances take precedence over the process of the group or discussion of the theme.

    d. Crucial concerns (15 minutes): Ask the group to brainstorm to identify the types of problems most frequently experienced by couples separated by incarceration. If the group is resistant to naming problems, facilitate the process by suggesting possible topics. Inform the group that part of next week's agenda will entail identifying the five or six specific topics that the group is most interested in addressing. Wives should be encouraged to exchange phone numbers to help establish an outside support system. Therapists should briefly discuss the purpose of building an outside support network of group members, both wives and husbands.

- Homework. Ask the members to think during the week about the topics identified in this first session. Ask them to identify personal strengths and resources (experience, expertise, and so on) that relate to the topics and that may be helpful to the group.

2. Session 2: Sharing the Real Me
   - Objectives
     a. To continue in rapport building and development of trust among group members.
     b. To identify the subthemes that will be addressed in Sessions 4 and 5.
     c. To create an awareness of the clarity and bonding attainable through explicit, self-disclosing messages and of misperceptions resulting from implicit communication.
   - Role of leaders. The group leaders should model openness and warmth, while facilitating group participation in each of the activities. Also, they can fulfill an important function in clarifying and organizing members' comments. One of the leaders gives a brief "lesson" on explicit self-disclosure (see below).
   - Procedures
     a. Review and rapport building (30 minutes): The group members, seated in a circle, should have an opportunity to become reacquainted. This process can occur by challenging someone to name everyone in the circle. The chances are slim that anyone will accomplish this on the first attempt. Continue until someone accurately names all the group members. Follow the same sequence in recalling the adjectives or pictures that the members used to identify themselves in the first session. Select each person to be in focus, one at a time until all have had a turn. Ask the other members to tell as many good things as they can about the person in focus (for example, "She smiles a lot,"

"He's gentle with his wife," "Her hair is pretty," "He seems so easy-going," and so on).

b. Identification of subthemes (20 minutes): Ask the group to reflect on the main theme of the group, "my own ability to cope with prison separation." By doing this, they should become aware of specific difficulties resulting from the incarceration. As noted in the first session, these difficulties will serve as subthemes for the final sessions of the group. Use chalk and chalkboard to write down and appropriately consolidate the suggestions. Begin a brainstorming session to identify the difficulties that are most prevalent in the lives of group members (loneliness, sexual deprivation, discipline for the kids, financial panic). Then ask the group to identify the issues that are of greatest concern. These will serve as the focus of future group sessions. Facilitate this discussion by interpreting and rephrasing suggestions until a consensus on three to five topics has been reached.

c. One-on-one sharing (70 minutes):

   (1) Ask the group members to pair off with their own spouses, facing each other, holding hands, and leaning slightly forward toward each other. Instruct the couples to close their eyes and to begin to think of the things that are *most* valuable to them. Here is a suggested introduction to this exercise: "I would like each of you, while continuing to hold hands with your spouse, to close your eyes for a few minutes. During this time I would like you to think about the things that are most important to you. These should not be material things or anything that money will buy. Instead, I would like you to think of experiences, memories, relationships, or feelings that are valuable to you. These are things that make you the happiest, that feel the warmest or sweetest. They may even be thoughts or ideas that you have never shared with anyone else. Think about these most important things and enjoy for a few minutes the sweetness and joy of your thoughts. Now, when you are ready, open your eyes and face your partner."

   (2) At this time, instruct the husbands to share with their wives one important thing—one experience, idea, or feeling—that is very near and dear to them. Afterwards, the wives should share with their husbands the one thing that is very important to them. After all group members have shared their feelings sufficiently, instruct the couples to

repeat the process, this time sharing something even *more* important or even more valuable. Finally, after both partners have shared a second time, they should be instructed to repeat the process one final time, each person expressing something extremely important to that person. This series of dyadic exchanges is intended to involve each couple in an intense self-disclosure experience. The outcome is frequently a bonding or uniting experience.

(3)   After the couples complete the task, reassemble them in a circle and briefly discuss their feelings about the assignment, about themselves, and about their partners. The leaders should accentuate those comments that affirm the cohesive, unifying, warm, and tender aspects of the experience. Then sum up the discussion by giving a brief lesson about the value of self-disclosure. In this way, the group participants can begin to recognize the underlying reasons for the unity and warmth they are experiencing. It is important to include at least these specific ideas:

(a)   Self-disclosure entails honestly, openly, and kindly sharing the "real me" by explicitly stating the person's feelings and ideas.

(b)   This type of sharing is a bonding experience, resulting in feelings of tenderness and warmth for each other.

(c)   This type of sharing usually occurs in dyads in which each person can receive total attention from the other and give the same.

(d)   Trust is best developed by such genuine sharing.

- Homework. Request each couple to find an opportunity to be together, holding hands or touching in some way (for example, by linking arms) once more before the next group session. This time together should be at least 30 minutes in length and should consist of the members telling their spouses one thing they want *from* them.

3. Session 3: Long-Distance Intimacy
   - Objectives
     a.   To define intimacy and the determinants of intimacy.
     b.   To facilitate an awareness among group members of the essential aspects of nurturing intimacy-at-a-distance.
     c.   To identify practical means of nurturing long-distance intimacy.

- Role of leaders
  a. To lead supportively a group discussion on the previous assign-
      ment, reframing and rephrasing comments so that self-disclo-
      sure information (trust, bonding, and so on) is reviewed for the
      group.
  b. To give a brief lesson on the nature of intimacy.
  c. To facilitate a group brainstorming session about the variety
      of intimacy-producing activities that are possible for the family
      experiencing long-term separation.
  d. To identify the social support systems that are available
      throughout the crisis of separation.
- Procedures
  a. Homework review (20 minutes): Greet each couple in a warm
      and caring manner, accentuating the overall objective of learn-
      ing to appreciate and implement social support systems. Also,
      give the couples a brief opportunity to exchange greetings and
      support. Then ask each couple to report on the homework
      experience. The couples should focus particularly on feelings
      that resulted from the experience. After the couples have related
      their experiences, it is helpful to summarize the advantages of
      self-disclosure, especially with regard to emotional bonding
      and trust in a dyadic relationship.
  b. Intimacy defined (20 minutes): Prepare in advance a brief les-
      son about intimacy. The lesson should include the following
      points:
      (1) Intimacy involves a detailed understanding of one another
           that results from close personal connection or familiar
           experience.
      (2) Loneliness occurs when the marriage relationship lacks
           intimacy.
      (3) Intimacy requires special effort for couples who are sep-
           arated for long periods of time.
      (4) This special effort should focus on sharing feelings and
           affection when together; structuring affectionate or simi-
           lar experiences that unify the relationship, even when
           distance separates the couple (for example, similar hob-
           bies, jokes, books, or sports); and developing support
           systems in which each partner can freely discuss and
           reflect upon the goodness of the long-distance relation-
           ship.
  c. Intimacy-building suggestions (50 minutes): Following the brief
      lesson on intimacy, ask the group: "How can this warmth and

emotional closeness be maintained in your marriage? What are the things that you can do *for* each other and *with* each other to encourage this intimacy between you?'' The brainstorming session that follows may require some initial direction and coaxing by the group leaders. The following are activities that might be shared when the couples are together: pursuing the same hobby and comparing notes (stamp collecting, coin collecting, pottery making, and so on), nurturing private ongoing jokes or holiday traditions, reading similar books and discussing them, joint planning for the years to come when the family will again be together.

d. Support Systems (30 minutes):

   (1) Stress how important it is that separated families frequently interact with other individuals who can affirm or validate the relationship with the missing member. Often the prison sentence of a husband or father results in well-meaning, protective individuals ridiculing or in some way harassing the continuance of the relationship. This type of input or feedback is obviously eventually damaging to the tenderness and intimacy of the relationship. It is crucial that separated couples guard against this sort of input by seeking out support systems or relationships that encourage, affirm, and validate the marriage.

   (2) Conclude this session by sharing the above information and discussing the need for support systems. Each couple should analyze the relationships with others that take up a significant amount of time. They should then determine whether these relationships are supportive or disruptive of the marriage. Discuss strategies for restructuring or eliminating those relationships that undermine the marriage.

• Homework. Each person should follow strategies developed in the group to change or eliminate destructive, nonsupportive relationships.

4. Sessions 4 to 8: Problem Solving
   • Objectives
      a. To help members learn ways of understanding, dealing with, and overcoming problems in a warm positive atmosphere.
      b. To gain support from other members of the group in dealing with problems after the group terminates.

- Roles
  a. Leaders
    (1) To set a tone of positive rapport in the group.
    (2) To make the members responsible for their own feelings and actions.
    (3) To keep a balance between the group's dwelling on individual feelings (''I''), the group process and interaction (''we''), and the fulfillment and understanding of the theme (''it'').
  b. Participants. The participants are responsible for their own behavior in the group; they receive from the group and give to the group what they want (see discussion above on ''being your own chairman''). They are to adhere to the commitments they made in Session 1 and to express common experiences and resources honestly to help the other group members understand and deal with problems.
- Procedures
  a. Silence exercise (similar to that in Session 1): Use three silent periods of two minutes during which the group is to think about the subtheme for the week and how it relates to the members and their experiences. For example, if the subtheme is ''handling family finances,'' encourage the members to think about it for the first two minutes, to let their minds focus on and try to ''get in touch'' with the subject and how it relates to them. Then, for the second two minutes, with their eyes still closed, ask them to notice and become aware of the bodily sensations and emotional feelings they are presently having. Finally, with their eyes still closed, instruct them to ponder (for the last two minutes) their own resources (past experience, training, expertise, and so on) that could be of help to the group in understanding and overcoming problems associated with the subtheme.
  b. After the silent periods, have the group communicate about the experience until they notice one member (or couple) relating or demonstrating an anxiety associated with the subtheme. At this point, focus mildly on those feelings, experiences, or attitudes and encourage the person or couple to talk about and explore them in the group.
  c. After sufficient time has been spent focusing on the one individual or couple and the group understands the problem under discussion, shift the group into a ''we'' (group) mode by asking the members to express how they feel about what the person or couple has been saying: how it makes them feel, what it

does to them, and so on. (If the group is a verbal group, this will probably be spontaneous; if it is resistant, it might be wise to go around the group and ask for feelings and comments in turn. However, this should be unnecessary after two or three times around the group.) Allow the group to explore reactions to the person or couple and the problem until all members have had a chance to talk about their feelings. This is a good time to remind the group of those interactions that need ground rules and of the basic ground rule, "be your own chairman." Comment on those reactions that shed light on each individual's unique situation and ability to deal with a particular problem.

d. Shift into an "it" (subtheme) mode by asking the participants to state some general considerations and principles that have emerged in the above interaction and that relate specifically to the subtheme. As these are mentioned, make a list of them and instruct the group to apply them to the problem of the individuals or couples identified in c. above. Ask them to think of possible ways they could deal with the cited problem and how each member could use these means to help them cope with similar problems as they arise (or now exist). It may be that not enough interaction will have taken place concerning the first problem of the session to enable the members to develop enough general statements or principles to help solve the problem. In this case, list the statements or principles that do emerge and retain them until the next person or couple deals with a problem or until the process is repeated enough to enable the retained statements to be beneficial.

e. As the group discusses the principles of the subtheme and how they can help members solve related problems, ask the members of the group to share experiences that are similar to those discussed and also any relevant resources (training, expertise, insight, ability to help, and so on). Each member can respond in turn, or it can be left up to the group to respond spontaneously. No one should be pressured to respond, since some will not have helpful experiences or resources related to the subject. However, each person who would like to share these ideas or resources should be allowed ample opportunity to do so. Encourage the members to help each other outside the group and to utilize this support to help them get through crisis situations related to the subject. The members themselves may set up ways of helping each other, but no pressure should be applied to see that this happens. However, leaders can facilitate the process by helping those members who want to help work out a good plan of action with those who need help. (It may be advisable to wait until the last 15 or 20 minutes of the session to follow this procedure, rather than apply it after each individual problem has been discussed. This delay will allow all needs and resources to be identified and thus permit a more adequate system of help to be utilized and coordinated.)

f. Allow the conversation to be free again and to deal with other aspects of theme, feelings, and so on, until another individual or couple emerges with strong feelings or needs to be focused on. Help the group go through all of the above procedures until the end of the session. However, any interruptions from group members who are experiencing stress or conflicts should take precedence.

g. Discuss briefly the subtheme for the sessions to follow and stress the value of using, not abusing, members for support outside group. Save some time in the final session (1 hour) to allow members to fill out post-MMPI and questionnaires for research purposes. This will aid in analyzing how effective the approach was and how well the members have been helped to understand and deal with the problems of separation. Because of the nature of the group, support of each other after termination is desirable and should be encouraged. Initiate a discussion of how to utilize this support and help set up ways of doing so. The wives may wish to meet together on the outside as a group, in smaller groups, or as dyads to help each other during their husbands' prison terms. The husbands may wish to do the same inside the prison. Strategies for doing this should be discussed until satisfactory decisions are reached. This will also help reduce separation anxiety.

Chapter 13

Responsible Assertiveness for Couples

Sally H. Barlow

This education program consists of six sessions designed to help marital partners whose patterns of behaving are best described as passive/aggressive. The sessions, each lasting two hours, should be held in two private comfortable rooms, each big enough to accommodate seven to ten participants and two facilitators, male and female. The participants, seven to ten couples, are divided into two groups with equal numbers of males and females, but with no couple in the same group.

The couples are dealt with in separate groups so that they can try out new behavior without having to attend to the history of their own marital relationships. The chance to role play with unrelated partners aids in confidence building and allows people to learn from other couples' situations. The couples may be volunteers responding to the advertised sessions or may be referred by counselors, teachers, or former participants of assertiveness training.

The intent of this structured program is to enable the participants to improve their communication patterns in relationships, in particular, in their marriages. Couples often get caught in a history of interaction that has become comfortable, though it may not be mutually beneficial. The behaviors that are learned in the program depend on the individual's needs. This may mean learning how to express directly anger, needs, wishes for behavior change, and so on. The focus of the sessions is on learning and then role playing the new learned responses that communicate the participants' personal rights, feelings, and desires. The ability to use such responses enables the participants to assert themselves more confidently, comfortably, and responsibly in their marriages and in a variety of other social situations.

Couples who could benefit from this program include partners who experience tension or awkwardness when encountering a situation that requires an expression of their needs, wants, or rights. The sessions would also be helpful to partners who are accustomed to getting their needs met through aggressive demands as well as partners who are timid, shy, or passive and who forgo having their needs met because of lack of skill. The sessions are geared toward both ends of the spectrum, toward passive as well as aggressive persons. Both interpersonal types are amenable to change. There have been several successful attempts to use assertive training with couples (Mace & Mace, 1976; Muchowski & Valle, 1977; Russell, 1981).

Assertiveness training can be taught by either professionals or graduate students. The most important prerequisite for leading such a group is the ability to distinguish, behaviorally as well as cognitively, passive, aggressive and assertive responses. With this program's facilitators manual in hand, any professional or graduate student with underlying skills in empathizing, understanding behavior change, and using the tools of role playing and processing could conduct the program's sessions.

The educational process in the program has the following schedule: Each session begins with a short lecturette describing that week's particular assertiveness skill, for example, the cognitive ideas underlying a person's right to refuse or make requests. This is accompanied by a handout that the participant uses as a guide and keeps for later reference or as a reminder. The participants are encouraged to put the handout material within view during the week, for instance, on the bathroom mirror.

Next, the facilitators model a few "impossible situations," thereby gaining the confidence of the group members and persuading them that a person can use an assertive response in almost any situation. The rest of the sessions are devoted to dyadic or triadic role playing, group discussion, verbal commitment by each member regarding the next week's homework, and reminders to keep current the diary entries that are processed in each group meeting.

Session 1 is devoted to introductions, an overview of the program, the establishment of group norms, the building of cohesion and trust, and creation of a relaxed and somewhat playful climate in which to practice new skills. Sessions 2 through 6 follow the format as indicated above, with enough time in the last session to process each participant's commitment to transfer learning to experiences in the outside world.

By the end of the sixth session, the participants should have achieved specific outcome objectives. They should be able to:

- define the differences among aggressive, passive, and assertive behaviors

- role play the differences among aggressive, passive, and assertive behaviors
- establish and experience support within a group of peers
- develop an increased self-awareness (know when they are behaving aggressively, passively, or assertively and also identify these behaviors in others)
- develop an ability to keep a diary for the purpose of accurately recording their feelings
- internalize the diary's subjective assessment of anxiety to enable them to keep track of their feelings and thereby modify their responses in the future
- act in an appropriately assertive way in and outside the marriage after leaving the group

The participants are given the Rathus Assertiveness Scale and McFall's Behavioral Role-Playing Test as preprogram and postprogram measurements to assess individual change. Potential marital changes are assessed by the Marital Adjustment Test and Caring Relationships Inventory. See Appendix B for descriptions of these instruments.

PROGRAM OUTLINE

The following outline describes the content, procedures, and materials used in each program session.

1. Session 1
   - Objectives. Session 1 is an introductory session in which the participants learn each other's names, something about each person in the group, something about assertive training, how to give effective feedback, and how to role play in an actual assertive training situation. The session ends with "impossible situations," in which the leaders role play situations generated from the participants' experiences. Homework assignments are then handed out before members leave.
   - Materials
     a. Blackboard and chalk
     b. Handout 1. The facilitator prepares several pages, stapled together, that list definitions of assertive as contrasted to passive and aggressive behaviors, with the points of view, social patterns, aims or goals, social consequences, and personal outcomes for each type (see Appendix 13-A). The five major

areas of assertive training that the group concentrates on are
(1) making simple requests, (2) refusing requests, (3) giving and
receiving compliments, (4) coping with criticism, and (5) asking
for a change in behavior. (See Appendix 13-B.) The last page
of the handout contains a list of books on assertiveness for
members who are interested in reading about the skill.

c.   Handout 2. This handout is a diary in which participants are
to record situations in which they feel anxiety and their responses
to such situations.

- Procedures

a.   Welcome and name exercise (45 minutes)

(1)   *Greet:* Greet people as they arrive.

(2)   *Ask:* Once the majority of members have arrived, ask
them to move their chairs into a circle.

(3)   *Name exercise:* Ask the members to tell a little something
about themselves—what their names are and whether
they like their names. Feel free to suggest any other topic
in addition to or instead of this one. The purpose is simply
to give them enough structure to get started. Go around
the circle until all members have had a chance to participate. Then ask if there is anyone who would like to try
to go around the circle and restate everyone's first name.
Once that is done, ask for another volunteer, until all
members have had a chance to try naming the participants.

(4)   *Note:* As the members are doing the above exercise, note
how individual members approach the name-remember-
ing task. Some may apologize for having forgotten; some
may express anxiety and embarrassment non-verbally.
The intent of the exercise is to give the participants an
immediate opportunity to combine introductions with
assertive skills.

(5)   *Process:* After the members have finished, process out
loud for them what you saw occur during the exercise.
For example, "Tom, I noticed that when you forgot Sue's
name, you looked flustered."

(6)   *Lecturette:* Give them a short lecturette on the societal
expectations we have about name remembering. Elicit
personal responses about how they feel when they meet
someone on the street whom they think they should know.

(7)   *Say:* Then say, "There is a more rational approach to
names. In fact, most people don't remember names. It is

quite normal to forget. A better way to deal with such situations is to practice a way in which to ask for a person's name in a direct way without apology or embarrassment.''

(8) *Coleader role play:* As coleaders, role play an example. The setting is two people meeting in a classroom:

> Jon: ''I know we've met before but I can't remember your name. Would you tell it to me again?''
>
> Sue: ''Yes, certainly. It's Sue Cameron. What's yours?''

(9) *Process:* Have the group members express any feelings or thoughts that might have occurred to them as they watched you. For example, ''How do you dare be that direct?'' ''Don't you think that hurts someone's feelings?''

(10) *Dyad practice:* If there are no comments, go on to the next group exercise. Ask each member to turn to another group member (preferably someone they do not already know) and practice exchanging names.

(11) *List:* List the following statements on the board to remind the participants of the intent of the exercise: (1) It is not a sign of disrespect to forget someone's name. (2) Most of us have trouble remembering names. (3) Asking directly for the person's name is better than mumbling an incorrect name or being apologetic or embarrassed.

(12) *Ask:* Once everyone has had a chance to complete the exercise, ask for any comments or questions. If comments or questions go on more than two or three minutes, cut them off by saying, ''I understand that you are curious about these aspects of assertiveness. We will answer most of your questions as we go through the planned exercises.''

b. Coleader lecturette (15 minutes): Divide the material between the two coleaders. The one who is speaking directs comments to the members. The one who is not, is responsible for handouts, if there are any for the particular lecture, and writes key points on the board. At a time predetermined by the coleaders, they switch roles.

(1) *Lecturette:* ''You have just experienced an example of assertive behavior. Our main purpose is to teach you skills that help you to be direct about your needs and wants in an assertive rather than a passive or aggressive way. Let's go over the definitions of the three terms.

(Coleader's name) will pass out a handout to help you understand the differences."

(2)   *Read handout:* Refer to first page of the handout and go over each area systematically, that is, points of view, social patterns, goals, social consequences, and personal outcomes of being nonassertive (passive), aggressive, or assertive (see Appendix 13-A). Encourage the members to follow along with the material in their handouts.

(3)   *Ask:* Ask if there are any questions so far. Again, if the questions or comments go on too long, gently cut them off in an assertive way so that you, as the facilitator, in fact model the behavior you are trying to teach. For example, "I would like to stop you now so we can go on to another section of the material." Do not say, "I don't mean to cut you off but . . ." Be direct. Remember, you are their most powerful tool for learning the new behaviors.

c.   Group responses, role playing and processing (45 minutes)

(1)   *Say:* Say, "Now (coleader's name) and I would like you to think of a time when you wished you would have acted assertively rather than aggressively or passively in your relationship with your partner in the other group. See if you can get that situation in mind and let us try to role play it a different way."

(2)   *Clarify:* Most members will have several situations in mind. Be sure you understand each situation's specifics by asking for clarification or further detail as necessary. For example, if someone says, "I don't get along with my wife," ask the person to think of a particular incident that occurred recently. Ask for a little background (only enough to know how you should act if you are playing the spouse). Set the scene by finding out if the incident occurred in the living room, at midnight, and so on. Then turn to your coleader and decide who will play which role.

(3)   *Model:* Negotiate in front of the group about who does which part so that the members can see you model the behavior of asking for something you would like to do, thereby showing that even the little things in life are often negotiated. Next, role play the scene as it appears to have happened. In this way, the participants can see graphi-

cally the differences between the "right way" and the "wrong way." The role play might proceed as follows:

> *Scene 1:*
> Wife: "John, you never clean up your dishes. It makes me so mad. Just get out of the kitchen if you can't clean up after yourself."
> Husband: "Okay, you can have your crummy kitchen to yourself. I'm getting out."

(4) *Coleader role play:* Now role play the scene with one of you (the person playing the role of the participant) behaving in a responsibly assertive way. The coleader who is playing the wife might, for example, continue to act aggressively or passively for a short time, but then give up the stance once a compromising tone has been set. Thus:

> *Scene 2:*
> Wife: "John, you never clean up after yourself. It makes me so mad. If you can't clean up after yourself, just get out of here."
> Husband: "I clean up after myself sometimes!"
> Wife: "You *never* do."
> Husband: "I can see that it really bugs you that I don't. I really am sorry."
> Wife: "Well, you should be!"
> Husband: "I am. But you know, sometimes I have a lot of work to do and I need to get started as soon as I finish eating."
> Wife: "That's true. But then I'm left with your mess, plus I feel lonely when you bring work home."
> Husband: "You have always wanted me to do well at work. And sometimes I'm afraid I just can't do it all."
> [Wife is now ready to compromise]
> Wife: "I can understand that. I think I'd be willing to compromise. For instance, if you clean up on Wednesdays when you don't have to go to work early, and then on the other nights just put your dishes in the sink, I'd settle for that. In addition, I'd like to schedule some play time for the two of us just to goof off and relax."
> Husband: "Okay, that sounds good. How about a movie Friday night!"

(5) *Ask:* "What were the differences you noticed between the two role plays? Can you identify verbal as well as nonverbal responses that were assertive rather than aggressive or passive?"

(6) *Process:* Let the group members talk about what they saw and heard.

(7) *Ask:* "Okay, who has another impossible situation they would like us to role play?"

   (8) *Role play:* Again, set the scene, determine who will play
         which part, and, if time permits, role play a contrast, for
         example, aggressive or passive first and assertive second.
         Role play as many situations as time permits.
   d. Summary, diaries, and homework (15 minutes)
      (1) *Wrap-up:* Encourage the participants to note their partic-
            ular reaction styles by keeping track of how they respond
            during the next week.
      (2) *Handout:* Distribute the Subjective Units of Discomfort
            (SUDS) Diary (Appendix 13-C) and explain briefly what
            SUDS mean. Ask the members to determine the subjec-
            tive discomfort they feel when in a certain situation by
            assigning a number to the situation and comparing that
            situation to another. For example, being confronted by a
            partner about a sensitive subject might rate a 75 SUDS
            rating, while talking to a salesperson might only rate a
            20. Ask them to write down, in the places provided on
            the handout, the situation and the response they had to
            it and then to attempt to distinguish between high SUDS
            (90–100) and lower SUDS (0–9, 10–19).
      (3) *Remind:* Encourage them to carry the SUDS handout
            with them during the week and remind them to bring it
            with them to the next week's meeting.

2. Session 2
   • Procedures
      a. Welcome, group sharing, and first exercise (45 minutes)
         (1) *Welcome:* Greet the members as they arrive. See how
               many names you are able to remember. Model asser-
               tively, asking for names if you have forgotten them.
         (2) *Sharing:* Ask the members to share the experiences they
               encountered during the week. Encourage them to use
               their diaries to remind themselves of what happened and
               how they felt. Go around the circle if the members are
               unable to answer spontaneously.
         (3) *Reward:* Be sure to reward members' responses that are
               assertive.
         (4) *Exercise:* Ask the members to take out their handouts
               from the first meeting (have extras on hand for those who
               have misplaced or forgotten to bring the handout). Go
               over the first area, making simple requests (see Appendix
               13-B).

(5) *Lecturette:* Read the ideas in the first area one by one. Ask for any comments or questions that come to mind. Reinforce the participants' right to make simple requests by noting the following: "As we have stated before, you have a right to ask for things you need or want. By doing so, you increase your chances for getting your needs met and having your preferences respected. You increase closeness and satisfaction in relationships. And even if you don't receive what you requested, at least you've expressed your preferences and thus strengthened your sense of integrity."

(6) *Ask:* Ask the members to think of situations in which they needed help or of something they had to ask for and to remember what they actually did. Were they passive, aggressive, or assertive?

(7) *Group responses:* Allow the members to talk about different situations and their fears about asking for things directly.

(8) *Explain:* At this point, explain an additional response that falls between aggressive and passive, called passive-aggressive. By now, several members may have tried to articulate this stance; but, since it does not fit into existing categories, they may not understand it.

(9) *Say:* "Passive/aggressive is a difficult response to pinpoint because we are often not sure when we display it or when it is being displayed by others. That is one of its characteristics: you're not sure what has happened. Essentially, it is a manipulative stance we take when we are angry but afraid to show it, so we smile while we stab someone in the back." Many people use it when they feel that they do not have direct access to power. Thus, the concealed attack may look something like this (the coleaders role play):

> Boss: "Ian, could you work late tonight? I have some things I need to have done by tomorrow morning."
>
> Ian (sullenly): "Sure, I'd be glad to. My old boss always managed to get his work done during the day, but I guess you have more to do."

Or it might look like this:

> Isadora (sarcastically): "Hi, Sherrie, your husband sure looks good when he goes to work. Do you spend all your clothing allowance on him, since you dress so plainly, I mean . . . practically?"

> Sherrie (unsure how to take remark): "Well, yes he does look good, doesn't he."

(10) *Ask:* "What was the indirect person's underlying feeling? How did Sherrie feel?"

(11) *Process:* Encourage members to explore why the indirect person felt as though they couldn't afford to be direct?

b. Group practice and impossible role playing (45 minutes)

(1) *Dyad role play:* Ask the group members to pair off. Instruct one person in a pair to ask for something that might be particularly difficult to ask for. Instruct the answering person not to comply right away so that the person "making a request" has to struggle a bit with the negotiation. Then ask the two to exchange places.

(2) *Process:* Encourage the members to talk about how they felt when asking, and how they felt when refusing, initially, and then how they felt complying or compromising.

(3) *Model:* Ask for "impossible situations" that came to members' minds as they went through the "request" exercise and discussion.

(4) *Clarify:* Make sure you understand each setting and help the people identify the behavior they displayed in the situation (passive, aggressive, passive/aggressive).

(5) *Role play:* Again, decide in front of the group who will take which part and role play the situation in an assertive way. Make sure the role player who is being asked something does not comply too quickly, so that the members can see that assertive negotiating takes time but is worth it in the end. Do several role plays if time permits. Allow for different kinds of role plays, requesting things from partners, family members, colleagues, neighbors, strangers, and so on.

(6) *Discussion:* Ask the members what they noticed verbally and nonverbally as the coleaders role played the various situations.

(7) *Write on board:* To emphasize the importance of their remarks, write them on the board, under the headings verbal and nonverbal. This way, they will begin to make the important distinctions among the ways we communicate.

(8) *Model:* If there are questions about nonverbal assertiveness, demonstrate the differences between various power plays, for example a boss who stands, looming over her

secretary, who is seated and literally "one down;" two persons who are having an argument and the aggressor puts hands on hips and spreads legs slightly to appear in control; and an assertive exchange in which both people are at the same level (standing or sitting together, maintaining eye-to-eye contact at the comfortable distance of two feet apart).

c. Questions and answers (15 minutes). By now, the members have had considerable experience watching themselves and they are becoming aware of many of the subtle aspects of assertive training. They may have many questions. Ask them to bring up anything they are thinking about. Be careful to keep a time frame in mind. For example, if a person asks specifically about how to refuse a request, remind the person assertively that you will be dealing with that particular topic the very next week.

d. Homework assignment (15 minutes)
   (1) *Remind:* Remind the members to maintain their diaries. Those who have filled up their first sheet will need another one. If there appears to be resistance to the keeping of a diary encourage the members to figure out their own way of "keeping track." The important point is that the members learn how to differentiate between different kinds of anxiety-producing situations and their responses to them. For example, they may act passively in a well-established personal relationship that they fear might end and act aggressively in a confrontation with a stranger who does not matter to them.

   (2) *Circle commitment:* Go around the circle and ask the members to describe particular situations in which they are planning to assertively make a request during the week with their partner or in some social situation. Encourage them to anticipate what might happen and how they might behave differently now that they have a new skill.

   (3) *Keep a copy:* Jot down what the members say so that at the next session the coleaders can ask how they did with specific situations. This not only fosters trust (the members see that the leaders think enough of them to keep track) but also helps the members to engage in the new behavior.

3. Session 3
   • Procedures
     a. Welcome, sharing, and first exercise (45 minutes)
        (1) *Welcome:* Try to remember everyone's name. If you have forgotten, ask assertively what their names are.
        (2) *Sharing:* Encourage the members to share what happened during the week as they practiced the assertive skill of making simple requests. Use your notes regarding the circle commitments made last week by each member.
        (3) *Reward:* Reward members for having tried the new skill.
        (4) *Exercise:* Use the following exercise to introduce the next behavior, refusing requests. Ask each member to ask another member for something and instruct the other member to refuse. Then instruct them to switch roles. Note how they respond.
        (5) *Process:* Ask the members to discuss what it feels like to say no. Do they feel guilty? Was it easy for some and not for others? Did it depend on what it was that was requested? For example, how can someone refuse a request as simple as, "Could you open the door for me?"
        (6) *Lecturette:* Go over the handout on refusing requests (see Appendix 13-B). Read the cognitive ideas underlying this skill.
     b. New skill, role playing, and impossible situations (45 minutes)
        (1) *New processing skill:* Inform the group members that you are going to teach them a new processing skill to aid them in giving each other feedback when they are role playing.
        (2) *Handout:* Hand out the material on feedback as effective communication (Appendix 13-D).
        (3) *Say:* "This is a handout that shows you the differences between helpful feedback and not-so-helpful feedback. Let's go down the sheet and read the two ways to give feedback and talk about why one way is more helpful than the other."
        (4) *Discussion:* Encourage the members to compare the lists and discuss why being descriptive, for example, is more helpful than being evaluative. If they are not sure of the differences, role play: For example, "Boy, that was a stupid thing you said in class." (evaluative) Or, "When you spoke up in class the other day, I noticed that your facts were not those that were presented in the chapter." (descriptive)

(5) *Triads:* Ask the group members to get into groups of three. One member in each group is to act as the observer, practicing the skills of giving feedback; the second is to act as the asker, and the third is to act as the refuser. Once each person has had a chance to play one of the parts, ask them to exchange roles until they have played all three parts.

(6) *Process:* Encourage the members to discuss how it felt to be refused, to be the refuser, and to be the observer giving the feedback.

(7) *Impossible situations:* Now that they have had some first-hand experience with the skill, they will have some situations in mind. Ask them to present them clearly, with enough specificity to work with.

(8) *Model:* Model from the situations given you the correct way to refuse assertively a request. For example:

Laura: "Tom, could you give me your notes from Geology. I missed class because I slept in."

Tom: "I spend a lot of time on my class notes, and I think it might be more to your benefit if you'd be sure to get to class on time."

Laura: "You mean I can't borrow your notes for one day?"

Tom: "Yes, that's what I mean."

Laura: "Well, what a meany!"

Tom: "I'm sorry you see it that way. It bothers me when I work hard to get to class every day and take good notes, and you want to use something I've worked very hard on."

(9) *Process:* Ask the group members what they saw and how they felt about watching the role play.

c. Questions, answers, homework (30 minutes)

(1) *Questions and answers:* Ask if there are any general questions or comments. Watch your time frame.

(2) *Homework:* Explain to the members that they are to keep a new diary on refusing requests during the next week.

(3) *Circle commitments:* Go around the circle and ask each person what particular situation they can anticipate coming up during the week in which they would be willing to practice refusing a request.

(4) *Keep a copy:* Write down each group member's commitments.

4. Session 4
   • Procedures
   a. Welcome, sharing and first exercise (45 minutes)

    (1)   *Welcome:* Do you know all their names by now?

    (2)   *Sharing:* Ask the members to share their experiences in refusing requests during the week. Encourage them to use their diaries to remind them of specifics and how they felt.

    (3)   *Reward:* Reward their efforts. Remember, even an attempt to refuse is a start.

    (4)   *Exercise:* Ask the members to turn to the person next to them and give them a compliment. Note the responses: uncomfortable laughter, requesting you as a coleader to clarify the exercise, and so on. These can be interpreted as resistance to doing a difficult thing.

    (5)   *Process:* Discuss their responses. How did the giver of the compliment feel? How did the receiver feel? What were some of the typical responses?

    (6)   *Lecturette:* Read the cognitive statements in the handout on giving and receiving compliments.

    (7)   *Discussion:* What are some of the things that come to the members' minds as they read over these ideas? For example, "I hate compliments, I never know what to do," or, "I don't know how to sound sincere when I give compliments."

b.   Role playing and impossible situations (45 minutes)

    (1)   *Triads:* Ask the members to divide into triads, using the same format as last week, in which one person is the observer, a second is the giver of the compliment, and the third is the receiver of the compliment. Encourage them to give real compliments. For instance, even though they may not know each other well, they can still say things like, "I like your sweater." Ask them to switch roles until everyone has had a chance at each part. Remind them that the observer must give feedback after each exchange so that it is current.

    (2)   *Process:* Encourage group discussion on how it feels to practice the new assertive training skill.

    (3)   *Impossible situations:* Ask for impossible situations from the group members—times when they have either given or received a compliment that they handled in an inappropriate way, but do not see how they could have handled it appropriately. Role play the situations assertively.

c.   Questions, answers, and homework (30 minutes)

(1) *Questions and answers:* Ask if there are any questions, comments, or criticisms in this particular area of assertive skill building. If the group runs out of comments and you have plenty of time left, pose some questions yourself, for example, "Do you forget to compliment your spouses?"

(2) *Homework:* Explain the need to keep a diary of the coming week's attempts at assertive ways to give and receive compliments.

(3) *Circle commitments:* The members may say that they cannot predict that they will receive compliments in the coming week. Remind them that then they can practice giving them. Get verbal commitment from the members as to which particular situation they can anticipate in which they can practice the skill.

(4) *Keep a copy:* Write down the commitments for next week's sharing period.

5. Session 5
   ● Procedures
      a. Welcome, sharing and first exercise (45 minutes)
         (1) *Welcome:* Surely, you know all their names by now!
         (2) *Sharing:* Ask the group members how their week's commitments went. Encourage them to use their diaries.
         (3) *Reward:* Reward successful attempts. Help those members who perceived their attempts as unsuccessful to process what could have been done differently.
         (4) *Exercise:* Ask the group members to pair off and think of imaginary criticisms of the other person and to state the criticisms aloud. Imaginary criticisms allow for faster learning of this skill. We are likely to take real criticism so seriously that we do not learn the skill, we just think of the deficit in our character that is being criticized.
         (5) *Process:* Ask the group members how it felt to give and receive criticism.
         (6) *Lecturette:* Read from the handout on coping with criticism (see Appendix 13-B).
         (7) *Discussion:* What are some of the things that the group members think or feel when dealing with criticism? Do they think the statements from the handout are accurate?
      b. Role playing and impossible situations (45 minutes)
         (1) *Triads:* Ask the group members to form triads. One person is to be the observer, the second is to give a criticism,

and the third is to respond. Make sure the groups have plenty of time to change roles and give feedback in between. Remind the observers to look for nonverbal as well as verbal behavior. This time, encourage them to pick a criticism that has some reality to it, for example, "I don't like your sweater." Remember that the practice is in responding to the criticism, not giving it.

(2) *Process:* Ask how the experiences of giving, receiving, and observing felt.

(3) *Impossible situations:* Request another round of impossible situations from the group members, that is, situations in which they did not act as they would have liked to, or imagined situations that they have always feared. In either case, they should be situations that they feel could not have been handled in a responsibly assertive way.

c. Questions, answers and homework (30 minutes)

(1) *Questions and answers:* Ask if there are any questions, comments, or criticisms. Remember that you are the group's most powerful model, so, if there is a criticism, model how to take it.

(2) *Homework:* Explain that next week the group members will work on responding to criticism, and remind them to keep track of their attempts in their diaries.

(3) *Circle commitments:* Go around the circle and ask what particular situation the members can anticipate might occur during the coming week, particularly in their relationships at home, in which they will have the opportunity to respond to criticism. This exercise not only helps them commit to practicing the new skill, it also helps them realize that they can predict some of the things that may happen to them during their week.

(4) *Keep a copy:* Be sure to write down the various situations to remind you of who is committed to do what.

6. Session 6
    • Procedures
    a. Welcome, sharing, and first exercise (45 minutes)
        (1) *Welcome:* If you do not know their names by now, maybe you need to participate in a memory building workshop.
        (2) *Sharing:* Ask the group members to talk about what happened during their week. Refer to your list of last week's

commitments. Encourage the members to use their diaries. Also, encourage them to report on the other assertive skills they have learned in the past weeks. Say, "This is a good chance for you to model two new skills." Reward their efforts (for example, when they receive compliments with a simple but appropriate "thank you") or criticize their efforts (so they can practice accepting criticism.)

(3) *Exercise:* Ask the group members to think of a behavior they would like to change in themselves. Ask them to take out a piece of paper and list the things that would need to happen in order for the change to occur, that is, under what circumstances would they be most likely to change? This hopefully will sensitize them to how difficult it is to ask for a behavior change in others.

(4) *List:* List on the board the different things they come up with so they are graphically confronted with the variety of circumstances that presuppose behavior change.

(5) *Lecturette:* Read the items from the handout on asking for behavior change (see Appendix 13-B). If the group members do not understand the cognitive part of this assertive skill, go over each thought carefully and illustrate the major points.

(6) *Discussion:* Ask, "Are there some behavior changes you would like to ask of someone you know?" This should initiate discussion.

(7) *Triads:* Ask them to form triads, using the same roles as in the previous meetings. Instruct them to use the ideas from the previous discussion in their role playing. For instance, if they would like to ask their spouse to stop leaving dishes in the sink, have them practice asking this with another group member. Make sure they rotate roles. Circulate among the triads so that you can be of assistance if they are having any problems. Note that this is the most difficult of the five skills the members have learned so far. It has, therefore, been reserved until last, after the members have had successful experiences with previous skills.

(8) *Process:* Ask the members how they felt when asking for the behavior change. What were some of the things they were afraid of (relationship in jeopardy, and so on)?

(9) *Impossible situations:* While practicing, several group members may have thought of situations, particularly in

their ongoing marriages, in which it seems impossible to ask for a behavior change. Ask them to set the scene and role play a possible assertive solution for these situations. Take as many situations as time will allow. Use some that are not directly related to a marital situation to enable them to (1) experience distance so that they can learn more and (2) realize that assertiveness is appropriate in many settings. For example:

Secretary: "Mrs. Smith (his boss), I was wondering if you had a minute."

Boss: "No! I'm busy."

Secretary: "Actually, that's exactly what I'd like to talk to you about. You are so busy that I rarely have time to check things out with you before I need to have them ready for the board meeting. Is there a way we could set aside 15 minutes on board meeting day before the agenda is set so that I could go over it with you?"

Boss   (surprised at his directness): "Oh, I didn't realize that it was such a problem for you. Yes, I would be glad to."

Secretary: "Okay, when can you do this on Thursday?" (The secretary may be fearful of asking for a behavior change in the person who holds the power to hire and fire, but it can be done!)

(10) *Process:* Allow the group members to talk about their fears, thoughts, and reactions to watching the coleaders role play their situations.

b.   Wrap-up and goodbyes (30 minutes)

(1)   *Summary:* Go over the five areas that the group members have covered in their assertive training workshop. Reinforce the idea that it takes practice to retain what they have learned, but that they have a good arena in which to practice—the marriage—and that their spouses have been learning the same material in a different group. Encourage them to use their diaries until the skills feel spontaneous.

(2)   *On the board:* Write the four stages of learning on the board:

Don't know that you don't know
Don't know that you know
Know that you don't know
Know that you know

Learning a new set of skills involves all four stages of learning. Right now, the members feel as though they are at the awkward stage of "knowing that they don't know" everything about assertive training skills. But this is a normal feeling on the developmental trail to acquiring new skills.

(3) *Role playing in front of the group:* Ask the group members if they would like to volunteer to role play with a coleader or another group member. Ask them to select one of the five skill areas. Encourage the members to participate in front of the group in role playing making a simple request, refusing a request, giving or receiving a compliment, coping with criticism, and asking for behavior change. This will demonstrate that as a whole they are a lot more skilled than they think, and surely more skilled than they were at the beginning of the workshop.

(4) *Challenge:* Encourage and challenge the members to work on their newly learned skills.

(5) *Goodbyes:* Express your positive feelings about having been able to work with them, and thank them for the things they have taught you!

Appendix 13-A

Descriptions of Nonassertive, Aggressive, and Assertive Behaviors

Table 13A-1 Descriptions of Nonaggressive, Aggressive, and Assertive Behavior

	Nonassertive	Aggressive	Assertive
Point of View	I'm not okay.	You're not okay.	I'm okay—you're okay.
Social Pattern	Ignores own wants, desires, feelings; allows others to infringe upon interpersonal rights.	Expresses self at the expense of others; attacks others directly or indirectly.	Expresses self freely, honestly, and responsibly; does not violate the rights of others.
Aim or Goal	The avoidance of conflict at all costs.	Domination, winning, ventilation of anger.	Honest communication; acknowledgment of respect for self and others.
Social Consequences	Other person may feel guilt, anger, frustration, disrespect.	Other person may feel hurt, defensive, humiliated, confused, manipulated; may counteraggress.	Mutual respect; honest satisfying relationships with others.
Personal Outcomes	Feels hurt, anxious; the "doormat" syndrome.	May have temporary feeling of power and success but in the long run suffers alienation.	Self-enhanced.

Appendix 13-B

Ideas To Keep in Mind

1. Making Simple Requests

- You have a right to have preferences, wants, and desires.
- You deny your own importance when you keep yourself or others unaware of your wants.
- The best way to get exactly what you want is to make a direct request.
- Indirect ways of asking for what you want may be misunderstood, for example, complaining of a heavy workload rather than asking for help.
- Asking for what you want is a skill that can be learned.
- Directly asking for what you want can become a habit with many rewards.

2. Refusing Requests

- You have a right to say no to unreasonable requests.
- You deny your own importance when you say yes and you really mean no.
- Saying no does not imply that you reject another person—you are simply refusing a request.
- When saying no, it is important to be direct, concise, and to the point.
- If you really mean to say no, do not be swayed by pleading, begging, cajoling, compliments, or other forms of manipulation.
- You may offer reasons for your refusal, but do not get carried away with numerous excuses.

- Do not become overly apologetic; this can be offensive.
- Saying no is a skill that can be learned.
- Saying no and not feeling guilty about it can become a habit—a habit that can be very growth enhancing.

3. Coping with Criticism

- You have a right to be the final and sole evaluator of your behavior.
- Evaluations—criticisms of your behavior from others—may be quite useful to you. They may improve your work performance and relationships with others.
- It is important to listen carefully to criticism and evaluate it realistically and objectively. Avoid automatic denial, magnifying (making it worse than it is), and overgeneralizing (extending it to other situations).
- If criticism is given to you in an indirect manner, help the person communicate more directly with you. Ask questions and prompt specific behavioral descriptions and requests.
- Some criticism from others may be unrealistic or invalid.
- "Fogging," or offering no resistance by agreeing to the criticism, may be used as a coping mechanism for avoiding criticisms, but use it sparingly.
- Assertively coping with criticism means maintaining your self-esteem by giving yourself permission to make mistakes.

4. Asking for a Change in Behavior

- When you experience negative feelings as a result of other people's behavior, you have a right to ask those persons to modify their behavior.
- When you do not exercise this right, you deny the importance of yourself as well as the relationship.
- The following four part guidance is crucial:
  (1) Describe the behavior observed in the other person. It is important that you use descriptive rather than labeling words. For example, "You have been critical of me in front of the staff and patients," rather than, "You insensitive blockhead!"
  (2) Describe the effects and feelings you experience as a result. For example, "I feel embarrassed and humiliated." Note the "I feel" rather than "you make me feel."

(3) Ask for a specific change in behavior. For example, "I want to hear your thoughts about how I might improve my work. But in the future I'd like this to happen in private without an audience."

(4) It may be necessary to spell out specific and reasonable consequences should the person not comply with your requests. For example, "If you continue to do this, I will simply leave the situation."

- Giving other people direct messages about how their behavior affects you prevents resentment build-up and makes for more satisfying relationships.

Appendix 13-C

A Sample Subjective Units of Discomfort (SUDS) Diary

Subjective Units of Discomfort (SUDS) Diary
Sample

Date	SUDS	Describe situation briefly	Describe anxiety you felt	Describe what you'd like to do next time
	0-9	Went sailing with my husband and oldest son.	Slow breathing	It was OK.
	10-19	Driving on the freeway to go shopping.	Normal breathing; muscles in hand, back, and neck tense	Wish I could avoid rush-hour traffic.
	20-29	Opened bill that I knew would be large.	Slight hand shake on opening envelope, stomach tight	Could have left bill for when I felt bad.
	30-39	Phone call from high pressure salesperson; couldn't say no.	Voice trembling, stomach tense, breathing faster	Next time I'll just say, "Thank you, but no," and hang up!
	40-49	Waited in line at department store ten minutes while others cut in ahead of me.	Stomach tight, back muscles tense, arms, and legs slightly trembling	Wish I could have said, "Excuse me, I was here first."
	50-59	Stopped by police for speeding; got a ticket.	Light-headed, mouth dry, sweaty palms, stammering, voice cracking	I deserved it! Guess I'll need to slow down.
	60-69	Oldest son told me he hated me and took my car without my permission.	"Tight-band" feeling in head, trembling, tears in eyes, tight stomach	I wish I could have calmed down and told him how I felt.

70-79	Husband yelled at me for over-drawing on the checking account when it was his error.	Heart beating fast, tight stomach, mind went blank, couldn't think	Next time I am going to stand up for myself and voice my opinion.
80-89	Had fight with husband; he told me I couldn't go to school this year.	Dizzy, heart racing, crying	I am going to talk to him later about how important school is to me.
90-100	Husband demanded to have sex with me when I told him I didn't feel like it.	Cried, stomach tight, felt like running out of room, shaking all over	Next time, I will tell him I love him but don't want to make love right now.

Subjective Units of Discomfort (SUDS) Diary
Blank Form

Date	SUDS	Describe situation briefly	Describe anxiety you felt	Describe what you'd like to do next time

Note: Enter under SUDS your own judgments as to what is very anxiety provoking (70-100), moderately anxiety provoking (30-69), and minimally anxiety provoking (0-29).

Appendix 13-D

Feedback As Effective Communication

More helpful if it's:
1. requested, desired
2. descriptive
3. a personal reaction
   I see . . .
   I hear . . .
   I feel . . .
4. specific, concrete
5. here and now
6. appropriately timed
7. based on the motive to help
8. focused on behavior that can be changed at relatively low cost

Less helpful if it's:
1. imposed
2. evaluative, judgmental
3. advice, inference, or attribution
4. general
5. accumulated, stored up
6. without regard for timing
7. based on the motive to punish
8. focused on behavior that cannot be changed or only changed at great cost

Balancing Professional and Private Lives: An Education Program for Professional Couples

Camille C. Delong and Thomas J. Delong

This is a family life education program for professional couples, with either one or both members working. It requires six weeks total time, with the first week for orientation and preassessment, five weeks for lecture/ workshop, and a final session for postassessment data collection. Each weekly session is two hours in length, with enrollment restricted to 20 couples. Male and female instructors are recommended. The program is applicable in business organizations, public and private agencies, and colleges and universities.

The program deals with couples trying to maintain some degree of balance between executive, family, and organizational life, and with the constant confrontation of competing choices, commitments, and conflicts. The program is concerned with current issues and dilemmas and teaches specific strategies for helping couples assess where they are in balancing professional and private life. The sessions are designed to help them achieve the balance they desire.

Traditionally the husband in our society has been minimally accommodative to family needs because his primary commitment has been to his work. Though the purpose of his labor is to provide for the physical needs of his family, his decisions as to how best to do this have characteristically been based solely on the requirements of his work and have usually ignored the more subtle, psychological needs of himself, his wife, and his children. Organizational policies have reinforced this nonaccommodative position by selectively rewarding those employees who demonstrate such "commitment" to their work. Traditional wives' roles have been necessarily complementary, since the wives have had to place total emphasis on the family. The results of these two roles have been exciting work and professional opportunities for men, financial rewards and prestige for both men and women, and reflected glory for women. The price for both men and women has been loneliness, divorce, alcoholism, alienated children, and coronaries.

However, times are changing, and more and more people are asking, "Is it worth it?" and, "Must success cost so much?" Research indicates that couples generally navigate the first decade of their marriages successfully. The status of the family in that period depends on the handling of certain life investments and problems along the way. If decisions about launching careers, family marital priorities, other family priorities, and life style priorities are handled effectively as they come up, the prices are not so high, and the cumulative effect of those life choices keep the interaction of work and family in balance (Evans & Bartolome, 1980).

STAFF AND SUPPORTIVE RESOURCES

To implement this program, the leaders must have training in organizational theory that gives them an understanding of the guides and constraints of life in an organization. They also must have some knowledge of marital and family systems, to be aware of the interaction effects of work choices on the family, and vice versa. Finally, they must understand group process, so that they can facilitate small group discussions. An awareness of the restricted choices for women and men in the traditional type of living situation and the new choices now available to them, as well as the physical and psychological implications of these choices for the family, will increase the effectiveness of the leaders.

Ideally, the leaders will be a married couple (traditional or nontraditional) that can serve as one of several models for the class. They must be able to model negotiation, partnership, and collaboration with each other. Competitiveness between the leaders or one-upmanship would seriously hamper the effectiveness of what is being taught in the class. Also, the leaders need to assess the local community for couples who live traditional and nontraditional life styles and schedule them to come and talk about their choice of life style and how it works for them.

The cost of materials for participants is about $9 for a packet that should include the following for each couple: excerpts from the Schein (1978) article (permission will be needed), a sample genogram, a list of genogram symbols, a list of questions to be answered on the genograms, a copy of the Family Interaction Tally Sheet (Appendix 14-A), and a copy of the class syllabus. The packet should also contain, for each person, a genogram, the Uses of Resentment, Gripes, and Envy Exercise Sheet (Appendix 14-B), the Life Goal Exercise Sheet (Appendix 14-C), and a Quit, Keep, Start (QKS) Evaluation Form (Appendix 14-D). (For information regarding the use of genograms, see Guerin & Pendagast, 1976, and Pendagast & Sherman, 1978).

GENERAL OBJECTIVES

The program has the following three general objectives:

1. To help the participants establish priorities and clarify their goals and desires in relation to their work, career, and family.
2. To identify and confront some of the current issues involving the professional family. For example, What is the effect on the home when a person is trying to establish a career? Is there any difference once the career has been established? What accounts for the differences between people who seem to "succeed" without paying the high prices and those who "succeed" but also have emotional and health problems? What happens to the housework, children, and husband when a previously unemployed wife starts to work?
3. To focus on the couples' options and alternatives and give them specific tools to help them manage themselves better.

THEORETICAL MODELS AND ASSESSMENT INSTRUMENTS

The theories used in the program are cognitive theory, experimental learning, and behavioral rehearsal and modeling. (See Appendix A for descriptions of these theories.) The main assessment instrument is the Dyadic Adjustment Scale by Spanier (see Appendix B for a description of this instrument). This is given in the first session and again in the last session. It is recommended that it also be given again one month after the program ends.

The Quit, Keep, Start (QKS) Evaluation Form (Appendix 14-D) should be handed out and collected at the end of each session. The participants should use it to evaluate each session's presentation in terms of what they liked, what they would like to have changed in the presentation, and what they would like to have omitted.

The Family Interaction Tally Sheet (Appendix 14-A) is used to collect information about at-home behavior. The leaders should have the couples keep track of their time together for one week before the program. The sheet should be collected at the first evening and then administered again three weeks into the course, after the self awareness activities. As a third measure, the couples should be asked to keep track of the same kind of behavior for one week after the class is over and to mail the data to the leaders. If possible all these instruments should be readministered again one or two months after the program has ended.

Before teaching the course, the leaders should have read the articles and books from which information for this course was drawn (see references and selected reading lists at the end of the book).

PROGRAM OUTLINE

The following outline describes the content, procedures, and materials used in each program session. Some of these sessions have been abbreviated. (To obtain the complete program, follow the instructions given in the Preface.)

1. Session 1: Introduction
   - Objectives
     a. To administer the pretest and collect the Family Interaction Tally Sheet.
     b. To give an introduction and review of the class.
     c. To provide a model for the issues and format of the class, through use of a panel discussion in which the leaders explain how they have personally dealt with the issues of balancing professional and private lives.
   - Materials
     a. Excerpts from Schein's (1978) article; pretest (Dyadic Scale); pencils; Quit, Keep, Start Evaluation Forms (Appendix 14-D); Family Interaction Tally Sheets (Appendix 14-A); and the class syllabus.
   - Information
     a. Instructions to Leaders. You will need to emphasize repeatedly that you are *not* espousing a particular life style. You are rather emphasizing choice making that fits each individual's marriage and family. Your job is to dispense information that will shed new light on old issues, raise new issues, give the participants tools for handling the new information, provide role models from various types of life styles, and facilitate the group process.
   - Outline of class activities
     a. greeting to class members
     b. administration of Dyadic Adjustment Scale (see Appendix B) and collection of the Family Interaction Tally Sheets (Appendix 14-A) (20 minutes)

    c. introductions (45 minutes), handing out of class syllabus

    d. break (5 minutes)

    e. leader panel (40 minutes)

    f. commitment to class (5 minutes)

    g. homework (5 minutes)

    h. the QKS Evaluation Forms (Appendix 14-D) (5 minutes)

- Procedures

    a. Introductions. Give a very short presentation on why you decided to teach this class. Then move to a more personal introduction. Use some creative way to share personal information and to learn about the class participants.

    b. Leader panel. In a panel format, present some of the problems and issues faced in deciding on a compatible life style. Make this a personal presentation, one that illustrates the problems individuals and couples in the class may be experiencing. After your presentation, open the rest of the time up for questions and comments from the group.

    c. Commitment to the class. Discuss with the class the importance of attendance. Each class session should build upon the previous one, so consistent attendance is important. The participation of the class members is an essential ingredient of the success of the class. Expression in the class of differences in perceptions and life styles benefits everyone. Such discussions increase everyone's choices and alternatives.

    d. Homework. Ask the class members to observe and talk to friends and acquaintances about the issues brought up in class. Ask them to read the information in their packets on life cycles before coming to class next week. Introduce next week's session by telling the class that the focus will be on three important life cycles: biosocial, career, and family. One objective is to determine how these three cycles may be creating stress in couples' lives.

2. Session 2: Life Cycles

- Objectives

    a. To examine the participants in the larger context of their biosocial cycle, career cycle, and family cycle.

    b. To give the participants an understanding of how these forces guide and constrain their lives.

    c. To help the participants pinpoint their own positions in these cycles.

    d. To improve the participants' understanding of their resources, feelings, and needs in individual situations.
- Materials
  - a. a previously prepared transparency to help the participants follow the lecture
  - b. a lecture that follows a prepared outline (not provided in the present shortened version of the program)
  - c. four transparencies for use with the discussion on the prototype family (not included in this shortened version)
  - d. overhead projector and screen
  - e. a QKS form for each person
- Outline of class activities
  - a. greeting of class members
  - b. presentation of lecture material (30 minutes)
  - c. couple role playing by the leaders (15 minutes)
  - d. break (10 minutes)
  - e. discussion of role play (20 minutes)
  - f. small group discussion and class activity (30 minutes)
  - g. announcement of next week's topic (5 minutes)
  - h. the QKS forms (Appendix 14-D) (5 minutes)
- Procedures
  - a. Couple role play. Role play a prototype couple in their early thirties who are launching the husband's career while parenting three young children. The children should not appear in the role play but should be alluded to. If this prototype does not fit your class participants, make up one that does.
  - b. Discussion of the role play. Discuss the dilemmas of the hypothetical Jones family. Do this by starting the discussion with the first transparency, and combine it with a presentation of how the Jones family handled the tasks in the role play. Then move to the next transparencies, noting the cumulative and interaction effect of all the stages. Highlight the discussion of the interaction effect with the final transparency (the transparencies are not included in this shortened version).
  - c. Small group discussion. Divide the group into two or three small groups. Ask a couple to make a diagram identifying their present life cycles and some of the tasks and questions they are struggling with. Discuss the diagrams and ask specific questions to stimulate discussion.
  - d. Next week's session. Announce that next week the class will engage in activities that will help them become more aware of what they want and need in their marriages.

3. Session 3: Self-Awareness Activities
   • Objectives
     a. To help the participants know the difference between what they really want and what they are "supposed" to want because of family and societal pressures.
     b. To become more aware of personal needs and wants by utilizing the positive aspects of resentments, gripes, and jealousies.
   • Materials
     a. pencils
     b. a blank genogram (per person)
     c. a sample genogram the leader has filled out (per person)
     d. a page of genogram symbols (per couple)
     e. a list of questions to be answered on the genogram (per couple)
     f. a copy of the Appendix 14-B exercise, The Uses of Resentments, Gripes and Envy (per person) and a copy of the Appendix 14-A Family Interaction Tally Sheet (per couple)
     g. one QKS form (Appendix 14-D) (per person)
   • Outline of class activities
     a. greeting of class members
     b. genogram exercise (45 minutes)
     c. group discussion (15 minutes)
     d. break (5 minutes)
     e. the Uses of Resentments, Gripes, and Envy Exercise (45 minutes)
     f. group discussion (10 minutes)
     g. homework (5 minutes)
     h. the QKS Evaluation Forms (Appendix 14-D)
   • Procedures
     a. Introduce the use of a genogram. Tell the participants that in this session they will participate in an exercise that will give them a systematic way of mapping the influence their family of origin has had upon them in handling conflict, money, emotions, manliness, womanliness, child rearing, occupation, relationships, and leisure. Their methods of coping have also been determined by the models they had at home while growing up. In the same way, their parents' manner of management was greatly influenced by the models they had in the homes they grew up in. The genogram is a way of investigating the patterns of behavior that families and parents' families use to manage the above-mentioned areas. The genogram is used here to identify the patterns the participants have been exposed to and probably implemented and to evaluate those patterns to deter-

mine how useful they are. It is especially important for the class members to notice how similarly or differently their spouse's family managed the same areas. If the participants are dissatisfied with the patterns and choices they are presently making, subsequent discussions will give them other alternatives.

b. Couple exercise
   (1) Give each person a copy of a blank genogram, a sample genogram that one of the leaders has filled out, the page of genogram symbols, and the list of questions they are to answer on the genogram.
   (2) Using the sample genogram, explain how to fill out their own. Some of the participants may not know the answers to many of the questions and may want to know how to find them. Tell them to go back to members of their families and ask questions. If a parent is reluctant to discuss certain issues, they can go to an uncle, aunt, or a friend of the family and get their perceptions. Emphasize discretion and caring. Do not force information out of people.
   (3) Provide one-half hour for each couple to fill out a genogram, using the sheet of questions as a guide. The couples may discuss their perceptions with each other about their families, but each couple must have a separate genogram. Stop the work session at a stipulated time. If some couples did not finish, encourage them to finish their genogram at home.

c. Group discussion
   (1) Use the same small discussion groups as last week, unless there is a good reason to change a group's membership.
   (2) Discuss the exercise and the new information learned.
   (3) Clear up any misconceptions about the purpose of the exercise.

d. Classroom exercise—The uses of resentments, gripes, and envy
   (1) Remain in small groups.
   (2) Introduce the exercise, The Uses of Resentment, Gripes, and Envy (Appendix 14-B), by saying "Now that you are getting a better idea of what your patterns of living are and where you got them, it may be useful for you to identify more explicitly what it is you want."
   (3) Read the instructions for Part 1 to the class and have them fill in the answers for that part.

(4) After the class has had 15 to 20 minutes to fill out the first part of the answer sheet, stop them and move into the second part.

(5) Give instructions for the second part: "As you filled in your answer sheet, you probably experienced a range of emotions—anger, pain, sadness, or amusement. You should now feel a sense of release. You've been letting out a lot of pent-up pressure. Pressure produces energy that can be turned into directed productive use. This is a chance for you to discover meaning, to plan how you can benefit from the complaints you expressed, to learn from your envy just what your deepest wishes are, and to use these discoveries to help you find the best direction for future choices. To help you get started, I will give you some examples from possible responses."

(6) Give examples from Part 1:
   (a) *Gripes about my job.* "I am angry that I don't have more time to spend with my wife and children. Even when I am home on weekends, I see my briefcase overflowing with work that needs to be done; and so, even when I don't do the work, my mind is on it and not with my family. I get work-related calls at home, and I am never free from work."
   (b) *People and situations I envy.* "I envy Joe Smith who comes home on weekends and really seems to enjoy his family. I see the Smiths out in the yard playing together, frequently with laughter and fun. Joe and Ilene joke with each other and go places together. I envy them because it seems that they would rather be with each other than with anybody else."
   (c) *Gripes about my family and marriage.* "We don't play together and I'm not sure anyone cares about this. Sometimes I think as long as I bring money home, that's all that my family cares about."

(7) Give examples from Part 2:
   (a) "I asked myself the questions in Section a and learned that I value my family but I don't put them high in my priorities. Because I let my briefcase dictate my weekends, they don't know how much I care about them. I want to have fun and receive assurance that my family can play together and love each other."

(b) "From answering the questions in Section b, I learned that I envy Joe's and Ilene's fun and laughter. I also learned that my pain about my family is deep, and that I want to do something about it. I decided that I could put my briefcase in a new place out of sight, or leave it at the office. To protect our time at home, I could either let it be known that business calls will not be acceptable at home, or, for a regularly designated time, we could unplug all of our phones. I do not enjoy playing outside, but there are other activities I could do that would be fun. The good feelings seem to just be continuations of how Joe and Ilene feel about each other and spend time together. Jane and I need to spend some time just with each other. We have not taken time to enjoy each other by ourselves."

e. Homework. Hand out the Family Interaction Tally Sheet (Appendix 14-A). Ask the couples again to keep track of their interactions and to bring the sheet next week.

4. Session 4: Guest Speakers
   - Objective
     a. to expose the participants to different models of marriage and family life in order to expand their repertoire of alternatives
   - Materials
     a. one QKS form (Appendix 14-D) per person
   - Information
     a. Instructions to leaders for sessions 4 and 6.
        (1) As you decide on the dates to run your class, contact couples in your community who would be interesting guest speakers. Schedule them well in advance so that you will be able to get the varied representation of life styles that you need. The guest speakers should include a traditional couple (full-time female homemaker, full-time male provider), a dual-career couple (both male and female engaged in full-time careers, as well as in raising children), a househusband and wife (full-time male homemaker, full-time female provider), an executive couple (the husband a high executive in industry, government, or education and the wife in a support role or in a career, but with emphasis on the husband's career), a commuting couple (a dual-career couple who have jobs in different

cities or states and who maintain two residences, preferably with children), and a childless, dual-career couple.

(2) The above categories are not exhaustive. For instance, they do not consider the single parent. Also there will be variation in how your couples fit into the categories. Thus, the categories are representative and are not meant to be restrictive. You may have a dual-career couple, with one person working only part-time. Hence, use the categories only to find as great a variety of guest speakers as you can.

(3) Other criteria that are crucial in selecting the guest speakers are that they should have   fairly healthy, stable relationships so they will not embarrass themselves or the class; they should be articulate about themselves, their life styles, how they chose them, and the costs and benefits; they should self-disclose appropriately and not use the time for grandstanding, dumping resentments, or putting down their spouses; and they should be able to portray cooperative efforts in their decision making and life style choices.

(4) Contact your guest-speaker couples and acquaint them with the class format. Ask them in their ten-minute presentations to address the following questions: How would you describe your life style? What made you choose this way? What are the benefits you find and the prices you pay? What do your children, friends, colleagues, and relatives think of your choices? If a couple, or one member of a couple, is uncomfortable with these questions, you should find other couples who can respond to them.

- Outline of class activities
  a. greeting of class members
  b. collection of Family Interaction Tally Sheets (5 minutes)
  c. requests for any questions or insights that participants may have accumulated during the previous week's exercise (15 minutes)
  d. guest couples' panel (50 minutes)
  e. break (5 minutes)
  f. small group discussion (30 minutes)
  g. next week's topic (5 minutes)
  h. the QKS form (Appendix 14-D) (5 minutes)
- Procedures
  a. Couples panel. Introduce the guest couples in the following manner:

(1) "We have a panel tonight consisting of a couple living in a traditional life style (the woman full-time homemaker, the man a full-time provider) and a couple living in a dual-career life style. Each couple will give about a ten-minute presentation on how they view their life style, how and why they made the decisions to live the way they do, and the prices and benefits of their particular choices. After this presentation, time will be available for questions from the group."

(2) When the allotted time has passed, divide the group into two parts. Ask the men to stay in one room with the female speakers, and ask the women to go to another room with the male speakers. Typically, the women at this time will question freely, express their difficulties in balancing their lives, and share ambivalences about some of the roles they are expected to fulfill. The men also ask questions they might not have asked with their wives present; however, in our experience, the emotional tone is much more contained with the men than with the women.

b. Next week's session. Next week the class will participate in some exercises to help them get a perspective on their life's goals and some specific strategies to help make their present situation less stressful.

5. Session 5: Life Goal Exercise, Demand System and Negotiation
   - Objectives
     a. To build on the self awareness exercises done in past sessions, help the participants to:
        (1) Get a long-range perspective of their life goals.
        (2) Establish priorities so that they will be able to work on the most important things first and *not* overwhelm themselves by thinking that everything must be done at once.
        (3) Provide a negotiation model for the couples to use to generate alternatives for themselves.
   - Materials
     a. one Life Goal Exercise (Appendix 14-C)
     b. a Demand System Exercise (Appendix 14-E)
     c. one QKS form (Appendix 14-D) per person
     d. one Family Interaction Tally Sheet (Appendix 14-A) per couple

- Outline of class activities
  a. greeting of class members
  b. review of the self-awareness exercises (genogram and the use of gripes and envy) and queries as to whether the last week's speakers added new insights or alternatives of behavior (15 minutes)
  c. life goal exercise (Appendix 14-C) (20 minutes)
  d. group discussion (10 minutes)
  e. break (5 minutes)
  f. the demand system (Appendix 14-E) (15 minutes)
  g. small group discussion (10 minutes)
  h. present negotiation model (15 minutes)
  i. couple negotiation exercise (15 minutes)
  j. small group discussion (10 minutes)
  k. announcement of next week's topics
  l. a QKS form (Appendix 14-D)
- Procedures
  a. Life goal exercise
      (1) Introduce the life goal exercise by reading the instructions from Appendix 14-C. Give the group 15 minutes to fill out the form. They will not be able to finish the whole exercise, but direct them to provide at least two themes for the last question. Also instruct them to answer the questions as specifically as possible. One-word answers are not acceptable.

  b. Group discussion. Ask the group to discuss the differences between their future goals and how they spent their time last week. Have them spend time working on priorities "highlighted" by each couple, knowing that other priorities will have to be "highlighted" at a different time.

  c. Demand system. This exercise (Appendix 14-E) is to help the participants assess where they spend their time each day, to help them see clearly where pressures keep getting in the way and preventing them from doing what they want. Read the instructions from the demand system exercise sheet and invite the class to follow them. Then divide the group into the same two or three small groups and discuss the exercise.

  d. Couple exercise. Stay in the same small groups. Use a volunteer couple to identify a common pressure to exemplify the steps of negotiation. Then have each couple, on their own, practice the steps of negotiation.

    e. Next week's session. Announce that next week there will be another set of guest speakers who will give the participants additional exposure to different life styles.

6. Session 6: Guest Speakers and Wrap-Up
- Objectives
  - a. To review the couple negotiation exercise.
  - b. To have guest speakers present information.
  - c. To administer post-tests.
- Materials
  - a. Pencils
  - b. Dyadic Adjustment Scale
  - c. QKS forms (Appendix 14-D)
- Outline of Class Activities
  - a. greeting class members
  - b. review of couple negotiation exercise from last week (15 minutes)
  - c. introduction of guest speakers (75 minutes)
  - d. summary of guest speaker presentation
  - e. administration of post-tests (15 minutes)
- Class activities
  - a. In introducing the guest speakers, use the same format as in Session 4. However, you may need to keep the whole group together for the entire discussion, since this time there is more time pressure. Allow your guest speakers to leave before you summarize their presentation.
  - b. In administering the post-tests, have the participants take the standardized tests in class. Send home with each couple a copy of the Family Interaction Tally Sheet (Appendix 14-A) with a self-addressed, stamped envelope. Ask them to fill it out in the second week after the course has ended. Make sure you have all the participants' names and phone numbers so that you can call them to remind them to fill out the sheets and mail them in.

Appendix 14-A

Family Interaction Tally Sheet

Please record on this sheet the amount of time you, as a couple, have spent together each day in talking, playing, planning, or in active contact of any kind (not TV). Also record the number of minutes father spends with the children, mother spends with the children, and the family spends together. For example, meal times, when the family talks with each other, would count as family time.

	Sun.	Mon.	Tues.	Wed.	Thurs.	Fri.	Sat.
Couple Time Together							
Father with Children							
Mother with Children							
Whole Family							

Appendix 14-B

The Uses of Resentment, Gripes, and Envy

Instructors: When you prepare this handout, leave space for answers.

Part I: Fill out this part by focusing on your negative associations. Don't try to be "fair." Don't try to see the other side. Unload your feelings, whether they are about people, lack of time, or your unrealized expectations. Pour out your thoughts and feelings about the situations or people you envy and about the times when you have wanted something so much it gave you pain. Focus on:

- my gripes about my job: _____

- people and situations that I envy (occupation related): _____

- my gripes about my family/marriage: _____

- people and situations I envy (family/marriage related): _____

- my gripes about my self-development: _____

- people and situations I envy (self development-related): _____

Part 2: In this part of the exercise, examine your gripes and envy and turn them to your advantage by learning something about yourself from each situation.

- Section a—Say to yourself the following statements as you read over the resentments and gripes you have written down:

189

—From this I can learn: _____
_____

—From this I can get in touch with: _____
_____

—From this I can tell myself that: _____
_____

—From this I can change my situation by: _____
_____

Continue to fill out this section by saying the above phrases to yourself and then writing down the completed sentences for each resentment or gripe.

• Section b—Ask yourself the following questions when you read over the people and situations you envy.

—What part of this situation is triggering in me a pain of deep longing?

—What do I really want? How can I get it? Write down your responses to these questions. You may not be able to tell at first what part of the picture generates the envy, but through your own rational process of elimination you will be able to reduce the broad picture into the components that most attract you.

Appendix 14-C

Life Goal Exercise

Instructors: When you prepare this handout, leave space for answers.

The following questions will assist you in determining the differences between your life aspirations and your present behavior. Try to answer the questions in the order they appear.

The first set of questions focuses on your long-range aspirations:

1. What kind of a person do you want to be at the end of your life?
2. What kind of career do you want to have had at the end of your life?
3. What kind of a family do you want to have had at the end of your life?
4. What will your spouse be like at the end of your life?
5. What will your relationship with your spouse or significant other person be like at the end of your life?
6. How much time will you have spent with your children at the end of your life?
7. What will your relationship with your children be like at the end of your life?
8. Will you be happier at the end of your life than you are now?

The second set of questions focuses on your professional and private lives five years from now:

9. What kind of a person do you want to be five years from now?
10. What kind of career do you want to have five years from now?
11. What kind of a family do you want to have five years from now?
12. What will your spouse be like five years from now?
13. What will your relationship with your spouse or significant other person be like five years from now?

14. How much time will you spend with your children five years from now?
15. What will your relationship with your children be like in five years?
16. Will you be happier at the end of your life than you will be five years from now?

The final set of questions focuses on last week's behavior in relation to your professional and private lives:

17. What kind of a person have you been this past week?
18. Have you been pleased with your work or career this week?
19. How much time have you spent with your family, and what kind of time was it (TV, other activities)?
20. How much time have you spent alone with your spouse this past week?
21. How much time have you spent alone with each of your children this past week?
22. Have you been satisfied with the past week in relation to your career, your family, and your spouse or significant other?

Quit, Keep, Start (QKS)
Evaluation Form

I would like to have the leaders in this session quit doing the following:

_____
_____
_____
_____
_____
_____

I would like to have the leaders in this session keep doing the following:

_____
_____
_____
_____
_____
_____

I would like to have the leaders in this session start doing the following:

_____
_____
_____
_____
_____

Appendix 14-E

Your Demand System

Instructions: Make a list of five to ten pressures or worries that make a demand on you—the more specific the better. In the middle of the blank part below, draw a small circle and label it "me." Place the worries or pressures on your list (represented by circles) around you. The bigger the circle, the greater the *importance* of the worry or pressure. The closer each circle is to you, the more *immediate pressure* it exerts. This diagram is to represent the way you experience things right now.

Now redo your diagram the way you would like it to be.

Chapter 15

A Premarital Education Program

Margaret H. Hoopes and Barbara L. Fisher

The procedures for delivering a community-based premarital program were developed by the authors at the Family Consultation Center at Brigham Young University (BYU). (Many of the functions of the Family Consultation Center, which no longer exists, have now been taken over by the BYU Comprehensive Clinic.) This eight-week program was designed to provide practical information to engaged couples about marriage. Although students at BYU had previously taken marriage preparation classes, many of them were not engaged at the time. The present program was developed in response to requests and in recognition of a need for couples to know more about marriage in order to enhance their relationships and to be better prepared for marriage. One of its major foci was to provide engaged couples with appropriate information and to promote a meaningful interpersonal discussion about that information.

This chapter presents a basic format for premarital education. It is designed to help communities and agencies organize and administer their own programs. A committee from within the community is best equipped to design the specifics of a program for the community's population. In this way, the program can more appropriately address the issues and problems relevant to a particular audience. Facilitators of the program's miniworkshops are selected on the basis of their expertise in specific areas and their knowledge of the community.

The procedures and content of the program that was delivered at BYU to an audience of engaged university students may or may not be applicable to every community or agency. It is suggested that the directions for the program be read with this in mind, and that communities apply those procedures that are helpful and adapt others as necessary.

ORGANIZATION

To facilitate the premarital education program, the following are needed: (1) a sponsor, (2) a community committee, (3) a director, and (4) miniworkshop facilitators.

Sponsor

An effective sponsor would be an existing organization that has the interest in and commitment to a premarital education program such as a church, a mental health organization, a private agency, a community school, a school district, a college, or a university. The Family Consultation Center at BYU was the sponsor for the present premarital education program.

The role of the sponsor includes one or all of the following functions: (1) organizing the workshops, (2) contacting interested people, (3) responding to requests, (4) providing information, (5) organizing a committee, and (6) providing a contact source (for example, a telephone number for additional information). The sponsor may be asked to provide a program to meet the needs of selected premarital couples or it may be responsive to needs observed in the community. The Family Consultation Center at BYU responded both to requests from many engaged couples and to the recognition by professors and clergy in the community of the need for such a program.

Community Committee

The community committee is made up of people interested in organizing a premarital education program that will meet the community's needs. At least half of the committee should consist of individuals from the premarital group. Other members could be people from the sponsoring organization and interested adults from the community who can promote, advise, and facilitate the development and presentation of the program.

The community committee for the BYU program consisted of graduate students and faculty members of an existing advisory committee for the Family Consultation Center. Although the committee had input from engaged students, such students did not formally participate in the initial development of the program. However, we recommend that other community committees do have formal representation from this group.

The duties of the committee are to (1) decide on general goals for the program and for each miniworkshop, (2) decide on topics for the miniworkshops, (3) suggest people in the community to be facilitators of specific miniworkshops, and (4) make decisions about fees for participants and honorariums for miniworkshop facilitators. Selection of the facilitators may be made by the committee, or that responsibility may be assigned to the program's director.

Director

The director should have prior experience in administering community or educational programs in order to undertake the key responsibilities for the program. These responsibilities include (1) managing all details required to operationalize the program (place, time, dates, contracting with facilitators suggested by the committee, publicity, public relations, and so on); (2) introducing the facilitators at the beginning of each miniworkshop; (3) enrolling those interested in the program, answering their questions, making any necessary weekly contact with them, and collecting fees from them if appropriate; and (4) managing all other details of the program (arranging for equipment, materials, and space, administering and collecting evaluations, and so on).

Miniworkshop Facilitators

The facilitators should have demonstrated expertise in the topic area covered in the particular workshop assigned to them. For most of the workshops, a female-and-male team, some of them married couples, would be a valuable asset. The team approach enables each couple to model, when appropriate, what they are presenting. The presentations should be personal and practical, but could be adapted to different formats as appropriate.

THE MINIWORKSHOPS

Selection of Topics

Before organizing the premarital education program at the Family Consultation Center, specific topics were selected for the miniworkshops. In order to determine which topics would be useful and relevant to engaged couples, a questionnaire was given to approximately 50 married couples and 50 divorced individuals. It was believed that those who had participated in marriage both successfully and unsuccessfully could identify areas in which more information would have been helpful. The areas covered in the questionnaire were:

- money (budgeting, bills, bank accounts, stocks and bonds, insurance, investments, and so on)
- in-laws
- children (birth control, discipline, responsibility)
- sexual relationships (physical, psychological, and emotional aspects)
- communication (expressing needs, fighting, building and maintaining close relationships, resolving conflict, and so on)
- food
- religion

Ideas for additional topics were also requested of the respondents.

Based on the responses to the questionnaire, eight areas of interest were selected for the premarital education program. These areas were later further refined, based on evaluation of the program after it was administered. The following areas of interest were selected for the eight mini-workshops following evaluation of the first completed series of sessions.

1. *Planning for the wedding,* including making arrangements, photography, catering, flowers, and bride and groom responsibilities.
2. *Building and maintaining a close relationship,* including communication, partner responsibility, and spiritual oneness.
3. *Conflict resolution,* including an examination of conflicts and the skills that couples can develop to resolve their own problems.
4. *Premarital counseling,* including a discussion of the advantages of counseling, a live demonstration of premarital counseling, and some discussion of available resources for married couples needing help.
5. *Budgeting, investment, and insurance,* including how to prepare a budget, realistic examination of insurance needs, and the wise investment of money.
6. *Meal planning and food storage,* including food buying, nutrition, variety in meal preparation, and creativity in food storage.
7. *Interior design,* including budget-decorating with regard to color, fabrics, and furniture selections.
8. *Sexual concerns in marriage,* including examination of roles, expectations, responsibilities, sexual behavior, special considerations involving the honeymoon, and premarital physical examinations for both the man and the woman.

Each time the program was presented, these workshops were given in a different order and by different couples. For example, "planning the wedding" was requested by one group as the first presentation because a number of the group members wanted to begin their wedding arrangements. In another group, this topic was presented third. On several occasions, a male-and-female team, both of whom were professionals in arranging weddings, were used. Other times, several couples, representing a variety of options for weddings, presented what they had done, including their disasters, mistakes, and successes. To make these kinds of decisions about topics, the committee should assess both the needs of their anticipated audience and what is available in the community.

Formats

The facilitators for each miniworkshop were requested to use the following format (the times are approximate but help to illustrate the timing of the schedule):

- **8:00–8:15 P.M.** Announcements, return of questionnaires, homework assignments, distribution of articles or forms for the next week's workshop, forms or questionnaires for this evening's workshop. This part is presented by the director of the program.
- **8:15–8:20 P.M.** Introduction of facilitators by the director.
- **8:20–9:45 P.M.** Miniworkshop. Facilitators follow the following format: (1) 20 minutes of information, (2) an activity that involves an exercise by the couple participants, (3) a discussion between the facilitators and the couples, integrating the couples' experiences and the information given by the facilitators. This format may be difficult for some facilitators, and the director may need to help them adapt their material and personalities to the indicated format. However, the power of the miniworkshop format is in the participation of the couples. Couple participants consistently rated the workshops that engaged the couples in discussion and interpersonal dialogue higher than workshops that did not provide these activities.
- **9:45–10:00 P.M.** Evaluation of the miniworkshop. The completed evaluations are returned to the director at the end of the session.

ORGANIZING THE PROGRAM

In organizing the program, one of the first steps is to determine who will be the director of the program. Sometimes, the sponsoring organization will have someone who has administered a similar program or someone they would like to have as director. Other times, it falls to the committee to determine who would be a good director and to ask that person to attend planning meetings. Other important aspects to consider are the development of the program's content and planning its presentation, including facilitator selection, meeting arrangements, and publicity.

Content

The content areas should be selected by the community committee. The content areas in the BYU program may serve as guides, or the committee may choose others. The rationale for choosing the content areas should be clear. That is, the selection should not be whimsical, but rather should be based on questionnaire results or a needs assessment. These may be acquired through research or from information provided by a committee member.

The general objectives of the overall program and of each miniworkshop are then determined. A question that should be asked about each content area is, Will this presentation prepare engaged couples for a successful marriage? The managers of each miniworkshop may present their own objectives for the workshop, but they must adhere to the general goals set by the committee. The order of presentation of topics must then be decided. In some cases, there may be a logical sequence of topics. In others, the order may be determined by the availability of facilitators.

Presentation

Selection of Facilitators

People in the community who have expertise on a selected topic are usually chosen as facilitators. After discussing possible candidates, the committee makes recommendations for specific facilitators. The director of the program then contacts and contracts with these people to do miniworkshops in the program.

It is the director's responsibility to provide the facilitators with one-page guidelines on the program, including dates, times, and places. The facilitators are thus aware of the content that precedes and follows them. The guideline also helps them to understand the format of the miniworkshops and the program's overall objectives. They can then determine whether or not they can fulfill the objectives that have been established for their particular miniworkshops. If a facilitator has alternative objectives, adaptations should be made through negotiation.

Meeting Arrangements

The director should ensure that there is adequate space and facilities for the type of program to be presented. The meeting arrangements should include installation of microphones and audio-visual equipment and the provision of other materials that may be requested by the facilitators.

Publicity

Publicity is an important part of the program. As soon as the program is developed, the committee should decide on the type of publicity needed and who will be responsible for each aspect of that publicity. Both newspapers and local radio stations, which are usually quite willing to make public announcements, should be used. Community or church leaders and agencies that might have contact with the program's audience are also good sources of publicity.

The following is an announcement that was used to publicize the BYU premarital program:

FROM: Family Consultation Center Director and Program Director
TO: All stake presidents, branch presidents, bishops, BYU faculty, instructors, and potential participants

Please announce this program to all interested people, or read it in your classes if you are faculty or an instructor.

The Family Consultation Center of Brigham Young University announces the beginning of their premarital education program. The eight-week program will begin on Tuesday, October 22, 1974, and end on Thursday, December 12, 1974. Because of the large turnout last year, the center is offering the same presentation on both Tuesday and Thursday nights of each week. The only exception is the week of Thanksgiving. There will be a single presentation on Tuesday, November 26, 1974, in the "step-down lounge" of the Smith Family Living Center. All other presentations will take place in Room 260, Education Building, on lower campus. Each session will start at 8:00 P.M. and end at 10:00 P.M.

Couples are asked to phone in Tuesday or Thursday preferences. They will be committed to that preference for the entire program. Please phone 374-1211, ext. 3888, and ask for Dorine.

We would like to emphasize that the presentation will begin promptly at 8:00 P.M., and we ask that all couples be punctual so as to avoid unnecessary delays. A 75-couple limit is set for each night, and preferences will be acknowledged on a first-come, first-serve basis. Our preregistration procedure only involves phoning in your preferences. This should be done immediately.

The following page provides a short description of each week's presentation, the name of the presenters, and the dates the programs will be presented.

The announcement then continued with descriptions of the eight mini-workshops.

EVALUATION

The committee should decide how much and what type of evaluation they desire. Sometimes the sponsoring organization or an interested person will want to do some research to find out the effects of the program. We recommend that each miniworkshop be evaluated in some way. A simple process of evaluation should be used to determine whether or not the program is effective. The BYU program consistently used a goal sheet (Exhibit 15-1) and an evaluation form for each miniworkshop. In addition, some of the facilitators made their own evaluations.

The goal sheet was used to help the participants operationalize the information they received in the workshops. In order to meet the goals, the couples were asked to apply what was presented. The goal sheets were thus personalized for each miniworkshop.

The Exhibit 15-1 goal sheet was adapted for the miniworkshop on building and maintaining a close relationship. Shortly after the beginning of each workshop, the couples were asked to complete Part A, which assesses the couples' present behavior relative to the topic to be discussed, for

---

Exhibit 15-1 Miniworkshop Goal Sheet

Date _____ Name of miniworkshop _____
Couple file # _____
Instructions: Complete two copies of this and leave one copy in your folder. When making duplications, be sure to allow room for responses.

A. Present behavior (to be filled out by the couple near the beginning of the presentation): What are you now doing as a couple to help you build and maintain a close relationship?
B. Future plans (to be filled out after the presentation):
   1. Immediate goals: List the things that you agree to do as a couple, beginning this week, to help you build and maintain a close relationship.
   2. Long-range goals: List the things you agree to do as a married couple to help you build and maintain a close relationship.
C. Think carefully before you answer these questions:
   1. What will each of you do to help achieve the goals?
     Woman: _____ Man: _____
   2. What will get in the way of achievement of your goals?
     Woman: _____ Man: _____
   3. How much agreement do you have with your partner about these goals?

Woman	0	25	50	75	100%
Man	0	25	50	75	100%

   4. How difficult do you think the achievement of these goals will be for you?

Woman	1	3	5	7	10
	Easy				Difficult
Man	1	3	5	7	10
	Easy				Difficult

example, What are you presently doing as a couple to build and maintain a close relationship? The facilitators were responsible for relating this part of the goal sheet to what they presented in their respective miniworkshops. The couples were encouraged at this point to be as specific as possible. At the end of the workshop, the couples were given time to complete Parts B and C of the goal sheet. Again, the facilitators encouraged the couples to be very specific.

Immediate goals are the kinds of things that couples can do during their courtship until the time they will be married. The second section of Part B asks them to list the goals that they would set for themselves as a married couple. These would be defined by their own desires and by the information given to them in the workshop. Again, they should be encouraged to be very specific.

Part C is to help them negotiate and determine their goals and to operationalize how they will achieve the goals. Since the couple has just one goal sheet, the goals are not personal goals but rather goals for the couple. They need to determine each goal and who will do what to achieve it. They then must take a look at how much agreement they had on it and how difficult they think its achievement will be.

Research and experience indicate that when people set realistic but difficult goals they are more apt to achieve them than if they do not set goals or if they set easy ones. In introducing the program to the participants, this point should be made very clear. The couples should be encouraged to be specific in their answers and to follow all the directions on the goal sheet. To facilitate follow-up research, the instructions on the goal sheet ask the couple to make one copy for themselves and to leave one copy with the program directors.

The evaluation form asked the following five questions:

1. What was most helpful to you in this presentation?
2. What would you like more information about?
3. What suggestions do you have to improve the presentation?
4. What are your general impressions or comments?
5. Based on its usefulness to you, how would you rate this presentation on a scale from one to five?

The evaluation forms were used:

- to evaluate the workshop and determine its usefulness to couples
- to motivate the couples to negotiate and achieve meaningful goals

- to learn of the needs of the participants so that further sessions could be adjusted to meet those needs
- to develop future programs

The facilitators and the director of the program should encourage the participants to be honest in their evaluations and to take the time to give helpful information.

RECOMMENDATIONS

Based on our experience with the premarital program, the following recommendations may help to guide those who wish to establish similar programs.

Practicality

Make the workshops as practical as possible. The content should be meaningful; the couples should practice during each session skills that can be utilized in achieving their immediate and future goals.

Tardiness

Couples have a way of straggling in late. Follow a procedure of starting on time and of beginning with something important so that the introductory part of the session is high-keyed and valuable. If the straggling in continues, determine by questioning the couples—not in a punitive way but in a concerned way—what can be done to facilitate everybody being there on time.

Evaluation

Let the participants know that the director is reading the evaluations and that they are meaningful. Reflect the results of the evaluations in the program as it progresses.

Variations

Variations of the premarital education program should reflect the needs of the community. One community adapted the program for engaged couples and single people interested in marriage. Most of the participants in that program were from a rural area and were working full-time. The presenters of the program's miniworkshops adapted their information and exercises to these aspects of their audience, to meet the needs of both engaged and prospectively engaged participants.

Supplementary Miniworkshops or Services

Some audiences may need or request one or more supplementary workshops after the initial series. The director should be alert to these requests, and the community committee should plan to meet them if at all possible.

If a community has a number of divorced individuals who are planning marriage, supplementary workshops can be focused on their particular needs. Also, referral sources for consultation or counseling could be made available for those who desire such services.

Part V

Structured Family Facilitation Programs: Enrichment

Chapter 16

Executive Families: From Pitfalls to Payoffs

Reba L. Keele

This enrichment program is for entry level and middle-level managers' families with children above the age of 14. It takes ten weeks to present. The first week is for orientation and preassessment; the next eight weeks are devoted to two-hour, weekly sessions with five or six families (15–20 individuals); and the final week is for postassessment data collection. The sessions may be conducted by one facilitator, though two are preferable. The facilitators may be the same sex or be male and female, and should have family facilitation qualifications, particularly knowledge and experience of communication skills. The program may be offered through the community, a corporation, church groups, or in university or college settings.

PROGRAM RATIONALE

The purpose of the program is to improve the skills needed by the executive family—skills that encourage healthy family functioning. The executive family is likely to be one with traditional sex roles; the wife usually is not involved in a career, though she may work (Gullotta & Donahue, 1981; Margolis, 1979; Vandervelde, 1979). The wife's involvement in traditional roles may lead to some frustration with those roles. One survey has revealed that about half of the wives of top corporate executives are satisfied with the effects of their husbands' careers on their marriages and themselves, but only about a third are totally satisfied with the effects on their children and family life. "For these women, contentment doesn't appear to depend on the amount of sacrifice, or the degree of burden. Rather it seems to be determined by how well the couple manages these conditions and how equitable the wife considers the arrangement" (Allen, 1981, p. 29). This implies that involving husbands more meaningfully in the family will increase wives' satisfaction with their marriages.

The husband's job (the overwhelming number of executives are male) usually takes from 50 to 70 hours a week and involves him in travel up to ten weeks of the year (Allen, 1980; Gullotta & Donahue, 1981; Margolis, 1979; Sussman, 1979). Even though higher costs of relocation are resulting in more reluctance to move (Ricklefs, 1980), the frequent transfer is still important in some corporations' advancement policies for the lower-level manager, and such relocation means that there is a great deal of dependence on the family to provide stability and continuity (Margolis, 1979). However, this dependence on the family may not include the father in any involved way; it is likely that the higher he advances the more he defines his contribution to the family as financial, and the more he becomes "a privileged guest in the family, holding the power to make decisions but deferring the authority to his wife" (Gullotta & Donahue, 1981, p. 153).

Even though the father/husband works as a manager, and thus with people (at least in most cases), bringing "people" skills home does not often happen. There appears to be a burnout factor; the more involvement there is at work with intensive human relations, the more likely that he does not use those same skills at home (Kantor, 1977). In addition, he may see sharing his work world with his spouse as potentially draining (Feinberg & Dempewolff, 1980). The content of communication can thus become limited and superficial (Margolis, 1979).

The father's working hours are frequently such that he does not see or interact with his children, particularly when he brings home work from the office. Yet, in spite of the stresses placed on the family, Gullotta and Donahue (1981) suggest that "all family members are deeply invested in the quality of their lifestyle. Further . . . the members are aware that the maintenance of their lifestyle demands that Dad be a 'guest' in the home" (p. 155). In other words, it may be unrealistic to expect that the father will become deeply involved, will begin to spend more time with the children and spouse, or will turn down the relocation offer in order to keep the family in a good setting. The family has a great deal of pressure upon it to meet the needs of family members, yet the time, frequency of interaction, and emotional energy needed to build the family as a support system are often limited.

As a consequence of transfers and the severing of community and neighborhood ties, the spouse and children may feel isolated and have difficulty forming new relationships (Gullotta & Donahue, 1981; Margolis, 1979). Bringing groups of families together who share common backgrounds, experiences, and responses may help in forming new support systems, and in understanding that the consequences of similar pressures are shared. The goal of the present program is to provide instruction and practice in some skills that may help family members to build new support systems and connect better with each other during the times that are available.

PROGRAM ORGANIZATION

Goals

The program has the following three goals:

1. To teach families communication skills that will enhance the possibility of developing greater cohesion and adaptability. The communication skills include attentive listening; listening for affect and content; valuing the sender, message, and self; speaking for self; and expressing feelings. These skills should contribute to the ability of the family to respond with flexibility, to negotiate decisions, and to develop cohesion through the demonstration of supportiveness, psychological safety, and family identification.
2. To teach the process of negotiation and flexibility by having the family practice goal setting and evaluation at the conclusion of each session.
3. To provide, through interactions and shared activities, connections with other families who face similar problems.

Staff Resources and Setting

You may utilize one or two facilitators, as needed. The cost of materials is minimal. The major costs involve the reproduction of minor items and the provision of newsprint, paper, and pencils or crayons for each person. The room should have movable chairs and enough room (or separate rooms) so that the families can work together. A blackboard would be helpful, but newsprint can serve the same purpose.

Theoretical Models

The theories used in this program are communication, experiential, growth, and healthy family functioning (see Appendix A).

Selection Criteria

The following criteria should be followed in selecting family participants:

- Either the husband or the wife in each family should be a manager or be self-employed in business.

- Although the families may have younger children, only children 14 years or older will benefit from this program.
- The families should be fairly healthy.

The Symptom Checklist 90 (SCL-90) should be administered to all eligible family members (see Appendix B). The profiles should be examined to determine if any families should be excluded. If the facilitators are not familiar with the SCL-90, a psychological consultant should be used in the selection process. Families that are not eligible for the program should be advised of alternative services available to them.

Evaluation

To evaluate the program, demographic information—names, ages, educational level, number of moves since married, length and number of marriages—is needed about each family participant. With these data, the effects of the program are determined by using the Family Adaptability and Cohesion Evaluation Scales (FACES) as preprogram and postprogram measure. In postprogram testing, the family members are asked to rate the effectiveness of individual activities on a rating scale developed by the facilitators.

Initial Session

Objectives

(1) To administer the preassessment instruments to all families, and
(2) To get to know each other and to share expectations.

Materials

(1) paper for listing family names, addresses, and phone numbers;
(2) name tags;
(3) the FACES instrument, and, if needed,
(4) personal data forms.

Information

In this session, it is important to communicate enthusiasm about the process and to obtain commitments to positive results. The facilitators need to remember that the participants are busy families, whose own commitments have not often enbraced this kind of activity.

Procedure

- Introduce yourself and have all participants do the same. (30 minutes)
- Administer the FACES instrument and collect the personal information needed, including family addresses and phone numbers. The facilitators should be available to the families at this time to answer questions and collect the papers as the participants finish. (30 minutes)
- Introduce the program by describing what will happen in the next nine sessions (eight weeks plus one week for postassessment). Note the topics, the time and place of each session, and the commitment needed from the families to attend and complete agreed-upon tasks each week. Make it clear that, even if all members of a family cannot come (though full attendance is expected, it may become necessary for someone to miss), those who can come, should. (20 minutes)
- Ask the families to discuss together what they think will be happening in the next nine weeks and what they expect to gain from participation. They should appoint one person to share their perceptions and expectations with the whole group. (20 minutes)
- Conclude the session, reminding them of the time, place, and topic of next week's session. (5 minutes)

As noted, the group meets eight times for the enrichment program, then again one month after the end of the program for post-testing and to report on how they are doing with their agreed-upon goals. The leaders will have to remind them of the post-testing session by mail and phone to ensure that they return the questionnaires. If they do not, the leaders will have to visit the home to administer the tests.

PROGRAM OUTLINE

The following outline describes the content, procedures, and materials used in each program session. Information for some of the sessions for this program has been deleted. To obtain the complete program, follow the instructions in the Preface.

1. Session 1: Attentive Listening and Attending to Affect and Content
   - Objective
     a. To be able to interpret correctly what is meant by another speaker.
   - Materials
     a. Paper and pencils for writing goals.

- Procedures
  a. Introductions. As the facilitators for the program, introduce yourselves by telling one thing you want the group to know about yourselves; then ask each participant to do the same. Ask them to pay attention to what is meant by a statement as well as what is said in the statement. (20 minutes)
  b. Concepts. Present the following concepts:
    (1) We cannot not communicate.
    (2) Communication can be with verbal or nonverbal messages.
    (3) Listening is distinguished from hearing. Speak French or another language; ask how many of them heard, how many understood.
    (4) A critical aspect of attentive listening is to pay attention to everything the person does as well as says. (Any good book on communication will refer to these principles; see, for example, Stewart (1977).) (30 minutes)
  c. Activity. Instruct the family members, in pairs, in a number of communication skills. Follow this with a general discussion. (60 minutes)
  d. Conclusion. Reminding them of what was just learned about listening carefully, have the family members discuss what they can do to practice what they have just learned. Have them write down what they decide to do and who will report next week on how it went. Collect the written goals. The format of developing goals from the content and experiences of the session will be followed throughout the program. (10 minutes)

2. Session 2: Valuing of the Sender, Message, and Self
   - Objective
     a. To learn that disagreeing with others does not mean that you do not value them.
   - Materials
     a. Bomb shelter exercise reproduced for each individual, together with pencil and paper for writing goals (see Appendix 16-A).
   - Procedure
     a. Review. Review last week's concepts, and collect reports from the family members on how they did in meeting their goals during the last week. Review the goals and talk about making them realistic and achievable. (5 minutes)
     b. Concepts. Present the following concepts: (1) Value systems differ even for persons in the same family. (2) The valuing

process includes freely choosing from among alternatives (the consequences of which are known), affirming what we value, prizing those things, and acting consistently with what we say we value. (3) We need to learn to deal with value differences, information differences, and differences in approach. We do this by maintaining respect for other people, and feeling that there is something to learn from them. (4) Each family member contributes something of value to the family (Raths, Harmin, & Simon, 1966). (30 minutes)

3. Session 3: Speak for Yourself
   - Objectives
     a. To be able to use "I" messages to avoid speaking for others or to appeal to authority.
     b. To learn to link feeling feedback to observable behavior.
   - Materials
     a. Newsprint, felt-tip marker, paper, and pencils for each person.
   - Procedures
     a. Review. Review last week's concepts. Take reports from each family about accomplishments during the past week. Offer encouragement to any families who have not met their goals. (5 minutes)
     b. Concepts. Present the following concepts:
        (1) There is a difference between accepting responsibility for my own feelings and thoughts, as expressed by saying, "I'm angry," and telling you what you do, as expressed by saying, "You make me mad."
        (2) We should not tell others what they mean or feel, but rather ask them to tell us what they mean or feel. Ask the families to give examples of when they have been told what they feel instead of asked.
        (3) Appeals to authority can be escapes from responsibility for self. Examples of this are the frequent statement from children, "All the other kids get to do that," or the statement from parents, "No other kids get to do that!" It is better to say, "I would like to do that," or, "I don't feel comfortable with you doing that, for the following reasons." Ask the group if they can think of ways they might appeal to authority to avoid taking responsibility. (20 minutes)

  c. Activity.* Explain that there will be four rounds of communication and that each round will be interrupted as necessary. The exercise will take place in mixed family groups of about five persons each (Pfeiffer & Jones, 1974–1975, vol. 3). (40 minutes)

   (1) *Round 1.* Write on newsprint the phrase, "Now I see." Each participant is to describe to the group the nonverbal behavior of the others in their group by statements that begin with the phrase, "Now I see." Illustrate briefly by describing the movements of nearby participants. Allow about five minutes for this round. Interrupt if the participants begin to move away from behavior description toward discussion. Take two minutes to process what happened.

   (2) *Round 2.* Write, "Now I think," and instruct the groups to continue their conversation by beginning each sentence with the phrase, "Now I think." An example may be given. (5 minutes for the round, followed by 2 minutes for processing)

   (3) *Round 3.* The third phrase is, "Now I feel." After about two minutes of interaction, interrupt to explain that groups that focus on feeling data commonly confuse thoughts and feelings. Suggest that the members avoid the following two phrases in the remainder of this round. "I feel that . . ." and, "I feel like . . ." Instead, the group members should use the phrase, "Now I feel," followed by an adjective. They should remember the tendency to focus their attention on the other person instead of their own feelings. (10 minutes, followed by about 3 minutes for processing)

   (4) *Round 4.* The final phrase is, "Now I think you feel," which is used at the beginning of each communication to other group members. Conversations should be two-way, to determine how accurately group members perceive each others' feelings. (10 minutes, followed by 3 minutes for processing)

  d. Activity in family groups. Give the group members paper and pencils. Ask them to write down five things they like to do,

*Reprinted from J. William Pfeiffer and John E. Jones, *A Handbook of Structured Experiences for Human Relations Training,* Vol. III, San Diego, CA: University Associates, Inc., 1974. Used with permission.

five things they think another member of the family likes to do, and five things that mother, father, or a sibling of their choice would say that the writer likes to do. Have them compare the three lists, and as a family discuss the comparisons. How accurate were they in guessing the likes of the other members of the family? How accurately were their likes guessed? What do they think are the reasons for the accuracy or inaccuracy? How often do people in their family say what they like or do not like? What are the reasons for that? Do they as a family want to do anything about it? Do they as individuals want to do anything about it? (30 minutes)

e. Discussion.
   (1) Ask the family members to talk about times when they might use authority appeals justifiably and when they might use them to avoid taking responsibility. (5 minutes)
   (2) Have the families discuss what they can do as individuals or as families to practice speaking responsibly and using "I" messages. They should determine their goals for the next week and decide how they can help each other remember without being obnoxious. Write down their goals and practice methods. (5 minutes)

f. Collect the goals. (5 minutes)

4. Session 4: Expressing Feelings
   • Objective
      a. To practice sharing feelings openly and clearly by using feeling words.
   • Materials
      a. Pencils and paper
      b. Copies of incomplete sentences for each participant.
   • Procedures
      a. Review. Review last week's concepts, and take reports from each family about goal accomplishments during the past week. Offer encouragement to families that have not met their goals and discuss if necessary. (5 minutes)
      b. Concepts. Present the following concepts:
         (1) We cannot depend upon on nonverbal information or our own guesses for communication of feeling because everyone expresses feelings differently, and our guesses may not be accurate. Nonverbal communication is important, but cannot be used alone.

(2)   We often ask others to guess what we are feeling, then we are disappointed when they do not guess correctly.

(3)   The hiding of feelings magnifies their power; sometimes they feel overwhelming because of lack of exposure.

(4)   The hiding of feelings prevents people from responding to them, which often makes them feel angry or betrayed. (20 minutes)

c.   Activity. Give each family member a list of incomplete sentences to complete with paper and pencil. You may want to adapt the sentences to topics or concerns raised in the preceding weeks. Then discuss together how each member has completed the sentences. Examples of incomplete sentences that could be used are shown in Exhibit 16-1. (30 minutes)

d.   Activity. Describe the following strength exercises to the entire group, but complete the activity in the family groups. First, the family members write down five strengths that they think they have. Then Father begins by telling the family one strength that he thinks he has. Each member of the family then tells Father a strength that they think he has. Then, one by one, the children state strengths that they think they have, and the other members of the family add strengths to each child's list. This continues until each person in the family has been the focal person. No one is allowed to deny a strength or in any way discount what is said. Ask the whole group to discuss how they feel after one strength round. How do they feel about the things said about them? Did they already know that members of their family felt that way about them? Why or why not? Repeat the whole process four more times, until each person has listed a total of five strengths and has five more expressed by each member of the family. Discuss how the members feel at the conclusion. (40 minutes)

Exhibit 16-1 Incomplete Sentences

The time I was most frightened was _____. One thing I feel angry about is _____. When I am with people I love, I feel _____. One of the reasons it is hard for me to express feelings is _____. When I love someone I _____. When I am hurt, I _____. One thing that frightens me is _____. I think it is sad that _____. I am happiest when I _____. When I feel happy, I _____. When others in my family express feelings, I feel _____. One of the things I miss most is _____. The thing I like best about our family is _____. The thing that most concerns me about our family is _____. The most important thing for you to know about me is_____.

e. Discussion. Plan with the family how they will practice expressing feelings during the next week and later. What are some feelings that are easier to express? How will they know when they are getting better at expressing feelings? Instruct them to write down their goals and practices and give them to the facilitator. (5 minutes)

5. Session 5: Flexibility
   • Objective
   a. To generate new ideas and change patterns of behavior and interaction among family members in the face of new situations or modified assessments.
   • Materials
   a. Cards for role playing, cash register worksheets, copies of developmental cycle (or the cycle may be placed on newsprint or a blackboard).
   • Procedures
   a. Review. Review the previous week's concepts and take reports from the families about their homework during the week. Discuss realistic goal setting. (5 minutes)
   b. Concepts. Present the following concepts:
      (1) Something is not a mistake unless we continue to act the same way when new information tells us a different course of action should be followed.
      (2) New situations (change of job, moving, new demands on the family, and so on) require new actions, but we often continue as if everything were the same. In this context, refer to the developmental stages of families in Carter and McGoldrick (1980) p. 17.
      (3) We can learn to perceive what the situation is now and to modify our behavior and interpretations.
      (4) Basic decision-making skills involve defining what the real problem is, gathering information about the various alternatives proposed, selecting an alternative, trying it out, and adjusting according to the new information that results from trying it out. (20 minutes)
   c. Activity.
      (1) The following activity provides a clear picture of the value that comes from working together as a group and in understanding the assumptions of decision making. Give a copy of the football worksheet (Exhibit 16-2) to each person and put them in groups of about five persons each. The

Exhibit 16-2 Football Worksheet

The Story

Four teenagers were playing football in the street near their homes, when a person appeared and demanded their money and football. The teenagers turned their pockets inside out, the contents were scooped up, and the person ran down the street. As soon as they returned home, the teenagers told their parents.

Statements about the Story

1. The four boys were playing when approached.	T F ?
2. The man who approached them was a robber.	T F ?
3. The person wanted money and the football.	T F ?
4. The teenagers gave the robber money.	T F ?
5. One of the boys owned the football.	T F ?
6. The robber scooped up the teenagers' property.	T F ?
7. The parents did not know of the incident.	T F ?
8. While the man got money from the boys, we don't know how much.	T F ?
9. The people referred to in the story are the boys, the robber, and the parents.	T F ?
10. The whole incident took only a few minutes.	T F ?
11. The following events in the story are true: The teenagers were playing, the contents of their pockets were scooped up, and the man who robbed them got completely away.	T F ?

---

participants have ten minutes to read the story paragraph and then to indicate whether each of the statements about the story is true, false, or unknown (indicated by a question mark). Then give another copy of the worksheet to the group. Again, they have ten minutes to arrive at a consensus as to whether each statement is true, false, or unknown. At the end of that time, announce the "correct" answers—No. 7 is false, No. 3 is true, everything else is unknown. Then lead a brief discussion of the experience, during which comments can be elicited about assumptions and the value of group decision making. Ask the families to make the connection to their own family decision-making process. (20 minutes)

(2) Prepare a set of role play cards, along with a second set of cards that change the circumstances of the role play. Two or more families work together in this role play. One family is placed in the center of the circle, with a situation to role play. At any point, the other family, which is outside the circle, can interrupt to suggest a change in the

circumstances the family faces. For instance, the family members in the center may receive role play cards that tell them that they have just been given an opportunity for a transfer, which will mean a big promotion for the father/husband. The wife/mother has just started a new job in her own field, after a series of part-time jobs. The children are seniors and sophomores in high school. The cards of changed circumstances distributed to the observing families might include at least the following: the children are juniors and freshmen; the children are 6 and 10; her new job is part-time; there is a chance that the father/husband will be up for another promotion in about a year; the company won't say how short a time he might be at the new job; she has just started college to earn a master's degree, which will take two years; the children have finished high school; she is pregnant and has two children, 10 and 12 years of age; at any time, grandmother may have to come to live with them. As the family members in the center try to make decisions, the observers can, at any point, tell them what has changed and they must try to adjust to the different circumstances created by the new information. Each family has a chance to be in the center in a different role-play situation. (40 minutes)

d. Discussion. Discuss the following questions: What kinds of changes were the most difficult? What did it feel like to be forced to be flexible? How is this like real life, and how is it different? Can they think of a time when their family has had to be flexible? Were they able to be flexible? Why, or why not? (10 minutes)

e. Family goals. The families should then discuss the following questions: What is the most immediate important decision that their family will face? Can they start the process of decision making tonight or during the coming week? Who needs to do what for that process to begin? The families should write down what they will do and hand the results to the facilitators. (25 minutes)

6. Session 6: Negotiation
    • Objective
      a. To successfully negotiate differences by reaching a decision that is acceptable to all, rather than continue in limited or endless negotiation.

- Materials
  a. Jigsaw puzzle pieces, either from pictures or actual puzzles, for each family.
- Procedures
  a. Review. Review the previous week's concepts and take reports from the families. (5 minutes)
  b. Concepts. Present the following concepts:
     (1) There are many conflicting needs in a family.
     (2) To establish a setting for negotiation, the communication skills that they have been practicing are required.
     (3) Negotiation involves bargaining for their own needs while taking into account the needs of others.
     (4) Negotiation is a way to help all parties achieve their goals. (20 minutes)
  c. Activity. Within each family group, distribute portions of the jigsaw puzzle to each member. Each member is to assemble as much of the jigsaw puzzle as possible alone. The members must negotiate for pieces they need through bargaining, but they may not give up pieces without receiving something of equivalent value in return, either in numbers of pieces or important pieces needed for completion of their portion of the puzzle. When the individual portions are completed, the entire puzzle can be assembled. (45 minutes)
  d. Discussion. Discuss with the whole group how they got each other to give up pieces and what they gained from giving and getting. (20 minutes)
  e. Family rules. Give the remainder of time to the participants to decide what rules about negotiation they want to make explicit in their own families. (25 minutes)

7. Session 7: Supportiveness
   - Objective
     a. To nurture and validate each other verbally and nonverbally as family members to fill emotional and physical needs.
   - Materials
     a. List of statements
   - Procedures
     a. Review. Review the previous week's concepts. Obtain brief reports on last week's homework. (5 minutes)
     b. Contents. Present the following concepts:
        (1) We need to know that the people we care about also care about us.

        (2)   Caring is demonstrated by actions, words, and touching.

        (3)   Frequent expression of caring through actions, words, touching, and valuing each other builds a supportive atmosphere in the family. (20 minutes)

   c.   Activity. Each person in the family group takes five statements from a list provided by the facilitator. (Example: I am happy you did that.) The family members then (1) demonstrate, without using words, how a statement is true; (2) express how it is true, using their own words; and (3) demonstrate how a statement is true by combining touching with words. The five statements could be tailored for individual families. (20 minutes)

   d.   Activity. Repeat the strength exercise from Session 4, this time adding whatever nonverbal messages the family members are comfortable with as they tell each other the strengths they have. Repeat the exercise four times, trying to use different strengths each time. (20 minutes)

   e.   Discussion. Have participants discuss these activities in family groups. Supply questions as needed to stimulate their responses. (40 minutes)

   f.   Family decisions. Ask the families what will have to happen during the week to increase the amount of support that is expressed verbally and nonverbally in the family? Have them write their answers down and hand them to the facilitators. (5 minutes)

8. Session 8: Psychological Safety and Family Identification
   - Objectives
     a. To help the family members feel security, safety, and trust in one another's presence by using the principles of communication they have learned.
     b. To give the family members a sense of belonging to the family by working together on a task that requires consensus and individual contributions.
   - Materials
     a. Newsprint, crayons, pencils with erasers, and copies of the handout.
   - Procedures
     a. Review. Review previous week's concepts: Tell the group it will integrate all the concepts in this session while learning a new concept. (5 minutes)
     b. Activity. Pass out the newsprint, crayons, and pencils with erasers. Give the participants the handout (Appendix 16-B) and

go over the instructions orally. Have them complete the task indicated in the handout. (45 minutes)

c.   Family discussion. Supply the families with questions to facilitate discussions about the handout task. Focus the questions on the positive activity that facilitated completion of the task. (30 minutes)

d.   Activity. For the whole group: Draw together some concepts from the activities and the discussion—about family cohesion, specifically psychological safety or the creation of a family in which the members feel welcome, loved, protected, trusting, and trusted. Ask what concepts about psychological safety can be drawn from the discussion. (15 minutes)

e.   Discussion. Talk about your experiences with the group and what you appreciate about them. Stress that the purpose of the group has been to learn to develop a more cohesive family, one in which all members feel as if they belong, are welcomed, loved, and protected, trusting, and trusted. Note that, to this end, the participants have practiced and improved many skills. (5 minutes)

f.   Goal setting. Have the families talk together about the skills they feel need the most practice and those they think their family is best at. They should decide which they will be practicing most and how they will maintain a record of accomplishment. They should then write their conclusions down and hand them to the facilitators. (20 minutes)

g.   Termination. Remind the group that it will meet together in a month to talk about what it has learned and to retake the survey it took at the beginning of the program. Allow time for the families to say goodbye to each other.

Appendix 16-A

A Bomb Shelter Exercise

One evening a year from now you invite eight acquaintances to your home to talk with a psychology professor whom you know personally. In the midst of your discussion you hear the air raid siren. You turn on the radio and the Civil Defense station broadcasts that enemy planes are approaching. Fortunately, you have a well-equipped bomb shelter in your basement, so immediately you direct the professor, your eight companions, and a mechanic who has been repairing the air-conditioning unit, to go downstairs. Shortly after you are all in the shelter, a terrific blast shakes the earth, and you realize that the bomb has fallen. For four frantic hours you get static on the radio in your shelter. Finally you hear the following announcement: A bomb of great magnitude has hit the Air Force base. Damage is extensive; radiation is intense. It is feared that all those not in shelters have suffered a fatal dose of radiation. All persons in shelters are warned that it would be fatal to leave before at least a month. Further bombing is anticipated. This may be the last broadcast you will hear for some time.

Immediately you realize that you have 11 persons in a shelter that is equipped with food, water, and—most important—oxygen enough to last 11 people two weeks or six persons one month. When you reveal this information, the group unanimously decides that in order for anyone to survive, five must be sacrificed. As it is your shelter, all agree that you must stay and choose the other five who are to be saved.

Source: Adapted with permission from Klemans, P., & Beidler, E. A question of values: A unit in written composition, *The English Journal* (September 1962); and the National Council of Teachers of English.

1. Mary, the psychology professor, is a few years older than the rest of the group. It has already become evident that the others respect her and recognize her grasp of the situation and her ability to take control. Although she is rather cold and impersonal, she has helped to quiet the group's nervousness and settled an argument between Don and Hazel. Even though no one seems close to her, you feel she would be valuable as an organizer and a pacifier.

2. Hazel is studying home economics—nutrition and dietetics. She is a very sexy, attractive woman. One of the first things she did was to appraise the food supply. You realize that her training has given her practical knowledge of how to ration food to avoid waste; also, she is an imaginative cook who can fix even canned foods appealingly. She is efficient to the point of being domineering and bossy.

3. Alberta is a brilliant woman who has been given a graduate study assistantship to do research on radiation. She has been pampered all her life and is horrified at wearing the same clothes for a month, being unable to take a bath or wash her hair, and sleeping in a room with five other people. Her scientific knowledge of the situation would be a definite asset; her whims and attitude would be trying.

4. Laura is a literature major, has read extensively, and writes well herself. Already she has entertained and diverted the group by retelling one of the books she has recently read and analyzing the author's sensitivity to human experience.

5. Nancy, Chet's wife, has a pleasant personality. She is expecting a baby in two months and is thus more concerned and nervous than many others in the shelter.

6. Chet, Nancy's husband, is a medical student. He has had two years of medical study, three summers in a camp as medical director, and close association with his father, who is a doctor. He refuses to stay unless Nancy also remains.

7. Jack, the mechanic who had been working upstairs, also has a great deal of practical know-how to recommend him. Although his formal education ended with high school, he has had experience with air-filtration systems, air purifiers, and oxygen supply. He has already been reprimanded by Hazel for snitching a Hershey bar from the food supply. He fails to grasp the necessity for self control as far as the food and water supply is concerned.

8. Paul, a young minister, is easy going. His calmness, optimism, and faith are an inspiration to the group. In an intangible, yet perceptible, way, his presence is reassuring. While helping calm Nancy's nervousness he revealed that he has learned to remain calm of neces-

sity, because he is diabetic. He would require a special diet and easily becomes tired. Over-excitement causes him to faint.

9. Joe is a clean-cut, husky black football player, the star center of the college's team. He is highly respected by everyone on campus. Joe was the only one able to lift the heavy metal plate that had to be placed over the shelter door. At one point, when Chet took it upon himself to set the oxygen tank valve, Jack flew at him, shoved him out of the way, and reset the valve properly. A fist fight might have ensued had Joe not parted the two.

10. Don is romantic. His smile, lively guitar music, and scintillating sense of humor have helped improve everyone's mood. He gets along well with everyone—too well with some of the women. He has already offended Hazel by being fresh, and everyone has noticed his flirting.

Four assumptions: 1) Accept the hypothetical situation as a fact. 2) Be candid. Your physical and mental well-being and survival will depend on your companions. 3) Accept all facts concerning the ten persons as actual. Assume nothing which would conflict with the information presented. 4) Do not overlook your own strengths and weaknesses in making your choices.

You will be given time to rank your choices from 1 to 10, 1 being the person you most want in the shelter, 10 the least wanted individual. After you have made your own choices, your work group will come together to arrive at a *consensus* decision about who stays.

Family Coat of Arms*

Handout

This is an exercise in communication, trust, negotiation, revelation of self and so on through the whole list of skills we have learned. You will be drawing, but artwork is not the emphasis of this exercise, so feel free to use stick figures or whatever will represent what you want to communicate. You will be drawing an individual coat of arms. Draw a shield on the newsprint, as large as you'd like. A sample is below. You may either use imaginary lines or actual lines, but the shield has six sections, numbered as below. You will be doing something different   in each section. Please follow the instructions below the shield. Do not discuss.

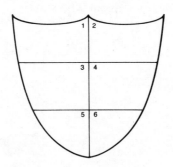

*Note: For information about current Values Realization materials and a schedule of nation-wide training workshops, contact Sidney B. Simon, Old Mountain Rd., Hadley, MA 01035.

Source: Adapted with permission from Simon, S.B., Dinner table learning. In S.B. Simon & H. Kirschenbaum (Eds.), *Readings in value clarification*. Minneapolis: Winston Press, Inc., 1973.

1. In the first section draw a picture which represents your view of your family's greatest achievements.

2. To the right of the first section, draw pictures to represent two things your parents (or children) are good at.

3. Draw a picture showing your favorite relative outside the immediate family.

4. Make a drawing symbolizing one issue about which you feel strongly and others in your family disagree.

5. In the fifth section, draw a picture representing something you are striving to obtain (material goods, personality trait, abstraction, etc.)

6. This is the only block in which to write words. Pick three words which you think should become the family motto. They can be three separate words or three words which make a sentence. They should be three words the whole family could believe in.

Each member shares his/her coat of arms, explaining why they drew what they drew.

After sharing individually, discuss as a family what you think the IDEAL coat of arms would be for your family. When you have agreed upon the ideal, arrive at a consensus for the REAL family coat of arms, using individual and ideal information. Finally, divide the six blocks among the family for completion of the artwork agreed upon. Remember, art is not the important idea; the expression of family consensus in a loving atmosphere is.

Chapter 17

Family Enrichment with the Hopscotch and Little League Generation

Barbara L. Fisher and Charles Ronig

This program is designed to be administered to whole families (including all family members over six years old). Several families may participate at one time. The number of families depends on the preference of the leader and the available facilities. The program is six weeks long, with weekly, one-hour meetings. This length of time seems appropriate for the attention span of school-age children (and their parents). One or two facilitators may be used. If two facilitators are used, a male-female team is recommended.

Each session has a similar format, consisting of facilitator presentation, family exercises, discussions, and homework. The facilitator presentation is designed to provide content information about the topics or exercises. The family exercises and discussions are designed to facilitate the development of skills. The homework assignments are designed to assist the family in practicing the skills at home.

OBJECTIVES AND FORMAT

The specific purpose of this program is to improve family functioning in four areas: communication, self-disclosure, positive reciprocity, and cooperation. These are stated objectives and are pursued directly. There is at least one lesson devoted to each of these objectives.

The unstated objectives include: improved family cohesion, increased information flow, improved self-esteem, and increased awareness of family strengths. These are pursued indirectly, or through the process of the program. There are no exercises specifically designed to teach these skills. However, they are part of the outcome of the program, since they are developed through the means or process of achieving the stated objectives and skills.

The stated and unstated objectives are well-documented in recent research as aspects of healthy family functioning. They were chosen for this program because they frequently appear as variables in research studies.

The program is designed for families with school-age (kindergarten to sixth grade) children. It is based on both developmental and healthy family functioning literature. Developmental literature indicates that families with school-age children need to develop good communication skills. They must help the children learn to be cooperative members of the family and to handle feelings and impulses appropriately. They must also assist the children in acquiring a sense of competence. The program is designed to help families acquire the skills needed to achieve these developmental tasks.

The program has been field tested. The testing instruments were the Piers-Harris Self-Concept Scale (to measure self-concept of children) and the Kvebaek Family Sculpture Technique (to measure family cohesion). See Appendix B for descriptions of these instruments.

Each session has a stated purpose and a list of needed materials. Each session, except the first, begins with a brief review of the previous session. All sessions end with a brief summary and a homework assignment. The facilitators should follow the format and structure of each program, but should be flexible enough to allow for family differences and needs. In the following program outline, estimated times for each presentation, exercise, and discussion are provided as guidelines.

PROGRAM OUTLINE

The following outline describes the content, procedures, and materials used in each program session:

1. Session 1: Communication
   - Objectives
     a. To introduce the program facilitators and family members.
     b. To introduce basic rules of communication and begin developing skills in communicating.
   - Materials
     a. Pencils, 3 × 5 cards (one for each participant), overhead projector and screen, two blank transparencies, transparencies of the "Blind Man Story" (Figures 17-1 through 17-8), transparencies of communication rules (Figures 17-9 and 17-10), the transparency of a sample homework contract (Figure 17-11), a set of Tinker Toys (one set per family), two Tinker Toy structures in boxes, and the homework contract (Exhibit 17-1).

- Procedures
  a. Introduction (10–15 minutes)
    (1) Introduce yourself and provide relevant information to the participants in an informal and relaxed manner.
    (2) Explain the nature of this enrichment program. For example: "The goals of the program are to assist the families in developing additional skills in being healthy and happy. The program is six weeks long and will consist of mini-lectures, exercises, and assignments. Each family is asked to attend all six sessions, and to try each exercise. We welcome comments about the program."
    (3) The family members should choose someone in the family to introduce them and to say a little about each of them and their family. The information to be shared should include nicknames, unusual hobbies, and so on. Or a family member may talk about a TV or movie personality each family member resembles or about a nickname for the whole family. The families may be given a few minutes to decide what will be shared. Let them know that this is more a playful than a serious exercise. Lead the exercise accordingly in an enthusiastic mood.
  b. Warm-up exercise (5 minutes)
    (1) Exercise. Pass out a 3 × 5 card or piece of paper and a pencil to each person. Have the participants write their names three times, as quickly as they can, on the card. When everyone is finished, make a few comments on how easy it was and how well everyone did. Next, tell them to write their names again, this time with their other hand, again writing it three times as quickly as possible.
    (2) Summary. Have the whole group discuss what was different the second time. Why was it harder and slower? Get across the idea that writing with their natural hand is easy because it is a habit that they practice all the time. When they tried to use their other hand, it was not natural; hence, it was strange to do and also quite difficult. Emphasize to them that much of what they will be doing in this workshop will feel unnatural and strange. Some of the things they will be asked to do will be like asking them to write with their other hand. Many of the new things will be awkward or difficult to do until they have had time to practice them.

Figure 17-1 The Blind Man Story: Transparency 1

c. Minilecture: The basic rules of communication (15 minutes)
  (1) Say to the group, "There are several rules of good com-
       munication. Today we will look at two rules. The first is
       that the message sent is not always the message received.
       This means that, sometimes when we say something, the
       other person will not understand it the way we mean it.
       There are lots of reasons why this happens, but first let's
       look at an example." Place Transparency 1 (Figure 17-1)
       on the projector and read:

> It was six men of Indostan
>   To learning much inclined,
> Who went to see the Elephant
>   (Though all of them were blind),
> That each by observation
>   might satisfy his mind.

Place Transparency 2 (Figure 17-2) on the projector and
read:

> The first approached the Elephant, and
>   Happening to fall
> Against his broad and sturdy side,
>   At once began to bawl:
> "God bless, me! But the Elephant is very
>   Like a wall!"

Figure 17-2 The Blind Man Story: Transparency 2

Place Transparency 3 (Figure 17-3) on the projector and read:

> The second, feeling of the tusk cried,
>   "Ho! What have we here,
> So very round and smooth and sharp?
>   To me 'tis very clear
> This wonder of an Elephant is very like
>   A spear!"

Place Transparency 4 (Figure 17-4) on the projector and read:

> The third approached the animal
>   And, happening to take
> The squirming trunk within his hands,
>   Thus boldly he spake:
> "I see," quoth he, "the Elephant
>   Is very like a snake."

Figure 17-3 The Blind Man Story: Transparency 3

Figure 17-4 The Blind Man Story: Transparency 4

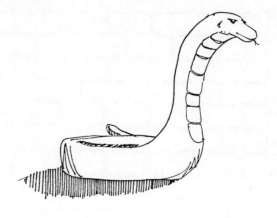

Place Transparency 5 (Figure 17-5) on the projector and read:

> The fourth reached out an eager hand
>   And felt about the knee.
> "What most this wondrous beast
>   Is like
> Is very plain," quoth he,
>   " 'Tis clear enough the Elephant
> Is very like a tree!"

Figure 17-5 The Blind Man Story: Transparency 5

Figure 17-6 The Blind Man Story: Transparency 6

Place Transparency 6 (Figure 17-6) on the projector and read:

> The fifth, who chanced to touch the ear,
>   Said, ''E'en the blindest man
> Can tell what this resembles most.
>   Deny the fact who can
> This marvel of an Elephant
>   Is very like a fan!''

Place Transparency 7 (Figure 17-7) on the projector and read:

> The sixth no sooner had begun
>   About the beast to grope,
> Than, seizing on the swinging tail
>   That fell within his scope,
> "I see," quoth he, "the Elephant
>   Is very like a rope!"

Figure 17-7 The Blind Man Story: Transparency 7

Figure 17-8 The Blind Man Story: Transparency 8

Finally, place Transparency 8 (Figure 17-8) on the projector and read:

> And so these men of Indostan
>   Disputed loud and long,
> Each in his own opinion
>   Exceeding stiff and strong.
> Though each was partly in the right,
>   They all were in the wrong!

(2)   Summary. Say to the group, "This is the composite elephant the blind men saw. It reminds us that the world we live in is built up of the different experiences that people have had and managed to communicate with each other. But let us also consider that, if the blind men had exchanged places and individually experienced a portion of the elephant they had not felt previously, they ultimately would have been able to agree upon a much better looking ele-

phant than the one depicted in Transparency 8. Thus, as we read, listen, and experience, we establish the basis for a better understanding of what others experience, and we can—in the end—find that we have much more to agree on than to disagree about. It is when we stop learning that we begin to build the barriers that keep us from understanding other people—and perhaps finding common agreement with them.''

(3) Minilecture. Next, present the following to the group: ''The second rule of communication has to do with the fact that messages have two aspects—one is what we say, and the other is how it is said. Our voice tone, facial expressions, and gestures are important in communicating. If I say 'I'm not angry' (use a loud, gruff voice and pound the table with a fist), what message do you hear? (allow for an answer) Why? What if I say, 'Gee, I love the way you cleaned your room' (use sarcastic tone), what message do you hear? Why? (allow for an answer) In these instances, the words I say are not believable because the way I say them is contradictory. As a further example, let's play a game with the children called 'Two Messages.' I want you (each child) to pretend you are coming home from school, and it has been an awful day. Mom asks how the day went, and you give her two messages—say 'fine,' with your mouth, but have your actions say, 'It was terrible.' The fathers can help decide what actions to use.'' Give the families enough time for one or all of their children to play.

(4) Summary. Ask the family's parents whether their children had a fine day at school, or whether they think something was wrong. Point out again that the nonverbal (actions) sometimes contradicts the verbal (words). This can be very confusing. Thus, tell them that the second rule of communication is to make sure that words and actions go together.

d. Family exercise: Communication rules (20 minutes)

(1) Give each family a set of Tinker Toys. Bring out your box with a prebuilt Tinker Toy structure inside. Invite the mothers to come up and see your structure. Inform each mother and her family that she will have to describe the object to the family and have them build the same object based on her description. She cannot help them

build, and they cannot ask her questions. The family members can talk to each other but not to the mother. The mother may go back to view the original structure three times. Allow about seven minutes for the exercise. Now, bring out the second Tinker Toy structure in a box and repeat the exercise. Again, invite the mothers to view the object. The rules this time are that the mothers may return to see the object three times but cannot help build the family's object. The family members, however, can ask her questions. Again, allow seven minutes for the exercise.

   (2) Discussion. Ask the group the following questions, and make a list of their answers to c on newsprint:

     (a) Which time was easier?

     (b) What was different about the second part?

     (c) What made it difficult to copy the object in the first exercise?

  e. Summary (5 minutes). Announce that the session is coming to a close and you want to go over the rules of good communication. Ask the group to name the rules of good communication that they learned earlier. As they repeat the rules, put the two transparencies on communication rules (Figures 17-9 and 17-10) on the overhead.

  f. Homework (5–10 minutes). Put the transparency of the sample homework contract (Figure 17-11) on the overhead, and hand each family a homework contract form (Exhibit 17-1) for Session 1. Have them choose one of the rules of communication to practice during the week. Explain the example and how the contract works. Explain that two copies of the contract are to be completed and signed by all family members and the group leader. One copy will stay with the leader and one should be taken home and left in a conspicuous place to remind everyone of their contract. Thank the families for attending.

2. Session 2: Communication Skills

  • Objectives

    a. To practice communications skills derived from the basic rules taught in Session 1

    b. To introduce sender and listener skills

    c. To demonstrate the importance of nonverbal communication

  • Materials

    a. Overhead projector and screen, transparencies of communication rules (Figures 17-9 and 17-10), transparencies of listener/

Figure 17-9 Communication Rules: Transparency 1

The message sent is not always the message received.

Figure 17-10 Communication Rules: Transparency 2

Communication has two levels - what we say and how we say it.

Figure 17-11 Transparency of Sample Homework Contract

Exhibit 17-1 Homework Contract

We have learned two communication rules:
1. The message sent is not always the message received.
2. Make sure words and actions go together.
In order to practice rule #___ (choose one), we will each do the following:
_____
_____
_____

If we successfully complete our goal, we will reward ourselves with:
_____
_____

Signed:
_____
_____
_____
_____
_____
_____

_____
Group Leader

sender skills (Figures 17-12, 17-13, and 17-14), two gossip stories (Exhibit 17-2), one copy of a role play (Exhibit 17-3), a "Noisy Nerf" football (one ball per family), and a copy of the Communication Steeplechase Game (Figure 17-15) (one per family).

- Procedures
  a. Review (5 minutes)
     (1) Place the communication rule transparencies from Session 1 (Figures 17-9 and 17-10) one at a time on the overhead projector. Ask the children in the group to state the communication rules depicted on each. Ask why the rules are important and what happens when family members do not follow them.
     (2) Ask the group if they completed the homework assignment. If the families successfully completed the homework, have the family members say what they did and what the exercise was like. If families had difficulty, ask which parts were difficult.
  b. Warm-up exercise (10 minutes)
     (1) Send all of the fathers out of the room except for one volunteer. Read to the volunteer Gossip Story 1 (Exhibit 17-2). Call in one of the other fathers and have the first father tell the story to the second father. The second father cannot ask questions. Have the first father return and sit down with his family. Call in a third father and have the second father tell him the story. Repeat this process until all the fathers have heard the story. Have the last father tell the story to the entire group. Next, read the original story to the group and compare it with the story told by the last father.
     (2) Ask one child from each family to go outside. Repeat the above exercise, using Gossip Story 2 (Exhibit 17-2). This time, allow the child being told the story to ask questions of the child telling the story. You can help each child ask questions, for example, by saying "That's pretty complicated. You can ask questions about the story so you are sure you heard it all."
  c. Discussion of listener and sender skills (10 minutes)
     (1) Explain that you want to talk first about what the fathers did, then about what the children did.
         (a) Ask the fathers if the storytelling was easy or hard. Ask them what made the storytelling hard. What made it easy? Was it always clear what they were being

Exhibit 17-2 Two Gossip Stories

Gossip Story 1

A 21-year-old man in a leather jacket and blue jeans rode his Yamaha motorcycle to the forest to take a walk. The forest was filled with oak trees and pine trees. He had to cross a small stream and got his feet wet. After a few minutes, he saw squirrels and rabbits scurrying for cover because it was beginning to rain. He found a small cave to crawl into for protection. He waited for the rain to stop and then continued to walk. When he was deep in the forest, a brown bear and two baby cubs appeared from behind a pine tree. The man stood very still, pretending to be a bush. The bears came up and sniffed him. Just when he thought they would eat him, one baby cub gave him a big kiss on the face and all three bears strolled away.

Gossip Story 2

A boy named Ralph who was seven years old and a girl named Cindy who was six years old lived next door to each other. They were the best of friends. One day, Cindy's parents invited Ralph to go to a lake with their family. They drove to a large lake. Cindy's father went fishing and caught six fish. Cindy's mother stayed on the shore to get a suntan. Cindy and Ralph went exploring. They saw lots of trash and decided to help the lake look prettier. They gathered up cans, candy bar wrappers, and other trash. A woman saw them cleaning up the lake and asked Cindy's mother if she could buy the children ice cream cones. Cindy's mother said it was okay, and Ralph and Cindy had a treat.

---

told? Was it difficult to tell the story clearly? Did it take work? Then ask the mothers how the first story ended up so differently from the original.

(b) Ask the children if the storytelling was easy or hard. What made it hard? What made it easy? Do they think it was easier because they could ask questions?

Point out that asking questions or "checking out" helped get the story right. The dads didn't get to check out, and their story lost a lot of meaning.

(2) Points to emphasize

(a) It is not easy to be effective as a sender and listener. It takes work.

(b) In the exercise, the message sent was not the same as the message received. This was not done intentionally; it occurs naturally in everyday communication. No matter how hard we try, the original message often gets lost.

(c) Neither the sender nor listener is to blame for miscommunication; both tried to make sure the message was clear.

(d) Asking questions or "checking it out" helps to get a message right. Remind the group of the Tinker Toy exercise in Session 1. When the family members could ask the mother questions, building the Tinker Toy structure was easier and it looked more like that of the leaders.

d. Minilecture: Listener Skills (10 minutes)

(1) Say to the group, "We are going to learn some specific sender and listener skills that you can practice at home. I have my friend 'Noisy Nerf' here tonight, and he is going to help us learn communication skills. The first is a listener skill called *paraphrasing* (show Figure 17-12 transparency). I'm going to make a statement and then throw Noisy Nerf at someone, and they have to repeat back in their own words what I said. I will let you know if you are accurate when you throw 'Noisy Nerf' back to me. Okay, here goes."

(a) "I surely enjoy winter. I like to ride in a snowmobile and to cross-country ski." (Throw the Noisy Nerf to a mother in the group. If she paraphrases well, have

Figure 17-12 Gossip Story: Transparency 1

Paraphrasing—
reflecting back
the message

her throw the ball back. If not, repeat the statement
and have her try again.)

(b) "I am looking forward to fall. The trees turn such a
pretty color, and the air feels so good." (Throw the
Noisy Nerf to a father this time; repeat as above.)

(c) "I like to watch Muppets® on TV because Miss Piggy®
is so funny." (Throw Noisy Nerf to a child and repeat
as above.)

(2)   Say to the group, "Our second skill is also a listener skill.
It is called *checking out* (show Figure 17-13 transparency). It is used to help someone see if they understand
what the sender means, thinks, and feels. This is difficult,
so we will practice it. First, let me demonstrate." Ask a
mother to come up front and role play (use Exhibit 17-3).

(3)   Summarize by saying, "I asked the mother several questions so that I would know what she thought, felt, and
meant. This took more time than if I had just assumed I
knew what she meant, but it helped me understand her a
lot better, and I'll bet it also helped her feel more understood and cared about."

Figure 17-13 Gossip Story: Transparency 2

Exhibit 17-3 A Role Play

Mother:	I am upset, I try to be a good mother, but don't always do a good job.
Leader ("checking out" what she means, thinks, and feels): Are you saying that you try hard but don't always measure up to what you would like to be?	
Mother:	Yes. I don't always measure up to my standards or the standards of my husband.
Leader:	Sounds as if you are discouraged and disappointed in yourself.
Mother:	Well, yes, I'm not very happy with myself.
Leader:	Anything else you mean by your first statement that we haven't covered?
Mother:	No, that covers it.

    e.   Exercise (10 minutes). Pass out one ball to each family. Explain that now they will play a game of checking out and paraphrasing. Give the ball to the father. Ask him to make a statement about himself, and then throw the ball to another family member and say "paraphrase" or "check out." The member receiving the ball is to either paraphrase or go through the checking-out process described above. Once that member has successfully completed the task, the member makes a statement and throws the ball to another family member. Go around to each family and help the members with the skills.

    f.   Minilecture: Sender skills (5 minutes)

        (1)   Explain to the participants that they will now learn one last skill: a sender skill. Tell the group the following: "A sender should not overwhelm a listener (show the Figure 17-14 transparency). The sender should take care to not say too much at one time. The sender should give the listener time to think about what the sender has said. If a sender says too much at one time, the listener may get lost and not listen."

        (2)   Provide the following example (read or paraphrase very quickly):

> Last night I had a great time. John and I went to see a movie. Well, before we went we picked up Jim and Randy, and they were excited. They had been to a basketball game, and their team won. I thought it was great. Then we went to Baskin-Robbins® and talked. This guy was terrific. He was handsome and intelligent. He tried to warn a group of people that these other guys were going to hurt them unless they went to this one guy and paid them. Well, they didn't believe him because the guy didn't really want to be paid: he was

Figure 17-14 Transparency on Overwhelming the Listener

trying to go to this other guy to convince them that he should convince the other group to go see the guy!

(3)   Ask the group, "Are you confused? Me too! What was wrong?" Let the participants explain how they got lost with so much information.

g.   Summary. Explain that the participants have learned three important communication skills. Ask what they are. Show the transparencies on paraphrasing and checking out (Figures 17-12 and 17-13). Finally, remind them that they should not overwhelm the listener with too much information (see Figure 17-14 transparency).

h.   Homework. Explain the homework assignment as follows: "The homework assignment for this week is the game of communication steeplechase. (Hand out copies of the Figure 17-15 game.) The assignment is to play the game once during the next week. Each person is to have a playing piece. Roll the dice and move as many spaces as it says. If you land on a space with instructions, do as instructed. Some of the instructions let you know what communication will help you move ahead or cause you

Figure 17-15 Communication Steeplechase Game

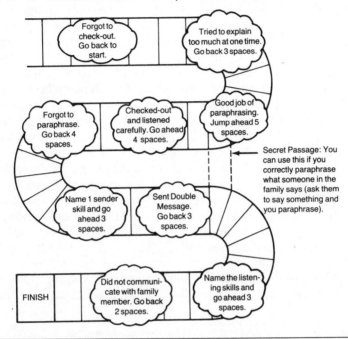

to go backward. In these cases, you do not have to do anything but be aware of the impact of different communication skills and rules. Other instructions require you to do something in order to move ahead. The first to finish wins.

3. Session 3: Self-Disclosure (Part 1)
   - Objective
     a. To facilitate self-disclosure between family members.
   - Materials
     a. Transparencies on listener/sender skills (Figures 17-12, 17-13, and 17-14), two scripts (Exhibit 17-4) (two per family), over-head projector, blank transparencies and marking pen, roll of toilet tissue, a handout on self-disclosure (Exhibit 17-5), and a homework handout (Exhibit 17-6).
   - Procedures
     a. Review (10 minutes)
        (1) Ask the families about the homework game from last week. Did they enjoy playing it? Did they practice any of the skills throughout the week?

(2)   Hand each family copies of two role play scripts (Exhibit 17-4). Ask the families to choose two members to play the roles in the first script. (Children can take the part of a mother or father.) When all the families have completed the first role play, ask what is wrong with the way the two people talk to each other? Cover the following points: they interrupt each other, they do not "check out," they are not very patient and understanding, and they overwhelm the listener. Now ask the family to read Role Play 2, with two family members playing the roles. When they have finished, ask them how the second role play is different from the first. What did the people do right? What did they do that was good communication? Cover the following points: they "checked out" meaning, they seemed to care about each other's interests, they talked about feelings rather than acted them out, and they listened to each other.

Exhibit 17-4 Two Scripts for Communication Role Playing

Role Play 1

Mother:	What did you think of our homework game?
Child:	I thought it was goofy! I didn't win, and Joey cheated. Besides I think I communicate real well. Dad needs to listen better.
Mother:	Oh, you never like anything. You are always . . . .
Child (interrupting):	I like lots of things. I just didn't . . . .
Mother (interrupting):	You are a grouch!

Role Play 2

Mother:	Hi Honey. Are you hungry?
Father:	Sure am. What's for dinner?
Mother:	Chopped steak.
Father:	Sounds good! Where is the newspaper?
Mother:	I put it by your chair.
Father:	It is difficult for me to find it when you put it under the cushion. How about leaving it on the table after you read it?
Mother:	Sorry. I just tried to make the house look neater. There is an interesting article about that fire downtown last week.
Father:	Sounds as if you are really interested in that.
Mother:	It was a building my father used to have his office in.
Father:	I didn't know that. How long was he there?
Mother:	How about if I tell you about it over dinner? You look tired, are you?
Father:	Yea, I think I could get real grouchy, too.
Mother:	Oh, oh. Hard day at the office.
Father:	Grrrrrrrr!

b. Minilecture: Introduction to self-disclosure (3–5 minutes)

    (1)   Say to the group, "Thanks for your help with the role plays. There are a great many communication skills, as you can tell from this exercise and our discussion. Tonight, we will use the communication skills we have learned to practice a different skill—self-disclosure. Self-disclosure means to share important things about ourselves with others. This includes thoughts, feelings, experiences we have had, or other things that are important to us. In order to share or self-disclose, family members have to trust each other, care about each other, and be supportive. Also, they must use good communication skills and value the other person, even if they disagree. These make self-disclosure easier."

    (2)   Ask, "Why do you suppose self-disclosure is important in a family?" Let the family members come up with ideas.

c. Family exercise (5 minutes)

    (1)   Explain that you will call out two words. The family members must decide which word they are most like. If they think they are most like the first word, they should walk to the right side of the room. If they think they are most like the second word, they should walk to the left side of the room. If they cannot decide which of the two words they are most like, they should stand in the middle of the room.

    (2)   Say, " For example, if you are most like RED, go to this side (right) of the room. If you are most like GREEN (the paired word) go to that side (left) of the room. If you cannot decide, stand here (middle)." Read the following paired words; allow everyone enough time to walk to their choice of sides and stand for a few seconds.

RED	GREEN
DOG	CAT
STEAK	PIZZA
WORK	PLAY
TELEVISION	BOOKS
SANTA CLAUS	SCROOGE
SUMMER	WINTER
DICK TRACY	SUPERMAN
DILL PICKLE	POPSICLE
BEAR	TIGER

Then ask everyone to return to their seats.

d. Discussion (5 minutes). Explain that they have just self-disclosed. They have shared with everyone some things about themselves. Ask the family members the following questions to spark a discussion: Did you learn anything about yourself? Were you surprised at some of the choices of other family members?

e. Minilecture and exercise (30 minutes)

    (1) Minilecture. Explain that we are all different in how we see ourselves and in what we like. This does not make one family member right and another wrong—we are just different. The first guideline of self-disclosure is that we must allow others to feel and to think as they wish. We cannot and should not try to change their feelings or thoughts. Write Guideline 1 on a Transparency: Respect and accept another person's self-disclosure.

    (2) Family exercise. Pass around the roll of bathroom tissue. Indicate that each square, or sheet, will represent some description of themselves. Ask the family members to take as many sheets as they think they will need. Instruct them to separate them into squares. For each tissue square they have, ask them to choose one word that describes themselves. They are to tell their family one word for each square, then drop the tissue on the floor. Give them an example: After all members have taken sheets, tear off three or four sheets of tissue and say a word for each square that describes you as a leader. Have each family do the exercise.

    (3) Discussion. Ask the families the following questions: Was it difficult to think of words to describe yourself? Why do you think this is true? What types of words were most difficult to talk about? What did you learn about other family members? Allow the family members to discuss their answers within their families.

    (4) Minilecture. Say to the group, "It isn't easy to talk about ourselves. It makes us uncomfortable sometimes, but it helps others understand us. Thus, the Guideline 2 of self-disclosure is that we must be willing to risk." Write Guideline 2 on the transparency: "The final guideline is to let others volunteer their self-disclosure. It is not fair to require someone to share; they should do it only when they want to." Write Guideline 3 on a transparency.

(5) Family exercise. Hand out copies of the self-disclosure questions (Exhibit 17-5). The family members should share the reading of the questions. Begin with Question Unit 1; have all members answer the questions. Then go to Units 2 and 3. When the families have had enough time, call for order.

(6) Discussion. Ask the families to tell you what kinds of feelings they experienced. What was easy to talk about? What was difficult to talk about? What do other family members do that make it easier to share with them?

f. Summary. Ask the group to remember the three guidelines of self-disclosure. Tell them that you will be very interested to hear how the guidelines work for them. Show transparency and review: (1) respect and accept, (2) risk, and (3) volunteer.

g. Homework. The homework for this week is to practice self-disclosure. Hand out a list of questions for the family to answer (Exhibit 17-6). Suggest to them that at one time during the week, maybe at dinner, they should all share their answers to the questions on the sheet.

4. Session 4: Self-Disclosure (Part 2)
   • Objective
     a. To continue the focus on self-disclosure that began with Session 3 and to provide additional opportunity for in-depth self-disclosure.

Exhibit 17-5 Self-Disclosure Questions

Unit 1:
   1. What type of music do you really like?
   2. Where would you like to go for a vacation if you could go any place in the world?
   3. What is your favorite season of the year and why?
   4. What do you like to eat?

Unit 2:
   1. If you could be any kind of animal, which one would you be? Why?
   2. What do you like to daydream about?
   3. Describe three things for which you are very thankful.
   4. What is the worst habit you have?

Unit 3:
   1. What do you most like to do with your family?
   2. Give one word to describe each family member.
   3. Finish the sentence, My family is special because _____.

Exhibit 17-6 Homework Assignment

Instructions: Some time during the week, have each family member share with the whole family the answers to the following questions. Remember the rules of self-disclosure: (1) Respect and accept the self-disclosure of others. (2) Be willing to risk. (3) Self-disclosure is voluntary; you do not have to answer a question if you do not wish to do so.

  1. Describe your ideal breakfast, lunch, and dinner.
  2. How do you like to spend your spare time?
  3. What is your favorite sport and why?
  4. Who do you admire and why?
  5. What do you like most about yourself?
  6. What is something that really excites you?

- Materials
  a. Overhead projector, blank transparencies and marker, the transparencies from session three, a set of cards for each family with feelings printed on each (Exhibit 17-7), magazines with pictures, glue (one bottle per family), crayons, colored paper, paperbacks (one per person), a collage on a paper bag representing something about the leader, a homework handout for each member (Exhibit 17-8).
- Procedures
  a. Review (5 minutes)
     (1) Remind the participants that last week they learned about self-disclosure. Ask them to repeat the rules of self-disclosure. Show the transparencies from Session 3 on respect and acceptance, willingness to risk, and voluntary self-disclosure.
     (2) Ask how they did with the homework assignment. Ask the families to describe their experiences with self-disclosure.
  b. Family exercises
     (1) Pass out a set of cards to each family (Exhibit 17-7). Place them face down. Then say to the group: "When I say go, each member in turn draws a card and acts out the feeling printed on the card while everyone else tries to guess the feeling. If you have trouble reading your card to know what to do, raise your hand and I will help. Keep taking turns until all the cards are gone. This is like the game of charades. The feelings are all fairly common; we express

Exhibit 17-7 Feelings

Cards for the Family Exercise on Feelings	
ANGRY	MEAN
SAD	HAPPY
SHY	GROUCHY
CONTENT	BORED
PROUD	EXCITED

them or see them expressed frequently, don't we?" (10 minutes)

(2) Then say, "I want each family member to choose a TV or movie star or a book character that that person would like to be. Tell your family who you have chosen and why. Who do you want to be like and for what reasons?" (5 minutes)

(3) Finally, say the following: "We are practicing self-disclosure. Now I have one last exercise that will help you understand each other better. Everyone is to use these magazines, colored papers, crayons, and glue to develop a collage on a paper bag. Do you know what a collage is? It is a group of pictures or designs. Here is an example of a collage. (show leader's collage) This collage shows several things that are important to me. (For example point out various things about the collage and self-disclose about it. The leader should have developed a good collage as a model.) Using pictures and crayons, each of you will now develop a collage that represents you. After you are finished, show and explain the collage to the others in your family."

c. Summary. The past two weeks, the participants have shared a lot of themselves with others in their families. Self-disclosure has a lot of benefits. Ask the group to tell what they are. Allow time for the family members to respond voluntarily. If they have trouble, you may add some suggestions (it helps you feel closer, helps to understand each other, and so on). Ask them to leave their collages with the leaders for return to them at the next meeting.

d. Homework. This week the homework assignment is to say something nice to each family member at least once during the coming week. Pass out the assignment form (Exhibit 17-8) for each family member to fill out for the next meeting.

5. Session 5: Positive Reciprocity
   - Objective
     a. To increase the exchange of positive comments in the family.
   - Materials
     a. Collage bags from Session 4, the story "A Fuzzy Tale" (Steiner, 1974), crayons, 3″ × 5″ cards (at least ten per participant), fake fur strips (4″ × 8″), paper eyes (2 per person), glue (one bottle per family), tissues, needle and thread, and "warm fuzzies." To create the fuzzies, start with a piece of fake fur 10″ × 24″. Fold it in half (so it measures 10″ × 12″) and stitch the sides together. Stuff the interior with tissue and sew the final side closed. Glue on two large eyes. Then comb the fur so it lays flat.
   - Procedures
     a. Review. Discuss the exercise on self-disclosure and note that you hope it was fun and helpful. Ask for their homework assignments.

Exhibit 17-8 Homework Handout

Homework Assignment

Family Member's Name	Compliment I Gave Her/Him This Week
_____	_____
_____	_____
_____	_____
_____	_____
_____	_____

My Name _____

b. Minilecture: Positive comments (5 minutes). Announce the following: "Tonight we are going to talk about giving each other positive comments. It is good to have someone say something nice about us. But, it does not happen often enough. It is too easy to criticize, or to not pay attention to those things we like about each other. However, researchers have found that those families who are the healthiest psychologically frequently compliment each other. Last week you had the assignment to give each other compliments. How did you feel when someone paid you a compliment?"

c. Family exercise (15 minutes). Tell the group the following: "I am going to place your collages from last week up here in front of the room. Then I will pass around 3 × 5 cards and crayons. Each of you will need to take two cards for each member of your family. On each of the cards you are to write or draw two things you like about each family member, including yourself. For example, if you like yourself because you are friendly, on your card write "friendly" or draw a picture of yourself that shows you being friendly. If you like Mother because she is helpful, write "helpful," or draw a picture of her being helpful. After you have written or drawn two compliments for each member of your family, including yourself, place your cards in the collage bag of the person to whom the compliments belong. When everyone is finished, go get your own collage bag and read the cards. Share the compliments you received with the rest of your family. Maybe they will want to explain their compliments further."

d. Minilecture: Warm fuzzies (10 minutes). Explain that you have brought a friend to tonight's session (show your "warm fuzzy"). Then read "A Fuzzy Tale" (Steiner, 1974). Ask the participants to finish the story of the warm fuzzies. Ask them what a warm fuzzy would be in their homes (for example, when one member says another member looks handsome or pretty). Allow time for the participants to respond.

e. Family exercise (20 minutes). Say "So you will remember to give Warm Fuzzies, I want each of you to make a small, warm fuzzy like mine tonight. Take a piece of fur, a needle, thread and tissue and two eyes. Sew two sides of the fur together, stuff it with tissue and then sew it shut. Glue on two eyes . . . Okay, have fun!"

f. Homework. When the group finishes the discussion, give them the homework assignment. Ask them to take home their collage bags and several 3 × 5 cards. Instruct them to use the cards to make thank-you notes. Each person is to write one thank you note during the week, thanking someone in his or her family for something that person did.

6. Session 6: Cooperation
   • Objectives
   a. To teach the importance of cooperation between family members.
   b. To give the family a chance to see the importance of each member as an individual, yet as someone capable of contributing something special to the family.
   c. To close the program by emphasizing the importance of working as a family.
   • Materials
   a. One set of Tinker Toys per family, a Tinker Toy model (already made), old magazines, scissors, glue, and posterboard.
   • Procedures
   a. Review. Ask the group about the thank you notes from the previous week. Did everyone write them? How did they feel when they received them?
   b. Family exercise: Cooperation (20 minutes)
      (1) Show an object made with Tinker Toys. Have separate sets of Tinker Toys for each family and divide the individual parts among the family members. Each family member gets a different set of parts necessary to create a copy of the model; no other member of the family gets the same part. The goal of the exercise is for each family to make an exact likeness of the model.
      (2) Explain that the goal is to work together to copy the model, using the parts that each family member has. However, the individual family members do not have to help if they do not want to; they can give as many or as few of their own parts to the project as they wish.
      (3) Instruct the families that they are not to ask any other members to give up one of their parts for the project. Each member, if he or she chooses, is to freely give up the parts without being asked.
   c. Discussion (10 minutes)
      (1) Ask the group how the exercise went. How many were able to copy the model? Did it take long, and was it easy

or difficult to do? Who took charge and made sure the exercise was completed? Did any families have members who did not want to give up their parts? Who helped the most? What role did the children play in the exercise?

(2) Ask the participants how well they think they did in working together. Was it unusual for the family to work together in this way? Is it easy for the family to work together like this? What makes it easy or difficult to cooperate in this way?

(3) It might be helpful to write their comments and thoughts on the overhead or on newsprint—especially those that might help them to work together in the future.

d. Family exercise: Creating a collage (20 minutes)

(1) Explain that the goal of this exercise is to have the family members create a picture of what their family looks like. The picture, in the form of a collage, should describe how close the family is, who is closest to whom, what the family likes to do, and who is in charge of the family. The collage is to represent the whole family.

(2) Each family member is to pick out things from magazines to include in the collage. The members then are to come together and negotiate about what should be included in the collage. Each member must include something, but not everything a member wants in the collage need be included. Provide old magazines, scissors, glue, and posterboard for the families to use.

e. Discussion (10 minutes)

(1) Ask the group what they learned from doing the collage. Point out that all family members have pictures of what their family looks like; in fact, the pictures usually are different. Was anyone surprised by what another family member wanted to include in the collage? Did they have something they wanted to include but the rest of the family did not want it included? How did they decide what to include and what to leave out?

(2) Make the point that every family member contributes something different to the family picture and that this is what gives the family its charm and life.

(3) Make the point that, in order for a family to have a picture of itself, these different contributions must be integrated in some way. However, sometimes this integration is

difficult, and sometimes it is not possible to integrate all the contributions.

(4) Explain that it takes cooperation by all family members to develop and maintain a picture of the family. Some family members may even have to change a part of their own picture in order for the entire family to share a family picture. Finally, it should be remembered that family pictures change because family members change and the world they live in changes.

f. Summary. Thank the family members for their participation. Remind them that, in the past weeks, they have learned about communication, self-disclosure, complimenting and cooperating. Extend your best wishes to them in using these skills.

Chapter 18

Family Clustering for Growth and Development

Dorothy S. Becvar

The present program lasts 12 weeks, with weekly meetings of two to three hours each. Cofacilitators, preferably one male and one female, are recommended. The program is applicable to a variety of settings, including churches, schools, and community agencies.

The family clustering program described in this chapter is an expanded version of the model created by Margaret Sawin (1979) in 1970. One of this model's greatest assets is its flexibility, and hence adaptability. Though originally designed for use in a church setting, the family clustering model lends itself to implementation in a variety of secular settings with only minimum modification. Its specifically religious aspects are readily translated into a more general spirituality that is applicable to all human beings, regardless of their religious stance.

BACKGROUND

Family clustering is a developmental model of intergenerational experiential education for groups of four to six family units that contract to meet together over an extended period of time. The family units should vary in composition, including couples with no children, young children, children of various ages, or grown-up children; single-parent families; and families with grandparents and single adults. This provides a context for mutual support, for training in skills that facilitate relational living, and for sharing and celebrating individual and family beliefs together.

Family clustering is not a therapy model. It is best suited to families who are not experiencing serious dysfunction. It can be used as a means of enhancing a feeling of community among families in communities where isolated nuclear units are generally the rule. The particular needs of the target populations will shape the programming, the development of a curriculum, and the formulation of specific goals and objectives.

As an example, let us consider a church with a large congregation in which several families have expressed a desire or concern to explore a particular experiential area, such as anger or feelings in general, in some depth. Family clustering can respond to such a need in that it provides a model both for writing a curriculum that can be tailored to the concerns of the particular group and for creating a context of intimacy and trust, so that sharing, learning, and commitment to one another are fostered. In this case, the church benefits by having fulfilled the needs of some of its members in a manner consistent with its own goals of service to the community and enhancement of a community feeling.

Working with a group of families is the modality of choice to overcome the isolation of family units from each other or from various social institutions, for example, schools, with which better working relationships would benefit all parties. The whole family is included, in contrast to traditional models of education by peer group, thus providing a means of overcoming the so-called generation gap.

Churches are particularly well-suited to the use of family clustering in that they are the only institutions in our society that regularly include whole families among their members. In other contexts as well, as we begin to think in more ecological terms, the inclusion of the entire system seems a more useful way of working with both individuals and families.

PROGRAM DESCRIPTION

Basic Staff and Resource Needs

A family cluster program requires facilitators and a room large enough and comfortable enough for the group to relax and enjoy themselves. Although not essential, audiovisual resources—such as a record player, tape recorder, slide or movie projector, or a piano—might be helpful. Old newspapers or magazines, newsprint, paper, pencils, paint, crayons, chalk, magic markers, clay, scissors, glue, tape, and other art supplies can also be utilized to great advantage. Children's books and records on topics related to the concerns of the group, or to family life in general, make particularly good resources. A coffee urn for heating water, or instant coffee or soup, tea, milk, sugar, cups, and spoons may be provided where budgets allow. These basic resources are often available in church and other community settings. Additional resources may be provided by the sponsoring agency or by charging each family a minimal fee to cover costs.

General Objectives

The general objectives of family clustering are:

- to let each person know that they are unique and special
- to let each person know that they have personal values
- to let each person know that their values are rooted in their family of origin

Theoretical Bases

The theoretical and philosophical assumptions underlying family clustering include systems theory and family dynamics, group dynamics, humanistic and transpersonal psychology, experiential education, process theology, values clarification, and communication.

- *Systems theory and family dynamics.* The family is not only a group of individuals; it is also a system of related parts that must be understood in terms of the interaction of the whole. The family is one of many systems existing in the context of a larger social or cultural system or supra-system. A happy family is one in which happy things happen (Becvar & Becvar, 1982).
- *Group dynamics.* Group process can be very important in fostering human growth and development (Shaw, 1976). Both interfamily and intrafamily dynamics are operative in a family cluster.
- *Humanistic and transpersonal psychology.* The potential for and achievement of growth and change in terms of both individual and family development are fundamental assumptions of family clustering. Several theories of the stages of individual, cognitive, moral, marriage, and family development are implicit in these assumptions (see selected readings at the end of the book). As an education and enrichment model, family clustering provides a context for the facilitation of human growth and development.
- *Experiential education.* Education is most productive when understood as a process of "leading out" through a combination of experience and reflection (Groome, 1980). Its elements include reflecting on an experience by identifying a specific event, analyzing the event to deepen understanding, and then generalizing the meaning of the event so that it is available for future use (Sawin, 1979).
- *Process theology.* Belief processes are facilitated by an individual's experiences, and all of these experiences can be given a religious

(spiritual) interpretation. Sawin (1979) claims that the process of believing, sharing the meanings of that belief through words and behavior, and receiving feedback on behavior are ways to further growth in faith. She asserts that each person is on a faith pilgrimage, that sharing that journey is growth promoting for others, and that persons absorb and internalize the values of others who help them meet their needs. It is this process that constantly fashions a person's own value or belief system, from which evolves a behavioral stance.

- *Values clarification.* The family, as the primary unit of socialization, is the principle teacher of and influence upon value formation and clarification. A goal of family clustering is to make explicit the valuing process in the context of one's own and other families (see selected readings).

- *Communication.* As one cannot not communicate in some way, communication is the basis of interpersonal relationships. It also defines the nature of the relationships within the family system (Becvar & Becvar, 1982).

Measurement Techniques

In systems theory, change occurs in response to a change in context. Such change is facilitated when all members of a system experience a context that is different; a change in one member can have ramifications for the entire system. These elements define the context created by family clustering to achieve its goals and objectives.

In family clustering, change is measured by the following:

- Assessment of individual and family strengths by participants at the beginning and end of the cluster, using cognitive, affective, and behavioral measures in a paper and pencil questionnaire designed by the cofacilitators.

- Systematic observation, through review of video or audio tapes, of participation and commitment of members, as indicated by frequency and type of interaction, attendance, and willingness to assume leadership roles.

- Inventory of change, through interviews or pencil and paper questionnaires, of individuals and systems who interface with members before and after the family cluster.

Publicity

Families should be notified of the impending formation of a cluster at least one month prior to its initial meeting. The notification—including a brief description of the cluster and its purpose and the limitation on participants (25 to 30 people)—may be made by letter or by an announcement in a church bulletin, school newsletter, or agency brochure. Interested parties should be asked to contact the cofacilitators by a specific date.

Orientation Procedures

The cofacilitators should meet with interested family members in their own home to explain the details of the program and ascertain the family's level of commitment. Each member of the family must agree to attend all sessions; no one is excluded because of age.

An effort should be made to include several generations, as well as single individuals and nontraditional, single-parent families. The aim should be to bring together a group of individuals and families who will respond well to one another. The cofacilitators must make judgments about reasonable compatibility.

When the cluster members have been selected, each family member is asked to sign (an X for small children) a contract that commits that member to meet for the 12 weeks at a specified time and place. This contract signifies membership in the family cluster. The signing might take place either in the family's home or in the presence of the whole group at a preliminary meeting. Those families that are not selected should be so notified and informed of future opportunities for family clustering.

Forming the Group

Family clustering should take place in a room, usually at the sponsoring agency, that has a "homey" feeling, with the potential for hanging contracts and other "creations" on the walls as the program proceeds. The room should have tables and chairs, so that the group may eat together as one large family. Other furnishings should include a rug and cushions for floor sitting and, if possible, some couches or easy chairs for older folk. There should not be undue concern about neatness, since the room is to be lived in, permitting family activities and celebrations that are often distinctly untidy.

Meeting time is optional, although it is preferable to meet around either the lunch or dinner hour, as sharing a meal together can be a powerfully binding experience. As noted, the meetings are held once a week and should last from two to three hours, depending upon whether or not a meal is included. Punctuality in beginning and ending on time are important aspects of the cluster members' commitment to one another.

Involvement of Cofacilitators

The cofacilitators have primary responsibility for formation of the cluster and for curriculum preparation in response to the needs and desires of the members and sponsoring agency. Once the basic curriculum has been designed, they will need to schedule time at least once a week for program planning prior to each session. The coleaders should also spend a period of time debriefing one another and sharing reactions following each session.

It is best not to plan in more than general outline form very far in advance, since the ability to respond to evolving needs and the continuing process of contracting are important aspects of family clustering.The coleaders, acting as facilitators at all sessions, should encourage leadership among members of the group as it begins to emerge.

PROGRAM OUTLINE

As the family cluster program proceeds, there is an increase in mutual understanding and regard for one another, as the members begin to think of themselves as one large family. With growing familiarity and trust come greater risk-taking, sharing, and learning, as the individuals and families support each other on their respective faith or growth journeys. The cofacilitators facilitate this process in their roles as parental models for the cluster family.

Specific Objectives

The following four specific objectives apply to each session in the family cluster program:

1. to increase individual and family self-esteem
2. to increase understanding of the self in the context of the family system
3. to increase understanding of the family in the context of other family systems
4. to learn how to achieve growth consistent with the goals and objectives contracted by the cluster at its inception

Sessions

The following is an outline for a cluster that is scheduled to take place on 12 consecutive Sunday evenings from 4:00 to 7:00 P.M. Each family is to bring enough sandwiches for its own members as well as something to share with the rest of the group (cookies, chips, condiments). Milk, coffee, tea, and soup are to be provided by the sponsoring agency. The cluster members will share the tasks of meal preparation and cleanup in whatever manner is agreed upon in the opening session.

3:45-4:00 P.M.	Drifting in and greeting exercise
4:00-4:15 P.M.	Opening ritual: Welcome, prayer, meditation, song, and so on
4:15-4:30 P.M.	Icebreaker or warm-up exercise
4:30-4:45 P.M.	Introduction of topic and presentation of agenda: Discussion, questions and answers
4:45-5:15 P.M.	Theme activity
5:15-5:45 P.M.	Supper: Grace, socializing, cleanup
5:45-6:15 P.M.	Family Council Meeting: Housekeeping details, family business
6:15-6:30 P.M.	Playtime or freetime
6:30-6:50 P.M.	Reflections on the activities of the day
6:50-7:00 P.M.	Closing ritual: Prayer, meditation, song, goodbyes

Although it is often difficult to judge time accurately, it is important that the cofacilitators stick to their agenda schedule as closely as possible and that each session begin and end on time. Members must recognize their obligation to the group in terms of attendance and punctuality as part of the process of commitment and mutual respect.

Each session should be given a title, and the activities and objectives should be planned accordingly. An agenda for each session, clearly printed on a blackboard or large sheet of newsprint, should be introduced at the beginning of each cluster session. Sessions 1, 2, and 3 should focus on inclusion activities, building trust, and an explanation of the dynamics of family clustering. Contracting about the general direction and specific details of the course that the members wish the cluster to take occupies a large portion of time in these early sessions.

Sessions 4 to 11 should focus on the specific areas of interest to the cluster, using a variety of experiential activities to introduce and explore topics. The activities may include role playing, discussions in large and small groups, task performance, creative arts, movies, slides, storytelling, and so on.

Equipment and materials for each session will vary according to the curriculum design. The cofacilitators must plan how they will set up each session and should discuss member assistance with the group as the need arises. They must also decide in advance who will be responsible for which activity and the role that each member is to take in relationship to the others. Modeling by the facilitators is an important element in the educational process; thus it is essential that the cofacilitators have a clearly defined and compatible working relationship.

Questionnaires to collect before and after data should be administered in the first and last sessions, perhaps during family council meetings. The final session should be focused on aspects of termination, with discussions and activities dealing with separation and closure. Plans might also be made at that time for a "family reunion" and follow-up survey at some future date.

FACILITATOR TRAINING AND MODEL EVALUATION

According to the model's originator, "any person who wishes to train others for the task of Family Cluster leadership must be cognizant of the following:

- "the dynamics of leading family growth groups;
- "the knowledge and skills important in leading family growth groups;
- "the influence of one's family of origin in relating to families;
- "ways to divide the knowledge and skills into training components;
- "the kind of staff needed and the necessary skills;
- "the dynamics of guiding persons-in-training through the training components" (Sawin, 1979, p. 118).

Family Clustering, Inc., runs training laboratories and provides a variety of resources and information for training facilitators and forming clusters in various settings. Those interested should address inquiries to P.O. Box 18074, Rochester, New York, 14618.

The present author became a cluster leader by coleading several clusters with a trained leader. She then attended a weekend training workshop conducted by Margaret Sawin. Since that time, she has co-led clusters, acted as consultant on family clustering for community agencies such as the YMCA and schools, and has taught graduate courses using the cluster model—to learn about family clustering and how to adapt it and build other models for individual, marriage, and family development and enrichment. It is her belief that, having once learned the basic skills, experience is the best teacher. Correspondence should be addressed to the St. Louis Family Institute, 7349 Dale Avenue, St. Louis, Missouri, 63117.

Family clustering in a variety of forms has been widely implemented throughout the United States, Canada, Australia, and other foreign countries during the past decade. However, like many other models of marriage and family education and enrichment that have suffered from a scarcity of research (Hof & Miller, 1981), little empirical data have been reported on the outcomes of cluster programs. Those of us who endorse the model are thus challenged to design suitable methods of measurement and to make public the results of our findings.

Part VI

Structured Family Facilitation Programs: Treatment

Chapter 19

Finding Personal Strengths in Adjusting to Divorce*

Margaret H. Hoopes

This treatment program requires ten weeks to administer: the first week for orientation meetings and preassessment, the next eight weeks for the structured treatment, and a final week for the collection of postassessment data. Follow-up data should be collected three to six months later. Each session, lasting two hours, should be held in a private, comfortable room that is big enough to accommodate six to eight persons and two cofacilitators, male and female.

OBJECTIVES

The treatment is designed to help men and women cope with the stress of divorce or separation, caused either by estrangement or death. The program's general goals are to teach people (1) to ask for and give support, (2) to be committed to the group and its purposes, (3) to learn and apply a problem-solving model, and (4) to apply their personal strengths to each of the other three objectives. It should be noted that some divorced people are not ready for this kind of group experience.

The facilitators explain the program to interested people in an orientation meeting where the SCL-90 and the Fisher Divorce Adjustment Scale are administered (see Appendix B for descriptions of these instruments). If it is impossible for people to attend a group meeting for orientation, the same information should be given and data collected in an individual session. These instruments and the peoples' responses to the description

---

*This treatment appears in a shortened version with only the second phase in its entirety. The reader may secure a complete treatment by following the instructions in the Preface or by referring to the selected readings and references (Steele, Vogel-Moline).

of the program provide enough information for the therapists to select the participants. The same instruments can be used as preoutcome and post-outcome measures. A number of other instruments have been used with this treatment program, including T-JTA, DACL, self-concept measures, and open-ended questionnaires (Vogel-Moline, 1979). (See Appendix B for descriptions.) Therapists can select appropriate instruments and procedures of their own choosing, or they can replicate the project as described by Vogel-Moline (1979) and Feinauer (1980).

Research and Evaluation

This program has been used extensively in a variety of clinical settings. It has been found to be significantly effective in decreasing depression (.01), as measured by the Depression Adjective Check-List (DACL); in increasing the level of self-esteem (social worth and social competence) (.05), as measured by the Rosenberg Scale and a modified version of the Osgood Semantic Differential (Vogel-Moline, 1979); and in decreasing nervousness (.01), depression (.05), hostility (.05), subjectivity (.02), inhibition (.006), submissiveness (.02), and domination (.03), as measured by the Taylor Johnson Temperament Analysis (T-JTA) (Feinauer, 1980). Over a 15-month period, the experimental group continued to improve significantly or maintained improvement in their level of depression as measured by the DACL and in all but the nervous/composed trait measure on the T-JTA (Steele, 1981).

PROGRAM DESCRIPTION

Instructions for Cofacilitators

The instructions for this structured group treatment program for single people who are adjusting to separation through death or divorce are documented to facilitate treatment objectives. The following guidelines will help facilitators effectively administer the treatment:

- Read the instructions until the procedures are very familiar.
- Participate in training sessions until you are at ease with the concepts and appropriate phases.
- Learn and practice supportive behaviors in the training sessions.
- Map out a plan for each session with your cotherapist. Decide (1) who will do what, (2) how to keep to the time limit, (3) what to do to help your partner and (4) what to expect from your partner.

- During the training sessions, conceptualize relevant information in order to understand the psychological dynamics of separation.

Before each session the cofacilitators should arrive early and prepare the room. They should procure audio tapes from the project leader and tape each session.

Procedures

The following general instructions should guide the cofacilitators:

- Follow the order given in the treatment.
- Watch the clock. The sessions are to be finished within two hours, and the members should not be dismissed less than ten minutes before that time. It is important that all groups have approximately the same amount of time together.
- Tape all sessions (optional). Be sure the recorder is working and the tape is turned over.
- Contact absent members by phone the day after the group meeting.

The treatment is provided in the following phases:

- Phase 1: Support. This phase of the treatment is included in the first session and is then emphasized in every session. The phase's underlying value is the theme that divorced, separated, or widowed persons have lost their support system and the group is going to provide that support for them while, at the same time, teaching them how to develop their own support system outside the group. The major concept that the members learn is that, in order to feel support in one's environment, one must learn how to give, receive, and ask for support. These principles are taught and practiced in the group.
- Phase 2: Problem solving. This phase extends from Sessions 2 through 5. In this phase of the treatment, the members learn a method of problem solving. One of the effects of divorce or separation is that the persons find it difficult to solve the accompanying problems produced by the divorce or separation. The process of problem solving introduced in this phase is as follows: (1) Specify what the problem is. (2) Discuss what has been done in the past to solve the problem. (3) Discuss how the person would like things to be. (4) Present solutions to the problem. (5) Allow the person to evaluate each solution (disadvantages and advantages). (6) Encourage the person to decide

which solution will best solve the problem. (7) Ask for verbal commitment from the person to act upon the solution(s) chosen to solve the problem. The ideas about support presented in Session 1 are utilized in this phase; that is, the members ask, give, and receive support from one another.

- Phase 3: Strengths. In Sessions 6 through 8, the group members learn how to develop an understanding of their personal strengths to help them in the period following the divorce, death, or separation. The members are helped by other group members to become aware of their strengths. If there are personal weaknesses they wish to overcome, they can discuss them with the group and receive suggestions to overcome them. However, the main focus of this phase is on the positive—to help the members realize that they have the potential to solve their problems and overcome their weaknesses.

Each of these phases builds upon the other phases, with the goal of enabling the group members to learn ways of dealing with their problems and of gaining support in their environment. Also, the members become aware of their potential as self-sufficient beings, able to help themselves and others. These three phases are particularly important for individuals who are going through separation from a spouse because of death or divorce.

PROGRAM OUTLINE

The following outline describes some of the content, procedures, and materials used in each program session:

1. Session 1: Instructions, Expectations, and Commitments
   - Objectives
     a. To have the participants introduce themselves, discuss their expectations, and make commitments to the group and its goals.
   - Materials
     a. Tape recorders (optional)
   - Activities
     a. Introductions (35 minutes). Give the participants an opportunity to introduce and talk about themselves. Give a sample introduction that includes interaction guidelines. Then have the members introduce themselves, using their first names only.

Use whatever method you wish, but, by the time you finish, each participant should know everyone else's name.

b. Use of tape recorders (1 minute): Explain to the group that the tape recorders (if used) are there to help the facilitators, and assure them that confidentiality will be honored.

c. Expectations of participants (10 minutes): Discuss the group process and the major aspect of the treatment, the support system, thereby confirming or disconfirming the expectations of the participants. Define support and discuss the concept.

d. Commitment (50 minutes).

(1) The objective of this exercise is to commit each participant to the group and its goals. Before the commitment process, discuss the activities that will help to develop support systems and to which members will later commit themselves. For example, discuss what will help or hinder them from attending each session; proposing solutions to problems; sharing experiences; giving support by being honest, empathic, and responsible; expressing gratitude or acknowledging support received; identifying a meaningful problem; and asking for the kind of help needed.

(2) After the discussion, *get a detailed personal commitment from each person*. That is, ask each person, one at a time, a series of questions pertaining to the above activities. Some of the participants may not be able to commit themselves wholeheartedly. Their feelings of inadequacy may inhibit them, and they may decide that the group is not for them. Respond appropriately, but make sure that everyone in the group has had an opportunity to make a commitment. Reinforce any commitment they make, and redefine the lack of commitment in a positive manner, for example, by saying "Your ability to be honest with us is an indication of strength you have, which will be important to all of us." Do not confront persons who are resistant. Finally, you, as cofacilitators, should make your commitment to the group.

e. Challenge (10 minutes). Invite the participants to practice the group rules with other people during the week, for example, by refraining from talking about other people in a blaming way, by being honest and responsible, and so on. Indicate that several of them will talk about their problems at the next session. Tell them that in succeeding sessions the group will learn a process of determining explicit solutions for problems. Encourage each person to be supportive in some way to at least one person during the week.

2. Sessions 2 to 5: Problem solving
   • Objectives
     a. To model supportive behaviors.
     b. To reinforce supportive behavior by the participants in and outside the group.
     c. To learn and practice problem-solving skills.
   • Activities
     a. Greetings (3 minutes): Say hello to everyone individually by name; and in some way, verbally or nonverbally, let them know that you are glad to see them back. Reinforce upon their minds how important their attendance is.
     b. Review (10 minutes): Review the importance of a support system. Ask the group members what impressions they have from last week. Emphasize that a support system includes a lot of people and that they will be able to build support systems by both giving and asking for support. Remind them that the small group, like the one they are now in, provides an opportunity for them to ask and give support. Check to see if any of them are aware of adding to their outside support system in the past week by asking for or giving support in some way.
     c. Types of supportive behavior. Make the participants aware of the various types of nonverbal and verbal supportive behavior that they can use to create support systems (see Exhibit 19-1).
     d. Discussion. Discuss the following with the group: The facilitators and group members are very similar in the things they can do to be supportive to other group members. Emphasize that the members will get better at doing the things they presently see a therapist doing. Following are some of the things that both therapists and group members can do to be supportive:
        (1) Listen carefully.
        (2) Be responsible for your own understanding of the problem. This means that, if you do not understand, you should ask for information or make clarifying statements that can be checked out by the person who is telling you something or explaining a problem. (In this way, the therapist can teach responsible behavior to the group.)
        (3) If you sense that the person who has been talking has risked something, be sure to point this out and compli-

Exhibit 19-1 Types of Supportive Behavior

Nonverbal

Touching:	Touching in a positive, supportive, empathic, and understanding way
Head nodding:	Recognizing, agreeing with, relating to, listening to the other person(s)
"Um hum:"	Relating to or understanding what is being said
Smiling:	Indicating warmth and acceptance of the person(s) receiving the smile
Tears:	Weeping with or in response to another person because of feelings of empathy and understanding
Voice tone:	Being aware of the change in the general quality of the voice in response to support toward a group member
Body position open:	Becoming aware of the open position of arms, of legs not being crossed, or of legs loosely crossed, in relation to acceptance of an individual (possibly acceptance of feedback)
Proximity close:	Being aware of the close physical distance between persons (20 inches or less)
Hugging:	Placing arms around another person and applying pressure with the arms
Leaning forward:	Reclining of the body torso toward the group or individual
Finger snapping:	Indicating agreement or support

Verbal

Concern:	Using statements that express care, such as, "I like you," "I accept you," or, "I am glad to be in this group with you"
Confrontation:	One person verbalizing two sets of incongruent behavior of another (must manifest helpfulness and non-attacking in intent)—for example, a person smiles but sounds angry
Positiveness:	Creating a positive emotional experience for the recipient by making positive statements
Agreement:	Two or more persons reaching the same conclusion and having at least one of them verbalize it
Similarity:	Discovering common points of interest, background, knowledge, belief, or activity between two or more people
Understanding:	Indicating that statements are heard and correctly deciphered by persons in an exchange of statements

---

ment the person for taking the risk. If you have had an experience similar to the person who is talking, let the person know that. In every way possible, present an optimistic, positive approach to the solving of problems.

e. Volunteers to present problems. Indicate that this is the first opportunity for the members to indicate what problem they want to work on and to ask for help from the group. Some participants may not be ready for this. If you do not get a volunteer to present a problem, you might talk about the resistance or fear they may feel in being the first in the group to volunteer. To overcome such resistance, have them prepare statements asking for help on specific problems.

f.   Problem solving. Present the following steps in solving problems. Tell the participants that they will learn the steps as together you and they solve problems that the members bring up.

(1)   As the group member talks about a problem, the others will note all relevant information.

(2)   The description of the problem should be complete. That is, the therapists and other group members should encourage the person who is talking to be specific, to give useful information, about the problem.

(3)   This step has two parts. The first is to have the person describe how that person would like to be. The second part is to have the person describe the solutions thus far tried in efforts to solve the problem. To get a description of how the person would like to be, the therapist should feel free to use imagery, role playing, sculpturing, or anything else that helps to make clear what the problem is.

(4)   Discuss ways to change the problematic behavior, attitude, or feeling. Try to develop as many solutions as possible, by brainstorming and drawing on the group members' own experiences. The group members and therapists should both be highly involved in this process. Before moving on to the next step, one of the therapists should write the ideas and solutions that have been developed on a note pad and present a summary.

(5)   Weigh the advantages and disadvantages of the suggested solutions. Then have the person develop a plan of action, based on what is reasonable and possible for the person to do.

(6)   Instruct the person in how to proceed in implementing the plan. Use the other group members to act as people outside the group in role-playing or skill-learning situations. The group member with the problem should then practice implementation of the plan. Though you, as therapist, are highly involved in this teaching-training situation, be careful not to discount ideas that come from the

group. Some of the ideas may not work, and some may divert you from the path you are on, but be sure to take time to comment on the fact that the members are thinking and presenting ideas.

(7) Now that the person has a plan and has been instructed in how to implement it, get a commitment that the person will try out the plan in an environment outside the group. Find out what obstacles there might be and what kind of help may be needed from the group and have other group members volunteer to do whatever is necessary.

g. Discussion. If you have time remaining in the session, move to another person and follow the same procedure. If you do not have time, summarize what the group has done. Talk about some things you have seen happening in the group that were supportive and helpful. Indicate that you recognize that other people are also wrestling with problems and that they will have an opportunity to solve them in the group. Keep in mind to stop the group discussion ten minutes before the scheduled ending time. Collect any written material the members may have prepared or any measurement data assigned. In this phase, the role of the facilitators diminishes from one session to the next. As members learn the problem-solving steps, they help keep the person in focus on track. The practice of supportive behaviors also allows facilitators to be less active.

h. Challenge. Emphasize the need for the group members to continue to practice communication skills and supportive behaviors in their own support systems and to apply the problem-solving steps where appropriate during the week.

3. Sessions 6 to 8: Strengths
   - Objectives
     a. To develop and reinforce supportive behavior among the group members.
     b. To learn about and accept one's personal strengths.
     c. To utilize personal strengths in problem solving and in maintaining support systems.
   - Procedures
     a. Review (10 minutes). Summarize the problem-solving process they have been learning and comment on the problems they are trying to solve. Be supportive as you summarize. Emphasize that persistence and time, coupled with their own strengths

and support from within and outside the group, will do much to solve their problems.

b. Activity. Introduce the final phase of treatment (strengths). Give the participants forms (Exhibit 19-2) to record and share their strengths. Assign someone to make the entries as each member talks. Give the participants time to discuss this procedure.

c. Instructions for therapists
   (1) Participate by pointing up strengths and weaknesses, but do not dominate.
   (2) If the group does not follow the procedures, make process comments to pull them back to the structure.

d. Instructions for group members
   (1) Step 1. Say the following to the group: "We have been stressing the need for support. One way of getting support is to volunteer information about your strengths and then to enlist the help of others in eliminating your remaining weaknesses. This exercise is designed to help you do this. The group members will volunteer to tell the group about their strengths—their talents, abilities, hobbies, interpersonal skills, and so forth. Each person will start by saying something like, 'I have some strengths I want to tell you about.' " Have someone in the group write each person's strengths on the Exhibit 19-2 form as the person talks. The group may ask questions but are not to negate or

---

Exhibit 19-2 Form for Recording Strengths

	Group _____
	Group Leaders _____
Name _____	
Strengths:	
	Need to work on:
	Specific things to do:
	What resources will you use outside the group?

qualify the statements. If the members have seen the strength the person has mentioned, they should say so. Present the following guidelines:

(a) "We need not display a strength constantly in order to call it a strength. None of us is totally consistent. Therefore, do not qualify your strengths. An example of a qualifying statement would be, 'Sometimes I speak clearly and distinctly,' or 'once in a while I can say what I want to say.' "

(b) "You are not to say anything negative about yourself. Everything is to be put into a positive context."

(2) Step 2. When the person has finished listing personal strengths, the other group members should then add to them. They should be specific, citing incidents that have occurred in the group or been observed outside the group.

(3) Step 3. The person who has been telling about personal strengths now tells the group some things that person wants to improve. These may be things already mentioned on the strength list that need strengthening, or they may be things regarded as weaknesses. Problems that have been dealt with previously in the group may be included if the person needs to continue to work on them. When the list is completed, the individual may say to the group, "Are there other things I should be working on? What are your suggestions?"

(4) Step 4. The group then adds to the list the things the person needs to work on. They should cite specific incidents that have happened in the group related to the person's behavior. If the thing to be worked on is not clearly defined, it should be discussed. The person and the group members should then try to define it more clearly.

(5) Step 5. The person now indicates the specific things to be done to improve the person's behavior in the areas indicated as weaknesses. The group helps by asking clarifying questions and by giving suggestions. As a group, the participants examine the list of strengths to see which ones will help the individual strengthen the problem behavior. In this context, relevant resources that are available outside the group should be identified. The person who has been recording this information then gives the list with the specified behaviors to the individual, and

another person in the group goes through the same procedure.

e. At the beginning of the eighth session, get commitments from everyone to complete the research measurement instruments distributed by the therapists. The last few minutes of Session 8 should be reserved for final goodbyes, plans for reconvening if the group wishes, or information from the facilitators about additional group or individual services available to group participants.

Chapter 20

Husbands and Wives at War: A Peace Plan

David J. Gardner

This structured group treatment is for couples who are experiencing conflict in their relationships. The specific etiology of conflict is not relevant, since this treatment deals with overall dynamics. The treatment requires a total of seven consecutive weeks. All sessions are two hours in length. The first and last sessions are designed to gather assessment data. The initial session is also used as a screening interview. There are five actual therapy sessions. Finally, there is a three month follow-up session for the couples in the group. Cotherapists (male-female combination) are recommended. The treatment is applicable in a number of settings, including private practice, public and private agencies, and colleges and universities.

ORIENTATION, INTAKE PROCEDURES, AND SELECTION CRITERIA

It should be stressed at the outset that this treatment program is designed for couples who are experiencing conflict in their relationships, not for those who exhibit severe pathology individually or as a couple. The couples therapist who recommends participants for the group serves as an initial screening point to exclude those with the latter type of difficulty.

It is also important to note at this point that it is not unusual for clients in concomitant therapy to experience a sort of "therapeutic bind" between their two therapists. Because of the possible damaging effect of this dynamic, the therapist referring the couple is asked to suspend therapy until the completion of the group. This request should be included in the letter sent to therapists informing them of the group.

A letter should be sent to each participating couple, informing them of the time and place of the screening interview. A telephone follow-up is essential to determine if the couple is coming. Each couple meets with the cotherapists of the group. This session is one of the seven sessions in the program. During this interview, the couple is informed of the general objectives of the group and the basic group format. Questions are answered, and a determination made as to whether this form of treatment is appropriate for the couple. The interview should last about 30 minutes. At that point, the coleaders should ask the couple to decide privately if they would like to participate in the group. While the couple is conferring, the therapists decide if the couple could benefit from the group. If both the therapists and the couple agree that the treatment would be beneficial, the therapists then administer selected instruments as pretest measures of the couple dynamics. The cotherapists should be alert for possible pathology not previously screened. At the same time, they should assess the couple's sociability, openness, and commitment. If any of these things are lacking, or if the therapists feel their personalities would clash with those of the couple, the therapists should suggest that the best line of treatment would be for them to continue in marital therapy with the therapist who referred them. On the other hand, the therapists must respect the feelings of the couple if they decide they do not wish to participate.

INVOLVEMENT OF THERAPISTS

The cotherapists in this treatment group are expected to be equal in every way. This means that the two therapists have similar levels of sophistication and similar orientations, or at least are comfortable with each other's style. It is essential that they are both thoroughly familiar with this group treatment and have a solid knowledge of the theme-centered, interactional approach to groups, group and interactional dynamics, and the determinants of healthy and dysfunctional marriages.

All duties in setting up the group should be shared equally. If the treatment is being sponsored by a clinic or agency, the problem of dividing the initial duties of informing professionals and prospective group members is alleviated, since these tasks can then be done by supportive personnel under the direction of the therapists. It is important that, once potential group members have been contacted to set up the initial interview, the therapists do the interviews conjointly. This allows both therapists to have a say in who the members of the group will be. This mutual selection process establishes a sense of "our group," which is very helpful in motivating the therapists to be committed to the group.

ATTITUDES AND OBJECTIVES

The general tone of the group should be supportive and casual, with the therapists directing the interaction of the group toward the specific theme of each session and the overall theme: how to resolve marital conflict. The attitudes of openness and support should be reinforced and encouraged through the ground rules, at the direction of the therapists.

The overall objective of the treatment program is a reduction in the conflict experienced by the couples in the group. In addition, the following specific objectives are to be achieved in the implementation of the program:

- Each couple, and each partner in the couple, will identify areas of concern to themselves and to their relationship. These need not be made known to the group, but they should be explicit to the couple and the therapists in the screening session.
- By learning new communication skills, the members of the group will become responsible for their own statements and will be "their own chairman," asking for and getting what they need from the group.
- The group members will develop trust and openness with one another, giving as well as taking from the group.
- All participants will give support and display empathic listening. Each member will be involved in checking out information that is not clear and resolving intergroup problems that may arise.
- Each couple will leave the group with new skills of communication, compromise, and giving-taking. The members will also better understand why they have conflict in their relationships and how they have supported that conflict. As they leave the group, the participants should have some basic skills to help them deal with their conflict constructively.
- Group members will be able to return to therapy outside the group with a more positive outlook and with renewed hope, should they choose to continue therapy.

RESEARCH AND EVALUATION

To date, this program has not been used in a clinical research setting. All elements of the treatment have been used in a number of groups from various populations, but the unique combination of exercises and theory as presented here has not yet been implemented as a complete program. Such implementation is planned for the near future.

Individually, the exercises and instruments of the program have been shown to have validity as effective elements in a structured group treatment program. However, their combination in the form presented here awaits verification and acceptance by the professional community. Pending full implementation, we believe this treatment program offers distinct benefits to both its clients and its practitioners.

PROGRAM OUTLINE

The following outline describes some of the content, procedures, and materials used in each program session: All the sessions are not complete. To receive the entire program, see instructions in the Preface.

1. Session 1: Screening and Preassessment
   - Objectives
     a. To screen those who will be invited to participate in the treatment group, using the following procedure:
        (1) Establish that the couple is in therapy at the time they begin the structured group treatment, and that they have the permission of their therapist to be in the group. It should be understood that the couple will suspend meeting with their outside therapist for the duration of the treatment group.
        (2) Identify through an individual interview with each couple what the areas of conflict are in each couple's marriage.
        (3) Encourage each couple to state their expectations from the treatment as well as their apprehensions concerning it.
     b. To help each couple better understand the orientation and rationale behind the structured group treatment, thereby making them better able to determine if they would like to participate in the group.
     c. To give the cotherapists an opportunity to gain information about the couple (mostly biographical), and to establish rapport with prospective members.
     d. To administer pre-treatment assessment instruments.
   - Procedures
     a. The cotherapists will:
        (1) Contact by mail those therapists who may have candidates for the program and provide them with an outline

of the proposed group treatment. Each therapist contacted is asked to return a list of possible group members. The therapist should agree that, if one or more of the couples he is seeing join the group, private conjoint marital therapy will be suspended for the duration of the treatment (this includes any form of therapeutic contact with those clients). The therapist should be asked to send a note with each referred couple, indicating compliance with the above criteria.

(2) Contact the potential clients and ask them to come in for a two-hour, screening/assessment orientation meeting with the therapists of the group.

(3) Evaluate the couple as to their "appropriateness" and compatibility in the group. Also assess their willingness to participate in the treatment.

(4) Once it has been decided that a couple will participate, the therapists should administer the three preassessment instruments: the MAT, the MHS, and the IMC (see Appendix B for descriptions).

b. The participants are expected to:

(1) Be honest in their detailing of the problems in their relationship and share openly and honestly the information requested.

(2) Decide whether or not they would like to participate in the group.

(3) Ask any questions they might have regarding the group, the therapists, or the procedures.

(4) Respond honestly to the instruments given.

c. Treatment

(1) Greeting and interview with the couple. (40 minutes)

(a) Introduce yourself to the couple.

(b) Ask the couple to present a document from their therapist allowing them to enter the group, with the understanding that they will not meet with the other therapist for the course of the program.

(c) Explain the rationale of the theme-centered approach and the dynamics of a structured group treatment.

(d) Deal with any questions or apprehensions.

(e) Ask the couple to consider privately (for 10–15 minutes) if they would like to be involved in the group treatment. The therapists should leave the room and confer, deciding if they should invite the couple to join the group.

(f) If all parties agree that the treatment would be efficacious, discuss some specifics of the group program and its basic rules with the couple (that is, being on time, attending all sessions, and so on). Ask them to sign an audiovisual taping release form (if the treatment is to be audio or video taped) and to provide on a form whatever biographical data is requested.

(2) Explanation and administration of the MAT. (15 minutes)

(a) Give the following explanation: "This test gives us some idea of how you see your marriage right now. You cannot answer the questions right or wrong, so just put down how you honestly feel about your marriage. Please don't compare answers or discuss the items on the test."

(b) Give each person a copy of the MAT.

(c) Answer any questions and have the couple take the test.

(3) Explanation and administration of the MHS. (10 minutes)

(a) Give the following explanation: "This test lets us know how happy you are with your marriage right now. Please indicate how happy you feel today in each of the areas asked about. Put down only how you are feeling today. Again, please do this independently from your spouse."

(b) Answer any questions about the test.

(c) Give each person a copy of the MHS and have them take the test.

(4) Explanation and administration of the IMC (45 minutes): This test is divided into two segments to facilitate pre/post measurements using the same instrument (Fisher, 1974, p. 29).

(a) Give the following explanation: "We are going to put you in separate rooms and give you a series of situations to read. Once you have read them, please answer the four questions on the answer sheet."

(b) When both persons have answered the questions, bring them back together and tell them that they have different points of view of the same problem. Ask them to resolve the problem by coming to some decision regarding the situation, and then to respond on a joint answer sheet. This session is audio or video recorded and is 20 to 30 minutes long. Independent raters judge the tapes later.

    (5)   Ending the screening/preassessment session. (10 minutes)

        (a) Tell the couple they will be contacted by phone about the group within the next few days.

        (b) Answer, if possible, any questions the couple may have.

        (c) Thank the couple for their cooperation, and end the session.

2. Session 2: Initial Therapy Session—"I Would Really Like To Get To Know You"

- Objectives
  - a. To establish a more comfortable, open, and trustful feeling among all group members.
  - b. To make explicit, or to review if necessary, all the rules that will govern the group (being on time, attending all meetings, confidentiality, owning one's own statements, participation in activities or discussion, and so on).
  - c. To gain a commitment from each group member to abide by the established rules.
  - d. To introduce group members to "break-the-ice" and to establish a feeling of group cohesion.
- Procedures
  - a. Greetings. (5 minutes)
  - b. Rules of the group (30 minutes): The ground rules for the group are introduced, discussed, and accepted.
  - c. Introductions (1 hour): The participants introduce themselves as if they were their partner. The group can ask questions, but only of the person being introduced.
  - d. Summary of the session and homework assignment (20–30 minutes): The participants process all the activities of the session, with emphasis on sharing personal reactions.

3. Session 3—"How Well Do I Really Know You?"

- Objectives
  - a. To share insights from last week's session and assignment.
  - b. To enable group members to understand how they feel and to express themselves.

    c.   To help the couples understand and become aware of different levels of communication.

    d.   To have the group members begin to recognize and to be able to state the strengths and weaknesses of their partners.

- Procedures
  a.   Greeting the group (5–20 minutes): Greet the members by name and discuss what was learned during the week in relation to last week's session. Introduce the theme for the current session.
  b.   Palm dance exercise (15–20 minutes): Nonverbal communication is created by the couples standing palms to palms and moving through a series of therapist and self-directed activities. First the partners and then the group members together discuss their reactions to the exercise.
  c.   Communication skills (15–20 minutes): Verbal and nonverbal communication, mind reading, perception checking, clarification, and reflective listening skills are introduced and role played.
  d.   Fish bowl exercise (45 minutes–1 hour): One couple at a time meets in the center of the group with the therapist and the partners discuss their strengths and weaknesses. They practice using the communication skills.
  e.   Summary of session and homework assignment. (5–10 minutes)

4. Session 4—"Maybe It's Not That Bad After All"
   - Objectives
     a.   To get the members to understand that, though they attribute meanings to their spouse's behavior, that meaning is not always correct.
     b.   To help couples understand the dynamics of how and why they fight: the major reasons for conflict, who initiates conflict in the relationship, and so on.
     c.   To show the couples different meanings for the same behaviors.
     d.   To get each couple to work on a compromise, and not to feel as though they are "being cheated."
   - Procedures
     a.   Greeting the group and processing the assignment. (15–20 minutes)
     b.   Reframing exercise (30 minutes): Instruct the couples to break up into groups of three or four. Tell the groups that they are to decide where they would like to go for dinner after the session tonight. Each person participates by practicing a role assigned

on cards distributed by the therapists. After discussing their roles, a group discussion focuses on how many ways the roles could be acted or interpreted. Use role play to dramatize reframing.

c. Compromise activity (1 hour): Ask the couples to pair up, husband and wife, and plan a vacation trip. Create groups of four with the same assignment. Keep adding couples until the entire group is trying to plan the trip. Process the experience by identifying how decisions were made, how compromises were made, and so on.

d. Summary of session and homework assignment. (10 minutes)

5. Session 5—"I'll Scratch Your Back If You'll Scratch Mine"
   - Objectives
     a. To help the couples change the focus of their relationship from "I" or "me" to "you"and "us."
     b. To show that giving can be as rewarding as receiving, that pleasuring involves giving to the other.
     c. To help the couples use the skills developed thus far: communication, compromise, and so on.
   - Procedures
     a. The therapists will:
        (1) Help the group members understand what pleasuring is and how they can foster it in their relationship.
        (2) Be sensitive to unspoken needs of group members and encourage them to ask for what they need from the group if it is not being given.
     b. The group members will:
        (1) Be responsible for themselves during the program.
        (2) Work on compromise and identify patterns of giving and taking in their couple relationships.
     c. Treatment
        (1) Greeting the group and processing the assignment (30 minutes)
            (a) Greet each group member in a personal way that is comfortable for the leader and the group member.
            (b) Ask the group members to discuss their attempts to compromise during the past week. The coleaders should leave the discussion to the group with little or no intervention.
            (c) Present the theme of this week's session and outline the session.

(2) Nonverbal giving/taking exercise (30 minutes)
   (a) Ask the couples to sit on the floor with one partner in front of the other.
   (b) Tell the partner sitting behind to give a loving backrub to that person's partner. Tell the person receiving the backrub to let the person doing the rubbing know how it feels, or to ask that person, without using words, to do something different.
   (c) After about five minutes of backrubbing, the partners are to change positions and repeat the exercise.
   (d) Allow the group to express how they felt during the experience. Was it more pleasurable to give or to receive? Did the person receiving the backrub demand more than the partner was willing to give? How did the partner know what felt good when giving the backrub? Do you see any similarities between this experience and your own relationship?
   (e) Allow time for processing by the group.

(3) I-Me, You-Us Exercise (30 Minutes)
   (a) Have the couples sit facing each other, holding hands, with elbows on knees.
   (b) For five minutes, one partner is to talk about whatever is important to that person, using only I-Me statements. When time is called, the other partner is to respond using only You-Us statements. The leaders should demonstrate how this is to be done.
   (c) After this interaction, the couples change roles and repeat the exercise.
   (d) Give time to process the feelings emerging from this experience. Ask how it feels to speak with only yourself in mind, as opposed to speaking in terms of someone else.

(4) Summary of session and assignment (30 minutes)
   (a) Ask the couples to verbalize and share what they have learned from this session. Again, the coleaders should allow the members to be "their own chairman" and allow them to say what they need to say.
   (b) Point out that next week's meeting will be the last session as a group. Encourage the couples to continue to use all the skills they have learned thus far. In this last week especially they should work on giving

pleasure to their partners and on seeing their relationship in terms of their partner's point of view.

6. Session 6: Final Therapy and Termination Session—"And They
   Lived Happily Ever After"
   • Objectives
     a. To process what has happened in the group.
     b. To terminate the group.
     c. To leave the couples with a good feeling and with a subliminal
         desire to have a more conflict-free relationship derived from
         the telling of a metaphorical story.
   • Procedures
     a. Greeting and processing assignment (45 minutes): Talk about
         the assignment regarding pleasuring and giving in the relation-
         ship. Outline the session and allude to the session's theme.
     b. Group discussion about what each person has gotten from the
         group (30 minutes): Ask each person to think of something that
         person has gotten out of the group; begin by asking someone
         to volunteer. The group members should proceed in a "whip"
         process (one person quickly following another) around the
         group, with each member expressing personal feelings on the
         subject to the group.
     c. The Polar Bear Story (30 minutes): One of the therapists tells
         the group that their sessions together bring to mind the story
         of the two polar bears. The therapist should then relate the
         following story: "Once upon a time, not so very long ago in a
         zoo not too far from here, there lived two polar bears. They
         were very famous, and people came from all over to watch
         them, because these bears knew many tricks. The children
         especially loved to watch the bears and would throw them all
         kinds of good things to eat. The polar bears were pretty happy
         in their cage; they had everything polar bears could want. One
         day, the large male polar bear noticed that his mate was getting
         much more food than he was, so he started to do more and
         more tricks so the people would look at him and throw him
         goodies. When the female polar bear saw this, she became very
         mad. She refused to share with him; and it eventually got so
         bad, they were sleeping on different sides of the cage. Now
         when the people came to see them, they could tell that the
         bears were mad at each other; instead of doing tricks to please
         the people, the bears were doing them to spite one another.
         Soon the people got bored and quit coming to see the polar

bears. The other animals in the cages around them began to avoid them whenever possible, because all they would do was quarrel about who did the best tricks. The zookeepers realized that something had to be done, since no one was coming to see the famous polar bears any more. They decided that they should teach the bears some new tricks, and also that they needed a change of scenery. Their new home would be behind the cage they were in now, so the workers lowered some bars to keep the bears in the front part of the cage while they were building the new complex. The bears' new home would have a large slide running into a pool of nice, cool water, a waterfall, a larger swing than they had in their old cage, a nice tree for them to climb in, and a shelter when the weather was bad. As the two bears watched the workmen, they just paced back and forth, back and forth. Instead of practicing the new tricks they had been taught, they just continued to walk back and forth, back and forth. Finally, the new complex was finished. The zoo spent a great deal of money to advertise the new building and the new tricks of their famous polar bears. Finally the big day came, and the zoo was filled with all kinds of people who had come to see the bears do their new tricks in the beautiful new complex. All the children in the town were there, waiting to throw goodies to the bears. At last the hour arrived, and the new complex was revealed. The bars were slowly raised and the people cheered, but, to the astonishment of the people and especially the zookeepers, the bears did not look happy, nor did they begin to show their new tricks to the people. They just continued to pace back and forth, back and forth, in their old little cage.''

d. This story may be varied in any way the leader feels is appropriate. More details or concepts may be added, but the basic outline of the story should be about the same. The story should not be processed, and no questions concerning it should be entertained.

e. Termination (15 minutes): The cotherapist who has not told the story should stand up immediately as the story ends and tell the group that they will now do their last exercise. Before the exercise begins, the group should be told that each couple will be contacted about when to come in for the individual evaluation and postassessment session. The therapist should then explain that each person is special and has a special way to say goodbye. Have each member of the group say goodbye in any way the person chooses. The only rule is that there can be no talking. When the group members are done saying goodbye, they should leave the room couple by couple.

7. Session 7: Evaluation and Postassessment Session
   - Objectives
     a. To meet with each couple individually and to discuss the group, what they liked, what they disliked, and so on.
     b. To thank each member for participating in the structured group treatment group.
     c. To gather postassessment data on the three assessment instruments.
   - Procedures
     a. Greeting the couple and discussion of the group (40 minutes): Discuss with the couple the role they played in the functioning of the group, paying particular attention to validating any good behavior seen by the therapists. Mention any change or evidences of growth that may have occurred. Encourage the couple to respond honestly and candidly.
     b. Explanation and administration of the MAT. (15 minutes)
     c. Explanation and administration of the MHS. (10 minutes)
     d. Explanation and administration of the IMC. (45 minutes)
     e. Termination of the evaluation, postassessment session (10 minutes): Thank the couple for their cooperation during the session. Remind them that in three months there will be a follow-up session that they should plan to attend. Explain that they will be contacted by mail, along with the rest of the group, about when that will take place.

8. Session 8: Follow-Up Session
   - Objectives
     a. To determine, following a significant period after termination of the program, if there has been any carryover from the group experience into the lives of the couples who participated in the group treatment.
     b. To allow the group members to experience the successes or failures of one another and to give support if it is needed.
   - Procedures
     a. Greeting the group members. (5 minutes)
     b. Processing the group. (1 hour and 45 minutes)

c. Give the remainder of the time to the group to use as they wish. If the group appears to be stuck at some point, you may wish to stimulate conversation; otherwise you should remain silent. Finally, terminate the session. (10 minutes)

Chapter 21

A Treatment Program for High-School-Aged Siblings in Conflict

Kayleen Mitchell

This treatment program for adolescent sibling dyads is applicable to public or private school settings and to government and private mental health agencies. The treatment covers a period of ten weeks. The first session is focused on orientation and preassessment, the next eight weekly sessions are devoted to structured treatment, and a final session is for postassessment data collection. Each session lasts one hour and forty minutes. Recommended group size is six to eight persons (three to four sibling dyads). The treatment can be conducted by one therapist, male or female, or it can be adapted for therapy by two therapists.

The treatment is focused on sibling, peer, and family relationships and on the factors that help in understanding, improving, and maintaining healthy relationships. Group members learn about themselves and improve their relationship skills through structured roleplaying, communication, sculpting, and problem-solving experiences. Members of each sibling dyad learn about and improve their relationship through structured sharing experiences.

Sibling relationships have a significant impact on an individual's development of social skills and self concept. Bank and Kahn (1975) reviewed the literature on sibling subsystems and family therapy and concluded that the influence of sibling interaction on family functioning is often underemphasized by family therapists in the American culture. Although the sibling subsystem can be treated in family therapy, some dysfunctional sibling relationships are not being reached because the parents of the siblings are not interested in family therapy. School settings provide a convenient vehicle for identification of adolescent behavioral problems and sibling relationship problems. Group treatment can also be conducted on a regular basis without demanding extra time from adolescents after school hours.

Bank and Kahn (1975) list the following functions that siblings serve for one another, relatively free of parental monitoring: (1) identification and differentiation between the siblings, (2) mutual regulation and experimentation with new roles, (3) provision of direct services through negotiating and bargaining with each other, and (4) establishment of coalitions in dealing with parents. Group treatment for sibling dyads can enhance and improve these functions insofar as they fail to result in positive behaviors and adaptive relationships.

PROGRAM DESCRIPTION

General Objectives

The overall treatment objective is to enhance relationships between sibling dyads. Three other general treatment objectives are:

1. To improve self image.
2. To increase compatibility in the sibling relationship.
3. To increase understanding of each member's own interactional behavior and needs and those of the sibling in the relationship.

Participants are encouraged to understand and improve their relationships with other family members and peers by applying the skills and knowledge gained in the group.

Theoretical Basis and Techniques

The major theoretical underpinning of this structured treatment is Cohn's (1972) theme-centered Interaction Model of Group Therapy. Several aspects of the Vinter and Sarri (1974) social work model are also incorporated in this adolescent sibling group treatment (see Appendix A).

In the treatment program the group therapist models interpersonal skills, support, and problem-solving skills. The therapist also facilitates the change factors in the group process and takes observational measures to determine whether progress is being made.

Selection Criteria and Orientation

The following selection criteria for a treatment group are recommended:

- voluntary commitment of both siblings to participate in the group

- either one or both siblings experiencing difficulties in peer or family relationships
- parental consent for the siblings to be in the treatment
- individual evaluation through assessments and interviews indicates no severe psychopathology that contraindicates group treatment

It is recommended that the group therapist be involved with the group from the beginning by orienting and interviewing potential group members. This gives the therapist an opportunity to assess more closely individual needs and to begin to establish a relationship with the adolescents. The commitment process for the adolescents is strengthened by their telling the group therapist at the outset of their intentions to attend all sessions.

Treatment

Each group session has a subtheme within the overall theme of "Improving My Relationships." In each session, there is a dynamic balance between the focus on the theme, discussion of group relationships, and sharing by the individual of their unique personalities. Sessions on accepting differences, understanding rules in relationships, identifying and improving communication patterns, and improving the ability to resolve conflicts are designed to help group members understand and improve their interactional behavior with their siblings in the group. Group members are also encouraged to apply their interpersonal understanding and skills in peer and family relationships. The structured treatment provides an opportunity for them to try out new behaviors and to learn through modeling and sharing.

Equipment and Materials

Materials required for every session include a tape recorder and audiotape to tape the session (use videotape if available) and the ground rules written on a posterboard or on the blackboard. The following additional materials needed for specific sessions include a record player or tape recorder and recordings of the following songs:

1. Session 1: "The Cat's in the Cradle." (A similar song about family relationships could be substituted, or the words of the song could be read to the group.)
2. Session 4: "Sounds of Silence" by Simon and Garfunkel.
3. Session 8: "Shower the People You Love with Love" by James Taylor.

Measurement Instruments

Sibling relationships, individual self-image, and the interactional behaviors of group members are assessed by the following five instruments*:

1. Family-Oriented Sentence Completion
2. FIRO-B, adapted to sibling relationships (see Appendix B)
3. Coopersmith Self-Esteem Inventory, adapted for adolescents (see Appendix B)
4. Sibling Perception Rating Scale (each person will rate sibling and self)
5. Therapist's behavioral observations, to be completed following each session.

The first four measures are administered prior to the first group session and again following the last session.

Pregroup Procedures

The following procedures are used to establish the treatment program:

1. Inform potential members about the group treatment opportunity (30 minutes).
   - Briefly describe the general purposes of the treatment.
   - Answer any questions the group might have regarding their referral, the length and time of treatment, and so on.
   - Hand out a student information sheet to those who are interested in the group and would like to be considered.
   - Ask the potential group members to take their evaluations home to their parents.

2. Call the parents to answer any of their questions. Arrange for an interview with them after their evaluation is completed.

3. Conduct an evaluation session with the whole group:
   - Completion of FIRO-B for siblings. (15 minutes)
   - Completion of Coopersmith Self-Esteem Inventory. (12 minutes)

---

*These instruments have been adapted by the author for high school students. The program is not presented in its entirety. To receive the complete program and the adapted instruments, see the instructions in the Preface.

- Completion of Family-Oriented Sentence Completion. (20–30 minutes)

4. Arrange individual interviews (30 minutes each):
   - Get acquainted.
   - Encourage the potential member to discuss any questions or hesitations about being involved in the group.
   - Deal with doubts and resistance, and help the potential member to identify some need for the group experience.
   - Discuss the results of the FIRŌ-B evaluation in general. Ask the potential member which areas need improvement.
   - Determine the commitment level by asking if the individual would attend every session if selected to be in the group.
   - Explain that both siblings must be committed to the treatment.
   - Discuss with the potential member any individual concerns that might be pertinent.
   - Have the individual fill out the Sibling Perception Rating Scale in reference to that person's sibling.

5. Arrange interviews with parents (45 minutes to one hour):
   - Become acquainted with the parents while answering their questions about the treatment program.
   - Ask the parents about their concerns for the children who are being considered for group participation.
   - Discuss with the parents any general problems they may have concerning their role as parents.
   - Assess the sibling relationship and its problems from the parents' point of view.
   - Discuss the general results of evaluations.
   - Ask the parents in which areas they would like to see their children improve and what they, as parents, are doing at home to encourage growth in those areas.
   - Ask the parents to sign the consent form for group treatment if it is determined that the siblings should be involved in the treatment.

PROGRAM OUTLINE

The following outline describes the content, procedures, and materials used in each program session. Sessions 3 and 8 are presented in complete form; the remaining sessions are abbreviated.

1. Session 1: Improving Relationships
   - Objectives
     a. To acquaint members with each other.
     b. To introduce the overall objective and the theme, "Improving Relationships."
     c. To decrease anxiety by dealing with any questions not discussed in individual interviews.
     d. To establish ground rules.
     e. To emphasize the positive approach of the treatment and the importance of support.
     f. To get commitments from the members to attend each session.

   - Procedures
     a. Introductions (5–10 minutes): Ask the members to give their names and share two things they enjoy doing with people.
     b. Introduce the theme (30 minutes): Briefly introduce the theme and play the song, "The Cat's in the Cradle." Help the group discuss aspects of their family relationships. Conclude this general discussion by asking them to think of their relationships with the siblings in the group.
     c. Establish ground rules (10 minutes): Introduce each ground rule and discuss it with the group members. (Have the ground rules written on a poster or the board.)
     d. Introduce the concept of support (15 minutes): Ask the group to discuss ways in which the group members can support each other. Instruct the group members to move into sibling pairs to discuss the kinds of support they would like from one another during the group. Conclude by asking the members to share some of the things they have learned about support from the group and sibling discussion.
     e. Discuss expectations of the group treatment and any questions that have not been answered (10 to 15 minutes).
     f. Commitment to attend group (15 minutes): Discuss with the whole group the importance of commitment. Then have them commit themselves in individual interviews to attend the group. It is important that everyone attends in order to support each other. Ask the members one at a time if they are going to attend all of the sessions and if they will follow the ground rules.
     g. Homework assignment (5 minutes): Ask the members to think of some strengths in their relationships with their brother or sister. Ask them to think of the areas they would like to work on in the relationship.

2. Session 2: Understanding and Accepting Differences
   - Objectives
     a. To speak for self regarding value choices and decisions.
     b. To listen to the differences expressed by others.
     c. To increase acceptance of differences between the members and their siblings.
     d. To discuss how values and differences influence family, peer, and sibling relationships.
     e. To set goals for sibling dyads in at least one area in which they would like to improve   their relationships.
     f. To set goals to improve relationships with siblings.
   - Procedures
     a. Introduction of the subtheme, "Understanding and accepting differences" (5 minutes): Discuss these questions: Are differences a strength or a weakness in a relationship? What is the value of similarities in a relationship? Think about the similarities and differences between you and your brother or sister.
     b. Either-or, forced-choice values exercise (30 minutes): For this exercise, select 10 to 15 items from page 96 in *Values Clarification* (Simon, Howe, & Kirschenbaum, 1973) or make up your own list of contrasting characteristics and interests. Ask the group members to stand, and arrange the room so that there is space to move from one side to the other. Then ask an either-or-question like, "Are you more like a clothes line or more like a kite string?" By pointing to the two sides of the room, indicate that those who feel they are more like a clothes line go to one side and those who feel they are more like a kite string go to the other side. Then give the participants an opportunity to discuss with someone why they made their particular choices.
     c. Group discussion about what was learned about group members during the structured exercise (10 minutes): The focus of this discussion is on expectations of the choices siblings would make and on the surprises related to those choices.
     d. Written exercise concerning behaviors valued in a relationship (15 minutes): Each member completes the written exercise, "Friendship Values." The members then go over the exercise a second time, placing a star next to the choice guessed to be the most important to their sibling. The siblings and then the group share the results.
     e. Group discussion of what kinds of behaviors are most important in relationships, along the dimensions of affection, inclusion, and control (15 minutes): Define the terms. Follow this

with a discussion of these behaviors with peers, siblings, and family.

f.   Group discussion of how differences influence relationships either positively or negatively (10 minutes): After a discussion about the influence of differences in relationships, ask the siblings to identify something they can do to improve their relationships. Each dyad then writes two goals that both are willing to work on in their relationship.

g.   Homework assignment (5 minutes): Ask the members to observe how their values influence their behavior in relationships with parents, brother(s) and sister(s), and peers during the week.

3. Session 3: Understanding Rules in Relationships
   • Objectives
      a.   To identify at least one rule in the members' family relationship and one rule in their sibling relationship.
      b.   To increase each member's awareness of that member's spatial relationship boundaries.
      c.   To discuss the subtheme, "Understanding Rules in Relationships," and to make connections to the overall theme of the group.
   • Procedures
      a.   Role of participants
         (1)   The group members are encouraged to take part in the boundary sculpting exercise, but they are not forced to participate against their will.
         (2)   In this session, the participants become more active and involved in the therapy process. Their creative ideas are encouraged in the sculpting, and they help each other to identify boundaries.
         (3)   The siblings work on an experience together by acting out a family rule for the group.
      b.   Treatment
         (1)   Follow-up discussion on what the members learned through their observations of the influence of values in relationships (5 minutes).
         (2)   Introduction of the subtheme, "Understanding Rules in Relationships" (5 minutes): Use one of the values previously discussed to make a connection between values and rules. For example, the question could be asked, "How does the value of loyalty influence your rules on whether or not to report something a friend has done

wrong?" "Is there a connection between your parents' values and the rules they enforce in the home?"

(3) Family rules (15 minutes)
   (a) Each person individually completes the family rules form.
   (b) Each sibling pair compares their rules and observes the similarities and differences in their impressions of family rules.

(4) Acting out of family rules (exercise from Hoopes, 1979) (15 minutes)
   (a) Ask for volunteers to act out one rule nonverbally. Encourage them to select a rule that influences how people relate to each other. Help them decide how they can represent the rule nonverbally.
   (b) Following the demonstration, direct each sibling dyad to get together and select one of their family rules to act out in pantomime for the group. They can play the part of other members of the family, or they can choose to play themselves. After each dyad does its pantomime, the group guesses and makes comments on what the dyad was trying to express.
   (c) After the members have acted their rules, discuss as a group what was learned about the rules in other families. What makes the rules different? What is similar about the rules? How do family values influence the making and enforcing of family rules?

(5) Discussion of members' rules in peer and sibling relationships (5–10 minutes): Ask the members about their rules in their relationships. What are their rules about how close people can get? How do they enforce their rules?

(6) Boundary sculpture (55 minutes)
   (a) Explanation of boundary sculpture: Boundary sculpture places the responsibility for awareness of a person on the person doing the perceiving. All systems have an ordering that can be formulated as "rules." Members of a family act under the influence of certain rules of behavior, whether or not these rules are verbalized. If rules are not clear and accepted by all, the members may run into conflict and invade one another in some dimension. When rules are verbalized, they may be changed to fit the present realities of the system. One way of clarifying the conflicting rules

that govern behaviors and manifest themselves as invasions between two or more people is to use boundary sculpture. Boundary sculpture shows that a person's rules governing that person's space may be only assumed by or be unknown to the other person, with the result that the behavior of the first person is judged in the context of the rules of the second person.

(b) Directions for the boundary sculpture (Duhl et al., 1973)

1) Ask one person to walk around the room and feel out, as a sculptor does, a personal space, that space the person always carries around. It is best if the first person volunteers. Ask the following questions to aid the person to feel the personal space and to describe it to the group: "How much space do you need in a group of people?" "Is there enough space in this room for you?" "How do you show people what your space is?"

2) Summarize what the sculptor has said, and ask if the summary was accurate.

3) Ask how the sculptor gets out of or leaves the space. This helps to determine to what extent the sculptor is in charge of the space. This control of space is vital to a person's self-esteem.

4) Ask the sculptor to describe who can enter the space and under what conditions it would be possible. To help the person in this differentiating process, you can use yourself or others in the room. However, it usually works best if the other sibling is included in the sculptor's descriptions. Ask the sculptor to react without words to the entry of a male or female stranger, an acquaintance, and close personal friend. Have each person, one at a time, and in a manner appropriate to the defined role, try to enter the sculptor's space without words as the sculptor reacts.

5) Enact what happens when the sculptor has several people trying to enter at the same time.

6) Throughout the sculpting, have information given to the sculptor regarding the other's perceptions.

7) Ask how the sculptor brings others into the personal space. Ask how the sculptor gets someone (acquaintance, friend, intimate, male, female, mother, brother, and so on) into the space without words. Observe the sculptor using this approach. Does the sculptor use force? Eye contact? Suggest alternatives if an approach does not work.

8) Then have the sibling enter the sculptor's space, without words, the way in which the sibling usually enters. If there has been some problem between the two, the entrance may be perceived by the sculptor as an invasion of some dimension. Ask the sibling to enter again, now using information from the therapist about the sculptor's boundaries and how the sculptor would like people to enter. Note that the sculptor will react more freely, in an accepting manner, if the boundaries are understood.

9) Repeat the exercise with another member of the group.

(c) The above directions are general guidelines to help the therapist. Some group members may do only a part of the process. A sculpture for an insecure person might be for the person to stand in the space and signal nonverbally when another person gets too close for the person to feel comfortable. The members will vary in the time they spend in the sculpting activity and in the number of entry roles they explore.

(d) Following the participation of all who desired to be involved, the group discusses what they learned from the experience. Ask what the members learned about the rules governing group members' personal spaces that they did not know before? How do they feel when their personal spaces were violated? If there are members who did not participate in the boundary sculpture, encourage them to talk about their boundaries in their relationships with peers and family members.

4. Session 4: Improving Communication in Relationships
   - Objectives
     a. To give and receive messages, both verbally and nonverbally, within the sibling dyad.
     b. To identify differences in the forms of communication members have on a daily basis with family and friends.
     c. To set goals to improve communication in the areas of sharing and giving feedback.
     d. To recognize the differences between partners that block effective and congruent communication.
     e. To measure the level of group sharing.
   - Procedures
     a. Introduce the theme (10 minutes): Play the song, "Sounds of Silence," by Simon and Garfunkel. Discuss the members' feelings and reactions to the song. Explain that communication in relationships is both verbal and nonverbal.
     b. Communication with others, an exercise about the types of communication with different people (15–20 minutes): Have the group members complete written exercises. Discuss the group's reactions and responses to the exercise.
     c. Communication exercise (20 minutes) (Hoopes, 1979): Talk with the group about how the members send messages and how nonverbal behavior could demonstrate what the messages are doing. Talk with the members about where they feel the messages were received; some messages are received in the head, others in the heart, others in the stomach. Instruct the siblings to give each other a message and to show the nonverbal motion that goes with it. Discuss what was learned from the exercise as a group. Ask the members what they learned about their brother's or sister's response to their message.
     d. Johari Window exercise (15 minutes) (Luft, 1969): Explain the four different dimensions of the Johari Window and relate them to the group. Direct the members to diagram the Johari Window dimensions of their sharing in the group in the first session. Then ask them to draw their level of knowledge about themselves in the present session. Ask them to diagram the Johari Window level of openness with their brother or sister at present and how they would like it to be in the future.
     e. Role playing family communication patterns (30–35 minutes): Explain the roles described by Satir (1972): placater, superreasonable intellectualizer, blamer, and distractor. Then have them practice these roles in make-believe families.

    f.   Homework assignment (5 minutes)

       (1) Ask the members to be aware of both verbal and nonverbal messages they send during the week.

       (2) Ask them to practice speaking for themselves and listening to the opinions of others.

5. Session 5: Understanding Roles in Relationships

- Objectives

    a.   To increase their awareness of the roles that members play in their families.

    b.   To share their feelings about their birth-order positions and responsibilities in their families.

    c.   To identify the roles they play in family conflicts.

    d.   To hear how the members' siblings feel about their roles, positions, and responsibilities in the family.

    e.   To increase the feeling of commonality.

- Procedures

    a.   Follow up on the homework assignment by discussing what the members learned about their communication roles. Ask them to share any experiences they had in speaking for themselves and listening to the feelings of others. (5–10 minutes)

    b.   Introduce the theme, "Understanding Roles in Relationships" (5 minutes): Ask the members what kinds of roles they play in relationships.

    c.   Give members handouts on roles to complete. Then ask members to share some of the roles they play in relationships.

    d.   Discuss birth-order positions, roles, and responsibilities in the family. (20 minutes)

    e.   Sculpting of a family conflict (45–50 minutes): Give each person the opportunity to sculpt a family conflict, using other members of the group as family members. It is recommended that the sculptures be minisculptures as described by Constantine (1978).

    f.   Discussion of roles in peer relationships (10 minutes): Ask the members if the roles in their relationships with friends are different from their roles at home. What do they do when they have a disagreement with a friend? Do they like the role they play in the peer group, or would they like it to be different in some way?

    g.   Homework assignment (5 minutes): Ask the members to think of one problem or area in their relationship with their brother or sister that they would like to work on in the group.

6. Sessions 6 and 7: Improving Problem-Solving Abilities
    - Objectives
        a. To recognize the importance of resolving conflicts and communicating about differences rather than avoiding conflicts or holding grudges inside.
        b. To learn a basic problem-solving method through a review of the steps at the end of Session 6 and by going individually through the steps).
        c. To give supportive comments and constructive suggestions during the problem-solving process.

    - Procedures
        a. Introduce the theme of problem solving (5 minutes): Review some of the themes that have been covered so far to improve relationship skills. Introduce the need to be able to work together in a relationship while understanding differences or resolving conflicts.
        b. Ask the members what skills they have learned in the group that may be helpful in dealing with hurt feelings and conflict. (15 minutes)
        c. Review steps of the problem-solving method. (10 minutes) (Hoopes, 1978)
        d. Remind the participants of the goals they set in the initial interview. Give the sibling dyads an opportunity to discuss the areas in which they have improved in their relationship. Ask them to select one problem on which they would like to have the group's support and help. (10 minutes)
        e. Review supportive and encouraging behaviors demonstrated by members of the group. (10 minutes)
        f. Use the remainder of the sixth session (except for five to ten minutes) to deal with problems shared voluntarily.
        g. Discuss with the participants what they have learned in the session. (5–10 minutes)

7. Session 8: Giving Support in Relationships
    - Objectives
        a. To identify strengths and to share some of them with the group.
        b. To demonstrate the ability to give support by sharing perceived strengths with the person in focus.
        c. To share what members have learned about themselves and their relationships while in the group.
        d. To discuss feelings about termination of the program.

- Procedures
  a. Role of therapist
     (1) Model support, but, as much as possible, let the partici-
         pants give the positive feedback. By this time, the group
         should have learned supportive behaviors and should be
         helping each other.
     (2) Deal with group termination issues.
  b. Role of participants
     (1) The participants should now be giving the majority of the
         supportive statements made in the group.
     (2) The participants should be more open in sharing their
         feelings about themselves than they were in the beginning
         phases of treatment.
  c. Treatment
     (1) Follow up on progress in the areas discussed in problem-
         solving sessions. (10 minutes)
     (2) Introduce the theme of focusing on strengths as a way of
         supporting. (10 minutes)
         (a) Play the song, "Shower the People You Love with
             Love," by James Taylor. Ask the group members
             how this song relates to how they share in relation-
             ships.
         (b) Ask the members how they like to be shown appre-
             ciation and love by others.
     (3) Focusing on strengths. (50–60 minutes)
         (a) Each person is "in focus" for 3–5 minutes and shares
             personal strengths with the group. The experience is
             voluntary, but all members are encouraged to partic-
             ipate.
         (b) Following each individual's sharing of strengths, the
             group members add to the strengths that have already
             been identified.
     (4) Sharing by group members of what they have learned in
         the group and how they have improved their relation-
         ships. (15 minutes)
         (a) Rediagram the Johari Window on group and sibling
             relationships to see if there has been any improve-
             ment since the fourth session.
         (b) Ask the members how they have improved their rela-
             tionships with siblings, peers, and parents.
     (5) Discussion of feelings about the group ending. (15 min-
         utes)

        (a) Plan for the postgroup evaluation session. (1 hour)
        (b) Plan a group party with refreshments. (1 hour)

8. Postprogram Activities
   * Evaluation session
     a. Administer the FIRO-B, the Family-Oriented Sentence Completion form, the Coopersmith Self-Esteem Inventory, and the Sibling Perception Rating Scale in the week following the eighth session. To encourage participants to come to the evaluation session, a party could be planned to follow completion of the assessment.
   * Posttreatment interviews
     a. The individual interviews with each person involved in the group treatment should assess the following: (1) how the group helped them, (2) any negative effects from the group treatment, (3) the desire to continue or not to continue working on the sibling relationship, and (4) present and future counseling needs.
     b. The interviews with the parents should include the following: (1) sharing of the general results of the treatment, (2) sharing the needs of the adolescents with the parents, (3) checking to see what progress has been made in the sibling relationship and in the siblings' relationship with the parents, (4) listening to the present needs of the parents, and (5) referral for family counseling if indicated and desired.

Chapter 22

Helping Couples Who Are in Crisis Because of a Life-Threatening Illness

Dana N. Christensen

This structured group treatment is designed to treat couples in which one member has been diagnosed as having a life-threatening illness, for example, cancer or heart disease. The program covers a period of 10 weeks with each session lasting 2½ hours. It is designed for five couples.

The setting for the treatment should be as noninstitutional as possible. Hospitals and clinics are not appropriate, due to the unpleasant memories associated with them in this treatment's population. The setting should instead be a pleasant, well-lighted, well-ventilated, large room with as much "life" as someone's living room. The room must be large enough for each participant to be able to find a private space in which to do the movement exercises. The setting also needs to be free of interruptions and possible violations of privacy. The room should be carpeted, and furniture in the room should be limited to a few tables and chairs around the outside of the room with soft pads or beanbags in the center of the room for the participants to sit on.

PROGRAM DESCRIPTION

Selection Criteria

All participating couples are required to attend an individual intake interview in which the treatment is explained and a clinical assessment is conducted to determine the treatment's appropriateness for each couple. The latter decision will be based on the following criteria. The couples must:

- be sharing their lives together
- be committed to each other out of love

315

- have one member who has been diagnosed as having a life-threatening illness, such as cancer, but who is not *currently* terminal
- be physically capable of participating in the treatment procedure over a ten-week period
- be psychologically healthy, not psychotic or borderline psychotic (as determined by extreme T-JTA scores and clinical interview)
- be motivated rather than coerced to attend
- be willing to bring the rest of the family to the final session

No decision is made concerning the couple until after the interview and until the therapists have had time to discuss the advisability of admitting them. If group treatment is not appropriate for the couple, marital therapy or referral is recommended. This initial interview also serves to clarify questions the couple might have and to allow the couple to establish a beginning relationship with the therapists.

Treatment Overview

The first session is devoted to introductions, an overview of the program, establishment of group norms, and the building of cohesion and trust. The second, third, and fourth sessions utilize gestalt techniques to enhance self-awareness and emotional expression. The activities are designed specifically for the treatment population.

Sessions 5 through 8 center on relational conflicts (for each couple) that may be, though need not be, related to the life crisis situation. These sessions are characterized by psychodramatic techniques focused on goal-oriented problem solving.

The ninth session concentrates on positive growth aspects of the group members. The tenth and final session consists of a pot-luck dinner attended by all the couples and their families. At this last dinner session, a general recapitulation of the members' experiences takes place in the presence of their families.

Outcome Objectives

By the end of the tenth session, each participant will have:

- learned skills in developing a support group
- established and experienced a support group
- developed an increased level of self-awareness
- enhanced and enriched awareness of the person's spouse as an individual

- increased emotive flexibility and diversity
- expressed emotional empathy
- had an opportunity to express anticipatory grief
- experienced goal-oriented problem solving
- begun to eliminate at least one relational conflict
- shared the treatment experience with the participant's family

Measurement Instruments

Four assessment instruments are used to measure change in the participants: The Taylor-Johnson Temperament Analysis and the Caring Relationships Inventory (see Appendix B for descriptions), a Self-Report Questionnaire (see Exhibit 22-1) and the therapists' session reports. In the latter reports (see Exhibit 22-2) the therapists make short statements about each couple and the couple's concerns and comment on the results of the group process. The reports should also include comments on any problems, concerns, or questions that may arise and notes on the efficacy of the treatment design.

Exhibit 22-1 Self-Report Questionnaire

(When preparing this form allow room for written responses)

A support group is an undefined group of people who care about each other and who share with each other the difficulties as well as the joys in life. Examples are families, relatives, church memberships, clubs, fellow workers, and friends.

1. What personal skills would a person need to develop a support group for themselves?

2. Do you currently have such a support group?

3. Of whom does it consist?

4. How often do you have conversations with someone about your personal feelings?

5. With whom do you have these conversations?

6. What are these conversations about?

7. What relationship conflicts have you resolved in the past two months?

8. What relationship conflicts do you wish to resolve in the next two months?

Exhibit 22-2 Therapists' Session Report

Session # _____ Date _____ Therapists _____

_____

Please comment on the following:

Couple A:

Couple B:

Couple C:

Couple D:

Couple E:

Group as a Whole:

Treatment Design:

Initial Interview

The purpose of the initial interview is to assess the treatment's appropriateness for each referred couple, to inform the couple about the treatment, to begin a therapeutic relationship prior to the first group meeting, and to obtain data necessary to evaluate the program.

Procedures and Instructions

The following criteria should guide the initial interview:

- Begin with an introduction to and an overview of the interview. Be sure to state that no decision will be made at this meeting as to whether the treatment is right for the couple.
- Give the rationale for the treatment and invite questions. Be sure to distinguish clearly the present treatment from medical/physical treatment.
- Inquire generally as to couples' interest.
- Conduct a clinical assessment interview (this depends on therapists' own methodology).
- Administer the assessment instruments if the clinical interview indicates a potential for meeting the criteria for membership in the group.
- Refer to other sources if the clinical interview clearly shows the present treatment is inappropriate.
- Do not accept potential couples immediately as group members. The couples should be informed of their acceptance only after the assessment instruments have been scored and interpreted and the therapists have had an opportunity to share their clinical impressions. This process ensures that the participant criteria are met and also serves to motivate the couples (Smith & Alexander, 1974).

Role of the Therapists

The therapists should adopt an attitude that is essential for any clinical assessment interview, that is, to be therapeutic but to avoid doing therapy. In addition to making the initial assessment, the therapists should, in the initial interview, establish an initial rapport and provide information concerning the treatment. To support their role, the therapists should have a knowledge of referral resources in their area.

Program Phases

The first phase (Session 1) of the program is devoted to introductions and the establishment of the basis for group support. Phase 2 (Sessions 2 through 4) have similar formats, though they begin with different exercises. The aim in this phase is to create an environment in which an exploration of self may take place. Projective exercises are used in a gestalt therapy framework to maximize self-awareness and to underscore and reinforce efforts at differentiation (Bowen, 1976). This treatment is based on the theoretical premise that differentiation is a healthy step and necessary to the process of both individuation and relationship dissolution (Bosormenyi-Nagy & Spark, 1973). This initial step of viewing oneself as separate yet interdependent becomes extremely important in anticipatory grief (Powers, 1977). The four sessions (Sessions 5 through 8) in Phase 3 have a common format and therefore common objectives. This phase is designed to build upon the awareness exercises of the first phase as well   as to draw upon and enhance the support system that has been established. The main objective here is to integrate emotional catharsis and awareness with cognitive restructuring (Blatner, 1973). This involves the experiential involvement of the whole group as individual couples grapple with relational conflicts. The emphasis is on defining conflict through psychodramatic enactment, and then drawing upon the support system to offer goal-oriented alternatives, again experientially.

The purpose of Phase 4 (Session 9) is to provide a positive inner growth experience for the participants and an opportunity for them to share support. Phase 5 (Session 10) serves as a therapy and support bridge between the treatment program and follow-up social and family action. The final phase, Phase 6 (Session 11), is devoted to postprogram assessment and follow-up services as appropriate.

PROGRAM OUTLINE

The following outline describes the content, procedures and materials used in each program session:

1. Session 1: Introduction (2 hours, 30 minutes)
   - Objectives
     a. This session is an introductory session in which participants will learn each other's names, learn something about each person in the group, participate in establishing group norms in areas of support, and commit themselves to helping each other. The session draws heavily on the treatment for divorce adjustment by Hoopes (see Chapter 19).
   - Materials
     a. Colored construction paper, scissors, glue, stapler, colored magic markers, pipe cleaners, and straight pins.
   - Procedures
     a. Name exercise (45 minutes)
       (1) Greet each individual and couple as they come in and help make them comfortable. Do *not* ask how they are doing or feeling.
       (2) As they come in, instruct them to get some materials and make name tags in the shape of an animal with their names on them and to pin the tags to their shirts.

(3) As new people arrive, instruct them to join the others in creating their own animal name tags.

(4) As the participants finish, ask them to join the circular seating arrangement in the center of the room.

(5) When all are present with name tags, welcome the group and mention the following topics: the intake interview, the commonality of the couples' experiences, the introductory nature of the first session, and the need to get to know each other as a first step.

(6) Suggest that they introduce themselves in the following way: "Hi, I'm (first name), the (name of name tag animal). I'm a (tag animal) because (some reason) and because I like to (some action)."

(7) When everyone, including the therapists, has had a turn, a "we" statement may be appropriate, such as, "I think we all deserve a hand!" or, "We have a lot of talent to draw from here!"

b. Expectation exercise (45 minutes)

(1) Make a transitional statement, such as "To get us all going in the same general direction, let's discuss some of our expectations for this group, and also some of the things we can do to make it a good group. Let's get started by discussing our expectations."

(2) If necessary, pose a more specific question, such as, "What would you like to happen here?"

(3) Facilitate a discussion, weaving in a general overview of the treatment as the discussion progresses. Be sure to remind the group that the focus is on emotional not medical concerns.

(4) Include in the discussion the important points of confidentiality, attendance, support (how to build it and how to ask for it), and recognition of one's own strengths.

(5) Inquire whether anyone has difficulty with anything discussed so far and, if so, how the group can help in dealing with that difficulty.

c. Sharing exercise (45 minutes)

(1) Make a transition statement, such as, "Let's take some time now to share something about your current situation and how it is affecting your relationship. Risk telling us about yourself as if we were old friends. Remember, our

focus here is on the emotional impact your diagnosis has had on your relationships."

(2)   Instruct each couple to take about five minutes to discuss their situation and problems in a general way.

(3)   Be sure to focus the couple's as well as each member's questioning on the relationships and affective components.

(4)   Monitor the time carefully (each couple should take around ten minutes).

d.   Closing comments (15 minutes)

(1)   Make an anticipatory closing statement, such as "We're near the end of the first session, and I want to discuss some things before we go."

(2)   Then review the discussion on receiving and giving support, and challenge each member to be supportive of one other person this week.

(3)   Mention that next week the group will be doing some exercises that require comfortable clothes. Suggest that the members dress casually and that women may be more comfortable in slacks.

e.   Role of the therapists. The therapist must be something of a conductor in this first session. The session's goals require a good deal of time management and emotional management. The focus of the group must be kept on the objectives while still allowing for depth sharing, which is necessary to begin the creation of trust and group cohesion. It is also appropriate for the therapists to share themselves in a joining operation.

2.   Session 2: Exploration (2 hours, 30 minutes)
   • Objectives
     a.   To serve as a vehicle for beginning self-exploration and awareness in the specific area of identity. A further objective is to move the focus of attention from a preoccupation with the illness to other facets of each participant's personality and experience. In terms of group development, the session's aim is to acknowledge individual characteristics and to imply commonality through similarities.
   • Materials
     a.   Scissors, glue, 15 to 20 picture magazines, and 24" by 28" posterboard.
   • Procedures
     a.   Opening exercise (15–20 minutes)

(1) Greet and welcome each member by name until all members are present.

(2) Begin the session by inquiring how the group members did in supporting someone else during the week. Use this discussion to review the concepts of asking for and giving support.

(3) Make an introductory transition statement, such as, "Let's begin tonight by doing an exercise in giving and receiving."

(4) Instruct the couples to give each other backrubs (for about ten minutes). Give them the following guidelines:

    (a) The persons receiving must be responsible for their own comfort.

    (b) The persons receiving must coach the givers as to the pressure, rhythm, and location desired.

    (c) The givers must be as sensitive as possible to the receivers' requests.

    (d) After ten minutes, the couples should switch roles.

    (e) The therapeutic team should participate in this activity.

(5) Call the group back together and spend a few minutes processing (do not go deeply into problem areas).

b. Collage exercise (1 hour, 55 minutes)

(1) Instruct each member to construct on the posterboard a "self-collage." Suggest that the participants look through the magazines, clipping out pictures and images that particularly strike them in some way. Advise them that they need not think a great deal about what they are doing, but merely choose pictures that they like or that remind them of themselves. Then have them arrange the pictures on the board in any way they like and glue them in place. The therapists should participate in this activity.

(2) When they have finished (in about thirty minutes), instruct them to sign their collages in the corner and place them in a circle, facing out, in the center of the room.

(3) Instruct the group members to take a few minutes and slowly walk around the circle, taking time to view each other's representation in silence (this should not be rushed).

(4) After they have finished (usually five minutes), ask them to take seats behind their self-collages.

(5) Ask for volunteers to share themselves with the group through their collages.

(6) As someone volunteers, have the person hold up the collage (or tape it to the wall) and describe it in the following way: "This is me, I'm _____ . I'm also over here: _____ . This down here is the part of me that _____ ." The description should not be rigid, but gestalt principles of ownership should be practiced. It may be necessary for one of the therapists to share a collage by modeling early in the process.

(7) Monitor the time so that everyone has an opportunity to share themselves (some will be quite brief).

(8) Encourage, model, and reinforce supportive statements.

(9) Provide feedback from your observations of the group members' collages as appropriate, with statements such as, "I feel great strength in your sun." The use of metaphor is very helpful in this exercise (Van Dusen, 1972). Another statement might be, "I sense a lot of live growing plants and other things in your representation." A comment on a painful symbol might be something like, "That surely is a dark cloud hanging overhead on the right there. Is that something you wish to share?" or, "What does that tree without any leaves on it mean to you?" Collages typically have many facets and your inquiry should be well-balanced.

(10) Acknowledge problem areas, but do not seize upon them in an effort to resolve the problem. Use helpful statements, such as, "You may want to work on that in the problem-solving sessions we will have in the next few weeks," or, "What in your collage helps you deal with that?"

c. Closing exercise (5–10 minutes)

(1) When all members have had an opportunity to explain their collages, ask them to take their collages separately to a place in the room where they each will have privacy.

(2) Instruct them to choose images or places on their collages from which they receive strength.

(3) Ask them to close their eyes, to let their muscles relax, and to become aware of their breathing (any short relaxation exercise is appropriate here). Then have them go to their private places to feel the strength that is there, and, when they are ready, to come slowly back into the room.

(4) Be silent for a minute or two, then say it is time to stop.

d. Role of the therapists. The therapists should work to create an
environment conducive to self-exploration and self-exposure.
They should model supportive behavior as well as active listening. Because of the nature of the collage exercise, it is
particularly useful to assist members in discussing their projections in a personal manner by providing direct or metaphorical references. No one should be confronted to the point of
becoming defensive or of being forced to discuss something.
Again, the use of metaphor is helpful here.

3. Session 3: Exploration
   - Objectives
     a. To continue the focus on self-exploration, self-awareness,
     emotional empathy, and the expression of emotions centered
     around the possibility of dying.
   - Materials
     a. Crayons, chalk, magic markers, and 24″ by 28″ posterboard.
   - Procedures
     a. Opening exercise (15 minutes)
        (1) Greet and welcome each member by name.
        (2) Start the session in the circle by asking if there is any
        unfinished business or news items that need taking care
        of. Comment on or question efforts to give support out-
        side of the group.
        (3) Conduct a warm-up exercise (any short physical warm-
        up is appropriate). The following is one possibility: "Find
        a place to stand where you have plenty of room to swing
        your arms at your side. Lift your arms straight out to the
        side and move them in a small tight circle, still straight
        out. Now turn them in the opposite direction. Now, keep-
        ing both arms straight out, write the word 'ridiculous' in
        the air with your right arm. Now do it with your left arm.
        Now write it with your left knee (keep your arms up).
        Now your right knee. Now write it with your nose. Now
        write it with your rear-end."
        (4) After the warm-up, instruct the members to stretch any
        muscles that are still stiff and to sit down somewhere
        comfortable.
     b. Road of life exercise (2 hours)
        (1) Instruct the participants to close their eyes; then conduct
        a short relaxation exercise.

(2)   When participants are relaxed and their eyes are closed, give the following instructions: "In a few minutes, I'm going to ask you to draw a road, your road of life. Imagine how the road begins. Imagine where you are on the road now, and imagine where the road is headed. What is the road made of? Are there side trails? Are there obstacles? Now, when you are ready, you will find posterboard on the tables and crayons and markers to reproduce your road. Take about 30 minutes to work on your road, and then we'll get back together and discuss it."

(3)   When the 30 minutes are up, arrange the drawings in a circle and instruct the group members to walk slowly around the circle viewing each other's road.

(4)   When the viewing is done, ask for a volunteer to begin the discussion. Explore the drawings (projections) within a gestalt framework, emphasizing awareness by reclaiming projections through the process of "being the symbol" (Perls, 1969). The therapist should encourage the members to present creatively, to involve others (at the request of whoever is in focus), and to underscore universality. Some useful techniques here are the use of split-half dialogues, dialogue between symbols, denoting polarities, and giving sound and movement to a graphic representation.

(5)   Do not expect (or encourage) all members to participate "in focus." Resolution of conflict is neither expected, nor avoided. Rather the gestalt principle of "staying with something" should be used as guidance (Polster & Polster, 1973).

(6)   Monitor the time so that the exercise is ended within stipulated time limits.

c.   Closing exercise (15 minutes)

(1)   Make a transitional statement, such as, "Before we process our experiences tonight, let's shake loose some cobwebs. Stand up, shake your body as if it had water on it after a shower. Shake both legs, shake your arms, your trunk. Now add sound to it (model this with a sound of relief). Now slowly come to a stop and take some deep breaths. Again. Okay, let's sit down and process tonight."

(2)   Suggest that each member take a minute to think about all that has happened in the session. Have them try to come up with one thing they have learned about them-

selves, their spouse, or their relationships and one thing they have come to appreciate in another person.

(3)   Have each person briefly share these thoughts.

d.   Role of the therapists. The therapists' leadership role in this session is a strong one, due to the structure and characteristics of the exercises. However, the therapists must be sensitive to possibilities of allowing the members to assume some leadership functions. This should be facilitated as a general trend whenever possible. During the exploration of the "road of life" drawings, the undue emphasis should not be placed on painful issues; however, neither should such issues be ignored. It is helpful to remember that, within the drawings, polarities can mean strength and hope as well as weakness and despair. The members' attention should be focused on the members' resources (present in the projection) that are useful to them in "meeting their obstacles." The growth of such strengths can be facilitated by the gestalt technique of "being the symbol," that is, "I am the rock, I am strong, I am enduring," and so on.

4. Session 4: Exploration
   • Objectives
     a.   This is the last session specifically designed for self-exploration, self-awareness, catharsis, and reclaiming projections, in preparation for the next problem-solving phase.
   • Materials
     a.   Colored construction paper, scissors, glue, stapler, string, tape, pipe cleaners, and magic markers.
   • Procedures
     a.   Opening exercise (30 minutes)
       (1)   Greet and welcome members as they arrive.
       (2)   Gather in the usual manner and ask about any unfinished business. You may model this by identifying something unfinished, such as thanking a person for something specific that person has done, expressing concern over someone who is absent, or sharing an emotion about something that has happened. Inquire about support-giving outside of the group (no longer than ten minutes). Ask the group to remember and schedule for the pot-luck dinner with families present in the tenth session.
       (3)   Introduce an exercise that emphasizes dependency or teamwork. It should be one that can be done in 20 minutes

or less. One of the following exercises may be appropriate:

(a) A "trust walk" in which one member of a couple is blindfolded and led around obstacles by the hand of the other. The positions are then alternated.

(b) The laughing exercise. This exercise is begun by one person lying down on the back, then the next person lies down with the head resting on the first one's stomach, the third person rests the head on the second, and this continues until all members are connected by head and stomach. The first person then says "ha," the second person says "ha-ha," the third "ha-ha-ha," and so forth in order, right up to the last person who must say ten or twelve "ha's." If someone does not say the correct number of "ha's," the chain reaction must start over again with the first person, with each person in turn again saying only the prescribed number of "ha-ha's". This usually proves impossible, and the chain must start over again. This exercise usually requires a break afterward.

(c) The machine. One person enters from the circle to the middle of the room, then takes an unusual position to which the person adds a movement and sound. A second person then becomes attached to the first, as if they formed part of a machine, adding more movement and more sound. This process continues until the first person begins to slow down, then the second, and so on until the machine stops.

(4) If the exercise chosen produces a high level of energy that might interfere with the next exercise, a short break may be scheduled.

b. Personal exercise (2 hours)

(1) Conduct a short relaxation exercise as described in Session 2, before beginning the following guided fantasy. Then give the following instructions: "Imagine you are an actor or actress who has just been given the part of playing yourself. In order to appear on stage, you will need to fashion a mask—a mask that represents how you try to appear to the rest of the world. What will the mask look like? What expression will it have? (give the members time to reflect) When you think you have enough

information to begin start to make the mask. Materials are on the back table. You have about 30 minutes.''

(2) When the group is ready, give the following directions: ''Put on your masks and mill around the room slowly in varying directions: avoid making contact with anyone. Now imagine this room is a stage and the people near you are fellow actors. Stop and describe to them just what sort of character you are; convince them that you are really that kind of person, that you really have the described qualities.''

(3) Allow this activity to go on for a few minutes, then ask them to stop where they are, sit down in small groups, remove their masks, and share themselves and their experience in ''wearing masks.'' Allow about 20 minutes for this.

(4) When this process is finished, suggest that each couple find a private place and discuss what the masks mean in their own relationship.

(5) Call the group back together and process what happened in stages: the fantasy, the mask, the milling, the convincing of others, the small group experience, and the couple's experience in their relationship. This processing should take the rest of the time—about 30 minutes.

(6) End the session by reminding the group that the next four sessions are devoted to considering their concerns about their relationships. Suggest that they consider over the next week what they wish to work on.

c. Role of the therapists. This is the last awareness session prior to the problem-solving activities. The therapists' role is increasingly low-key during these processing segments. The therapists give structure through their directions but refrain from entering the mask-making exercise, the small group discussion, or the couple discussions. In the large-group discussions, the therapists facilitate the discussion but do not become a part of it.

5. Sessions 5 to 8: Problem Solving
   • Objectives
     a. To enhance the group members' support systems.
     b. To integrate the members' emotional catharsis and awareness with their cognitive restructuring.

- Materials
  a. Blackboard and chalk.
- Procedures (2 hours, 30 minutes for each session)
  a. Opening exercises (15 minutes)
      (1) Greet and welcome the members as they arrive.
      (2) Begin with unfinished business. This should include reports from those who worked on a concern the week before. This is particularly important in Sessions 6 through 8.
      (3) Warm-up exercise. This is the stage in psychodrama in which an environment conducive to spontaneity and creativity is created. The exercise and methods chosen must be kinesthetically, emotionally, and cognitively stimulating. For example, the members may:
           (a) use any of the warm-up exercises already outlined.
           (b) divide into two small groups, one of which pantomimes a social situation peculiar to this treatment population, while the other one guesses the circumstances.
           (c) follow the leader through an imaginary obstacle course.
           (d) use   large, white butcher paper, 12' to 15', to create a mural on which the whole group creates something nonverbally together.

  b. Psychodrama (2 hours, 10 minutes): The following problem-solving exercises have three stages, within which the therapists' creativity and spontaneity should operate: (1) Enactment, problem definition or the presentation in the "here and now" of a relational concern; (2) Re-enactment, the behavioral practice of the changed situation or the reworking of the situation with help from the rest of the group; and (3) Commitment, the stage in which the couple partners commit to each other, and to the group, what it is they are going to do differently.

      (1) Enactment stage
           (a) The therapist asks a couple to volunteer. This volunteer couple's concern to be enacted may have grown naturally out of an awareness that surfaced in the warm-up exercises, or it may have emerged from experiences in Phase 2.
           (b) The problem is presented verbally by the two partners together. As they talk they are drawn to "center stage." Whenever they mention an occurrence in a time and place, the therapist directs them to "show

us" as if it were happening right now. Present tense is then used from that point on. The couple is led slowly through the interaction, with detailed description of the scene (time of day, placement of furniture, and so on) in an effort to recreate the emotional and contextual environment of the problem.

(c) As new people emerge in the problem situation, "auxiliary egos" are chosen by the couple to participate, and the enactment continues.

(d) If the couple tends to narrate or "talk about" the situation, auxiliary egos should be coached to address them in their role, to say, for example, "Hey, you're talking as if I'm not here!"

(e) If one or both members of the couple become emotionally blocked, or if the action is going circular with no depth, the therapists must use their creativity to "charge" the enactment. The following psychodramatic techniques may be useful: a soliloquy; the use of a double; substitution of another group member in a role; emphasis on the nonverbal (exaggerated); a shift from a current situation to a past similar situation, which may require recreating a primary family constellation; acting out or "going with" resistances; exaggeration of injunctions; fantasizing situations, such as, "at a funeral," "at St. Peter's gate," Judgment Day, or rebirth; and role reversal.

(f) When the problem is well-defined and the couple has fully experienced the emotional pain associated with the situation, the next stage, re-enactment, may begin. It should be remembered that problem definition is often reached when the couple experiences the "stuck" point (Perls, 1969).

(2) Re-enactment stage

(a) The couple is encouraged to seek alternatives from the group. The alternatives are sought in a "brainstorming" fashion, that is, they are not evaluated when offered. The blackboard may be used at this time to list alternatives quickly; spontaneity and creativity should be emphasized.

(b) The couple then "tries the alternatives on for size" by walking through them in action, not discussion. At this point, other problems may arise; however, it is suggested that the focus remain on the original concern if the new problems represent a diversion.

(c) During this stage other group members should be used and the "walk through" made as real as possible. Particular attention should be given to *both* members of the couple to identify what the alternatives feel like.

(d) The couple then decides what it is they wish to do differently.

(3) Commitment stage

(a) Once both members have decided on what it is they wish to change, they commit to each other and to the group their determination to change.

(b) This commitment may take creative forms such as wedding vows complete with the group singing the wedding march.

(c) If appropriate, the couple rehearses the changed behavior with various group members, or tense, difficult situations are enacted as "testing their determination."

(d) If time allows, the procedure is repeated with another couple.

c. Closing the sessions (15–20 minutes)

(1) Encourage the couples to continue their exercises throughout the week and to inform the group of their progress at next week's session.

(2) Depending on the group mood, a "group hug" may be appropriate. The members gather in a tight circle with their arms around the person next to them. Sounds or chants may be added.

d. Role of the therapists. The therapists are active in the role of director in these psychodrama sessions and thus serve as creative catalysts. The catalyst's main objective is the creation of an environment that inspires creativity and spontaneity. In this effort, the therapists must work toward the same goal. The key points to remember in psychodrama are (1) stay in the present, (2) "act it out" rather than talk about it, and (3) the group is a tremendous resource.

6. Session 9: Strengths and Termination
   • Objectives
     a. This session may be used to do one more problem-solving

exercise in the first half if there is a couple who has not had the opportunity (this may be the case if there are five couples and each couple takes a whole session). The session's main function, however, is to provide a positive inner growth experience, and an opportunity to share appreciation for support. On a metaphorical level, the session begins the dissolution process, since part of it is future oriented.

- Materials
  a. Assorted coloring instruments, colored paper, colored tissue, and 18″ by 24″ drawing paper. If the psychodrama is finished, the following additional materials are needed for the first exercise: wooden drums (especially a bass drum), a tambourine, hand-held percussion instruments, and long multicolored scarves and ribbons.
- Procedures
  a. If the psychodrama is incomplete, the first 90 minutes should be devoted to the final couples, followed by the guided fantasy and sharing exercise. In this case, omit the opening and final exercises.
  b. Opening exercise (45 minutes)
    (1) Greet and welcome the members as they arrive.
    (2) Ask for the report of the last couple that worked in problem-solving phase.
    (3) Have all the instruments and colored scarves arranged in the center of the room prior to the meeting.
    (4) Begin by instructing the members as follows: "Slowly close your eyes and imagine drifting back through time—all the way back to when people lived in tribes. Imagine gathering around the tribal circle. (begin to beat very softly and slowly the largest bass drum) Let the beat of the drum take you back . . . back . . . back to the tribal circle. (long pause) Here there are instruments with which to make rhythmic sounds. There are scarves here to help you dance. When you are ready, let the beat of the drum move you. Let your body move you."
    (5) As the members begin to join in, the drum beat is merged with other sounds and movements. Individual noises become syncopated rhythms. Expect the energy level to rise and fall, and then rise again, often to a high level. Let the process take its course. Finish the exercise when the energy level is low again and the group is ready.
    (6) Take a 15-minute break.

c. Guided fantasy exercise (20 minutes)
  (1) Gather the group together and begin the second exercise with instructions to the members to find a comfortable place in which they have plenty of room to move around.
  (2) Conduct a relaxation exercise with people on the floor and their eyes closed.
  (3) Begin very slowly with the following fantasy: "Slowly begin to contract your muscles. Contract your energy into as small a space as you can. You are a tight pocket of energy taking up as little room as possible. Imagine you are a seed, a plant seed, with a few inches of dirt above you. Now listen carefully. Off in the distance, a storm is coming. The thunder of a spring rainstorm is coming closer and closer. You hear the first drops hit overhead. Now more are falling. Now you begin to feel the cool, life-bringing moisture on you. It is a soft soaking rain. Begin to soak up the nurturing element. Slowly, ever so slowly you begin to grow. The storm has stopped, and the sun's rays are bathing the earth above you. Slowly grow towards the surface. Your contracted energy begins to expand. You break through the surface. Feel the warmth of the sun's rays. Now let yourself really grow. (voice a little louder and upbeat) Reach to the skies."
  (4) The finish of the fantasy may be more movement or may be just a silent special moment. The group decides this through its collective action.
d. Sharing experience (30 minutes)
  (1) Gather the group back together in a circle on the floor.
  (2) Make a transitional statement, such as the following: "This is one of our last meetings together, at least as a group, so let's take time out to share what we appreciate about each other. Let's go one person at a time." If no one begins, the therapist should begin with someone.
  (3) This is a group activity, and the therapists should participate as members.
e. Theme-drawing exercise (40 minutes)
  (1) While still in circle, introduce this exercise in the following way: "This is the last activity tonight. There are paper, crayons, and markers on the table. I'd like to have you draw a picture with the title 'How I Wish to Grow.' Take some time to think about it, to let your desires surface. You'll have about 20 to 25 minutes for this." The

group by now should need little prompting for this exercise.

(2) When the time is up, suggest that each couple adjourn to some private place in the room and share the drawings.

(3) Hand out directions to the pot-luck dinner, and remind them they contracted to bring their entire family with them. The directions should include a reference to a short discussion after the dinner.

  f. Role of the therapists. This session requires that the therapists be versatile and flexible in both unstructured and structured exercises. The unstructured, primitive exercise grows out of the interaction of the group as process, and will not happen if "led." The guided fantasy requires the therapists to operate in both fantasy and reality in order to assist the group members through the metaphorical experience. The therapists must also feel comfortable working in the hypnagogic state.

7. Session 10: Building Bridges
- Objectives
  a. This session is meant to serve as a bridge in many areas: between a therapy/support group and a social/support group; between the couple experience and the family experience; and between therapy and social action.
- Materials
  a. Pot-luck dinner in a big, friendly house with seating for 20 to 30 people.
- Procedures (3 hours)
  a. Dinner and discussion
    (1) Greet people as they arrive and begin the pot-luck dinner early in the evening.
    (2) After dinner and the washing of dishes, gather in the living room with everyone present.
    (3) Begin with the members of each family introducing themselves to the other families.
    (4) Begin discussion in the following way: "I thought it might be useful for each of us to share our thoughts about this group so that our families as well as ourselves could learn from it. We also want to hear from our families about what it was like to live with us these past ten weeks." Therapists should participate as "members."
    (5) When appropriate, turn the discussion as follows: "How can we take what we've learned from each other about

people who have serious illnesses and apply it to the community?"

(6) If possible, involve the families in the discussion.

(7) Before the people leave, remind them of the follow-up session in two weeks, and of how important the assessment instruments are to research.

  b. Role of the therapists. In this session, the role of the therapists shifts to that of being good hosts and friends. The discussion has minimal organization, and the therapists' role is more like that of a valuable member. The group chooses its own direction, with the therapists holding back from their earlier leadership roles.

8. Session 11: Follow-Up Assessment
- Objectives
  a. The primary objective of this final session is to complete the assessment instruments and to offer further service if desired. A secondary objective is to provide a vehicle for the support system to be maintained beyond the structured treatment.
- Materials
  a. Assessment instruments.
- Procedures (2 hours, 30 minutes)
  a. Assessment
  (1) Greet the members as they come in, have refreshments available, and allow some socializing. (10–15 minutes)
  (2) Discuss briefly how useful the assessment information will be to research, and thank them for coming.
  (3) Tell the members that they can go as soon as they finish the tests.
  (4) Then begin administering the instruments.
  (b) Role of the therapists. The therapists' role in this final meeting is largely that of being concerned and interested. If during conversation the group members indicate a desire for further service, the therapists should be prepared to make either necessary arrangements or a referral.

Chapter 23

Multiple Family Therapy for Female Adolescent Incest Victims

Leslie L. Feinauer

This is a multiple family treatment program for female adolescent incest victims and their families. It requires ten weeks total time. An initial screening and orientation session is followed by an eight-week structured group treatment and a final termination and evaluation session. The weekly sessions are two hours in length and are led by a male and female cotherapy team. The program is applicable to private and public agency practice.

The purpose of the program is to interrupt the negative effects of incest on the individual members and on the family unit as a whole. The focus is on the resolution of feelings, the restoration of internal controls and boundaries, and the restitution of a healthy family support system.

BACKGROUND

The extent of incest can only be estimated. The recent public focus on incest has encouraged individuals to acknowledge more openly sexual abuse within families. It has been estimated that ten percent of American families have experienced some type of incestuous relationship. The dynamics of the involved individuals and their families vary; however, the most commonly recorded and studied incest dyad consists of a father and daughter within a nuclear family.

In response to the unique problems that arise in a family when a history of incest exists, multiple family therapy requires more active participation on the part of the therapists than more traditional, nonstructured group therapy. A male and female cotherapy team that is able to work well conjointly is required. In addition, some relatively inexpensive materials—such as large pads of paper, colored marking pens, magazines, and audio-cassettes—are required.

In father-daughter incestuous relationships, one of two family patterns is generally apparent: (1) a pattern of a rigid, secretive, enmeshed family in which there is little nurturance and support but in which, because of insecurity, the family members are extremely dependent upon one another; or (2) a pattern of a chaotic, multiproblem family in which life is a recurring series of crises and acting-out behaviors (Gottlieb, 1980).

In such families, as Brown (1978) indicates, the family's emotional system has become dysfunctional in its search for warmth and closeness. Family communication is poor, often nonverbal, and characterized by double messages. The family meets very few of the members' needs, and tends to isolate itself from the community in an attempt to maintain a conspiracy of silence. Most authors (Brown, 1978; Gottlieb, 1980) agree that multigenerational nurturance deprivation of both spouses results in an inability to meet one another's emotional needs within their marital relationship. Often the mother in the incestuous family was sexually abused by someone in her family of origin and/or her extended family (Brown, 1978; Gottlieb, 1980).

There is some controversy about the most effective mode of treatment for incest victims. Various therapists favor individual therapy, dyadic treatment, marital therapy, family treatment, age-and-sex-cohort group treatment, or combinations and sequences of these treatments. This author believes that initial individual and marital therapy may be required to permit effective family treatment but that successful resolution and further growth may not occur without resolution of the family issues that created the dysfunction originally. In order to reverse the family isolation and withdrawal, it is important that both parents and children share with other people who have had similar traumatic experiences.

In group therapy, the therapeutic processes are less threatening; the focus is not always on heavy intrapsychic material; it may also extend to interpersonal conflicts and concerns. The young female adolescent who is very much concerned with her peers may have the opportunity to test and subsequently minimize her fears about revelations concerning the incest with less threat or pressure than might occur if she were confined to dealing exclusively with her own family group. This becomes very important in light of the past exploitation by the parents, with their verbal and nonverbal behavior and double messages that pressured her to respond to their needs at the sacrifice of her own.

Incest victims and their families have a sense of estrangement from others. They have lost their sense of community and belonging. Meeting in small groups of families with similar feelings, fears, and experiences provides a sense of support and shared experience. This may enable them to explore coping alternatives previously unknown to them. With these points in mind, the present structured multiple family treatment program was developed.

PROGRAM DESCRIPTION

General Treatment Objectives

The program has the following five general objectives:

1. To help the group members gain or regain a more positive sense of themselves within their families.
2. To help the family members learn to be in charge of themselves and express what they feel, physically or psychologically.
3. To establish appropriate roles in the family to allow the family members to get their needs met in more appropriate ways.
4. To resolve some of the family problems that arose out of the skewed family relationship and to teach the family members a method of problem solving.
5. To help the families focus on the future, to gain a perspective and direction toward growth beyond the incest experience.

Organization of the Group

Although the incest victims and their fathers are usually identified as the most sensitive members of the group, it is essential that the whole family be interviewed. This allows the therapists to determine how many members of the family need to be included and if multiple family therapy is suited to the needs and abilities of the family members. It is essential that all children who are aware of and concerned about the incestuous relationship work with the family.

The following are criteria for selection of group members:

- willingness of the family members to be open about their concerns
- ability to function as a family group in some way
- desire to change the current relationships
- ability of the incest victim to acknowledge and discuss her responses, concerns, and fears related to her incestuous experience

With respect to the last criterion, if the victim is attempting to maintain denial, unwilling to participate in discussion, and fearful of exposure, multiple family therapy is not advised.

A large, sound proofed, and well-ventilated room with comfortable, easily movable chairs is required. The room must be large enough to allow movement and activity outside of the chairs. A chalkboard should be available.

The group is composed of family units. Usually the family unit will include two parents and the incest victim along with two or three siblings, but it may include only a single parent. The desired group size is three families or about 12 to 15 members, depending on the number of members in each family.

Cotherapy Team

A cotherapy team composed of a male and a female therapist most effectively facilitates the group process. The male therapist may reassure and confront the incest victim simultaneously. Some victims are unwilling to relate to men in an intense, intimate, nonsexual way. They are unaware of alternative ways of achieving closeness. However, some victims are reassured to see a man respond in a sensitive, accepting manner and respond readily to him. The men may find the male therapist an effective model and thus experiment more willingly with new behaviors. They may also feel more supported with another man who is presumed to understand their shared sexual roles. On the other hand, the mother and daughter may find the female therapist an effective model and source of support. The female therapist may relieve some of the pressure of the daughter to save the family, thus freeing her to deal with her own individual separation and developmental issues. Generally, with both male and female therapists available, the women and men present are able to work through their issues in a safe environment.

The therapists guide the family in dealing with issues related to the incestuous relationship and the subsequent problems, rather than deal with clearly unrelated personal agendas that could distract from the achievement of the therapeutic goals. The cotherapy team conducts the selection interview and also may use this time to begin rapport building and to help resolve common misconceptions and expectations about the group experience.

Treatment Program

Phase 1 of the program is a period of building an accepting and safe environment into which the victim can release her thoughts and feelings without fear that she will be condemned. The focus is on the ventilation of feelings in that the incest represents a loss of her right to be in control of her body. This phase is a period of expressing anger and resentment, to relieve some of her inner rage more openly. In Phase 2, the families' interaction patterns are explored. The families are helped to understand how to alter their patterns of behavior to cope with their needs and feelings. Phase 3 focuses on increasing coping skills and utilizing the support available to solve the group members' problems. This period emphasizes the mobilization of effective skills for the family and aid to the families in being supportive without undermining the members' attempts to help and be in charge of themselves. The final phase of the program is directed toward defining individual and family futures. The emphasis is on helping the victim and her parents understand the importance of individuation and the need for personal control over one's environment if the young woman is to grow.

Outcome Objectives

The following are specific outcome objectives of the treatment program:

- to provide for open, direct communication among members of the group as they discuss their family interactions
- to provide opportunities for the ventilation of feelings, including resentment, anger, and helplessness connected to dependency
- to help the families be aware of communication patterns being used in the family
- to develop skills for active problem solving in order to change family patterns of interaction
- to increase the number of alternative ways to meet individual and collective needs
- to increase a sense of autonomy and separateness within the family
- to increase evidence of assertiveness and protection of the group members' physical and psychological selves
- to decrease the depressive (helpless, out of control) effect in the family
- to increase acceptance of differences within the family
- to increase a sense of satisfaction in the members regarding their own roles and family relationships

Measurement Instruments

Since intrapsychic and interactional changes are desired as a result of therapy, instruments that measure individual changes as well as perceived family environment and interaction are used to monitor change in the program. The following may be used as assessment instruments: the Psychological Screening Inventory (PSI), the Moos Family Environment Scale (FES), and the Depression Adjective Check-List (DACL) (see Appendix B for descriptions).

Research and Evaluation

This program was tested using two families within a community mental health agency population. Prior to therapy, both families had dysfunctional family units in which there was no allowance for, or appreciation of, differences. Over the eight weeks of multiple family therapy, the responses and relationships among family members of the two units seemed to have changed in different directions. This assumption was supported by the results of the evaluation instruments, which indicated that the members of the enmeshed family voiced more varied opinions and had an increase in conflict. They were uncomfortable with their relationships and increased their discussion of values and beliefs. The members of the disengaged family, on the other hand, were less conflictual and more aware of one another's needs and feelings.

Members of both families felt isolated, introverted, and lonely. Initially, they were defensive and exposed limited pictures of themselves. After the treatment they were more open and expressive. They also expressed less defensiveness, anxiety, and emotional discomfort.

All the family members were encouraged with their progress after eight weeks, but requested continuation of the group because they did not regard the short-term therapy as long enough to resolve all their problems. These results indicate that multiple family therapy as applied in this program is a promising approach to focus members of families with incest on ways to change their behavior without losing themselves in the process.

PROGRAM OUTLINE

The following outline describes some of the contents, procedures, and materials used in each program session. (Some sessions have been abbreviated. To obtain the complete program, see the instructions in the Preface.)

1. Initial Interview
   • Objectives
     a.   To interview and screen each family referred for this program.

    b. To discuss common misconceptions about procedures, purposes, and functions of the therapy groups.

    c. To review ground rules, the membership, and leadership roles.

    d. To provide an overview of the program and to get commitments from the families to attend all sessions and to participate actively.

    e. To administer pretreatment evaluation measures: the Moos Family Environment Scale (FES), the Psychological Screening Inventory (PSI), and the Depression Adjective Check-List (DACL).

- Procedures (1 hour and 30 minutes)
    - a. General
        - (1) Involve both therapists in interviewing the families and discussing their fears and expectations. (20 minutes)
        - (2) Review and discuss handouts (as indicated). (15 minutes)
        - (3) Administer the FES and DACL Form A. (40–45 minutes)
        - (4) Direct the family to come the next week to the session. Provide the time and place of meeting. (5 minutes)
        - (5) Send home with the family DACL Form B, to be filled out in three days and returned to the therapists at the first session. (5 minutes)
    - b. Treatment
        - (1) Read the instructions for the FES and DACLs to the families, or allow them to read them, and answer any questions they may have.
        - (2) The measurement instruments are to be filled out independently by each participant without consulting other participants.

2. Session 1: Introductions, Commitments, and Myths
- Objectives
    - a. To conduct introductions in the group, with everyone using first names by end of the session.
    - b. To review ground rules established in initial interview.
    - c. To discuss expectations and the group process.
    - d. To explore common misconceptions and myths about incest.
    - e. To establish verbal commitments to the group from each participant.
- Materials. Multicolored sheets of construction paper, felt-tip pens, scissors, pins, chalkboard, chalk, and eraser.
- Procedures
    - a. General

    (1)   Introductions with self-description exercise. (35–40 minutes)

    (2)   Review. (5 minutes)

    (3)   Introduce the concept of support. (5 minutes)

    (4)   Brainstorming. (35–40 minutes)

    (5)   Family commitment procedure. (20–30 minutes)

b. Treatment

    (1)   Introductions with self-description exercise (40 minutes): Participants cut symbols representing who they are from colored construction paper. They then introduce themselves to the group through the meaning of the symbols. (Adapted from Johnson, 1972, p. 27.)

    (2)   Review (5 minutes): Review the ground rules and answer questions. Invite the group members to discuss concerns they might have.

    (3)   Introduce and discuss the topic of support as an important part of the program. (5 minutes)

    (4)   Brainstorming the myths and misconceptions about incest (40 minutes): This brainstorming must be done in a general way initially and should be followed by discussion. To facilitate this, the therapists need to introduce the procedure carefully and allow the members to generate ideas quickly without evaluation. There may be a moderate-to-intense amount of diffused rage apparent, and its ventilation at this point will be helpful in future sessions. Acknowledgment of the affect is appropriate and useful. Discussion of the myths and misconceptions about incest is an important, emotion-laden experience, and the therapists should facilitate that experience. The therapists are responsible for clearing up misconceptions not clarified within the group. This process allows the members to understand cognitively erroneous conceptions commonly held while anonymously and safely examining their own conceptions.

    (5)   Family commitment procedure (20–30 minutes): Divide the group into family groups and give the participants a list of expected behaviors that reflect commitment. Give the families five minutes to discuss their willingness to do these things as individuals. Have them commit themselves to doing them in their family groups and then return to the group as a whole to make commitments to the total group.

3. Session 2: Expectations, Stress, and Secrets
   - Objectives
     a. To create for everyone an experience in which something "private" becomes known and produces potential vulnerability.
     b. To provide an opportunity for the victims to become aware that others share their fears of exposure and that they are not alone in their need for control over their environment.
     c. To explore the need for confidentiality and privacy about "personal" experiences.
     d. To provide an opportunity to explore the responsibilities, binds, and roles which people perceive for themselves because of external forces and expectations.
     e. To increase the group members' awareness (revelation of their own perceptions and meanings observed by themselves) of the way they respond to their environment.
     f. To focus on the stress experienced by each group member because of the dysfunction within the family.
     g. To provide an experience in which the group members are able to experience themselves as supportive, understanding, and empathic with others in the group.
   - Materials. DACL Form C, pieces of paper and pencils, and self-rating sheets (Exhibit 23-1).
   - Procedures
     a. General
        (1) Fill out DACL Form C.
        (2) Discuss last week's experience and deal with any questions or concerns brought up by the group.
        (3) Introduce the secrets exercise as outlined below. (50 minutes)
        (4) Discuss similarities between feeling vulnerable and a loss of control because "secrets" are known and feeling out of control because of external pressures and demands. (10 minutes)
        (5) Conduct the sculpting exercise as outlined below. (50 minutes)
        (6) Have the group members fill out the self-rating sheet (Exhibit 23-1) for use at a later date. (5 minutes)
     b. Treatment
        (1) Secrets (50 minutes): The following script may be used as a guideline in presenting the secrets exercise:
            (a) "We keep secrets because we imagine that, if we were honest and open, there would be some kind of

unpleasant consequence—others wouldn't like us, they would take advantage of us, or they would be disgusted and reject us, and so on. The activity you are going to participate in will give you a chance to become more aware of the fear involved in revealing secrets without suffering any consequences. By writing your secrets anonymously on these slips of paper (give out paper), you will be able to see how people in the group respond to your secrets without knowing whose they are. You can also get some idea of what kinds of secrets others are keeping from you. Close your eyes now and think of two or three secrets about yourself that you would *least* want the others in the group to know. What information about yourself do you think would be most difficult for you to reveal or be most damaging to your relationship with the people here?

(b) "Now I want you to write your secrets on the pieces of paper I gave you. Write them clearly and with enough detail that anyone reading them will know exactly what you mean. For instance, don't just write, 'I'm afraid of people.' Say exactly which people, without naming them, you are afraid of and what you fear from them, for example, 'I'm afraid of strong men who might injure me physically.' *Please don't lie or minimize your secrets.* Either write a real secret that is important to you, or just write that you are unwilling to write down any of your secrets. When you have finished writing your secrets, fold the paper twice and place it in a pile in the middle of the floor. As you put your papers on the pile, shuffle the pile a little and go back to your place. (Give the participants sufficient time to write their secrets.)

(c) "Now that everyone has put a paper in the pile, I want each person to go to the pile and pick up one piece and then sit down again. Now I want one of you to read the secret on the piece of paper you picked up *as if it were your own*. Begin by saying, 'This is my secret: I . . .' Try to imagine that you really are the person who wrote this secret, and see if you can express something more about how you feel *as this person with the secret*. Even if the secret doesn't seem important to you, it was to someone, so please respect that. After a person has read a secret, I want the others in the group to say how they feel toward this person who has just revealed the secret. Don't say anything except your *feeling response—* 'I feel disgusted,' 'I am surprised,' 'I don't care that you do that,' or whatever your response is to each secret. If you share any of the secrets and you are willing to admit it, please do so." After everyone in the group has given a response to 'your' secrets, we will go on to someone else who will read another listing of secrets as if the secrets were that person's own and the other group members will again give their feeling responses. Any questions? O.K. Go ahead."

(d) Use the following to guide the follow-up discussion (10 minutes): "Now take ten minutes to discuss anything you want to share concerning what you felt or discovered through this experience. How did you feel as someone else read your secrets and as the others responded? How did you feel as you heard others' secrets?"

(e) Processing after the secrets exercise should include the idea that listening, understanding, and sharing one's own inner turmoil may be an emotionally strengthening experience. To provide a transition from the processing of this exercise to the next one, focus on how being out of control is experienced by the group. Help guide the group members to see how external and internal forces work to create binds, responsibilities, and roles that they may or may not choose to have. The cotherapist who is not leading this exercise should participate in the experience to increase cohesion, contact, and sympathy.

(2) Individual sculpting exercise (50 minutes)

(a) Introduce this exercise using the following as a guideline: "I want you to try out something a little bit different tonight. All of you will be involved in some way in the experience. (Name of group member), would you come to the middle and act as the first sculptor? The rest of you stand up and move into whatever part of the room and whatever position you are directed toward. (Name of selected group member), I want you to show us how you feel as a man and a father (woman and mother, young woman and daughter) in our society today. I want you to do this by putting some or all of the group members into physical postures that would create a picture symbolizing how you see yourself. Do this exercise without commenting on the meaning or significance it has at this time. We'll talk about it when you are done. All of you will have an opportunity to show us how you see yourselves'' (adapted from Duhl, Kantor, & Duhl, 1973).

(b) In doing the sculpting exercise, the cotherapists may find the following guidelines helpful: Choose someone from the group who is most likely to respond spontaneously. The therapists' own enthusiasm and conviction will serve as catalysts to overcome the family members' initial hesitation. Encourage body movement and physical activity during the creation of the sculpture.

(c) The responsibility of therapists is to outline the activity, select the sculptor, and encourage the families to move out of their seating positions so that they can begin. After the rules are set, allow the sculptor to design the sculpture with the therapist in the role of observer, commentator, and interpreter.

(d) Reduce the anxiety of the sculptor by indicating you are aware that the group is being asked to respond to one person's view of the situation and that there are, of course, other views. This sets the stage for acceptance if the sculptor creates something others may not agree with.

(e) As the sculptor proceeds, engage in an ongoing dialogue with the sculptor, providing encouragement as difficulties are encountered and asking if all the participants have placed their bodies as the sculptor intended. Allow the design of the sculpture to unfold at its own pace. After the sculpture is completed and the sculptor indicates it is finished, have the sculptor find a position in it.

(f) Next, have the sculptor explain what the positions, gestures, and expressions are meant to represent. The participants are asked to share some of their

feelings about the physical positions and relationships they are in. Comments should be confined to
the immediate experience. Following this processing,
encourage the other members to show how they perceive their position in our society.

(g) Process any general comments from the group about
the sculpting experience including any new or different ways they perceive themselves or their experience.

(3) Self-rating (5 minutes): Hand out the self-rating sheet
(Exhibit 23-1) and indicate that this form will be used in
another exercise in several weeks. Explain that the
coleaders are responsible for keeping these forms and
will return them at that time.

Exhibit 23-1 Self-Rating Sheet

Please rate yourself on the scales listed below. Rate yourself as you are now. The ratings
apply only to yourself.

Place a check (√) in the appropriate space

acceptable	unacceptable
inaccurate	accurate
alert	unaware
tense	calm
incompetent	competent
confident	unsure
inconsiderate	considerate
kind	cruel
dependable	undependable
inefficient	efficient
friendly	unfriendly
unhelpful	helpful
illogical	logical
merry	sad
immature	mature
calm	nervous
abnormal	normal
optimistic	pessimistic
awkward	poised
reasonable	unreasonable
unworthy	worthy
useful	useless
irresponsible	responsible

4. Session 3: Coping with Stress
    - Objectives
        a. To encourage open expression of the affective and cognitive responses to the crisis experience (revelation of incest).
        b. To facilitate listening and understanding between the parents and their children as they discuss their unique perspectives of the incest.
        c. To examine the roles assumed by the members of the family in relation to one another.
        d. To review the ways the individuals currently communicate in their families.
        e. To explore the other people who are available and involved in the group members' support systems and how those people have responded to the disruptive occurrence in the lives of the family members.
    - Materials
        a. Large easel, pad of paper, and multiple-colored felt-tip pens or crayons.
    - Procedures
        a. General
            (1) Fill out DACL Form D. (5 minutes)
            (2) Review the previous session. (5 minutes)
            (3) Conduct the fish bowl exercise. (30–40 minutes)
            (4) Make the transition from parent-to-daughter communication to family communication and support systems. (10 minutes)
            (5) Conduct the family circle exercise. (60 minutes)
        b. Treatment
            (1) Fish bowl exercise (30–40 minutes): Split the group into two parts. The young women move into the center of the room in a small circle and talk about their feelings and experiences while the parents remain in the outside circle and listen without talking. The therapists observe and help only if needed. After about 10 to 15 minutes, the discussion is halted and the members of the inner circle are silent while the parents discuss what they have heard about their daughters that was previously unknown. This requires another 10 to 25 minutes. After this discussion is concluded, bring the entire group back together and discuss the experience (Egan, 1976).
            (2) The family circle (60 minutes)
                (a) For each family, a large circle is drawn on a large pad

of paper. Using different colored pens, the family members represent themselves inside the family circle and in the environment surrounding it. A social network is drawn in to represent other people. The exploration, the placement, and importance of the people represented stimulates family discussion and controversy. Using symbols and instructions from the therapist, communication lines are drawn and discussed.

(b) Process this exercise as a group. How do they like their current style of coping with pressure? What new information do they have about themselves? There may be some resistance to covering old ground in this exercise, but it is generally overcome if the therapists create an atmosphere of enthusiasm and commitment to the exercise and are actively involved in the participants' experiences. Continue to be supportive of the group process.

5. Sessions 4 to 7: Family Problem Solving
   - Objectives
     a. To focus on the unique problems perceived by the individual families.
     b. To begin looking at problems the family encounters in a systematic order that will help them arrive at solutions more quickly and effectively.
     c. To involve members of the group in supportive, confrontive, empathic, and clarifying roles.
   - Procedures
     a. General
        (1) Give DACL Form E (F, G, and A at the following three sessions). (5 minutes)
        (2) Teach a problem-solution strategy and apply it to family problems. (1 hour and 50 minutes)
     b. Treatment
        (1) Using one family, help them identify an issue (15–20 minutes): Discuss the roles of the group members, briefly indicating that the family presenting its problem is risking something. Be sure to give supportive and reinforcing comments to both family and members. Emphasize the need for clear identification of a specific problem. This may require use of multiple therapeutic techniques,

including role playing, sculpting, fantasy trips, role reversal, and so on. Have the family members describe how they would like their experience to be different.

(2) Gather information from previous sessions or experiences, including previously tried solutions, that will help solve the problem. (20 minutes)

(3) Have the family members analyze and select from the gathered information those things they feel would be helpful to them in meeting their problem. (15 minutes)

(4) Form a tentative solution to the problem. Make it very specific and operational so that the family members know exactly what they are to do differently. (15 minutes)

(5) Help the family members move through this experience in a way that leads to discovery about themselves—to learning about their interactions and how to use their own resources. Guide the group interaction toward solvable problems, defining limitations, unrealistic expectations, or limited resources that might interfere.

(6) Provide an accepting, safe environment into which the victim and family members can release their thoughts and feelings without fear of condemnation or critical response born out of shared helplessness. Model empathy and willingness to address difficult material with poise and gentle reassurance and avoid overdirectiveness.

(7) Support the solution and get a commitment for follow-through with a report to the group at the next session. Write down on the chalkboard the possible solutions and influencing factors as they are identified under the problem so that the group can see what has been prepared.

(8) Commit the family to try the solution and to report at the beginning of the next session (5 minutes). Note: At the beginning of the next session allow the family to take the first 10 to 15 minutes to discuss the experience, using the solution the family members agreed to try.

(9) Ask another family to repeat the procedure. Rotate the families in the exercise during succeeding sessions.

6. Session 8: Facing the Future with Strength
   • Objectives
     a. To bring the group members back to a review of their individual growth, uniqueness, and future orientation.

b. To provide an expressive medium that allows them to create or generate their feelings, fears, and expectations.

c. To allow group expression of support to the individuals within the group much as they have to the family groups in the previous sessions.

d. To begin termination.

- Materials. Scissors, a variety of magazines, posterboards in a variety of colors, and glue.
- Procedures
  a. General
      (1) Administer DACL Form B. (5 minutes)
      (2) Give direction for the future in collage. (90 minutes)
      (3) Discuss termination. (10 minutes)
      (4) Emphasize the need to return for the final session. (5 minutes)
  b. Treatment
      (1) Future direction in collage. Use the following script as a guideline for this exercise:
          (a) "Go to the stack of magazines at the front of the room and select several magazines. Now silently, without consulting with anyone else, select from the magazines the pictures, words, headlines, colors, or shapes that somehow represent where you see yourself headed in five years. If it is difficult for you to begin, you might try glancing through the magazines and cutting out things that you like or are somehow attracted to. After you have accumulated as many pictures, symbols, words, and headlines as you want, select a piece of posterpaper that you like. The color should fit into how you see yourself in your future. Begin to organize your assortment onto your paper in a way that reflects where you will be in five years if you continue in the direction you are going. Take 15 or 20 minutes to complete your project.
          (b) "Now hold your collage so others can see it. I want you to take three or four minutes to describe your project. Do this in the first person present tense as if you were describing yourself. For instance, you might say, 'I have a lot of red and yellow shapes surrounded by headlines on my right side. On my left side and at the top, I have peaceful blue and green mountain scenes that fill most of me with pleasant warm feel-

ings.' Be aware of how you feel and what you notice as you describe yourself. Now each of you take a few minutes to describe your collage in the first person present tense.

(c) "Now that each of you has described your drawing, I want you to reflect silently on this experience. What did you discover about yourself and others as you expressed yourself through these projects? What similarities and differences did you notice in the collages? Now take another five or ten minutes to share your observations and discuss them."

(2) Discuss termination. Invite the participants to indicate what has been helpful to them in the sessions. Encourage them to be specific and to thank directly those who have been helpful.

(3) Postassessment. Remind the group about the postassessment session. Provide the members with information about available therapy sources.

7. Postassessment Session
   • Objectives
     a. To obtain FES and DACL Form C results.
     b. To finish up the sessions and terminate the group.
     c. To provide the participants with feedback about their individual growth.
   • Procedures
     a. Postassessment
       (1) Administer the self-rating scales (Exhibit 23-1) to be filled out individually. (5 minutes)
       (2) Provide the self-rating sheets administered in Session 1. (5 minutes)
       (3) Discuss the changes they see in themselves and how they feel about them. (30 minutes)
       (4) Administer DACL Form C. (5 minutes)
       (5) Administer FES. (30 minutes)
     b. Termination. Provide refreshments for socializing. Then terminate the group.

Chapter 24

Helping Stepfamilies Get in Step

Marcia R. Stroup, James M. Harper, William R. Steele,
and Margaret H. Hoopes

This treatment program consists of meetings with stepfamily couples for the first four weeks and with the entire stepfamily for the last four weeks. The treatment takes ten weeks total time: the first week for screening and preassessment, eight weeks of structured group treatment, and the final week for postassessment data collection. The treatment sessions consist of two hours per session once a week with three to four couples and their families. A male and female cotherapy team is recommended. The program is applicable to private practice and public and private agencies. The cost of materials is estimated to be $30 to $40.

The program has been presented, revised, tested, and revised again as part of a stepfamily research project at the Comprehensive Clinic at Brigham Young University. For more information, see Stroup (1982).

PROGRAM DESCRIPTION

General Objectives

The focus of the treatment is a group experience in which couples and families can share special problems and issues of stepfamilies, develop constructive problem-solving skills, learn and practice communication skills, and increase support and cohesion within the family. The purpose of this structured group treatment is to increase family expressiveness, improve marital adjustment, reduce family conflict, and create a moderate amount of couple and family cohesiveness. The treatment provides the stepfamily with social support, factual information about shared life stress, and an opportunity for emotional interaction with others within the group focus (Schwartz, 1978).

Theoretical Basis

The major theoretical basis for this structured group treatment is the theme-centered, interactional approach. One of the basic principles of this approach is that people are both autonomous and interdependent. This concept fits very well with what the treatment tries to do for stepfamilies. (For further description of the theory see Appendix A.)

Forming the Group

Before the treatment begins, a two-hour screening interview is conducted. After the members for the group are selected, a two-hour session is conducted to complete posttesting.

The group is composed of interested stepfamily members who meet the following criteria:

- At least one person in the couple is a stepparent.
- Children in the family who are younger than six years of age are excluded, due to their lack of emotional and cognitive maturity.
- Families with individuals who have serious psychopathology are screened out.
- Families may not be in individual family therapy concurrently.
- Families must accept the focus of treatment on the family as a whole rather than on only one member.
- Each person in the family must be willing to commit to the ground rules of the group, including regular participation during the eight-week period. Each family member must demonstrate a willingness to participate by deciding on individual family goals for the treatment.

Through their involvement in the prescreening telephone interview, the screening interview, and the orientation session, the cotherapists can help select the families they feel will best benefit from a multiple family structured group treatment. Therefore, it is recommended that the cotherapists be involved in the preliminary preparations for the group.

Specific Program Objectives

The specific objectives for this structured group treatment are:

- to establish family goals for treatment
- to commit the participants to the ground rules of the group

- to impart information about family systems
- to allow for the sharing of mutual problems
- to clarify roles
- to encourage expression of feelings
- to teach problem-solving skills
- to increase cohesiveness by assisting family members to complete the mourning of the loss of the previous family unit
- to provide experiences in which group members can have an opportunity to forgive
- to aid the family members in recognizing their strengths as a primary source for solving problems

Assessment Instruments

The following assessments are recommended (see Appendix B for descriptions):

- The Moos Family Environment Scale (FES) may be used to assess the variables of family cohesion and family expressiveness.
- The Kvebaek Family Sculpture Test may be used to measure the variables of family expressiveness, family cohesion, and couple cohesion.
- The Locke-Wallace Marital Adjustment Test may be used to measure marital adjustment (Locke & Wallace, 1959).
- The SCL-90 may be used as a screening device for individual pathology.
- An assignment check sheet is sent home with the participants each week as a homework assignment.

PROGRAM OUTLINE

The following outline describes some of the content, procedures, and materials used in each program session. Sessions 6 and 7 are presented as complete sessions; the remaining sessions are presented in abbreviated form. (To obtain the complete program, see the Preface.)

1. Session 1: Introductions, Ground Rules, and Commitment
   - Objectives
     a. To know everybody's names

    b.   To know a little about family systems

    c.   To know the ground rules for the group

    d.   To commit to the ground rules

- Materials

    a.   Name tags for each person, a poster showing a family map of a simulated stepfamily, an easel, newsprint, felt-tip pens, a list of ground rules for each participant, a posterboard to display the ground rules.

- Procedures

    a.   Roles of the therapists. Initially, the therapists are very active, direct, realistic, and positive about what is being said or what is happening. Although they are more involved in this first session than in later sessions, they need to be able to move in and out of the group as the sessions progress in order to allow other members of the group opportunities to function as co-therapists and to allow group cohesion to take place. Leadership is to be shared by the therapists, so that their active involvement is rotated from exercise to exercise, week by week.

    b.   Activities

        (1)   Introduction (5 minutes): The therapists introduce themselves and describe their roles. They then take the group through an exercise of group members telling their names and something that will help others remember their names.

        (2)   Family systems concepts (15 minutes): One of the therapists introduces a definition of a family system. The concepts dealing with the family system are taught to the group and discussed with them. Form, purpose, goals, productivity, stability, energy, information, feedback, rules, redundancy, and individual goals are some of the concepts that can lead to a discussion of how families work, what happens when families break up, what happens when two family systems come together to form a new family.

        (3)   Family map (30 minutes): The families are taught to draw family maps of their reconstituted families, which are then used to introduce each family.

        (4)   Goal setting (15 minutes): The group members share the goals brainstormed previously by the couples. The couples are instructed to discuss goals with their families and choose three to work on.

(5) Commitment procedure (50 minutes): The therapists discuss with the participants the purpose of the group and some ground rules that will help the group to function. After a discussion of the ground rules, each person is asked to commit to keeping the rules. The participants are told to expect to adhere to the rules rather than to assume they can be perfect participants without them.

(6) Homework. At the end of each session, give this assignment: "Think about what you have learned tonight in relationship to your objectives and goals. Decide when during this next week you can sit down as a couple and discuss these things. Then follow through on your decision." Distribute the checklist homework form to be completed at home and returned the following week.

(7) Instructions. Take time at the beginning of each session (5–10 minutes) to follow through on any assignments made from the previous week. In addition, the therapists need to encourage the families to spend time together each week to practice the skills learned in therapy, to continue to process thoughts and feelings, and to decide strategies for accomplishing family goals. The weekly checklist form can serve as a reminder of the ways each individual can improve relationships in the family each week. The therapists can design these forms or adapt from Stroup (1982).

2. Session 2: Role Clarification and Expression of Feelings
   - Objectives
     a. To raise the participants' consciousness about roles and help them clarify roles.
     b. To encourage the expression of feelings.
     c. To increase a sense of commonality by sharing common feelings unique to stepfamilies.
   - Materials
     a. Strips of paper in different shapes, pieces of string or scotch tape, and lists of words on strips of paper attached with masking tape to cardboard or the wall.
   - Procedures
     a. Metaphors (45 minutes)
        (1) Objectives
            (a) To help clarify various roles in the group.
            (b) To expand understanding of the multiple expectations, roles, and memories that each person is carrying.

          (c) To increase the sense of being in control and having the power of choice in life.

          (d) To teach the positive and negative aspects of losses, memories, and so on.

    (2) Roles of the therapists. The therapists should emphasize these points: a person can choose to quit carrying around guilt about past failures; a person can give up dwelling on dreams of what "could have been" and instead face the challenge of today; a person can decide to forgive those who hurt that person in the past and to give up bad memories.

    (3) Description of exercise

          (a) Metaphoric garbage (30 minutes): The members identify roles they presently have in their homes and something from the past that represents "excess baggage" in the present. All the couples decorate strips of paper with symbols that represent roles, for example, metaphors, shapes, and animals. These are hung on one couple that then represents the other couples as well.

          (b) Process (15 minutes): Process the experience with the group.

  b. Feelings (60 minutes)

    (1) Objectives

          (a) To increase the ability to express, own, and share feelings.

          (b) To increase the feeling of closeness within the group.

    (2) Roles of the therapists. The therapists are to support the open expression of feelings by modeling the openness and expressiveness themselves.

    (3) Description of exercise

          (a) Feelings (60 minutes): Tell the group, "There are many kinds of feelings in couples and families. We have put different kinds of feelings on strips of paper that are attached to this piece of cardboard. Decide which feeling words have been experienced by someone in your marriage or family and share that experience with the group." Give the couples a few minutes to reflect. Each of the couples is to participate, one at a time.

          (b) Process (15 minutes): Process the experience.

  c. Homework: See Session 1.

3. Session 3: Learning To Express Feelings in the Family
   - Objectives
     a. To allow each person in the couple to practice expression of emotions in a direct way to the other spouse, owning thoughts and feelings.
     b. To create a safe psychological atmosphere with trust and caring so that the couple members can give as well as ask for and receive support and appreciation from each other.
     c. To teach participants to define their own needs and then express them openly to their couple partners.
   - Procedures
     a. Sharing wants and appreciation (2 hours; 20–30 minutes for each couple)
        (1) One couple enters an inner circle with a therapist. The remaining couples and therapist sit in an outside circle and act as silent observers during the exercise. The therapist in the circle should say, "I want each of you to think about the things you appreciate about your partner. Next, think of something you want from that same person. Express your appreciation and wants to that person. Make sure you begin by using that person's name, then use 'I appreciate . . .' and, 'I want . . .' statements. All members will have an opportunity to express themselves at least once. The person receiving the statements is to listen silently until the giver of the message is finished. The receiver is to then acknowledge the statements by responding in a verbal or nonverbal way." After the first couple is finished, the second couple and the other therapist enter the inner circle and go through the same exercise. Then a third couple and the other therapist do the same, and so on.
        (2) Processing (5–10 minutes): After each couple has completed the exercise, the group members and leaders then form one large circle and share their experiences.
     b. Homework. See Session 1. Remind the parents that their children are to come next week.

4. Session 4: Expanding Alternatives—Part 1: Problem Solving for Parents
   - Objectives
     a. To teach problem-solving skills and expand alternatives through the sharing of mutual problems.

b. To increase participants' feeling of commonality.

c. To develop and strengthen peer relationships within the group.

d. To increase the degree of expressiveness through group support during problem solving.

- Materials

    a. Write the problem-solving steps on the blackboard, on a poster-board, or on newsprint.

- Procedures

    a. Note: While one therapist works with the parents in Part 1, the other therapist meets separately in a different room with the children to work on Part 2.

    b. Introduction to problem solving (30 minutes): The steps in solving problems are introduced to the group, together with a rationale for the need to plan how to solve the particular problems identified by the group. Discuss with the participants what decision rules are and how the lack of acceptable decision rules can abort decision making and decision implementation.

    c. Fishbowl exercise (25–30 minutes per couple): As a group, the parents brainstorm to provide a list of common problems centered on being a spouse or parent in a blended family. Then, in turn, each parent couple goes to the center of the circle with a therapist, chooses a specific problem to solve, and applies the steps to solve the problem. The audience may contribute alternative solutions, advantages, and disadvantages when a couple has exhausted its resources.

    d. Process (5–15 minutes): Only one circle should be formed, so that all can process what they observed, what they experienced, and what they learned. This processing can be done either at the end of each couple's turn or when all the couples have completed the experience.

    e. Homework. See Session 1.

5. Session 4: Expanding Alternatives—Part 2: Problem Solving for Stepfamily Children

    - Objectives

        a. To utilize a warm-up exercise to get acquainted and to prepare the group for the fishbowl exercise.

        b. To teach problem-solving skills and expand alternatives.

        c. To increase participants' feelings of commonality and strengthen peer relationships through the sharing of mutual problems.

        d. To foster group support during problem solving.

        e. To increase the degree of expressiveness.

- Materials
  a. Name tags for each person. Put the name tags on the chairs before the participants arrive to make sure siblings are not sitting next to each other.
  b. Problem-solving steps written on the blackboard and a poster-board or newsprint.
- Procedures
  a. Note: While one therapist works with the parents in Part 1, the other therapist meets separately with the children to work on Part 2.
  b. Introductions (5 minutes): The therapists introduce themselves and describe their roles. They then use a game that helps everyone to learn each other's name; for example, the participants introduce themselves as an animal, a flower, a mode of transportation, a movie, and so on.
  c. Wheel interaction exercise (25 minutes): The chairs need to be arranged in the shape of a wheel, so that the chairs in the inner circle have their backs to one another and are facing outward. The outside circle is formed so that there is a chair facing inward opposite each chair that is facing outward. Participants are instructed to find a chair facing someone other than a sibling. The therapist asks a question that those in the inner circle respond to for two minutes while those in the outside circle listen. Then the outside people share their response. The outside people then move to the next chair, and the process is repeated with new questions.
  d. Fishbowl exercise (45 minutes): The objectives and roles of therapists are the same as those described for the parents in Part 1.
  e. Homework. See Session 1.

6. Session 5: Ghosts from the Past
   - Materials
     a. Name tags for everyone, family maps from Session 1, list of ground rules for each person, therapists' notes of what kinds of decisions and commitments were made during last week's sessions, posterboards supported by wooden strips to represent "ghosts," and a poster listing the five stages of loss—denials, anger, bargaining, depressions, and acceptance.
   - Procedures
     a. Getting acquainted (5 minutes)
        (1) Objective

        (a) To become acquainted in the total group.

    (2) Roles of the therapists

        (a) To introduce themselves and reiterate that, as leaders, they will facilitate the plans for each session.

        (b) To remind the group of the ground rules.

        (c) To assist in seeing that the group moves smoothly, staying on task.

    (3) Description of exercise. Use the family map that was made in Session 1. Have the participants hold the family map one by one, give their names, and show where they are represented on the map. Ask them to say what they would like to be called. For example, does Mr. John Doe want to be called John or Mr. Doe by the children in the group?

b. Commitment procedure (30 minutes)

    (1) Objectives

        (a) To give the group members a rationale for the group.

        (b) To explain a rationale for the ground rules, to make sure everybody understands them.

        (c) To get individual and family commitments in front of group.

    (2) Role of the therapists. The therapists are to function alternatively in the facilitation of the group discussion, giving personal examples when appropriate and asking for questions and clarification.

    (3) Description of exercise

        (a) Purpose. Use the following script as a guideline in explaining the purpose of the exercise: "During the first week the couples met, we reviewed the ground rules and committed ourselves to adhere to them. Tonight, the children and young people are joining the group for the first time. We will briefly review the purpose of this new group and its ground rules and give each of you an opportunity to commit yourselves to the new group. It is especially important for our new members to participate actively in the group. In this new group, we can support one another by sharing similar problems and experiences with our families. We can try out new behaviors and, consequently, have new experiences in a safe, accepting environment. This group allows us to share in other people's struggles, to help them, and to identify similar problems of our own.''

(b) Ground rules. Review the meaning and purpose of ground rules by asking the group members to repeat and summarize them. Explain that group members usually grow into the ground rules, but they do not necessarily keep them perfectly (see Session 1 for ground rules).

(c) Commitment. Ask each person and then each family to commit to following the ground rules and to attend the sessions.

  c. Follow-Up on Problem Solving (25 minutes)

    (1) Objective. To allow time to follow through with what was decided in the Session 4 problem-solving Parts 1 and 2.

    (2) Roles of the therapists. The therapists are to review what alternatives were decided upon in the problem-solving session and encourage the group members to continue following up on their commitment to the solution decided upon last week. If the solution did not work, some additional suggestions can be given and a new commitment made.

    (3) Description of exercise. Two groups should be formed: the first a group for the stepfamily couples, and the second, a group for the stepfamily children. Group members are to report back to the group and the therapist what they did during the week in regard to their problem-solving commitment, how it worked out, what they want to continue to do, and so on.

  d. Break (10 minutes). During the break, the therapists can introduce an active group game to increase the energy level, or the break can be a free time for restroom breaks, and so on.

  e. Ghosts and family ghost building (50 minutes)

    (1) Objectives

      (a) To help the child deal with loss by giving up the intimate day-to-day contact with the biological parent, by dealing directly with negative feelings instead of projecting onto the surviving parent and/or stepparent, and by encouraging the child to make use of the substitute relationship with the stepparent.

      (b) To enable the spouse to acknowledge the grief of loss and separation, work through it, and let it go.

(c) To encourage individuals to give up one kind of relationship or the dream of what might have been while at the same time developing a different kind of relationship with the same person.

(d) To allow a mutual sharing of the memories of each original family unit and to integrate those parts into the newly reconstituted unit.

(e) To create a safe psychological atmosphere in which feelings can be owned, expressed, and openly dealt with.

(f) To enable family members to have control over their "ghosts."

(2) Roles of the therapists. The therapist who presents the exercise should be well-acquainted with its basic concepts and background information so that the presentation is in the therapist's own words. The presenter can check the understanding of what has been presented by asking clarification questions of the group.

(3) Description of exercise. The therapist should give the following background information to help the families understand why they need to deal with family "ghosts:"

(a) Information about stages of loss. Briefly explain the five stages of loss: denial, anger, bargaining, depression, and acceptance. Explain that individuals can be encouraged to give up one kind of relationship or the dream of what might have been while, at the same time, developing a different kind of relationship with the same person (Adapted from Hozman & Froiland, 1976).

(b) Information about ghosts. Tell the group the following: "We want to bring into the session tonight family ghosts from the past that continue to affect us in the present. Although we may have many people in our past who have an effect on us in the present, tonight we will limit those 'ghosts' to family members not present tonight—the family members we used to live with. Each of you has some ghosts from the past that interfere with and interrupt your present life. Tonight we are going to decide who our ghosts are, and then one family will have a chance to introduce its ghosts to the group."

(c) Family ghost building (30 minutes). Instruct the members to divide into individual family groups. Each therapist will divide time between two of the families. With the aid of the therapist, each family should decide which are its ghosts. After the ghosts have been selected, a posterboard with a wooden support should be used to represent each ghost. A felt-tip pen can be used to write the first and last name on each ghost.

(d) The family members are to leave the ghosts in the group room. Remind them in each week's session thereafter that they can take the ghosts and keep them with them during the sessions if they are not willing to let go of them. At the last session, the children can make small ghosts out of paper to fold up and put in their pockets and keep with them if they wish. This will signify the importance of keeping a place for their biological parents in their hearts.

7. Session 6: Ghosts from the Past
   - Objectives
     a. To increase cohesiveness by assisting family members in the completion of mourning.
     b. To free the family members emotionally so that they can direct their energy toward meeting the new family.
     c. To help each child deal with loss by giving up the desire for parental reunion, giving up the intimate day-to-day contact with the biological parent, dealing directly with negative feelings instead of projecting onto the surviving parent and/or stepparent, and encouraging the child to make use of the substitute relationships with the stepparent.
     d. To enable the spouse to acknowledge the grief of loss and separation, work through it, and let it go.
     e. To encourage the members to give up one kind of relationship or the dream of what might have been while at the same time developing a different kind of relationship with the same person.
     f. To allow mutual sharing of the memories of each original family unit and integrate those parts into the newly reconstituted unit.
     g. To create a safe psychological atmosphere in which feelings can be owned, expressed, and openly dealt with.
     h. To enable family members to have control over their "ghosts."
   - Materials
     a. The ghosts that were built in Session 5.

- Procedures
  a. Roles of the therapists. The therapists work with the families by assisting and supporting them as they deal with unresolved issues from their past. The therapists function as they would with a family in therapy, helping the family members to own and focus on problems unique to each family. They facilitate individual family therapy, keeping the overall program objectives in mind. In this context, they can be creative in their use of the ghosts, sculpting, use of space, and so on.

  b. Working with family ghosts (Two hours, 30–40 minutes per family)

    (1) Collect all of the ghosts of one family, leave the room, then knock on the door, ask for the specific family by name, and re-enter the room with the ghosts for the first family. The family then introduces its ghosts, explaining the ghosts' effects. The family members place the ghost spatially where they think it is in their life at the present time. In order to have room for the sculpting, the family is to stand or sit in the inner circle while the other families observe in an outside circle. Give the family plenty of freedom to experiment in deciding how close or how far each ghost is from the different family members. This process will be something like family sculpting, only with the inclusion of the ghosts.

    (2) After the ghosts have been introduced, continue to do individual family therapy with the family, while the other families observe. The therapists should continue to use the space to move toward or away from ghosts. The family can be seated part of the time or be moving about, if it is relevant to the therapy. The therapists facilitate the therapy by dealing with the unique issues of each step-family and asking such questions as, Where are these ghosts? Where do you want them to be? If you could talk to them, what would you say? For example, if Sam were here right now, what would you talk about? Can you ask Sam for permission to keep the good parts and let go of the bad? What effects does each ghost have on the family? With you as an individual? How can you be in control of these ghosts? How can other family members help you to do that? Are you willing to give up the control your ghost has over you? How much do you want to keep?

Encourage the family members to share the good as well as the bad memories and effects.

(3)   The same procedure is repeated with each family. There will be time for processing during Session 7. As noted earlier, the family members are to leave the ghosts in the group room for use in later sessions.

c.   Homework. See Session 1.

8. Session 7: Ghosts from the Past, and Learning to Forgive
    • Objectives
      a.   To allow time for families to finish dealing with their ghosts from the past and to process the experience.
      b.   To provide a guided fantasy experience in which group members have an opportunity to forgive and then process the experience.
    • Materials
      a.   Tape recorder and tape of guided fantasy.
    • Procedures
      a.   Roles of the therapists. The therapists continue to work therapeutically with each family, assisting and supporting the families as they deal with unresolved issues from their past. The therapists introduce and then process the guided fantasy on forgiveness.
      b.   Working with family ghosts (40–60 minutes): Complete the exercise from Session 6 with the families that did not have a turn, and process it with the total group.
      c.   Guided fantasy and process (60 minutes)
        (1)   Objectives. To enable the participants to experience a guided fantasy in which they can have an opportunity to forgive and let go of ghosts from their past.
        (2)   Roles of the therapists. One therapist introduces the guided fantasy experience, plays the tape, and then facilitates the processing of the experience.
        (3)   Description of exercise. A transcript of the guided fantasy is presented in Exhibit 24-1 in order to standardize the experience for future group treatments. The transcript should not be read, but should be put on tape, using appropriate pauses, voice tone changes, and so on.
        (4)   Process. After listening to the tape, process the experience with the group members by asking such questions as, Who did you see as you walked down the path and opened the door? How did you feel when you saw that

Exhibit 24-1 Guided Fantasy on Forgiveness

Most of us carry around resentments, unforgiveness, and guilt. These feelings are often heavy burdens. They weigh us down and keep us tied to the past. Sometimes we don't even want to get rid of them. We're so angry or so used to them that they seem a part of us, even though they stop us from doing and feeling and thinking some of the things we'd like to do. One way to get rid of these burdens is to forgive those who have hurt us and to ask forgiveness of people that we've hurt. Forgiveness does not mean that we have to take the blame or that the person who has hurt us is right; nor when we ask forgiveness does it necessarily mean that we have to take all the blame or even some of the blame. Most of us don't intend to hurt others by our actions; rather we act out of a sense of what is right at the time.

Tonight, we want to talk about and do some things that will release us from these ghosts from the past that are keeping us from progressing and interacting with each other the way we want to. We want to test your fantasy skills tonight to see what you can imagine. What I'm going to ask you to do will happen within you. All you need to do is listen and let your mind fantasize pictures and places, sounds, feelings, and actions.

First of all, get in a very comfortable position so that your body won't be reminding you of other things. Some of you may want to sit with both feet on the floor, your hands on your laps or your thighs, others may want to try out other positions. Just be sure that you're comfortable, as comfortable as you can be for a few minutes.

Now, look up to your right. See a movie screen and imagine that you see, feel, hear—imagine—a very peaceful, special, comfortable place; a sandy beach with warm winds touching your hair and your body with the sun blessing your face with its warmth; a grassy knoll with your back against a tree, with white clouds piling against the sky, with the peaceful drone of bees and the whisper of silence; with a boat far out on the lake, and your body reclining back against a cushion, rocking peacefully with the swell—back and forth, back and forth, the ebb and tide of the water, dreaming dreams. Imagine, see, smell, listen, feel. Do that now.

Wherever you are, there's a path, a very inviting path, maybe on the ground, maybe on the water, maybe in the air. It's going to lead you to a series of doors. You can let those doors look like anything you want them to look like—a bank of clouds, a rustic gate, a carved, wooden door with an ornate handle, even a cardboard door—anything you want. Behind each door there is a person you know—someone you have some unresolved conflict with, someone you need to forgive. See, listen, feel, imagine. Imagine the path leading to the door. Move toward the door. The person behind the door is someone you need to forgive—someone who has hurt you in some way. It could be from a long, long time ago. The person doesn't even have to be alive—it could be someone who is dead, perhaps someone in your immediate family. The hurt could have happened yesterday, or it could have happened many, many years ago.

Imagine the person in great detail—clothes, posture, expression on the person's face. See, listen, feel. Now open the door! See, touch, and hear the person standing there. Now in any way that you wish, tell that person that you forgive him or her. Hear what you would say; see what you would do; hear it and do it. Each of you will have had a different experience. You may have even imagined what the person's response would be. The response isn't very important. The important thing is that you give forgiveness— you imagine it, you see it, you feel it, you hear it. You've lightened your load.

In forgiving this person, something that was heavy, something that held you down, is lifted and is gone. You can see it, you can feel it, you can hear it leaving. It may be something that floats away into the distance and is lost, or something that rolls down a

Exhibit 24-1 continued

hill—it's leaving, it's gone. Feel yourself lighten—a little more buoyant, a little freer, a little less burdened.

Now, prepare yourself to go to the next door. Behind that door is someone you've hurt—not intentionally. You've done something, something that you would like to ask forgiveness for. And as you approach the door and open it, see, feel, even hear that person in great detail. Will the person be standing, sitting? What kind of clothes does the person have on? Is the person looking you in the eye? Looking at something in the distance? What is the person doing?

Now do something to get that person's attention, and as you get the attention, you'll ask for forgiveness. You may have even imagined the response that you get. Again, the response from that person is not important. The important thing is that you have asked for forgiveness. As you do so, see that you've given up some of the guilt that you felt because of what you did—because of the things that happened between the two of you. You can let go of the anger, the bad feelings. In fact, you can move the anger around in your body just as if it were water that could float. Move it into your leg, move it into your arm. Your arm is like a faucet that you can turn on, and you turn it on and let the anger flow out of you onto the floor below. It's leaving. Imagine, see, hear it flowing onto the floor, lightening your load—freer, buoyant, less burdened.

Some of you have a number of doors left with people standing behind them waiting for you to either forgive them or to ask to be forgiven. I'm going to give you some time to think about that—to go to some of the doors and do what is necessary for you. Imagine in great detail who it is that you're talking with. And as you forgive or ask for forgiveness, your load will lighten. You can let those things go—the anger, the resentment, the hurt, the fears. Turn on that faucet—let them flow out of you.

Some of you have not finished this task. You can complete it at home or wherever you wish. Now, I'd like you to go back to your peaceful place—a place on the hill or wherever you were. Relax and rest. Check and see if you're lighter. Check to see if you've given up the load you were carrying. Check it out once, and then enjoy where you are for a few minutes. Enjoy being freer, a more complete you—someone who can imagine, see, feel, and even hear the burdens leave and flow out of you, giving up some of the burdens by forgiving and being forgiven, by forgiving and asking for forgiveness. And now will each of you come back here to this room with all of us? Share whatever you want to. Some of you may not want to share any of this, and you don't have to. But if you do want to, we will take the time for you to do so.

person? Were you able to forgive that person? Did you ask that person to forgive you for something and was it difficult or impossible to do that? If so, what kept you from asking forgiveness or forgiving that person? What feelings did you have after the experience? Were you able to release that person and give up your resentment or bitterness? What was the experience like for you? Encourage the family members to talk to each other about the exercise sometime during the week.

d. Homework. See Session 1. Also remind the family members that they are to spend time talking to each other this week about their fantasy experience. Time will be given at the beginning of Session 8 to share what they learned from this assignment. During the week each family is to look over their Family Goals and report back to the group next week what they think they have accomplished in meeting those goals.

9. Session 8: Integration of Strengths, Progress Report, Feedback, and Good-Bye
   - Objectives
     a. To aid the family members in recognizing their strengths as a primary resource for solving problems.
     b. To provide feedback about individual and family growth.
     c. To allow the group members to experience closure of the group by having an opportunity to say goodbye.
     d. To provide feedback about the group treatment to the therapists.
   - Materials
     a. None
   - Procedures
     a. Roles of the therapists. The therapists facilitate the integration of strengths contributing to the group process. They provide suggestions for follow-up of the treatment as the families assess their progress on family goals. The therapists ask for feedback about themselves as therapists and also about the group treatment. Finally, they help provide closure by allowing time for members to say goodbye and by giving alternatives relative to future therapy.
     b. Review of the homework assignment (15 minutes): The therapists help the group members share what they learned from the fantasy trip and from sharing it with their family members.
     c. Integration of strengths (30 minutes): The group members focus on the positive attributes of each family, sharing specifically with each other what they consider those attributes to be. The participants may also share what they consider to be the strengths of individuals in the other families. The group members also share with each other and the therapists the specific ways they were helped by others in the group. For example, someone may say, "I remember how much you helped me that second week when you shared with the group your past mistakes and failures in your marriage. I realized that others have feelings similar to mine. Your openness helped me to accept my mistakes."

    d.   Feedback on treatment (15 minutes): The therapists administer a questionnaire, "Postprogram Feedback on Treatment."

    e.   Termination (60 minutes)

        (1)   Progress report. The therapists facilitate a discussion with the group members about the changes that they have seen in themselves, in others, and in their families. One member from each family is to report to the group on the progress of that member's family on its specific treatment goals (see assignment at end of Session 7).

        (2)   Feedback. Ask the group members to discuss their experience with the structured group treatment as a whole. The members are to identify the things they liked, disliked, and how they would change the treatment for future use. The therapists ask for feedback on how the members functioned in the group.

        (3)   Saying goodbye. Suggest that group members take five to ten minutes to walk around and say goodbye in any way they desire. Group members may want to speak privately to someone in the group, express feelings, or say goodbye in some nonverbal way.

        (4)   Information. Provide information about opportunities for further counseling and other community resources. Tell the participants that Session 9 is for the purpose of post-testing. Instruct the families to complete the checklist homework forms at home this week and return them next week. All participants are to meet at the regular time next week in the group room to be assigned to therapists for the post-tests.

10. Session 9: Post-Testing
- Objective
    a.   To administer postprogram tests.
- Materials
    a.   Kvebaek Family Sculpture Test (60 minutes)
    b.   Relationship Intimacy Barometer (for couples) (10–15 minutes)
    c.   Moos Family Environment Scale (FES) (20–30 minutes). The therapist may need to help the younger child with this instrument by reading the questions to the child. No one else in the family should do this.
    d.   SCL-90 (10–15 minutes). This should be given to group members who are 13 years of age or older.

  e. MAT for couples, and MAT alternative form for children (10 minutes)
- Procedures
  a. Administer the above tests in the times indicated.
  b. Check on the termination or transfer of each family from the program.
  c. Collect feedback on the treatment program.

Chapter 25

Multiple Family Group Treatment in Residential Programs for Drug Abusers

Philip S. Klees

This multiple family group treatment program works best with three to five families who are confronting the disruptions in family relationships caused by the abuse of a drug, most often alcohol. The treatment focuses on the functional role that drug abuse has played in the family and how the family system has incorporated dysfunctional interaction patterns that have helped maintain the drug abuse. The adolescent drug-abusing member of the family should be involved in an all-day residential treatment program, and the entire family is required to participate in three-hour sessions, five nights a week, for four weeks.

Drug abuse is herein defined as an individual's chronic and dependent use of chemicals resulting in serious disruption of the person's supportive relationships. Chronic and dependent use of chemicals is not perceived as an individual problem. The fact that 50 percent of adolescent chemical abusers come from families with a history of alcoholism or some other form of substance abuse (Addiction Research Foundation, 1975) strongly suggests that family factors contribute to the development of drug abuse. Numerous empirical studies corroborate the family's indulgence in chemical abuse is a causative factor (Annis, 1974; Pendergast, 1974; Schwartzman, 1975). It is logical then to focus on the family unit in the rehabilitation of the drug abuser.

The rationale for treating the families of drug abusers in multiple family groups is threefold: (1) Multiple family groups can induce change in families within a shorter time frame (Bowen, 1976; Laqueur, 1972); (2) such groups can be more effective in dealing with resistance (Laqueur, 1972); and (3) it is financially more economical to treat three to five families at once than it is to treat each family separately (Laqueur, 1972). The theoretical rationale for the multiple family group approach is based on existential-experiential therapy group theory (see Appendix A).

GENERAL PROGRAM DESIGN

Procedures for Placing Participants

The identified patient, that is, the individual family member who is abusing drugs, is referred to residential treatment by school or employment personnel, police or court officials, or possibly a family member. It is crucial at this stage that someone with authority over the drug-abusing individual act boldly to intervene.

Multiple family therapy groups are structured within a four-week residential program serving males and females between the ages of 15 and 65 who have serious and chronic drug-related problems. The program attempts to keep a family focus during all stages of treatment. It involves three phases:

1. Phase 1 includes evaluation, problem identification, and goal setting.
2. Phase 2 identifies defenses and the feelings they protect and seeks a recognition of powerlessness and unmanageability.
3. Phase 3 focuses on problem solving, relationships, and growth.

The intake process of the program requires that all family members be present. The first message the family receives is that the family—not just the individual with the drug problem—will be a primary focus in treatment. During intake, specific evaluation of conflict areas within a family context, problem identification, and goal setting occur. This process can take up to one week.

Program Structure

Following intake, and contingent upon the family making a commitment of participating five nights per week for four weeks, the drug-abusing family member is admitted to the residential treatment program. Family treatment sessions, involving all family members, run from 6:30 to 9:30 P.M. each night. Each family group is made up of 25 to 30 people or four to six families. The goal is to assist each member in the family system to make those changes in attitude and behavior that will lead to a more satisfying family life. The evening sessions include a didactic presentation on the nature of chemical abuse (McAuliffe & McAuliffe, 1975) and a multiple family group therapy treatment.

A "bridge night" is structured in the middle of the week. The purpose of the bridge night is to allow concerned friends, referral persons, employers, and AA members to participate with the patients and their family members in identifying and effectively dealing with stress areas so as to facilitate a successful post-treatment transition.

A week of the program is structured as shown in Exhibit 25-1.

Objectives

The objectives of the multiple family group treatment of drug abuse relate to the curative factors involved (Shaffer & Galinsky, 1974; Yalom, 1970). Specific objectives include the following:

- to develop a supportive group based on the sharing of common struggles in dealing with the drug abuse of a family member
- to identify dysfunctional family interaction patterns that maintain abusive drug use
- to facilitate the development of new family interaction patterns that do not depend on drug-abuse behavior
- to support the new behavior patterns developed by family members
- to consolidate family changes by supporting participation in family-oriented self-help groups

Exhibit 25-1 Weekly Schedule of Multiple Family Group Therapy Program

	Monday	Tuesday	Wednesday	Thursday	Friday	Saturday	Sunday
A.M.	Didactic Presentation	-------------	---------------	-------------	-------------	--------->	
							Open
	Therapy Groups	-------------	----------->	Therapy Groups ---	-------------	--------->	
P.M.	Open------	-------------	---------------	-------------	-------------	--------->	Visiting
6:30 7:30	Didactic Presentation	-------------	---------------	-------------	--------->		
9:30	Multiple Family Group Therapy	--------->	"Bridge Night"	Multiple Family Group Therapy	--------->	Open	AA Meeting

Measurement Instruments

Treatment effectiveness is measured by the following three methods:

1. Pretest and post-test measures on the Goal Attainment Scales (see Appendix B for description)
2. Four (one each week of treatment) ten-minute audiotaped probes rated on supportive-defensive communication within the family (Alexander, 1973)
3. Pretreatment and post-treatment subjective evaluations of family functioning by each family member

The first of the above methods, goal attainment scaling, a structured system to assess the outcome of therapeutic goals, has been used effectively in family therapy evaluation. The four ten-minute audiotaped probes of supportive-defensive communication function as a process measure. Each probe is rated by three independent judges. This method has been used effectively to discriminate between normal and deviant families (Alexander, 1973; Doane, 1978). The final instrument, subjective evaluations, has been used reliably as a measure of satisfaction with treatment (Margolis, Sorenson, & Galano, 1977).

PROGRAM OUTLINE

The following outline describes four structured treatment sessions. Since each multiple family group is made up of four to six families that meet four times per week (Wednesday night being "bridge night"), each family in the group receives the treatment described. That is, each family is the focus of the structured treatment session on a particular day of the week.

1. Session 1: Sharing Common Experiences
   - Objectives
     a. To share family experiences in dealing with the pain and frustrations of attempting to control the drug use of a family member.
     b. To build group cohesion by stressing the similarities between the families, all having at least one member abusing drugs (alcohol).
     c. To begin to speak from the "I" position and to own one's thoughts and feelings.
   - Procedures
     a. Role of therapist
       (1) Facilitates the opportunity for each participant to share experiences.

      (2)   Highlights similarities between families.

      (3)   Models the "I" position in communication and encourages others in the group to do so.

  b. Role of participants

      (1)   Share specific personal incidents related to the drug abuse of a brother or sister, husband or wife, son or daughter.

      (2)   Support other families by validating what has been shared with the group.

  c. Activities

      (1)   Introduction. Explain general objectives. (15 minutes)

      (2)   Sharing of experiences. (60 minutes)

      (3)   Summary. Highlight similarities between families. (15 minutes)

2. Session 2: Sculpting—Visualizing the Role Drug Abuse Plays in a Family

- Objectives

  a. To visualize the role drug use has played in the relationships between families.

  b. To identify conflictual relationships within the family and become aware of behavioral sequences that maintain the conflict.

- Procedures

  a. Role of therapist

      (1)   Acts as director, facilitating the acting out of concrete family situations.

      (2)   Pinpoints areas of conflict revealed in acting out family interaction.

      (3)   Suggests alternative behaviors to change the behavioral sequence maintaining the conflict.

  b. Role of participants

      (1)   Identify and share their perceptions of the roles played by individuals within the family (Wegscheider, 1981).

      (2)   Role play another family's roles so that the family being sculpted may "objectively" observe the interaction.

  c. Activities

      (1)   Introduction. Explain general objectives. (10 minutes)

      (2)   Sculpting (65 minutes): Explanation of a drug-related situation by a family member (10 minutes), directing interaction (30 minutes), debriefing the meaning of interaction (15 minutes), prescribing alternative behaviors (10 minutes).

(3)   General sharing of the experience with the multiple family group. (15 minutes)

3. Session 3: Exploring Alternative Behaviors
    • Objectives
        a. To explore alternative behavior patterns that do not support abusive drug use.
        b. To identify specific behavioral changes family members need to develop.
        c. To continue building support between the families in the group by eliciting suggestions for alternative behaviors.
    • Procedures
        a. Role of therapist
            (1)   Facilitates sharing by families of the areas of difficulty within their families.
            (2)   Summarizes information and assessments compiled in previous sessions.
            (3)   Selectively supports suggestions for change proposed by group participants.
        b. Role of participants
            (1)   Share specific problem areas within their families.
            (2)   Begin to practice new behaviors suggested by the group.
            (3)   Support other family members in their attempts to change.
        c. Activities
            (1)   Introduction. Explain general objectives. (15 minutes)
            (2)   Sharing by a family of specific problem areas. (20 minutes)
            (3)   Group suggestions for change. (30 minutes)
            (4)   Practice of new behaviors. (15 minutes)

4. Session 4: Initiating Ongoing Support Groups
    • Objectives
        a. To introduce family members to appropriate ongoing, community-based support systems.
        b. To experience the various support groups of Alcoholics Anonymous, ALANON (for spouses and other adults of alcoholics/drug abusers), ALATEEN (for adolescents with alcoholic/drug-abusing parents), and ALATOT (for young children of alcoholic/drug-abusing parents).
        c. To identify the needs family members may have for ongoing support groups.

- Procedures
  a. Role of therapist
     (1) Identifies the need for ongoing support.
     (2) Clearly presents the purposes of AA groups.
     (3) Coordinates the initial AA group experience by moving between each of the three groups set up during the session: ALANON, ALATEEN, and ALATOT.
     (4) Facilitates the sharing of family experiences.
  b. Role of participants
     (1) Actively participate in an appropriate group by sharing personal experiences of living with a drug-abusing family member.
     (2) Evaluate the need for a personal support group.
  c. Activities
     (1) Introduction. Explain to the entire multiple family group the purpose of the various support groups. (30 minutes)
     (2) Break up into the appropriate groups (ALANON, ALATEEN, ALATOT) and begin sharing experiences. (30 minutes)
     (3) Return to the larger group and evaluate the preceding group experience. (30 minutes)

Chapter 26

Changing the Effects of Family Tree Influences in Religious Communities

Laura Huelsing

This structured group treatment program consists of eight two-hour sessions conducted over a period of eight weeks. It is designed to be used with 5 to 12 individuals from a single religious community. The structure is based on the theme of discovering how one's family of origin influences one's ability to function in a community. The objective of the program is to improve functional interaction, that is, to create an environment in which the members are willing and able to articulate differences and feelings in the community.

Prior to the actual group treatment, the community meets for an introductory session during which an overview is given, ground rules are established, and assessment instruments are administered.

During each of the eight treatment sessions, the "I-We-It" triangle that characterizes the theme-centered interactional approach is operative (see Appendix A). The specific exercises in each session apply the interaction patterns from the family of origin to the community. The following areas are subjected to treatment in the eight sessions: family relationships; birth order; relationships with specific individuals in one's family of origin; individual strengths; community relationships; basic interpersonal needs of inclusion, control, and affection; rules and differences; and change.

PROGRAM OUTLINE

The following outline describes some of the content, procedures, and materials used in each program session. Sessions 2, 6, and 7 are presented in their entirety; the remaining sessions are abbreviated. (To obtain the complete program, see the Preface.)

1. Introductory Session
   - Objectives
     a.   To get to know the participants in the group on a social level.
     b.   To review with them the rationale for the treatment.
     c.   To present and discuss rules to be followed during the sessions.
     d.   To have the participants commit themselves to the treatment.
     e.   To obtain data necessary to evaluate the program.
   - Materials
     a.   Demographic information sheets, typed copies of the ground rules, Moos Group Environment Scale test booklets and answer sheets (see Appendix B), FIRO-B test booklets (see Appendix B), Huelsing Cohesion/Expressiveness Scales (Huelsing, 1981) and slips of paper with questions. The N. B. Huelsing Cohesion/Expressiveness Scales are needed for each session.
   - Procedures
     a.   Socializing exercise (35 minutes): Each member is given three questions that are revealing about the person who answers them. Here are some examples: What is one of your earliest family memories? What book would you recommend as a must? What three things do you treasure most in your life? The facilitators can easily generate 15 to 20 questions (24 questions are contained in the original manuscript). Each member chooses one of the questions to ask all the group members to answer. However, first, the member reads the two questions that will not be asked and tells the group why the member chose the remaining question to ask.
     b.   Review of orientation topics (5 minutes): The therapists give the rationale for the treatment, talk about the treatment as a research project (confidentiality, and so on), and explain the limitations of the treatment.
     c.   Ground rules exercise (10 minutes): The therapists lead a discussion of the ground rules to make sure all participants understand them (examples of ground rules are contained in original manuscript).
     d.   Commitment exercise (10 minutes): The objective of this exercise is to get a verbal commitment concerning attendance, participation, and ground rules from each participant. The therapists should state their own commitment.
     e.   Assessment (50 minutes): The objective is to obtain information and data to be used in evaluating the program. The therapists administer Group Environment Scale Test, FIRO-B, and the Huelsing Cohesion/Expressiveness Scale.

2. Session 1: Sharing a Family Genogram
   - Objectives
     a. To have the participants draw a genogram.
     b. To share the genogram information with the group.
     c. To depict through sculpting the participants' perspectives of their relationships in their family of origin.
   - Materials
     a. Magic markers, 14″ × 22″ posterboards for each participant, individual copies of "Birth Order, The Family System, and Implications for Therapy" (Hoopes & Harper, 1980), and genogram sheets (Guerin & Pendagast, 1976).
   - Procedures
     a. Genogram exercise (45 minutes): This exercise requires each member to draw a three-generational genogram and then to share the information with the group. Use the genogram sheets provided.
     b. Family sculpting exercise (70 minutes): The members portray current relationships in the family of origin by using space. The participants use the other group members to represent their family members.
     c. Closing exercise (5 minutes): The therapists should provide closure to the session by acknowledging the many thoughts and feelings that have been expressed. The members are asked to take home sheets containing birth-order information to read and bring back to next week's session. Through a short exercise, the group members show their appreciation for all the families represented in the group (saying "thank you" to the people on either side, using group hugs, and so on).

3. Session 2: Influence of Birth Order
   - Objectives
     a. To give the participants the chance to reflect on ways the birth-order theory describes them.
     b. To begin to see how birth order may be influencing current behavior in the community.
     c. To apply to community relationships statements related to birth order.
   - Materials
     a. A few extra handouts of Hoopes-Harper birth-order material, newsprint, magic markers, and masking tape.
   - Procedures
     a. Opening exercise (5–10 minutes)

    (1)　Objective. To elicit general feedback concerning last week's sessions and to take care of unfinished business.

    (2)　Role of the therapists. The therapists solicit information and answer questions that may come up.

    (3)　Description

        (a)　Begin by asking if the participants found themselves talking to each other about last week's session anytime during the week.

        (b)　Ask if there are any questions they want to raise concerning anything that went on last week.

b.　Birth-order exercise (55 minutes)

    (1)　Objective. To reflect on the ways in which the birth-order theory is descriptive of them.

    (2)　Role of the therapists. The therapists first get general feelings and thoughts about the material read last week, then give directions for the exercise and circulate among the members as they work on the exercise.

    (3)　Description

        (a)　Begin by saying, "Let's spend a little time talking about your general reactions to the material you read on birth order." (Spend about 5 to 10 minutes on this. It is important to accept all remarks, regardless of whether the birth-order information made sense or not.)

        (b)　Then say, "For the first exercise tonight, you'll be working with that material according to your birth order."

        (c)　Tell them how you have divided them into groups, that is, all first, fifth, and ninth children will be in one group; all second, sixth, and tenth children in another, and so on. If for some good reason, someone thinks he or she should be in a different group, honor that decision.

        (d)　When they get in their groups, follow these steps: (1) Use material from Questions 1–12 and the last four pages of the packet (systems function, perceptual orientation, interpersonal responsibility, characteristic response patterns). (2) Have them write on newsprint any characteristics of their birth order that are true of them. If the trait is not characteristic of all in the group, they should indicate after that trait of whom it is true. It may be helpful for the therapists to give a few examples of areas in which the birth-order theory is true of them. (3) Encourage the members to talk among themselves about their similarities. It may be important for the therapists to spend more time with someone who ends up alone rather than in a group.

(e) Ask if anyone has questions about the procedure to be followed.

(f) Tell them they have 40 minutes to complete their task.

(g) At the end of 40 minutes, ask them to stop and to put their newsprint aside for now. They will need to use it during the week to complete their homework assignment. Tell them you will explain the assignment at the end of tonight's session.

c. Guided sharing exercise: (45 minutes)
(1) Objective
(a) To share information about relationships in the participants' families and their community.
(b) To become conscious of the birth order of the person they are talking about.
(2) Role of the therapists. The therapists furnish the statements to be completed and remind participants to tell the birth order of the person they're talking about.
(3) Description
(a) When all are assembled in a large group, make a transitional remark such as, "We'd like to continue your reflection on yourself in your family of origin, but with a little different twist."
(b) Then explain the exercise: "I will begin a sentence, and any of you who feel inclined may finish the sentence with a remembrance from your family of origin. It is important in this exercise to indicate the birth order of the person you're talking about."
(c) Encourage the participants to keep their remarks brief. Tell them you will throw out a new statement when it appears everyone who wants to has spoken. In this exercise, "no one" is a legitimate way to complete a statement. This, too, says something about the person.
(d) Then begin with the first statement. If necessary, model by completing the first statement. The follow-

ing are sample statements (as many more may be added as desired):

1) I had the most fun with . . .
2) . . . was the one who came to me with problems.
3) If I needed help with a practical matter, I asked . . .
4) I fought most with . . .
5) When I felt sad, lonely, or depressed, I talked to . . .
6) It was hardest for me to disagree with . . .
7) The person whose sense of time was most different from mine was . . .
8) The person I spent the most time with was . . .
9) The person who most often disagreed with me was . . .
10) I felt closest to . . .
11) I was responsible for . . .
12) I could express affection most easily to . . .
13) . . . was responsible.

(e) After about 15 minutes, begin again, but change the verb to present tense. Keep the statements geared to the family.

(f) After another 15 minutes, begin with the same lead statements, but this time apply them to present relationships in the community. Again, be sure the participants mention the birth order of the individual they are talking about.

(g) Stop after 15 minutes and say, "Well, that's the end of our first exercise dealing with the possible implications of your birth order."

d. Evaluation exercise (10 minutes)
  (1) Objective. To elicit feedback concerning the previous exercise.
  (2) Role of the therapists. The therapists initiate a discussion and then keep it going.
  (3) Description
      (a) Make a comment such as, "Were any new awarenesses developed in you during that exercise?"
      (b) Then ask, "Did you benefit in any way from that exercise?"
      (c) The therapist needs to pay particular attention to what is happening between the group members at this

point. The last 15 minutes of the previous exercise were most probably their first encounter with risk taking, as far as community relationships are concerned, so the therapists may need to deal with the feelings involved with this.

   e. Homework assignment and closing (5–10 minutes)

     (1) Remind the participants to put their homework assignments in the large brown envelope marked *Homework* and to take a sheet for the coming week. Ask them to be sure their names and the date are on the sheet.

     (2) Refer to the sheets of newsprint from the first exercise tonight and say, "An additional assignment for the week will be based on these sheets."

     (3) The following procedure is to be followed by each member:

       (a) Contract with a person for at least 15 minutes when the two of you can sit down to discuss the points printed on the newsprint.

       (b) When you meet the person, hold the newsprint up with these three things to do printed on it: (a) Give an example of how one of the traits influences the way you function in this community. (The other person simply listens and accepts.) (2) Ask the other person how one of the traits (choose a different one) affects the person. (Does the person find it hard to deal with you because of that? Does it make the person feel closer to you?) (3) Ask for feedback concerning one of the other traits, but this time have the other person choose the one that person would like to give you feedback on.

     (4) Ask the members if they understand what they are supposed to do. Make needed clarifications.

     (5) Close by saying something like, "That's the end of our session for tonight. Tonight we began to make some connections between family and community. Thank you for your cooperation."

4. Session 3: Sharing Family-of-Origin Memories

  • Objectives

    a. To have the participants reflect on the lessons they learned in their family of origin exercise.

    b. To have them share these with the group.

    c. To increase expressiveness through the sharing of feedback about homework assignments and by trying to find relationships between present community living and things learned about the family of origin.

    d. To increase group cohesion by soliciting help in completing an assignment.

- Materials
  a. Little slips of paper on which there are numbers from one to five (or the number of members in the group) and scrap paper to write skits on.
- Procedures
  a. Opening exercise (5 minutes): The objective of this exercise is to release some of the day's tension and to "loosen up." The members stand in a circle. When they hear the number of their birth order called out, they jump into the middle of the circle and jump back only when they hear their number again. Variations of this activity may be used (they yell in unison when they hear their number).
  b. Evaluation exercise (20 minutes): The group members will express their thoughts and feelings to each other concerning the homework assignment for last week. The therapists observe strictly for 15 minutes, then give the members feedback for 5 minutes on what they observed.
  c. Dramatization exercise (75 minutes): Each member demonstrates three incidents from that member's family life. These incidents are expressed in three brief skits (between 30 seconds and one minute each), in which other members of the group participate. The objectives of the exercise are to reflect on things learned in the family of origin, to increase expressiveness by exploring possible connections between these things and present community living, and to increase group cohesion by soliciting help to complete a task. Allow feedback about the skits.
  d. Processing exercise (15 minutes): The group members should focus on what happened within the group as they participated in the skits. Questions for discussion could be: (1) Why did you choose those particular people? (2) How did it feel to be chosen to play a particular role? (3) Did you learn anything about yourself?

5. Session 4: Personal Strength in Community Perspective
   - Objectives
     a. To increase the self-esteem of each community member.

    b. To rediscover forgotten strengths.

    c. To increase group cohesion.

    d. To see strengths in a community perspective.

- Materials
  a. Magic markers, paper strips big enough to write a few words on, newsprint, scrap paper, and glue.
- Procedures
  a. Opening exercise (5–10 minutes): The members are given the opportunity to share some thoughts about the treatment thus far. The members each make a "wondering" statement that reflects something they have been wondering about in regard to the purpose or effects of the activities so far.
  b. Strengths exercise (80–100 minutes): This exercise is designed to fulfill the general objectives of the session. Members write on scratch paper two strengths of each person in the group—one a family strength and one a community strength. The members are, in turn, "in focus" and receive their strengths with an explanation from each member.
  c. Closing exercise (10–15 minutes): The therapists ask questions to facilitate discussion about the preceding activity ("What were some of your thoughts or feelings while you were 'in focus'?" and so on.)

6. Session 5: Sharing Relationships Within the Community
   - Objective
     a. To have the participants share with the group their perspectives on relationships within the local community.
   - Materials
     a. None.
   - Procedures
     a. Warm-up exercise (5 minutes): To relax participants and get them to laugh, ask them to stand up in a circle and punch the air with their right hand, and then with their left, and then with both.
     b. Community sculpting exercise (1 hour, 55 minutes): This exercise enables the members to share their perceptions of community relationships by using space. The members first draw their sculpture of the community so that they will not be influenced by what someone does before them. Following the sculpting, the therapists may facilitate a discussion about the process itself and have the members determine if and how family of origin relationships are being acted out in present community living.

c. Conclude the session with observations similar to the following: "Theoretically, we all accept the fact that each person has both strengths and weaknesses. We know, too, that wherever we have a group of people gathered together, we have both the strengths and weaknesses of those people at work. It was true in our families; it is now true in your local community. These strengths and weaknesses are fertile ground for the cultivation of conflict, and they are also fertile ground for reaping the harvest of meaningful relationships. Some of this has come out strikingly in your community sculptures. Thank you for the ways in which each of you has shared tonight. You might want to spend a little time during the coming week thinking about this quotation from one of Virginia Satir's books. Satir is a well-known family therapist. She states, 'People get together on the basis of similarities and grow on the basis of differences' " (Satir, 1972).

7. Session 6: Interpersonal Needs
   • Objective
      a. To share reflections on the three basic needs of inclusion, control, and affection.
   • Materials
      a. The FIRO-B tests taken during the introductory session, typed copies of the description of FIRO-B scales, and the community-profile results printed on a large posterboard.
   • Procedures
      a. Opening exercise (5 minutes)
         (1) Objective. To have the participants express briefly their "positions" in the three areas of inclusion, control, and affection.
         (2) Role of the therapists. The therapist asks three questions and directs participants to answer without explaining.
         (3) Description
            (a) The therapist begins by saying, "Our session tonight focuses on the three interpersonal needs of inclusion, control, and affection. Let's begin by you answering three questions. The questions all deal with a personal preference. Though circumstances could change your answer, please answer as you would for most situations. Probably the first thing that comes into your mind will be the truest answer, so go with it."

(b) Then say, "Let's follow this format: I'll ask a question, ask one of you to answer, and then simply go around in a circle until everyone answers. Just answer the question without giving any explanation. O.K.? Any questions?" (If not, then proceed.)

(c) Ask these three questions: (1) Would you rather *invite* someone to do something or *be invited* by someone? (2) Do you prefer to *make decisions* for yourself or *have someone* else make them *for you?* (3) Do you prefer to *give* affection or *receive* it?

(d) When all have been asked and have answered the questions, say, "That was dipping our toes into the water, so to speak. Let's move now into our main exercise for tonight's session."

b. FIRO-B exercise (1 hour, 55 minutes)

(1) Objective. To investigate the implications of the participants' FIRO-B results on community living.

(2) Role of the therapists. The therapists educate, give directions, and facilitate discussion among the participants.

(3) Description

(a) Begin the exercise by preparing participants for its many parts. Say something like, "Our main exercise deals with the three needs of inclusion, control, and affection. The exercise has nine parts. I thought I would begin by telling you what each part is so that you'll have a road map for our activities tonight."

(b) Read through the list of parts: (1) definitions, (2) a brief explanation of FIRO-B theory, (3) five points for discussion, (4) what you learned in your family about these needs, (5) what you learned in your community about these needs, (6) prediction of scores, (7) community profile, (8) distribution of test results, (9) short tasks to complete.

(c) Distribute the sheet, "Description of FIRO-B Scales." Give the participants a chance to read the sheet silently, and then say, "Would you please underline the words *the degree of need an individual feels.* These are important words. We'll talk about them in a little while. Your *expressed* inclusion scores reflect your need to reach out to others, to include them in your activities or relationships, whereas your *wanted* inclusion scores reflect your need to have others reach out to include you in their activities and relationships. The same can be said for control and affection.''

(d) Then say, ''Let me very briefly explain to you the theory behind the FIRO-B. FIRO-B is based on the assumption that all human interaction may be divided into three issue categories: issues surrounding *inclusion,* issues surrounding *control,* and issues surrounding *affection.* The FIRO theory of group development states that a group proceeds through inclusion issues into control issues and finally into affection issues; then it recycles. To illustrate the categories, consider a group of people on a boat ride. The issue of control here is who is running the motor or operating the rudder. The affection issue concerns any close relations that develop between pairs of people. The diagram at the bottom of the page I just gave you shows that each of these areas has two dimensions of behavior: what you as an individual express to others, and what you as an individual want from others.''

(e) Then say, ''I have five points I would like to make right now. Let me read through them quickly just so you'll know what they are: (1) There are no good or bad scores in these areas. The scores reflect your personal needs. (2) It is O.K. to be the way you are. If you decide you don't like the way you are, it is your decision whether you want to change. (3) Remember that your scores reflect your needs in regard to the community as a whole. When I gave the test to you, I asked that you answer it in reference to this group of people. (4) It follows from the above statement that, if you took the test in relation to a specific individual in the community, your scores would be different. They would also be different if you took the test in reference to a different group of people. (5) The scores will fluctuate, depending on your surroundings and the time you take the test. For example, one of my professors told me that, right after Vatican II, she was working with a group of 45 to 50 nuns and she gave them the FIRO-B; their scores on control were all zeros and ones. She told me that was an abnormal response, but it was certainly real at the time."

(f) Say, "Let's go back and discuss each of those points. Any question, comment, feeling in regard to the statement is appropriate." Read the first statement again and then facilitate a discussion of that statement. Continue in this fashion until all the statements have been discussed.

(g) Say, "Could we spend about 15 minutes sharing what you learned in your home about these interpersonal needs? You structure the discussion any way you see fit. I'll simply listen." At the end of 15 minutes, call time and move to the next part.

(h) Say, "Now that you've shared a little about what you have learned in your homes, let's talk about what you've learned during your years of religious living." This time the therapist could add, "Would you like to handle the discussion the same way you did the last one?" This is a way of commenting on the area of control. Stop the discussion after 15 minutes.

(i) Then say, "O.K. Now it's time for you to predict your scores in these areas. There's a grid at the bottom of the sheet, 'Description of FIRO-B Scales.' Below the grid are the divisions: If you think your need to express inclusion is low, then you'll give yourself a 0, 1, or 2. Are there any questions?" When the questions have been answered, say, "Let's take a couple minutes for you to write your predictions on the grid." After everyone has finished, move to the next step.

(j) Then say, "What I'd like to do now is show you your results as a community." (Show the posterboard with the scores on it.) "All expressed scores are given in black, and wanted scores are the same color as the trait itself; that is, control is printed in red; the black lines show where you are as a community in expressing control; the red lines show where you are as a community in wanting control. Understand?" Read the results aloud for each scale.

(k) Ask questions like, "Do you like the way this community profile looks? What are some implications for your living? Would you volunteer where you think you are and talk about how that feels for you?"

(l) After the above questions have been dealt with, say, "I am going to give you the results of your test now. The first thing I'd like you to do is copy your actual scores on the grid next to your predicted scores." Give a minute for them to do this.

(m) Then say, "I think that, now that you know your scores, two decisions become important. The first is whether or not you personally are satisfied with your scores. The second is how your scores affect those you live with. I'm wondering if you agree that both of these are important." Take time for comments.

(n) Now give this assignment: "You now have ten minutes to decide how or when you're going to find out how others think and feel about your scores in relation to their own."

8. Session 7: Sharing Differences
   - Objectives
     a. To acknowledge differences among community members.
     b. To share with others one way in which they differ, and to let the others know where the members stand in relation to that difference.
     c. To share implicit and explicit rules operating in their families.
     d. To think of implicit rules operating in the community.
     e. To make these implicit rules explicit.
   - Materials
     a. Balloons, pencils, slips of paper (some with participants' names on and some blank), and straight pins.
   - Procedures
     a. Opening exercise (10–15 minutes)
        (1) Objectives
            (a) To give the members time to think about the persons in their families and in their community who are most different from them.
            (b) To consider some effects of these differences on their relationships.
        (2) Role of the therapists. The therapists give instructions and pose issues in which the participants are to reflect.
        (3) Description
            (a) Instruct the family members to close their eyes, relax, and think about the person in their family who is most unlike them. Say, "Now picture the person as that

person is now (or the last time you saw that person alive). Keep a mental image of the person as you quietly reflect on the questions I'm now going to ask you to think about."

(b) Then ask questions similar to these (after each question, pause about 15 seconds so that the members have time to think):

1) In what ways are you different?

2) Have those differences kept you from having a close relationship with that person?

3) Have you ever talked together about some of the ways you're different? How was that talk? Was it a good experience? Or did you wish that you hadn't had it?

4) If you haven't talked with that person, could you think of the reason? Is it because you tend to see these differences as threats? If you do, try to get in touch with what in you fears that difference or is unwilling to accept that difference. Or do you tend to see these differences as a chance to learn something new?

5) Now let go of the image of your relative and put in its place a picture of the person in this community who reminds you most of that person in your family. Give yourself time to get in touch with who it might be. If no one in the community reminds you of that person, then decide who in the community you see as most different from yourself.

(c) When the last question has been asked, ask everyone to open their eyes and say, "Make one statement about what was happening to you on the feeling/ thinking level during that exercise?" Go quickly around the circle asking the question.

(d) End this exercise by recalling the quotation from Virginia Satir mentioned at the end of the fifth session: "You may want to recall the quotation from Satir that I shared with you at the end of our session two weeks ago: People get together on the basis of similarities and grow on the basis of differences. In our next exercise, we're going to focus on ways you are different from each other."

b. Differences exercise (45 minutes)

(1) Objective. To share with each member one way you see them as different from you and to let them know "where you are" in relation to that difference.

(2) Role of the therapists. The therapists give instructions and keep the exercise moving along. It is also important that the therapists urge the members to take risks in this sharing, so that they may benefit from the exercise.

(3) Description
(a) Distribute envelopes containing slips of paper and straight pins. If the group consists of seven people, each envelope contains six slips of paper and six straight pins.
(b) Then say, "In your envelope are slips of paper with straight pins. On each slip of paper, your name is printed in the bottom right hand corner. In the upper left hand corner is the name of each other person in the community. Write one specific way you see that person as being different from you. Are there any questions?" During the question time, it is important to explain that the participants will get more benefit from this exercise if they write a difference that is in some way difficult for them to deal with.
(c) After the questions have been answered, say, "Let's take about five to ten minutes to think about and then write one way in which each person is different from you. Before you begin to think, I would like to encourage you to take some risks with each other. You could play this safe, but if that's what you choose, your benefits may be minimal."
(d) When everyone is finished, say, "Let's handle this exercise pretty much the way we did our strengths feedback. The person to my right will begin, and then we'll simply go around the circle. When your turn comes, go to the person on your right, pin the slip of paper on the person, state the difference you've chosen and let that person know where you stand on an acceptance level. You might say, for example, 'I accept this difference in you,' or, 'I want to accept this difference in you, but I'm having a hard time.' " During feedback, the one in focus only listens.

(e) Explain that the reason for pinning the difference on the individual is to make it visible, that is, in a sense, to have it out in the open for awhile. Say, "Too often I think our differences remain hidden or at least not articulated. The differences remain implicit. I personally believe it's healthier to make things explicit. So by wearing your differences, you will have them out in the open, and then you'll at least know what you're not dealing with. Who knows, you may even choose to deal with the differences."

(f) After everyone has completed the exercise, use the remaining time to process in the large group.

c. Rule exercise (between 45 minutes and 1 hour)

   (1) Objectives
      (a) To share rules that operate in their families of origin.
      (b) To make explicit some implicit rules operating in the community.

   (2) Role of the therapists. The therapists give directions and facilitate the discussion of implicit rules in the community. The therapists will need to help the members to own their own feelings and thoughts, not to blame others or defend themselves.

   (3) Description
      (a) Make a transitional remark, such as, "Because of differences, people choose to emphasize different rules in their lives. When you think about it, a rule is basically a guideline for behavior. The last exercise tonight deals with rules."
      (b) Before proceeding, it is important to stress that the rule (constitution) of the community is not being considered here, but rather individuals' personal rules.
      (c) Explain the difference between implicit and explicit rules. Note that a religious community's constitution contains explicit guidelines.
      (d) When all the members understand the distinction between implicit and explicit rules, say, "Let's take a short time to share with each other one implicit and one explicit rule that were operative in your families as you grew up. Let's begin with the explicit rules because those will probably be easier to remember, since they are out in the open."

(e) After each person has shared an explicit rule, say, "Now let's have a few examples of implicit rules that operated in your family." Allow no more than 15 minutes for Steps d and e.

(f) Then say, "We're now going to move this notion of implicit rules into life in this community. You have five minutes to think of as many implicit rules as you can that you think are present in this community. As you think of one, write it on one of the slips of paper, put it into a balloon, blow the balloon up and let it lie in the middle of the floor."

(g) After five minutes, ask each person to take one balloon and hold it.

(h) Explain that the next step of the exercise is symbolic. Say, "Each of you, one by one, will break a balloon and read the rule aloud. As soon as everyone hears the rule, it moves from being an implicit to an explicit rule." Steps f, g, and h should take only about ten minutes.

(i) Facilitate a discussion among the members about the effects of these implicit rules on the community. Questions such as the following may be used for this discussion: (1) Did this implicit rule operate in any of your families? (b) Do you think it may be present among you because of your experience in a previous community situation? (3) Do you think this is a rule worth keeping, or would you like to see it discarded? (4) How difficult do you think it would be for you to do something to change this rule? The exercise is completed when each implicit rule has been dealt with. It is important to devote some time to each of the rules.

(j) Conclude the session by saying, "I hope you've found the exercise on differences and rules helpful. I see both of these areas as having the potential to cause conflict and to keep people from getting closer to each other. If you decide to do anything with some things you have learned, you may be able to deal with your conflicts more appropriately and then you may find yourself closer to one or more people in the community. Thanks for your cooperation once again. See you for our last session next week."

9. Session 8: Sharing and Reflecting on Growth
   - Objectives
     a. To reflect on what the participants have learned about change.
     b. To offer further service if desired.
     c. To enable the participants to share ways in which the treatment has benefited them.
     d. To complete the postassessment instruments and an evaluation form.
   - Materials
     a. Evaluation sheets, copies of the Group Environment Scale and answer sheets, copies of the FIRO-B, two balloons, strips of newsprint 10″ × 2″, stapler or rubber cement, magic markers, and evaluation forms.
   - Procedures
     a. Opening exercise (10–15 minutes): The objective of this exercise is to facilitate a discussion about change. By popping a balloon and then slowly letting the air out of a second balloon, present the concept of gradual versus abrupt (startling) change in a relationship. End with something like the following comment: "These sessions have been valuable to you only if they have effected some change in you and in the system of which you are a part."
     b. Evaluation exercise (60 minutes): This exercise requires the members to complete an evaluation form, the Group Environment Scale, and the FIRO-B and to share with others parts of the evaluation form.
     c. Chain link exercise (15–30 minutes): The members bring closure to the group experience by expressing gratitude for what has occurred. The members write things for which they are grateful on the strips of paper and then create a chain by connecting the papers. The chain is displayed in a place where they will see it often, to remind them of the efforts they made as individuals and as a community to make stronger the links uniting them.

References
and Selected Readings

REFERENCES—CHAPTERS 1–10

. Avery, A.W., Ridley, C.A., Leslie, L.A., & Handis, M. Teaching family relations to dating couples versus noncouples: Who learns better? *Family Coordinator,* 1979, *28*(1), 41–46.

Bader, E., Microys, G., Sinclair, C., Willett, E., & Conway, B. Do marriage preparation programs really work: A Canadian experiment. *Journal of Marital and Family Therapy,* 1980, *6*(2), 171–179.

Bagarozzi, D.A., & Rauen, P. Premarital counseling: Appraisal and status. *American Journal of Family Therapy,* 1981, *9,* 13–30.

Bales, R., & Slater, P. Role differentiation in small decision-making groups. In T. Parsons & R. Bales (Eds.), *Family socialization and interaction process.* New York: Free Press, 1955.

Barlow, S., Hansen, W., Finley, R., & Fuhriman, A. Leader communication style: Effects on members of small groups. *Journal of Small Group Behavior,* 1982, *13*(4), 518–531.

Bednar, R.L. Experiential group research: Current perspectives. In S.L. Garfield & A.E. Bergin (Eds.), *Handbook of psychotherapy and behavior change: An empirical analysis* (2nd ed.). New York: John Wiley & Sons, 1978.

Bednar, R.L., & Battersby, C. The effects of specific cognitive structures on early group development. *Journal of Applied Behavioral Sciences,* 1976, *12,* 513–522.

Bednar, R.L., & Kaul, T.J. Experimental group research: Current perspectives. In A.E. Bergin & S.L. Garfield (Eds.), *Handbook of psychotherapy and behavior change* (2nd ed.). New York: John Wiley & Sons, 1978.

Bednar, R.L., Melnick, J., & Kaul, T.J. Risk, responsibility, and structure: A conceptual framework for initiating group counseling and psychotherapy. *Journal of Counseling Psychology,* 1974, *21*(1), 31–37.

Bednar, R.L., & Weinberg, S.L. *Ingredients of successful treatment programs for underachievers.* Unpublished manuscript, Arkansas Rehabilitation Research and Training Center, 1969.

Bell, J.E. A theoretical framework for family group therapy. In Guerin, P.J. (Ed.), *Family therapy: Theory and practice.* New York: Gardner Press, 1976.

Bentley, J. *Group counseling: Some tentative ideas in outline form.* Unpublished manuscript, University of Utah, 1974.

Bion, W. *Experiences in groups.* New York: Basic Books, 1961.

Bosco, A. *Marriage encounter: The rediscovery of love.* St. Meinard, Ind.: Abbey Press, 1976.

Bowman, T.W. A dream taking form: Family life education in community settings. *Family Relations,* 1981, *30,* 543–548.

Campbell, S.M. *The couple's journey: Intimacy as a path to wholeness.* San Luis Obispo, Calif.: Impact Publishers, 1980.

Carter, E.A., & McGoldrick, M. *The family life cycle: A framework for family therapy.* New York: Gardner Press, 1980.

Cauthorn, C.K. *A comparative study of two approaches to family life education: Traditional vs. the systems approach teaching five leadership skills to fathers.* Unpublished thesis, Brigham Young University, 1976.

Clinebell, H.J. *Growth counseling for marriage enrichment.* Philadelphia: Fortress Press, 1975.

Corey, G., & Corey, M.S. *Groups: Process and practice.* Monterey, Calif.: Brooks/Cole, 1977.

DeJulio, R., Bentley, J., & Cockayne, T. *The effect of pregroup interaction.* Unpublished manuscript, State University of New York at Genesee, 1976.

Dinkmeyer, D., & Dinkmeyer, D., Jr. A comprehensive and systematic approach to parent education. *American Journal of Family Therapy,* 1979, *7*(2), 46–55.

Drum, D.J., & Knott, E. *Structured groups for facilitating development: Acquiring life skills, resolving life themes and making life transitions.* New York: Human Sciences Press, 1977.

Duvall, E. *Marriage and family development* (5th ed.). Philadelphia: Lippincott, 1977.

Fisher, B.L. *Assumptions of family enrichment.* Paper presented at the annual conference of the National Council in Family Relations, Washington, D.C., October 1982.

Fisher, B.L. *The effect of an increase in observation skills upon change in marital satisfaction and decision-making ability.* Unpublished thesis, Brigham Young University, 1974.

Fisher, B.L., Giblin, P.R., & Hoopes, M.H. Healthy family functioning: What therapists say and what families want. *Journal of Marital and Family Therapy,* 1982, *8*(3), 273–284.

Fisher, B.L., Sprenkle, W., & Sheehy, P. *Basic assumptions of marriage and family enrichment programs.* Unpublished manuscript, Fort Collins, Colo.: Colorado State University, 1980.

Foley, V.D. *An introduction to family therapy.* New York: Grune & Stratton, 1974.

Gantman, C. A closer look at families that work well. *International Journal of Family Therapy,* 1980, *8,* 106–119.

Gibbard, S., Hartman, J., & Mann, F. (Eds.). *Analysis of groups.* San Francisco: Jossey-Bass, 1974.

Goldenberg, I., & Goldenberg, H. *Family therapy: An overview.* Monterey, Calif.: Brooks/Cole, 1980.

Griggs, M.B. Criteria for the evaluation of family life education materials. *Family Relations,* 1981, *30,* 549–555.

Guerney, B., & Guerney, L. Family life education as an intervention. *Family Relations,* 1981, *30,* 591–598.

Gurman, A.S., & Kniskern, D.P. Enriching research on marital enrichment programs. *Journal of Marriage and Family Counseling,* 1977, *3*(2), 3–12.

Gurman, A.S., & Kniskern, D.P. Family therapy outcome research: Knowns and unknowns. In A.S. Gurman & D.P. Kniskern (Eds.), *Handbook of family therapy*. New York: Brunner/Mazel, 1981.

Haley, J. *Uncommon therapy: The psychiatric technique of Milton Ericson*. New York: Norton, 1973.

Haley, J. *Problem-solving therapy: New strategies for effective therapy*. San Francisco: Jossey-Bass, 1976.

Hawkins, J.L., & Killorin, E.A. Family of origin: An experimental workshop. *American Journal of Family Therapy*, 1979, 7(4), 5–18.

Hill, P. *Verbal interaction styles of three marathon encounter groups*. Unpublished doctoral dissertation, University of Utah, 1971.

Hill, W. *Hill interaction matrix*. Los Angeles: University of Southern California, Youth Study Center, 1965.

Hof, L., & Miller, W.R. *Marriage enrichment: Philosophy, process and program*. Bowie, Mass.: Robert J. Brody Co., 1981.

Hoffman, L. *Foundations of family therapy*. New York: Basic Books, 1981.

Hozman, T.L., & Froiland, D.J. Families in divorce: A proposed model for counseling children. *Family Coordinator*, 1976, 25(3), 271–276.

Hynson, L.M., Jr. A systems approach to community family education. *Family Coordinator*, 1979, 28(3), 383–387.

Johnson, D. *The social psychology of education*. New York: Holt, Rinehart & Winston, 1970.

Kaplan, H., & Sadock, B. (Eds.). *Comprehensive group psychotherapy*. Baltimore: Williams & Williams Co., 1971.

Klemer, R.H., & Smith, R.M. *Teaching about family relationships*. Minneapolis, Minn.: Burgess Publishing Co., 1975.

Laing, R.D. *The politics of the family*. New York: Vintage Books, 1969.

Lee, F., & Bednar, R.L. Effects of group structure and risk-taking disposition in group behavior, attitudes and atmosphere. *Journal of Counseling Psychology*, 1976, 24(2), 191–199.

Leiberman, M. Group methods. In F. Kanfer & A. Goldstein (Eds.), *Helping people change*. New York: Guilford Press, 1975.

Leiberman, M., Yalom, I., & Miles, M. *Encounter groups: First facts*. New York: Basic Books, 1973.

Lewis, J., Beavers, W.R., Gossett, J., & Phillips, V. *No single thread: Psychological health in family systems*. New York: Brunner/Mazel, 1976.

Lippett, R.O., & Schindler-Rainman, E. Designing for participative learning and changing. In K.D. Berne, L.P. Bradford, J.R. Gibb, & R.O. Lippett (Eds.), *The laboratory method of changing and learning: Theory and application*. Palo Alto, Calif.: Science and Behavior Books, 1975, 189–212.

Luft, J. *Group processes*. Palo Alto, Calif.: Mayfield Publishing Co., 1963.

Mace, D. A long, long trail from information-giving to behavioral change. *Family Relations*, 1981, 30(4), 599–606.

Mace, D., & Mace, V. The selection, training and certification of facilitators for marriage enrichment programs. *Family Coordinator*, 1976, 25(2), 117–126.

Mager, R. *Goal analysis*. Belmont, Calif.: Fearon Publishers, 1972.

Melnick, J., & Woods, M. Analysis of group composition research and theory for psycho-therapeutic and growth-oriented groups. *Journal of Applied Behavioral Science,* 1978, *12*(4), 493–512.

Mills, T. Power relations in three person groups. *American Sociological Review,* 1953, *18,* 351–357.

Mishler, E.C., & Waxler, N.E. *Interaction in families.* New York: John Wiley & Sons, 1968.

Nye, F., & Berardo, F. *Emerging conceptual frameworks in family analysis.* New York: Macmillan Co., 1966.

Olson, D. Insiders' and outsiders' views of relationships: Research studies. In G. Levinger & H. Rauch (Eds.), *Close relationships.* Amherst: University of Massachusetts Press, 1977.

Perry, W. *Forms of intellectual and ethical development in the college years.* New York: Holt, Rinehart & Winston, 1970.

Porter, B.R., & Chatelain, R.S. Family life education for single parent families. *Family Relations,* 1981, *30*(4), 517–526.

Reid, C. The authority cycle in small group development. *Adult Leadership,* 1965, *13*(10), 1–18.

Ridenour, N. Mental health education. In H. Rifren (Ed.), *The selective guide to publications for mental health and family life education.* Chicago: Marquis Academic Media, 1979.

Ridley, C.A., Avery, A.W., Harrell, J.E., Leslie, L.A., & Dent, J. Conflict management: A premarital training program in marital problem solving. *American Journal of Family Therapy,* 1981, *9*(4), 23–32.

Rinne, C.H. Criteria for evaluating curriculum materials in human relations. *Educational Leadership,* 1974, *32,* 37–40.

Robin, A. Problem-solving communication training: A behavioral approach to the treatment of parent-adolescent conflict. *American Journal of Family Therapy,* 1979, *7*(2), 69–82.

Rogers, C. *On becoming a person.* Boston: Houghton Mifflin Co., 1961.

Schumm, W., & Denton, W. Trends in premarital counseling. *Journal of Marital and Family Therapy,* 1979, *5*(4), 23–32.

Schwartz, W. Social group work: The interactionist approach. In *Encyclopedia of Social Work* (Vol. 1). New York: National Association of Social Work, 1971.

Spitze, H.T. *Choosing techniques for teaching and learning* (2nd ed.). Washington D.C.: American Home Economics Association, 1979.

Sporakowski, M.J., & Staneszewski, W.P. The regulation of marriage and family therapy: An update. *Journal of Marital and Family Therapy,* 1980, *6*(3), 335–348.

Stahmann, R.F., & Hiebert, W.J. *Premarital counseling.* Lexington, Mass.: Lexington Books, 1980.

Steinmetz, S.K. *The cycle of violence: Assertive, aggressive and abusive family interaction.* New York: Praeger Publishers, 1977.

Stinnett, N. In search of strong families. In N. Stinnett, B. Chesser, & V. DeFrain (Eds.), *Building family strengths.* Lincoln: University of Nebraska Press, 1979.

Stredback, F. The family as a three-person group. In A. Ferreira & W. Winter (Eds.), *Family interaction.* Palo Alto, Calif.: Science and Behavior Books, 1969.

Sullivan, J., Gryzlo, B., & Schwartz, W. Certification of family life educators: A status report of state departments of education. *Family Coordinator,* 1978, *27*(3), 269–272.

Thibaut, J., & Kelley, H. *The social psychology of groups.* New York: Wiley Publishers, 1959.

Travis, R.P., & Travis, Y.P. The pairing enrichment program: Actualizing the marriage. *Family Coordinator,* 1975, *24*(2), 161–166.

Tuckman, B. Developmental sequence in small groups. *Psychological Bulletin,* 1965, *63*(6), 384–399.

Vogel-Moline, M. *The effects of a structured treatment on self esteem and depression of divorced/separated persons.* Unpublished doctoral dissertation. Brigham Young University, 1979.

Ware, J.R., & Barr, J.E. Effects of a nine week structured and unstructured group on measures of self-concept and self-actualization. *Small Group Behavior,* 1977, *8*(1), 93–100.

Weakland, J., Fisch, R., Watzlawick, P., & Bodin, A. Brief therapy: Focused problem resolution. *Family Process,* 1974, *13*(2), 141–168.

Westley, W.A., & Epstein, N.B. *The silent majority.* San Francisco: Jossey-Bass, 1969.

Witkin, S., & Rose, S.D. Group training in communication skills for couples: A preliminary report. *International Journal of Family Counseling,* 1978, *6*(2), 45–56.

Wright, L., & L'Abate, L.L. Four approaches to family facilitation: Some issues and implications. *Family Coordinator,* 1977, *26*(2), 176–181.

Yalom, I. *Theory and practice of group psychotherapy.* New York: Basic Books, 1970.

REFERENCES—CHAPTERS 11–26

Addiction Research Foundation (ARF). Drug abuse: A family affair. *Journal,* 1975, *4,* 8–9.

Alexander, J.F. Defensive and supportive communication in normal and deviant families. *Journal of Consulting and Clinical Psychology,* 1973, *40*(33), 223–231.

Allen, F. Executives' wives describe sources of their contentment, frustration. *Wall Street Journal,* December 15, 1981, p. 29.

Allen, R. Chief executives say job requires many family and personal sacrifices. *Wall Street Journal,* August 20, 1980, p. 25.

Annis, H.M. Patterns of intra-familial drug use. *British Journal of Addiction,* 1974, *69,* 361–369.

Bank, S., & Kahn, M. Sister-brotherhood is powerful: Sibling sub-systems and family therapy. *Family Process,* 1975, *25*(4), 311–338.

Becvar, R., & Becvar, D. *Systems theory and family therapy: A primer.* Washington, D.C.: University Press of America, 1982.

Benningfield, A.B. Multiple family therapy systems. *Journal of Marriage and Family Counseling,* 1978, *4*(2), 25–33.

Blatner, H.A. *Acting in: Practical applications of psychodramatic methods.* New York: Springer, 1973.

Bosormenyi-Nagy, I., & Spark, G. *Invisible loyalties.* New York: Harper & Row, 1973.

Bowen, M. Family therapy and family group therapy. In D. Olson (Ed.), *Treating relationships.* Lake Mills, Iowa: Graphic Publishing Co., 1976.

Brown, A. A family systems approach to incest victims and their families. *Family,* 1978, *6,* 9–11.

Carter, E.A., & McGoldrick, M. *The family life cycle: A framework for family therapy.* New York: Gardner Press, 1980.

Cohn, R.C. Style and spirit of the theme-centered interactional method. In C.J. Sager & H.S. Kaplan (Eds.), *Progress in group and family therapy.* New York: Brunner/Mazel, 1972.

Constantine, L. Family sculpture and relationship mapping techniques. *Journal of Marriage and Family Counseling,* 1978, *4*(2), 13–23.

Crostwaite, A. Voluntary work with families of prisoners. *International Journal of Offender Therapy and Comparative Criminology,* 1972, *16*(3), 254–259.

Doane, J.A. Family interaction and communication deviance in disturbed and normal families: A review of research. *Family Process,* 1978, *17*(3), 255–266.

Duhl, F.J., Kantor, D., & Duhl, B.S. Learning space, and action in family therapy: A primer of sculpture. In D.A. Block (Ed.), *Techniques of family psychotherapy.* New York: Grune & Stratton, 1973.

Egan, G. Interpersonal living. Monterey, Calif.: Brooks/Cole, 1976.

Evans, P., & Bartolome, F. *Must success cost so much?* London: Grant McIntyre Ltd., 1980.

Fagen, J., & Shepherd, I.L. *Gestalt therapy now.* New York: Harper, 1970.

Feinauer, L. *The relationship of risk taking behaviors of treatment outcomes in a structured divorce adjustment group treatment.* Unpublished doctoral dissertation, Brigham Young University, 1980.

Feinberg, M.R., & Dempewolff, R.F. *Corporate bigamy: How to resolve the conflict between career and family.* New York: William Morrow and Co., 1980.

Fenton, N. *The prisoner's family.* Palo Alto, Calif.: Pacific Books, 1959.

Fenton, N. *Group counseling: A preface to its use in corrective and welfare agencies.* Monterey, Calif.: Institute for Crime and Delinquency, 1961.

Fisher, B.L. *The effect of an increase in observation skill upon change in marital satisfaction and decision-making ability.* Unpublished thesis, Brigham Young University, 1974.

Geddes, M., & Medway, J. Symbolic drawing of family life spaces. *Family Process,* 1975, *6,* 219–228.

Goldenberg, I., Stier, S., & Preston, T.A. The use of multiple family marathon as a teaching device. *Journal of Marriage and Family Counseling,* 1975, *1*(4), 343–350.

Gottlieb, B. Incest: Therapeutic intervention in a unique form of sexual abuse. In C.J. Warner (Ed.), *Rape and sexual assault: Management and intervention.* Rockville, Md.: Aspen Systems Corp., 1980.

Groome, T.H. *Christian religious education.* San Francisco: Harper & Row, 1980.

Guerin, P.J., Jr., & Pendagast, E.G. Evaluation of family system and genogram. In P.J. Guerin (Ed.), *Family therapy, theory and practice.* New York: Gardner Press, 1976.

Gullotta, T.P., & Donahue, K.C. The corporate family: Theory and treatment. *Journal of Marital and Family Therapy,* 1981, *7*(2), 1515–1558.

Hof, L., & Miller, W.R. *Marriage enrichment.* Bowie, Md.: Robert J. Brady Co., 1981.

Holmstrom, L.L., & Burgess, A.W. Assessing trauma in the rape victim. In D.R. Mass (Ed.), *The rape victim.* Dubuque, Iowa: Kendall/Hunt Publishing Company, 1977.

Hoopes, M. Structured group treatment for divorce adjustment. Unpublished paper, Brigham Young University, 1978.

Hoopes, M. Personal communication, 1979.

Hoopes, M.H., & Harper, J.M. *Birth order and the family system.* Unpublished manuscript, Brigham Young University, 1980.

Hopper, C.B. *Sex in prison.* Baton Rouge: Louisiana State University Press, 1969.

Hozman, T.L., and Froiland, D.J. Families in divorce: A proposed model for counseling the children. *Family Coordinator,* 1976, *25,* 271–276.

Huelsing, L. *Evaluation of effects of family of origin group treatment on cohesion and expressiveness in religious communities of women.* Unpublished thesis, Brigham Young University, 1981.

Johnson, D. *Reaching out.* Englewood Cliffs, N.J.: Prentice-Hall, 1972.

Kantor, R.M. *Work and family in the United States: A critical review and agenda for research and policy.* New York: Russell Sage Foundation, 1977.

Laqueur, H.P. Mechanisms of change in multiple family therapy. In C.J. Sager & H.S. Kaplan (Eds.), *Progress in group and family therapy.* New York: Brunner/Mazel, 1972.

Leichter, E., & Schulman, G.L. Multi-family group therapy. *Family Process,* 1974, *13*(1), 95–110.

Locke, H.J., & Wallace, K.M. Short marital-adjustment and prediction tests: Their reliability and validity. *Marriage and Family Living,* 1959, *21,* 251–255.

Luft, J. *Of human interaction.* Palo Alto, Calif.: National Press Books, 1969.

Mace, D., & Mace, V. The selection, training, and certification of facilitators for marriage enrichment programs. *Family Coordinator,* 1976, *25*(2), 117–125.

Margolis, D.R. *The managers: Corporate life in America.* New York: William Morrow and Co., 1979.

Margolis, R.B., Sorensen, J.L., & Galano, J. Consumer satisfaction in mental health delivery services. *Professional Psychology,* February 1977, pp. 11–16.

McAuliffe, M., & McAuliffe, R. *The essentials of chemical dependency.* Minneapolis, Minn.: American Chemical Dependency Center, 1975.

Muchowski, P., & Valle, S. Effects of assertive training on trainees and their spouses. *Journal of Marriage and Family Counseling,* 1977, *3*(3), 57–62.

Pendagast, E.G., & Sherman, C.O. A guide to the genogram. *The family: The best of the family, 1973–1978.* Washington, D.C.: Georgetown University Family Center, 1978, 101–112.

Pendergast, T.J. Family characteristics associated with marijuana use among adolescents. *International Journal of the Addictions,* 1974, *9,* 827–839.

Perls, F.S. *Gestalt therapy verbatim.* New York: Bantam, 1969.

Pfeiffer, J.W., & Jones, J.E. (Eds.). *A handbook of structured experiences for human relations training* (5 vols.). San Diego, Calif.: University Associates, 1974–1975.

Polster, E., & Polster, M. *Gestalt therapy integrated.* New York: Vintage Books, 1973.

Powers, M.A. The benefits of anticipatory grief for the parents of dying children. *International Journal of Family Counseling,* 1977, *5*(2), 48–53.

Raths, L., Harmin, M., & Simon, E. *Values and teachings.* Columbus, Ohio: Charles E. Merrill Co., 1966.

Ricklefs, R. It takes big benefits to recruit executives who have to relocate. *Wall Street Journal,* June 3, 1980, pp. 1, 25.

Russell, R.A. Assertiveness training and its effects upon the marital relationship. *Family Therapy,* 1981, *8*(1), 9–20.

Satir, V. *Peoplemaking*. Palo Alto, Calif.: Basic Books, 1972.

Sawin, M.M. *Family enrichment with family clusters*. Valley Forge, Pa.: 1979.

Schein, E.H. *Career dynamics: Matching individual and organizational needs*. Reading, Mass.: Addison-Wesley Publishing Co., 1978.

Schwartz, M.D. Situation/transition groups: A conceptualization and review. *American Journal of Orthopsychiatry*, 1978, *48*(2), 744–753.

Schwartzman, J. The addict, abstinence and the family. *American Journal of Psychiatry*, 1975, *2*, 154–157.

Shaffer, J.B., & Galinsky, M.D. *Models of group therapy and sensitivity training*. Englewood Cliffs, N.J.: Prentice-Hall, 1974.

Shaw, M.E. *Group dynamics*. New York: McGraw Hill Book Co., 1976.

Silverman, D.C. Sharing the crisis of rape: Counseling the mates and families of victims. *American Journal of Orthopsychiatry*, 1978, *48*(1), 50–59.

Simon, S.B., Howe, L.W., & Kirschenbaum, H. *Values clarification*. Minneapolis, Minn.: Winston Press, 1973.

Smith, R.L., & Alexander, A.M. *Counseling couples in groups*. Springfield, Ill.: Thomas Books, 1974.

Steele, W.R. *A follow-up study of the effects of a structured group treatment on self esteem and depression of divorce/separated women 15 months after treatment*. Unpublished thesis, Brigham Young University, 1981.

Steiner, C. *Scripts people live by*. New York: Grove Press, 1974.

Stephenson, R., and Scarpitti, F. *The group basis of crime and correction*. Westport, Conn.: Greenwood Press, 1974.

Stevens, J.O. *Awareness*. Moab, Utah: Real People Press, 1971.

Stewart, T. *Bridges not walls* (2nd ed.). Menlo Park, Calif.: Addison-Wesley Publishing, Co., 1977.

Stroup, M.A. *A preliminary study comparing two structured group treatments for step families: Coupled family treatment and family treatment*. Unpublished doctoral dissertation, Brigham Young University, 1982.

Sussman, J.A. Making it to the top: A career profile of the senior executive. *Management Review*, 1979, *68*, 15–21.

Van Dusen, W. *The natural depth in man*. New York: Perennial Library, 1972.

Vandervelde, M. *The changing life of the corporate wife*. New York: Mecox Publishing Co., 1979.

Vinter, R.D., & Sarri, R.C. Beyond group work: Organizational determinants of malperformance in secondary schools. In *Individual change through small groups*. New York: Free Press, 1974.

Vogel-Moline, M. *The effects of a structured treatment on self esteem and depression of divorced/separated persons*. Unpublished doctoral dissertation, Brigham Young University, 1979.

Wegscheider, S. *Another chance: Hope and health for the alcoholic family*. Palo Alto, Calif.: Science and Behavior Books, 1981.

Yalom, I.D. *The theory and practice of psychotherapy*. New York: Basic Books, 1970.

SELECTED READINGS—CHAPTERS 11–26

These readings provide additional background information on programs presented in Chapters 11–26. The relevant program is identified by the chapter number in brackets following the reference citation.

Agler, C.F. Psychodrama with the criminally insane. *Group Psychotherapy,* 1966, *19*(3), 176. [12]

Alberti, R.E., & Emmons, M.L. *Your perfect right: A guide to assertive behavior.* San Luis Obispo, Calif.: Impact, 1974. [13]

Aldous, J. *Family careers: Developmental changes in families.* New York: John Wiley & Sons, 1978. [18]

Alger, I. Multiple couple therapy. In P. J. Guerin (Ed.), *Family therapy.* New York: Gardner Press, 1976. [20, 22]

Anderson, D.A. *New approaches to family pastoral care.* Philadelphia: Fortress Press, 1980. [18]

Arnstein, H.S. *Brothers and sisters/sisters and brothers.* New York: E.P. Dutton, 1979. [21]

Assert yourself: A handbook on assertiveness training for women. The first Assertive Rap Group of Seattle-King County NOW, National Organization for Women, 1974. [13]

Avery, A.W., Ridley, C.A., Leslie, L.A., & Handis, M. Teaching family relations to dating couples versus noncouples: Who learns better? *Family Coordinator,* 1979, *28*(1), 41–47. [15]

Bach, S., & Goldberg, H. *Creative aggression: The art of assertive living.* New York: Avon Books, 1975. [13]

Bader, E., Microys, G., Sinclair, C., Willet, E., & Conway, B. Do marriage preparation programs really work: A Canadian experiment. *Journal of Marital and Family Therapy,* 1980, *6*(2), 171–179. [15]

Banahan, R. (Ed.). *Divorce and after.* Garden City, N.Y.: Doubleday Co., 1970. [19]

Bates, M.M., & Johnson, C.D. *Group leadership: A manual for group counseling leaders.* Denver: Love Publishing Co., 1972. [11]

Becvar, R.J. *Skills for effective communication.* New York: John Wiley & Sons, 1974. [18]

Benningfield, A.B. Multiple family therapy systems. *Journal of Marriage and Family Counseling,* 1978, *4,* 25–33. [23]

Berne, E. *The principles of group treatment.* New York: Oxford University Press, 1966. [12]

Bowerman, C.E., & Irish, D.P. Some relationships of stepchildren to their parents. *Marriage and Family Living,* 1962, *24,* 113–121. [24]

Brook, R.M. Interpersonal relationships in religious life. *Review for Religions,* 1976, *35,* 904–913. [26]

Burgess, A.W., & Holmstrom, L.L. The rape trauma syndrome. In D.R. Nass (Ed.), *The rape victim.* Dubuque, Iowa: Kendall/Hunt Publishing Co., 1977. [11]

Corder, B.G., Whiteside, R., & Vogel, M. A therapeutic game for structuring and facilitating group psychotherapy with adolescents. *Adolescence,* 1977, *12*(46), 261–267. [21]

Danesh, H.B. Anger and fear. *American Journal of Psychiatry,* 1977, *134*(10), 1109–1112. [11]

Diedrick, R.C., & Dye, A.H. *Group procedures: Purposes, processes and outcomes.* Boston: Houghton Mifflin Co., 1972. [12]

Drum, D.J., & Knott, J.E. *Structured groups for facilitating development*. New York: Human Sciences Press, 1977. [21]

Eist, H.L., & Mandel, A.U. Family treatment of ongoing incest behavior. *Family Process*, 1968, *7*, 216–232. [23]

Epstein, C. *Nursing the dying patient*. Reston, Va.: Reston Publishers, 1975. [22]

Erikson, E.H. *Childhood and society*. New York: W.W. Norton & Co., 1963. [18]

Fast, I., & Cain, A.C. The stepparent role: Potential for disturbances in family functioning. *American Journal of Orthopsychiatry*, 1965, *36*, 485–491. [24]

Fensterheim, H., & Baer, J. *Don't say yes when you want to say no*. New York: Dell Publishing, 1975. [13]

Fisher, B.L., Giblin, P., & Hoopes, M.H. Healthy family functioning: What therapists say and what families want. *Journal of Marital and Family Therapy*, 1982, *8*(3), 273–284. [16]

Fisher, B.L., & Sprenkle, D.H. Therapist's perceptions of healthy family functioning. *International Journal of Family Counseling* 1978, *6*, 1–18. [16]

Framo, J.L. Marriage therapy in a couples group. In D.A. Block (Ed.), *Techniques of family psychotherapy: A primer*. New York: Grune & Stratton, 1973. [12, 20]

Gerritsen, J.L. Healing of relationships: Community life in a time of sifting. *Sisters Today*, 1979, *51*, 95–112. [26]

Gordon, M. *Theme-centered interaction*. Baltimore: National Educational Press, 1972. [12]

Grieff, B.S., & Munter, P.K. *Tradeoffs: Executive family and organizational life*. New York: New American Library, 1980. [14]

Guerney, B., Jr., & Guerney, L.F. Family life education as intervention. *Family Relations*, 1981, *30*(4), 591–598. [21]

Guerney, B.G. *Relationship enhancement*. San Francisco: Jossey-Bass, 1977. [21]

Gutheil, T.G., & Avery, N.L. Multiple overt incest as family defense against loss. *Family Process*, 1977, *16*, 105–116. [23]

Hagan, C.M. Religious community after Vatican II. *Review for Religions*, 1978, *37*, 357–364. [26]

Heilbrun, A.B., Jr. Identification with the father and sex-role development of the daughter. *Family Coordinator*, 1976, *25*(4), 411–416. [14]

Hersen, M., & A.S. Bellack (Eds.). *Behavioral assessment*. New York: Pergamon Press, 1976. [11]

Hynson, L.M., Jr. A systems approach to community family education. *Family Coordinator*, 1979, *28*(3), 383–387. [26]

Jacobsen, D.S. Stepfamilies: Myths and realities. *Social Work*, 1979, *24*(3), 202–207. [24]

Johnson, D.W., & Johnson, F.P. *Joining together: Group theory and group skills*. Englewood Cliffs, N.J.: Prentice-Hall, 1975. [12]

Kleinman, J., Rosenberg, E., & Whiteside, M. Common developmental tasks in forming reconstituted families. *Journal of Marital and Family Therapy*, 1979, *5*(2), 79–86. [24]

Klemans, P., & Beidler, E. A question of values: A unit in written composition. *English Journal*, September 1962, pp. 421-423. [16]

Kniker, C.R. *You and values education*. Columbus, Ohio: Charles E. Merrill Publishing Co., 1977. [18]

Krantzler, M. *Creative divorce*. New York: Evans, 1974. [19]

Kubler-Ross, E. *On death and dying*. New York: MacMillan Co., 1969. [22]

L'Abate, L. Skill training programs for couples and families. In A.S. Gurman & D.P. Kniskern (Eds.), *Handbook of family therapy*. New York: Brunner/Mazel, 1981. [20]

Lamb, M.E., & Lamb, J.E. The nature and importance of the father-infant relationship. *Family Coordinator*, 1976, *25*(4), 379–386. [14]

Lang, D.M., Papenfuks, R., & Walters, J. Delinquent females' perceptions of their fathers. *Family Coordinator*, 1976, *25*(4), 475–481. [14]

Laqueur, H.P. Multiple family therapy: Questions and answers. In D.A. Block (Ed.), *Techniques of family psychotherapy: A primer*. New York: Grune & Stratton, 1973. [11, 12, 23, 24]

Laqueur, H.P. Multiple family therapy. In P.J. Guerin (Ed.), *Family therapy: Theory and practice*. New York: Gardner Press, 1976. [11]

Mace, D. Marriage and family enrichment—a new field? *Family Coordinator*, 1979, *28*(3), 409–419. [18]

Masters, W.H., & Johnson, V.E. *Human sexual inadequacy*. Boston: Little, Brown & Co., 1970. [12, 23]

McFadden, J.R. Family life education and university outreach. *Family Relations*, 1981, *30*(4), 637–642. [15]

Meeks, J.E. *The fragile alliance*. Baltimore: Williams and Wilkins Co., 1971. [21]

Messinger, L., Rogers, J., & Walker, K.N. Remarriage after divorce: A review. *Social Casework*, 1977, *58*(5), 276–285. [24]

Muson, H. Moral thinking: Can it be taught? *Psychology Today*, February 1979, pp. 48–92. [18]

Narciso, J., & Burkett, D. *Declare yourself: Discovering the me in relationships*. Englewood Cliffs, N.J.: Prentice-Hall, 1975. [13]

Nass, D.R. *The rape victim*. Dubuque, Iowa: Kendall/Hunt Publishing Company, 1977. [11]

Noble, W., & Noble, J. *How to live with other people's children*. New York: Hawthorn Books, 1977. [24]

Notman, M.T., & Nadelson, C.C. The rape victim: Psychodynamic considerations. In D.R. Nass (Ed.), *The rape victim*. Dubuque, Iowa: Kendall/Hunt Publishing Company, 1977. [11]

O'Brien, P. *The woman alone*. New York: New York Times Book Co., 1973. [13]

Parke, R.D., & Sawain, D.B. The father's role in infancy: A re-evaluation. *Family Coordinator*, 1976, *25*(4), 365–372. [14]

Paul, N. The role of mourning and empathy in conjoint marital therapy. In G.H. Zuk & I. Boszormenyi-Nagy (Eds.), *Family therapy and disturbed families*. Palo Alto, Calif.: Science and Behavior Books, 1967. [22]

Phelps, S., & Austin, N. *The assertive woman*. San Luis Obispo, Calif.: Impact, 1975. [13]

Ransom, J.W., Schlesinger, S., & Derdeyn, A.P. A stepfamily in formation. *American Journal of Orthopsychiatry*, 1978, *49*(1), 36–43. [24]

Ridley, C.A., Avery, A.W., Harrell, J.E., Leslie, L.A., & Dent, J. Conflict management: A premarital training program in mutual problem solving. *American Journal of Family Therapy*, 1981, *9*(4), 23–32. [15]

Rojas, O. *The effects of a structured group treatment on depression among individuals divorced or going through divorce*. Unpublished thesis, Brigham Young University, 1979. [19]

Roosevelt, R., and Lofas, J. *Living in step*. New York: Stein and Day, 1976. [24]

Russell, C.S. A methodological study of family cohesion and adaptability. *Journal of Marital and Family Therapy*, 1980, *6*(4), 459–470. [16]

Santa-Barbara, J., Woodward, C., Levin, S., Goodman, J., Streiner, D., Muzzin, L., & Epstein, N. Variables related to outcome in family therapy: Some preliminary analysis. *Goal Attainment Review*, 1975, *1*, 5–12. [25]

Satir, V. *Conjoint family therapy*. Palo Alto, Calif.: Science and Behavior Books, 1967. [21]

Satir, V. *Peoplemaking*. Palo Alto, Calif.: Science and Behavior Books, 1972. [18]

Sawin, M.M. *Family enrichment with family clusters*. Valley Forge, Pa.: 1979. [18]

Scharf, P. (Ed.). *Readings in moral education*. Minneapolis, Minn.: Winston Press, 1978. [18]

Schlossberg, N.K., Troll, L.E., & Leibowitz, Z. *Perspectives on counseling adults: Issues and skills*. Monterey, Calif.: Brooks/Cole, 1978. [18]

Schulman, G.L. Myths that intrude on the adaptation of the stepfamily. *Social Casework*, 1972, *53*, 131–139. [24]

Schumm, W., & Denton, W. Trends in pre-marital counseling. *Journal of Marital and Family Therapy*, 1979, *5*(4), 23–32. [15]

Sennott, J.S., III. *Healthy family functioning scale: Family members' perceptions of cohesion, adaptability, and communication*. Unpublished doctoral dissertation, Purdue University, 1981. [16]

Shaffer, J.B.P., & Galinsky, M.D. *Models of group therapy and sensitivity training*. Englewood Cliffs, N.J.: Prentice-Hall, 1974. [12]

Simon, S.B. Values clarification in family groups. *Journal for Specialists in Group Work*, 1980, *5*(3), 140–147. [18]

Smith, A.B., Berlin, L., & Bassin, A. Hostility and silence in client-centered therapy with adult offenders. *Group Psychotherapy*, 1965, *18*(3), 195. [12]

Smith, M.J. *When I say no, I feel guilty*. New York: Dial Press, 1975. [13]

Stahmann, R.J., & Heibert, W.B. *Premarital counseling*. Lexington, Mass.: Lexington Books, 1980. [15]

Stanfield-Packard, K. *Temperament characteristics of clinical and nonclinical divorced persons*. Unpublished doctoral dissertation, Brigham Young University, 1980. [19]

Stanton, D.F. Strategic approaches to family therapy. In A.S. Gurman & D.P. Kniskern (Eds.), *Handbook of family therapy*. New York: Brunner/Mazel, 1981. [20]

Steidl, J., & Wexler, J. An overview of family therapy. *Family*, 1977, *4*, 59–66. [23]

Steinglass, P. Experimenting with family treatment approaches to alcoholism, 1950–1975: A review. *Family Process*, 1976, *15*, 97–123. [25]

Steirlin, H. The dynamics of owning and disowning. *Family Process*, 1976, *15*, 277–288. [23]

Stevens, J.O. *Awareness*. Moab, Utah: Real People Press, 1971. [11]

Sutherland, S., & Scheil, D.J. Patterns of responses among victims of rape. *American Journal of Orthopsychiatry*, 1977, *40*, 503–511. [11]

Visher, E.B., & Visher, J.S. *Stepfamilies: A guide to working with step-parents and step-children*. New York: Brunner/Mazel, 1982. [24]

Vogel-Moline, M. *The effects of a structured treatment on self-esteem and depression of divorced/separated persons*. Unpublished doctoral dissertation, Brigham Young University, 1979. [19]

Weiss, R. *Marital separation*. New York: Basic Books, 1975. [19]

Woods, N.F. *Human sexuality in health and illness*. St. Louis: C.V. Mosby Co., 1975. [11, 22]

Yalom, I.D. *The theory and practice of group psychotherapy* (2nd ed.) New York: Basic Books, 1975. [11, 12, 21]

Theories Used in Structured Group Programs

The importance of theories as parts of the conceptual process of program design was emphasized in Part I. To avoid redundancy, we have deleted authors' descriptions of their applications of theories in the text and referred readers instead to this appendix. Here, we have limited our description to a few basic assumptions, concepts of change, and activities common to each theory. References are provided for reading in depth. Of course, theories other than those included here may be appropriate and helpful in conceptualizing programs.

1. Behavior Modification and Social Learning
   - Basic assumptions
     a. All behavior (cognitive, motor, or emotional) is learned in response to environmental stimulus, internal or external.
     b. Behavior is modified by altering response patterns.
     c. Behaviors learned in a group and reinforced by that group will be maintained longer than those learned in individual treatment.
   - Key concepts for change
     a. Focus on overt behavior and the accompanying affect and cognitions.
     b. Keep a record of the frequency of the behavior and its context.
     c. Carry out a program plan.
     d. Evaluate the outcome.
   - Common activities: Behavior rehearsal, role playing, skill building, assertiveness training, and teaching of cognitive concepts.
   - References
     Harris, G.G. *The group treatment of human problems: A social learning approach*. New York: Grune & Stratton, 1977.

Rose, S. *Group therapy: A behavioral approach*. Englewood Cliffs, N.J.: Prentice-Hall, 1977.

Shaffer, J.B., & Galinsky, M.D. *Models of group therapy and sensitivity training*. Englewood Cliffs, N.J.: Prentice-Hall, 1974.

2. Client-Centered
   - Basic assumptions
     a. The individual's frame of reference is of major importance and should not be imposed upon by the facilitators or other group members.
     b. People have an inherent tendency to grow and develop, and this tendency is either hampered or enhanced by their environments.
   - Key concepts for change
     a. Encourage here-and-now experiences but do not discount past experiences.
     b. Honest confrontation is valuable, even though the feedback may seem negative and potentially hurtful.
     c. Primary emphasis is on awareness, expression, and acceptance of feelings.
     d. A trusting and cohesive group climate is necessary for successful therapy.
     e. The goal is to achieve genuineness (congruence), empathic understanding, and positive regard.
   - Common activities: Role playing, body contact, and interpersonal and personal expression.
   - Reference
     Hart, J.T., & Tomlinson, T.M. (Eds.). *New directions in client-centered therapy*. Boston: Houghton Mifflin Co., 1970.

3. Cognitive
   - Basic assumptions
     a. The accrual of knowledge influences a person's behavior.
     b. The individual is responsible for assessing and altering that individual's own behavior.
     c. Directive, (educative) leadership involvement elicits learning.
     d. Instructional objectives provide a specific group format.
   - Key concepts for change
     a. Classroom cognitive interchange prompts behavior change.
     b. Specific content (coinciding with instructional objectives) is defined/adhered to by the teacher/leader.

    c. Classroom management entails balancing of concept description and clarification.

    d. Idea exchange clarifies the concepts.

    e. Role modeling, case studies, and examples serve to demonstrate skills/concepts.

    f. The teacher/leader demonstrates enthusiasm for learning through the teaching style (movement, gestures, facial expression, voice inflection).

- Common activities: Explanations, discussion and evaluation, case studies, idea-exchange readings, verbal information exchange, role modeling, lectures, skill training, and examples.
- References

  Buckland, C. An educational model of family consultation. *Journal of Marital and Family Counseling,* 1977, *3,* 49–56.

  Klemer, R., & Smith, R. *Teaching about family relationships.* Minneapolis, Minn.: Burgess Publishing Co., 1975.

  Resources for Teaching About Family Life Education. Minneapolis, Minn.: Nat'l Council on Family Relations, 1976.

4. Encounter
   - Basic assumptions

         a. The purposes include both the psychotherapeutic aspect and the educational function of growth and development.

         b. The stress is on the need for people to be more in touch with their feelings and less conforming to popular standards.

         c. Emphasis is on experiential awareness processes rather than on reflective cognitive aspects.
   - Key concepts for change

         a. Focus on what one's body can reveal and translate meaning by physical activity to release bodily feeling and energy.

         b. Utilize fantasy and inner imagery to get more awareness.

         c. Dissolve blocks and free energy; be able to "read energy."

         d. Deal with interpersonal issues, such as inclusion, control, and affection.

         e. Utilize honest confrontation and group support.
   - Common activities: Guided imagery, trust fall, cradling, wrestling, blend walk, gestalt exercises, relaxation and deepening breathing, screening, pounding, pillow beating, and communication games.
   - References

     Mintz, E. *Marathon groups: Reality and symbol.* New York: Appleton-Century-Crofts, 1971.

Rogers, C. *Carl Rogers on encounter groups*. New York: Harper & Row, 1970.

Schutz, W.C. *Here comes everybody*. New York: Harper & Row, 1971.

5. Experiential
   - Basic assumptions
     a. Relationship attitudes and skills are gained through focused relationship practice.
     b. Individual and relationship *strengths* are acknowledged and implemented in structured experiences.
     c. New behaviors are most efficiently learned when practiced in a safe and accepting environment.
   - Key concepts for change
     a. Communication exercises, both verbal and nonverbal, are relationship-enhancing.
     b. There is a mutual reinforcement of strengths in structured activities.
     c. Self-disclosure and self-perception activities serve to strengthen the relationship.
     d. Trust and rapport building strengthens the group commitment and involvement.
     e. Conflict negotiation and problem solving are nurtured by the accepting environment of the group.
   - Common activities: Dyadic communication, problem solving, conflict resolution, self-disclosure, trust building, negotiation, perceptual congruence, role playing, nonverbal communication, self-actualization, giving and receiving of feedback, role taking, and touching.
   - References

     Ho, H.A. (Ed.). *Marriage and family enrichment: New perspectives and programs*. Nashville, Tenn.: Abingdon, 1976.

     Hof, L., & Miller, W.R. *Marriage enrichment: Philosophy, process, and program*. Bowie, Md.: Brady, 1981.

6. Gestalt
   - Basic assumptions
     a. By focusing on the "here and now," intrapsychic conflicts of the individual will surface into awareness.
     b. An individual has the capacity to draw meaning and interpretations once awareness is accomplished.
     c. Everyone yearns to be whole.

d. Emphasis is on demonstrating awareness by attending to immediate experience, rather than on just talking about it.
- Key concepts for change
  a. Nonverbal cues by the body furnish extremely important clues.
  b. Each person and object in a dream represents a projected or deserved aspect of the dreamer.
  c. Internalizing an object directs inwardly directed aggression outward, gets the individual in touch with conflicting behavior patterns, and permits the release of energy.
  d. Most people have unfinished business, usually unexpressed emotion. The completion of this business brings about change.
- Common activities: Hot seat, top dog, underdog dialogues; supportive behaviors of the "Greek chorus;" changing of "it" statements to "I" statements; splitting, or the expression of both sides of a conflict; and polarity or ambivalence.
- References
  Perls, F.S. *The gestalt approach*. Palo Alto, Calif.: Science and Behavior Books, 1973.
  Polster, E., & Polster, M. *Gestalt therapy integrated: Contours of theory and practice*. New York: Brunner/Mazel, 1973.

7. Growth/Strength/Human Potential
- Basic assumptions
  a. People grow through the actualization of dormant capacities, abilities, strengths, and resources that reside in everyone.
  b. Each person has an inherent tendency toward growth and self-actualization with respect to self and others.
  c. In every behavior, no matter how destructive it appears, there is some intent to grow.
  d. Growth takes place on two levels simultaneously, through the development of self-esteem and the ability to make relationships with others that are satisfying and enhancing.
  e. The individual is an energy system whose goal is aliveness.
- Key concepts for change
  a. The following qualities are necessary to have a good sense of self: authority, integrity, courage, spontaneity, responsibility, commitment, congruency, and explosion versus implosion.
  b. To have meaningful relationships, individuals need to experience differences as growth-producing; separateness as wholeness, not isolation; and assertion as vital to growth; they must have the ability to allow others to be in charge of themselves, to empathize with another's feelings without losing self, and to

accept the consequences of other individuals' actions without question and to take full responsibility for their own actions.
- Common activities: Identification and better utilization of strengths, encounter and gestalt techniques for mobilizing energy, a regard for discrepancies, and use of action plans.
- References

  Otto, H.A. *Group methods designed to actualize human potential.* Chicago, Ill.: Achievement Motivation Systems, 1968.

  Otto, H.A. *Fourteen new group methods to actualize human potential: A handbook.* Beverly Hills, Calif.: Holistic Press, 1975.

8. Psychodrama
- Basic assumptions
    a. Through dramatic, spontaneous role playing, individuals can become open and in touch with their feelings, be more spirited and creative, and expand themselves to their limits of emotional achievement.
    b. People should be helped to stretch themselves to their creative limits.
- Key concepts for change
    a. Experiencing in the moment and acting out those moments create an alive and vibrant experience for both actors and observers.
    b. One of the most important functions of learning is to be more spontaneous.
- Common activities: Audience participation; soliloquies, double, role reversal, mirror and behind-the-back techniques, "magic shop," sociodrama.
- References

  Greenberg, I. (Ed.). *Psychodrama theory and therapy.* New York: Behavioral Publications, 1974.

  Moreno, J.L. *Psychodrama* (Vol. 1). Beacon, N.Y.: Beacon House Inc., 1946.

9. Social Work Group
- Basic assumptions
    a. The environmental context, the interactions, and the individual all prompt and maintain behavior.
    b. The group serves as a structured support system, acknowledging the individuals, the group as a unit, and the greater social context (extragroup).
    c. The leader/worker maintains a balance between a direct and an indirect influence.

- Key concepts for change
  a. The group format is structured or programmed to accommodate goal setting and problem solving in accordance with the members' needs.
  b. A mutually acceptable contract is established between the leader/worker and each group member.
  c. Spontaneous interactions among the members provide a mutual strength and goal focus.
  d. Problem solving focuses on each individual's goals, eliciting membership input and acknowledging environmental influence (extragroup).
  e. Group cohesion strengthens the individual in goal attainment.
- Common activities: Programming, conflict resolution, problem solving, decision making, contracting, mutual-aid systems, and group cohesion.
- References
  Schwartz, W. On the use of groups in social work practice. In W. Schwartz & S.R. Zalba (Eds.), *The practice of group work*. New York: Columbia University Press, 1971.
  Vinter, R.D. *Readings in group work practice*. Ann Arbor, Mich.: Campus Publishers, 1967.

10. Theme-Centered Interaction
    - Basic assumptions
      a. Membership interdependence is efficiently created through the implementation of a common group theory and group goals.
      b. Membership autonomy is encouraged through insistence upon the individual's goals and responsibility for self.
      c. Ground rules and leadership efforts serve to balance the "I-We-It" focus (dynamic balancing).
      d. Group leaders participate as self-actualizing members.
      e. Spontaneous involvement and emotional release are the goals of intense silent reflections (triple silence) on the theme.
    - Common activities: "Be-your-own-chairman," speak per I, give statements behind questions, triple silence, stop action.
    - References
      Cohn, R.C. Style and spirit of the theme-centered interactional method. In C. Sager & H. Kaplan (Eds.), *Progress in group and family therapy*. New York: Brunner/Mazel, 1972.
      Shaffer, J.B.P., & Galinsky, M.D. *Models of group therapy and sensitivity training*. Englewood Cliffs, N.J.: Prentice-Hall, 1974.

Assessment Instruments

A variety of assessment instruments are available for use in assessing structural family facilitation programs. The instruments described in this appendix are selected by the designers of the programs in Chapters 11–26.

Caring Relationships Inventory

The Caring Relationships Inventory (CRI), developed by Everett L. Shostrom, is a measure of the elements of love or caring in heterosexual relationships. Five elements of love are measured: affection-agape, friendship, eros-romantic love, empathy-compassion, and self-love. In addition, there are two subscales based on Maslow's concepts of "being love" (the ability to accept the other person as that person is) and "deficiency love" (loving a person for what that person can do for you). The CRI is a self-administering, 83-item instrument that requires approximately 30–40 minutes for completion. Scoring requires approximately 5–10 minutes per subject, on easily read profile charts.

Publisher: Educational and Industrial Testing Service
P.O. Box 7234
San Diego, CA 92107

Reference: Shostrom, E.L. Psychotherapy: Theory, research, and practice. *Journal of Consulting and Clinical Psychology,* 1972, 9(3), 194–199.

Coopersmith Self-Esteem Inventory

The Coopersmith Self-Esteem Inventory is a brief self-report measure, constructed for use with children and adolescents. The instrument consists of 58 feeling/self-perception statements that the child is instructed to assess either "like me" or "unlike me." The administering time of this instrument is brief (10–12 minutes), as is the scoring time.

> Reference: Coopersmith, S. *The antecedents of self-esteem.* San Francisco: W.H. Freeman and Co., 1967.

Depression Adjective Check-List

The Depression Adjective Check-List (DACL) is a continuous measurement instrument, developed to assess depressed affect. The author, Bernard Lubin, has constructed seven varying lists or versions (Forms A–G) of the instrument, providing a means for repeated assessment. The DACL can be administered rapidly and is easily scored. The scoring parallels the specific population of the client, providing excellent normative data on a diversity of populations (age, sex, race, and so on).

> Publisher: Educational and Industrial Testing Service
> P.O. Box 7234
> San Diego, CA 92107
> Reference: Herson, M., & Bellack, A.S. (Eds.). *Behavioral assessment.* New York: Pergamon Press, 1976.

Dyadic Adjustment Scale

The Dyadic Adjustment Scale, developed by Graham Spanier, is used to access a dyadic relationship. This 32-item descriptive scale measures each partner's perception of the relationship. The scale asks respondents to determine the degree of agreement or disagreement and relative frequency of perceptions or behavior on four separate subscales: dyadic satisfaction, dyadic consensus, dyadic cohesion, and affectional expression. The author of this scale has completed an impressive study to establish validity and reliability for the instrument.

> Reference: Spanier, G. Measuring dyadic adjustment. *Journal of Marriage and Family,* 1976, *38,* 15–30.

Fisher Divorce Adjustment Scale

The Fisher Divorce Adjustment Scale (FDAS) is a 100-item questionnaire developed by Bruce Fisher. An overall adjustment score is obtained, with additional subscores in five categories: feelings of self-worth, disentanglement of love relationship, feelings of anger, symptoms of grief, and rebuilding social trust.

Publisher: The Family Relations Learning Center
450 Ord Drive
Boulder, CO 80303
Reference: Fisher, B. *When your relationship ends.* Boulder, Colo.:
Family Relations Learning Center, 1978.

Fundamental Interpersonal Relations Orientation-Behavior Instrument

The Fundamental Interpersonal Relations Orientation-Behavior (FIRO-B) instrument, developed by William C. Schutz and Marilyn Wood, focuses on both individual and relationship attitudes involving control, affection, and inclusion. The instrument produces six scores: three on behavior expressed toward others and three on the behavior wanted from others. The FIRO-B is a companion instrument to the FIRO-F, which focuses on feelings rather than behavior. Scores from the FIRO-B can be used both for self-understanding and for interpersonal awareness and understanding. The instrument is self-administered. It consists of 54 statements and requires 5–12 minutes to complete. Scoring requires 5–10 minutes per instrument.

Publisher: Consulting Psychologists Press, Inc.
577 College Avenue
Palo Alto, CA 94306
Reference: Gilligan, J.F. FIRO-B norms and reliability revisited. *Journal of Clinical Psychology,* 1973, *29*(31), 374–376.

Goal Attainment Scaling

Goal Attainment Scaling (GAS) is a technique for identifying and quantifying goals and for providing a follow-up measure of goal attainment. Although it has been implemented in management settings and overall program evaluations, GAS is specifically designed for specifying therapeutic goals. Authors Kiresuk and Sherman developed the instrument as an assessment device to quantify goal attainment both during the therapy process and as an outcome measure.

Publisher: Program Evaluation Resource Center
501 Park Avenue South
Minneapolis, MN 55415
Reference: Kiresuk, T., & Sherman, R. Goal attainment scaling: A general method of evaluating comprehensive community health programs. *Community Mental Health Journal,* 1973, *4*(6), 443–453.

Group Environment Scale

The Group Environment Scale (GES) is a paper-pencil, self-report inventory consisting of 90 items and producing ten scales of measurement. The GES assesses the type and intensity of personal relationships among members of a group. Outpatient therapy groups are clearly differentiated from task-oriented and mutual support groups, thereby accentuating the value of the GES for research purposes.

Publisher: Consulting Psychologists Press, Inc.
       577 College Ave.
       Palo Alto, CA 94306

Reference: Moos, R.H., Insel, P.M., & Humphrey, B. *Combined preliminary manual: Family work and group environment scales*. Palo Alto, Calif.: Consulting Psychologists Press, 1974.

Inventory of Marital Conflict

The Inventory of Marital Conflict (IMC) is a nonself-report instrument (interactions are coded by a trained rater). The dyad is presented with a series of vignettes, each of which represents a unique marital conflict situation. The authors have constructed 18 vignettes that can be divided and implemented as pretreatment and posttreatment measures. Each spouse is asked to respond to a vignette, assessing who is responsible for the problem, identifying a solution to the problem, and determining whether or not the responder (or someone the responder knows) has experienced a similar problem. The couple is then asked to discuss each vignette and reach a joint agreement on the solution. This interaction is recorded and subsequently scored on the Marital and Family Interaction Coding Scheme (MFICS).

Publisher: Family Social Science
       University of Minnesota
       218 North Hall
       St. Paul, MN 55108

Reference: Olson, D.H., & Ryder, R.G. Inventory of Marital Conflicts (IMC): An experimental interaction procedure. *Journal of Marriage and the Family*, 1970, *32*, 443–448.

Kvebaek Family Sculpture Technique

The Kvebaek Family Sculpture Technique (KFST), developed by Ronald Cromwell, David Fournier, and David Kvebaek, is an outsider-rated instrument that assesses the observed verbal and nonverbal interactions that occur during a family task. The specified task requires each family member to individually "sculpt" all the family members, using a chess-board matrix and people figures. The family is then required to jointly "sculpt" the family members. The observer-rater's task is to assess the configuration of figures, the distance between the figures, and the inter-actions that occur during the joint sculpting task. The total administration time of both tasks is about 30 minutes.

Publisher: Pilgrimage, Inc.
　　　　　Jonesboro, TN 37659
Reference: Cromwell, R.E. A framework for diagnosing marital and family systems: Multisystem-multimethod assessment. In E. Filsinger & R.A. Lewis (Eds.), *Marital observation and behavioral assessment: Recent developments and technique.* Beverly Hills, Calif.: Sage Publishers, 1980.

Marital Adjustment Test

The Marital Adjustment Test (MAT) is a self-report, dyadic instrument that measures general marital adjustment in the areas of sexual conge-niality, compatibility, and closeness. A primary consideration of the MAT authors (Harvey Locke and Karl Wallace) was to develop a brief, easily administered instrument that could offer reliability and validity. The test is self-explanatory and requires only five minutes to complete. Each part-ner responds to 15 scaled questions that personally assess the marital relationship.

References: Kimmel, D., & Van Der Veer, F. Factors of marital adjust-ment in Locke's Marital Adjustment Test. *Journal of Marriage and the Family,* 1974, *36,* 57–63.
　　　　　Locke, H.J., & Wallace, K.M. Short marital-adjustment and predictions tests: Their reliability and validity. *Marriage and Family Living,* 1959, *21,* 251–255.

Marital Happiness Scale

The Marital Happiness Scale (MHS) is a self-administering, continuous measurement device developed by N.H. Azrin, B.J. Naster, and R. Jones. The instrument is intended as a means of daily data collection, rating ten categories of daily marital interaction. The categories include household responsibilities, rearing of children, social activities, money, communi-cation, sex, academic/occupational progress, personal independence, spouse independence, and general happiness.

The specific function of the MHS is to provide a continuous measurement of marital satisfaction and to provide incentive for the marital dyad to focus on reciprocal positive interaction as opposed to critical, negative interaction. The daily use of the instrument by the marital pair is suggested, thus conceptually adhering to social learning/reinforcement theory.

References: Ayllon, T., & Azrin, N.H. *The token economy: A motivational system for therapy and rehabilitation.* New York: Appleton-Century-Crofts, 1968.

Azrin, N.H., Naster, B.J., & Jones, R. Reciprocity counseling: A rapid learning-based procedure for marital counseling. *Behavioral Research Therapy,* 1973, *2,* 365–382.

McFall's Behavioral Role-Playing Test

Richard McFall and Albert Marsten developed the Behavioral Role-Playing Test for the primary purpose of assessing assertive behavior. The test consists of 16 tape-recorded stimulus situations requiring assertive responses. The respondents are instructed to respond to each situation (for example, friends are interrupting your studying, the laundry has lost your cleaning, the waiter brings you steak that is too rare) as if it were actually happening to them. The respondents are also asked to rate each situation on two criteria: (1) how anxious you would feel if this situation actually happened, and (2) how satisfied you feel with the response you gave. These role-playing situations may be particularly valuable as a means for pretreatment and posttreatment assessment.

References: Efran, J.S., & Korn, P.R. Measurement of social caution: Self-appraisal, role-playing and discussion behavior. *Journal of Consulting and Clinical Psychology,* 1969, *33,* 78–83.

McFall, R.M., & Marsten, A. An experimental investigation of behavioral rehearsal in assertive training. *Journal of Abnormal Psychology,* 1970, *2,* 295–303.

Moos Family Environment Scale

The Moos Family Environment Scale (FES) was developed by Rudolph Moos as a measure of the social climate of the family, the directions of personal growth emphasized in the family, and the nature and intensity of personal relationships in the family. Four scales are included in the measurement profile: expressiveness, conflict, independence, and control. The instrument is in a 90-item, self-report format, requiring not more than 30 minutes for completion.

Publisher: Consulting Psychologists Press, Inc.
577 College Ave.
Palo Alto, CA 94306

Reference: Moos, R.H. & Moos, B.S. A typology of family social environments. *Family Process,* 1976, *16*(4), 357–371.

Piers-Harris Children's Self-Concept Scale

The Piers-Harris Children's Self-Concept Scale is composed of 80 simple declarative sentences that are worded to fit the way a child generally feels. It is a self-report, self-administered questionnaire, and it is a reliable and valid instrument for measuring the self-concept of children.

Publisher: Counselor of Recordings and Tests
Box 6184
Acklen Station
Nashville, Tenn. 37212

Reference: Piers, E.V. *Manual for the Piers-Harris Children's Self-Concept Scale (the way I feel about myself).* Nashville, Tenn.: Counselor Recordings and Tests, 1969.

Rathus Assertiveness Scale

The Rathus Assertiveness Scale (RAS) is a 30-item paper-and-pencil, self-report instrument, requiring approximately five minutes for completion. The subject is expected to rate personal behavior ($+3$ = very characteristic of me, -3 = very uncharacteristic of me) on each of 30 situational sentences. Scores for the RAS are indicative of the impressions respondents make on other people and of how they would behave in situations where outgoing, assertive behavior is profitable.

Reference: Rathus, S. A thirty item schedule for assessing assertive behavior. *Behavior Therapy,* 1973, *4,* 398–406.

Relationship Styles Inventory

The (RSI) was developed by Lynn Scoresby and Bernell Christensen as a means of assessing people's perceptions of their styles of interaction in a given relationship. The RSI yields scores for parallel, complementary, and symmetrical interaction. Essentially, it produces a profile of dyadic functioning (from one person's perception) based on those three concepts.

The RSI has been found to be reliable and valid. It takes approximately 20 minutes to complete.

Publisher: Unpublished scale
         Contact: A. Lynn Scoresby or James Harper
         Department of Family Services
         Brigham Young University
         Provo, Utah 84602

Reference: Harper, J.M. *Fitting a Markov chain model to complementary symmetrical, and parallel relationship styles in marital dyads.* Unpublished doctoral dissertation, University of Minnesota, August, 1979. (Dissertation Abstracts International order #DEM80-06620)

Symptom Check-List

The Symptom Check-List (SCL-90), developed by Leonard Derogatis, consists of a 90-item, self-report symptom inventory. The instrument assesses psychopathology on nine clinical scales and three global scales. Information gained from this instrument is intended to be used in making an assessment of a person's present psychological functioning based on a significant number of symptoms being exhibited. Additional uses include the screening of clients who might need more specialized professional help and the segregating of "normal" from clinical populations. The average time for completion of the instrument is 20 minutes.

Publisher: Leonard Derogatis
         Clinical Psychometrics
         1228 Wine Spring Lane
         Baltimore, MD 21204

Taylor-Johnson Temperament Analysis

The Taylor-Johnson Temperament Analysis (T-JTA) instrument was developed by Robert M. Taylor, Roswell Johnson, and Lucille Morrison as an efficient, self-report, personality-trait assessment device. The instrument is not designed to measure serious abnormalities or disturbances; it is rather intended to evaluate traits that influence personal, social, marital, parental, scholastic, and vocational adjustment. The T-JTA profile consists of nine scales and may be scored for both self-perceptions and perceptions-of-partner, allowing for crossplotting of spouse scores and other relationship scores (parent-child, and so on). The instrument requires 30–40 minutes to complete.

Publisher: Psychological Publications, Inc.
5300 Hollywood Blvd.
Los Angeles, CA 90028
Reference: Curtis, J.H. *Toward the construction of positive guidelines for assessing individual and dyadic marriageability using the T-JTA profile.* Unpublished doctoral dissertation, Florida State University, 1972.

Tennessee Self-Concept Scale

The Tennessee Self-Concept Scale measures self-concept with 100 self-descriptive statements that a subject rates on a Likert-type scale. The scale is intended for use with individuals at all levels of adjustment. The subscales include a total positive scale and scales for self-criticism, self-satisfaction, behavior, physical self, moral-ethical self, personal self, family self, and social self. The Tennessee Self-Concept Scale has been widely used and demonstrates adequate reliability and validity.

Publisher: Counselor of Recordings and Tests
Box 6184
Acklen Station
Nashville, TN 37212
References: Fitts, W.H. *The self concept and behavior: Overview and supplement.* Nashville, Tenn.: Dede Wallace Center, 1972. (a)
Fitts, W.H. *The self concept and performance.* Nashville, Tenn.: Dede Wallace Center, 1972. (b)

Walker Problem Behavior Identification Checklist

The Walker Problem Behavior Identification Checklist (WPBIC) was developed for use in schools, focusing on teacher-student relationships. The authors designed 50 checklist items, drawn from teacher descriptions of classroom behavior problems (behaviors that interfere or actively compete with successful academic performance). The checklist is completed by the observing teacher or adult supervisor, and the responses are rated on five scales: acting out, withdrawal, distractibility, disturbed peer relations, and immaturity.

Publisher: Western Psychological Services
12031 Wilshire Blvd.
Los Angeles, CA 90025
Reference: Walker, H.M., & Bull, S. *Validation of a behavior rating scale for measuring behavior within the classroom setting.* Unpublished manuscript, University of Oregon, 1970.

Annotated Bibliography for Chapters 1–10

Alger, J. Multiple couple therapy. In P. Guerin (Ed.), *Family theory and practice*. New York: Gardner Press, 1976.
The chapter describes a systems approach for working with couples in groups. It includes an examination of issues related to selection of couples, size of the group, time, and cotherapy. A description of how to work with the couples group covers evaluation; structure; goals; evolution of the group through early, middle, and later stages; role of the therapist; and special techniques (family members, subgroups, family choreography, television playback, time and space).

Beebe, E.R. Expectant parent classes: A case study. *Family Coordinator*, 1978, *29*(1), 55–58.
The Expectant Parent Program is an education model designed to increase the effectiveness of parenting. The article describes program development, needs assessment, goals, content, staff, and funding. Program results based on parent evaluations are discussed with recommendations for improving the program.

Bowen, M. Family therapy and family group therapy. In Olson, D.H. (Ed.), *Treating relationships*. Lake Mills, Iowa: Graphic Publishing Co., 1976.
Bowen describes the antecedents, early history, growth, and current status of family therapy. He describes his own research and how his theoretical notions developed and explains their meaning and application. In a discussion about family therapy, he describes theoretical trends, clinical aspects, family group therapy, multiple family group therapy, and network therapy.

Corey, G., & Corey, M. *Groups: Process and practice*. Brooks/Cole, 1977. The authors outline basic issues and key concepts of group process. Issues center on the group member, the group leader, formation and initial stages of the group, the working stages of the group, termination, evaluation, follow-up, and ethics. Suggestions for working with children, adolescents, college students, couples, and the elderly integrate the issues and concepts in practical applications.

DeYoung, A.J. Marriage encounter: A critical examination. *Journal of Marital and Family Therapy*, 1979, 5(2), 27–34.
The author provides a brief history of marriage encounter, followed by a description of a weekend from a participant-observation perspective. He questions recruitment and various proceedings during the encounter. Three areas that DeYoung indicates need attention are male-centered teaching, recruitment toward building a stronger religious community, and lack of focus on the social and occupational facets of life that may affect marital relations.

Diedrich, R., & Dye, H. (Eds.). *Group procedures: Purposes, processes, and outcomes: Selected readings for the counselor*. New York: Houghton Mifflin Co., 1972.
The readings in this book cover several dimensions of group phenomena: purpose and process, leadership and membership, evaluation and ethics.

Doherty, W.J., McCabe, P., & Ryder, R.G. Marriage encounter: A critical appraisal. *Journal of Marriage and Family Counseling*, 1978, 4(4), 99–107.
This article provides a description and evaluation of the marriage encounter movement from theoretical and clinical perspectives. The authors raise concern about potentially destructive and illusory effects, while admitting that marriage encounter meets the needs of some couples. They call for evaluation and more dialogue between professionals and leaders of the movement.

Drum, D.J., & Knott, J.E. *Structured groups for facilitating development*. New York: Human Sciences Press, 1977.
In addition to providing a conceptual overview of structured groups, the authors identify three kinds of structured groups for the individual: skill groups, life-theme groups, and life-transitions groups. Descriptions and sample programs for each type of group are provided.

Framo, J. Marriage therapy in a couples group. In D. Block (Ed.), *Techniques of family psychotherapy*. New York: Grune & Stratton, 1973.
Framo describes his rationale for marriage therapy as different from marriage counseling. He applies marriage therapy in a couples group with a discussion of issues and procedures.

Hassall, E., & Modar, D. Crisis group therapy with the separated and divorced. *Family Relations*, 1980, *29*(4), 591–598.
The authors examine the use of crisis intervention techniques, based on their experiences with groups of separated and divorced people. The steps in the treatment process begin with cognitive mastery of the normal spectrum of reaction, and continue through the stages of expressing and resolving grief to the restructuring of the individual life situation.

Hennion, C.B., & Peterson, B.H. An evaluation of family life education delivery system for young families. *Family Relations*, 1981, *30*(3), 387–394.
The authors report on a learn-at-home delivery system employed by the University of Wisconsin—extension that provided low-cost family-life information for young families. A series of 10 packets were developed, covering parenthood, family management, consumer decision-making, credit, and nutrition. The results of evaluation indicated that the delivery system was both efficient and effective.

Jacobson, N.S. Training couples to solve their marital problems: A behavioral approach to relationship discord (Part 2). *International Journal of Family Counseling*, 1977, *5*, 20–28.
This article describes intervention strategies that seem to be effective in teaching couples problem-solving skills.

Johnson, D., & Johnson, F. *Joining together: Group theory and group skills*. Englewood Cliffs, N.J.: Prentice-Hall, 1975.
In an attempt to develop an understanding of group dynamics and effective group skills, the authors provide numerous exercises, paired with the following concepts: leadership, decision making, group goals, communication within groups, controversy and creativity, conflicts of interest, use of power, cohesion and norms, and problem solving.

Kaslow, F., & Lieberman, E.J. Couple group therapy: Rationale, dynamics and process. In G. Sholevar (Ed.), *The handbook of marriage and marital therapy*. New York: SP Medical and Scientific Books, 1981.
The authors provide a rationale based on the number of marriages

needing help. Discussion of their intervention philosophy and strategy for working with couples in groups covers short-term, close-ended analytic treatment, open-ended groups, and couples group psychotherapy.

Kaslow, F.W. Profile of the healthy family. *Interaction*, 1981, *4*, 1–15.
Using a case illustration, the author describes a healthy family on the following dimensions: a system orientation, boundary issues, contextual issues, power issues, autonomy and initiative, affective issues, negotiation and task performances, and transcendental values.

Klemer, R., & Smith, R. *Teaching about family relationships*. Minneapolis, Minn.: Burgess Publishing Co., 1975.
This book is written for teachers of family relationship courses. It supplies an overall framework for planning and teaching with an empathic approach. It presents nine general areas of family relationships, within a framework subject matter, over 150 behavioral objectives, and over 400 teaching techniques. The philosophy of the relationships between objectives, learning experiences, and evaluation is also covered.

L'Abate, L., & Weeks, G. Testing the limits of enrichment: When enrichment is not enough. *Journal of Family Counseling*, 1976, *4*(1), 70–74.
This article considers some of the most glaring failures in enrichment that can be used to learn more about which families can be enriched and which cannot. Guidelines, based on specific cases, are provided for nonapplication of enrichment programs.

Laquer, H.P. Multiple family therapy. In P.J. Guerin (Ed.), *Family therapy: Theory and practice*. New York: Gardner Press, 1976.
This chapter gives a brief history and description of multiple family therapy. The author describes the structures of disturbed and healthy families, relates them to systems theory, and highlights the differences between multiple family therapy and other forms of psychotherapy. The process of therapy is examined, along with the mechanisms of change. Finally, some goals and results are described.

Leiberman, M., Yalom, I., & Miles, M. *Encounter groups: First facts*. New York: Basic Books, 1973.
This research report focuses on what actually happens to people in encounter groups. The authors describe the methodology used and the effects of leaders, group normative structure, group cohesiveness, and interpersonal climate. They raise the question of the effects on outcome of the attitudes, expectations, and personality characteristics of individ-

ual members. The experiences used to induce learning, expressivity, self-disclosure, insight, and feedback are examined. General meaning, practical applications for leaders and participants, and the overall effectiveness of encounter groups are also discussed.

Lewis, M.L. *How's your family? A guide to identifying your family's strengths and weaknesses*. New York: Brunner/Mazel, 1979.
A whole family questionnaire is provided for use by readers in evaluating their families by identifying strengths and weaknesses. A parental relationship questionnaire is provided to enable couples to focus on their relationship separately from the family. The author discusses the characteristics of a healthy family and how they can be distinguished from those of faltering, troubled, and severely troubled families.

Mace, D. The long, long trail from information-giving to behavioral change. *Family Relations,* 1981, *30,* 599–606.
The author explores the nature of education with particular reference to the contrast between didactic and dynamic objectives. Questions are raised about the effectiveness of the classroom as a vehicle for bringing about the behavioral and relational changes that appear to be necessary for significant improvement of family life. As a basis of comparison, the environment provided by a marriage and family enrichment group is cited as a more promising setting for initiating relational readjustment.

McFadden, J.R. Family life education and university outreach. *Family Relations,* 1981, *30*(4), 637–642.
The purpose of this article is to review family life programs and courses that are offered in a variety of college and university departments with an interest in the family. A discussion of the general rationale and history of these courses and programs shows the current and potential impact of the offerings.

Moore, P.E., & Robin, A.L. An approach to parent training for high school students. *American Journal of Family Therapy,* 1981, *9*(4), 61–69.
The authors report evaluation results showing the effectiveness of a combined behavioral-reflective, parent-training program with high school seniors. Lectures, films, class discussions, role-playing exercises, and examinations are used to teach concepts of behavioral and reflective child rearing. The results are discussed in the context of teenagers' developmental readiness to cope with the tasks of parenthood.

Ohlson, M.M. *Marriage counseling in groups*. Champaign, Ill.: Research Press Co., 1979.
This book covers processes and techniques for working with couples in groups. It is written for marriage counselors who wish to work with "reasonably healthy" couples in groups, for couples who wish to have some understanding of the processes, for couples who are looking for "self help" enrichment materials, and for clergy and lawyers who want to improve their conferences with couples and make appropriate referrals. Thought-provoking questions follow each chapter.

Papp, P. Brief therapy with couples groups. In P.J. Guerin (Ed.), *Family therapy: Theory and practice*. New York: Gardner Press, 1976.
The author describes a "brief" therapy format for a couples group that is designed to produce accelerated change through planned strategy. Three techniques—family choreography, prescribed tasks, and use of the group's setting—are used to produce change. Examples and discussion clarify the use of the techniques.

Price, D. Normal, functional and unhealthy? *Family Coordinator*, 1979, *28*(1), 109–114.
The author reviews the various meanings of the words *normal, functional,* and *healthy*. He discusses the implications for the marriage and family field and concludes that there is a need for common operational definitions in order to avoid ambiguity and erroneous implications.

Scoresby, A.L. *The marriage dialogue*. Menlo Park, Calif.: Addison-Wesley Publishing Co., 1977.
This book, describing marital communication skills, affirms that marriage can be a place of happiness. The content covers the role of communication, interpretation of marital messages, the language of intimacy and understanding, sexual communication, decision making, negotiation, metacommunication, time driving and its effect on the marital relationship, how to fight properly, and love and its place in the marital dialogue.

Sell, K.D., Shoffner, S.M., Farris, M.C., & Hill, E.W. *Enriching relationships: A guide to marriage and family enrichment literature*. Greensborough: University of North Carolina, 1980.
This is a reference list for enrichment literature.

Stinnett, N., Chesser, B., DeFrain, J., & Knaub, P. (Eds.). *Family strengths: Positive models for family life*. Lincoln: University of Nebraska Press, 1980.
The readings in this book are authored by family-life educators, practitioners, and researchers who took part in a symposium on building family strengths. The readings are divided into the following sections: the family, marriage relationships, parent-child relationships, parent-adolescent relationships, the middle and later years, building strengths in families with special needs, and the role of education in building family strengths.

Strelnick, A.H. Multiple family group therapy: A review of the literature. *Family Process,* 1977, *16*(3), 307–326.
In reviewing multiple family group therapy, the author focuses on its origin in the intersection of family and group therapies, its use in a variety of settings, its specific techniques and group development in individual and ongoing meetings, its goals and dominant themes, and its parallels in family and group work. The evaluation of outcomes of this treatment modality and areas for future investigation are also discussed.

Wolberg, L., & Aronson, M. (Eds.). *Group and family therapy*. New York: Brunner/Mazel, 1980.
This book presents chapters written by group and family therapists. Compared with past volumes, it marks a shift from a major focus on group therapy to a recognition of exciting new developments in the theory and practice of family therapy. The 33 chapters are grouped into the following categories: the contributions of Peter Laquer, theoretical and clinical issues in group therapy, specialized approaches to group therapy, supervision in group therapy, theoretical and clinical issues in family therapy, and abstracts of selected journal and anthology articles published in 1979.

Yalom, I. *Theory and practice of group psychotherapy*. New York: Basic Books, 1970.
This book approaches group therapy through a discussion of the derivation and operation of curative factors and of the inductive sequence of a therapy system based on those factors. The therapist's role and technique, the chronology of a therapy group, and the expanding world of the T-group or encounter group are included in a broad overview of group therapy.

Index

About the Authors

MARGARET HOWARD HOOPES is a Professor of Marriage and Family Therapy in the Department of Family Sciences and a member of the Comprehensive Clinic faculty at Brigham Young University. She has a Ph.D. in counseling psychology from the University of Minnesota where one of her areas of emphasis was small group theory and practice. A licensed marriage and family therapist and psychologist in Utah, she is an approved supervisor and a clinical member of the American Association for Marriage and Family Therapy, the American Psychological Association, the National Council on Family Relations, and Phi Beta Kappa. She has presented papers and workshops in Canada, Mexico, Guam, Japan, and throughout the United States. In addition to her academic responsibilities of teaching, research, and supervision in a marriage and family therapy program, she maintains a small private practice.

BARBARA L. FISHER is an Associate Professor of Marriage and Family Therapy in the Department of Human Development and Family Studies at Colorado State University. She received her masters degree (1974) and doctorate (1976) from Brigham Young University in marriage and family therapy, with additional emphasis on family relations. She has been involved in developing, delivering, and assessing marital and family enrichment programs for several years. Some of her recent projects include enrichment programs for intact families with adolescents, for stepfamilies, and for single-parent families. In addition, she trains professionals through workshops and enrichment courses. Dr. Fisher is a member of the Board of Directors, an approved supervisor, and a clinical member of the American Association for Marriage and Family Therapy. She is a member of the National Council on Family Relations and an associate editor for one of that organization's journals, *Family Relations*.

SALLY H. BARLOW, an Assistant Professor in Clinical Psychology at Brigham Young University, developed an interest in group dynamics while earning a Ph.D. in counseling psychology at the University of Utah. Dr. Barlow is a member of the American Psychological Association, American Personnel and Guidance Association, and Phi Beta Kappa. She has presented papers at the International Conference of Families in Israel and at meetings of the American Psychological Association, has published in the area of group dynamics, and is currently writing articles on group leader skills and group leader impact. Dr. Barlow lives on a farm and is the mother of a young son, Jack.